SHORT-TERM ECONOMIC INDICATORS TRANSITION ECONOMIES

SOURCES & DEFINITIONS

INDICATEURS ÉCONOMIQUES A COURT TERME ÉCONOMIES EN TRANSITION

ORGANISATION FOR ECONOMIC CO-OPERATION AND DEVELOPMENT
ORGANISATION DE COOPÉRATION ET DE DÉVELOPPEMENT ÉCONOMIQUES

ORGANISATION FOR ECONOMIC CO-OPERATION AND DEVELOPMENT

Pursuant to Article 1 of the Convention signed in Paris on 14th December 1960, and which came into force on 30th September 1961, the Organisation for Economic Co-operation and Development (OECD) shall promote policies designed:

- to achieve the highest sustainable economic growth and employment and a rising standard of living in Member countries, while maintaining financial stability, and thus to contribute to the development of the world economy;
- to contribute to sound economic expansion in Member as well as non-member countries in the process of economic development; and
- to contribute to the expansion of world trade on a multilateral, non-discriminatory basis in accordance with international obligations.

The original Member countries of the OECD are Austria, Belgium, Canada, Denmark, France, Germany, Greece, Iceland, Ireland, Italy, Luxembourg, the Netherlands, Norway, Portugal, Spain, Sweden, Switzerland, Turkey, the United Kingdom and the United States. The following countries became Members subsequently through accession at the dates indicated hereafter: Japan (28th April 1964), Finland (28th January 1969), Australia (7th June 1971), New Zealand (29th May 1973), Mexico (18th May 1994), and the Czech Republic (21st December 1995). The Commission of the European Communities takes part in the work of the OECD (Article 13 of the OECD Convention).

THE CENTRE FOR CO-OPERATION WITH THE ECONOMIES IN TRANSITION

The Centre for Co-operation with the European Economies in Transition (CCEET) was created in March 1990, as the focal point for co-operation between the OECD and the countries of Central and Eastern Europe. In 1991, the activities of the Centre were expanded to include the New Independent States of the Former Soviet Union and, the following year, Mongolia. In 1993, the Centre was renamed Centre for Co-operation with the Economies in Transition (CCET) to reflect its wider geographic coverage. Since 1991, the Centre has operated a "Partners in Transition" Programme for the purpose of providing targeted assistance to the countries more advanced in introducing market-oriented reforms and which desire to become Members of OECD. The "Partners" are now Hungary, Poland and the Slovak Republic.

ORGANISATION DE COOPÉRATION ET DE DÉVELOPPEMENT ÉCONOMIQUES

En vertu de l'article 1er de la Convention signée le 14 décembre 1960, à Paris, et entrée en vigueur le 30 septembre 1961, l'Organisation de Coopération et de Développement Économiques (OCDE) a pour objectif de promouvoir des politiques visant :

- à réaliser la plus forte expansion de l'économie et de l'emploi et une progression du niveau de vie dans les pays Membres, tout en maintenant la stabilité financière, et à contribuer ainsi au développement de l'économie mondiale ;
- à contribuer à une saine expansion économique dans les pays Membres, ainsi que les pays non membres, en voie de développement économique ;
- à contribuer à l'expansion du commerce mondial sur une base multilatérale et non discriminatoire conformément aux obligations internationales.

Les pays Membres originaires de l'OCDE sont : l'Allemagne, l'Autriche, la Belgique, le Canada, le Danemark, l'Espagne, les États-Unis, la France, la Grèce, l'Irlande, l'Islande, l'Italie, le Luxembourg, la Norvège, les Pays-Bas, le Portugal, le Royaume-Uni, la Suède, la Suisse et la Turquie. Les pays suivants sont ultérieurement devenus Membres par adhésion aux dates indiquées ci-après : le Japon (28 avril 1964), la Finlande (28 janvier 1969), l'Australie (7 juin 1971), la Nouvelle-Zélande (29 mai 1973), le Mexique (18 mai 1994) et la République tchèque (21 décembre 1995). La Commission des Communautés européennes participe aux travaux de l'OCDE (article 13 de la Convention de l'OCDE).

LE CENTRE POUR LA COOPÉRATION AVEC LES ÉCONOMIES EN TRANSITION

Le Centre pour la Coopération avec les Économies Européennes en Transition (CCEET) a été créé en mars 1990 pour être l'axe de la coopération entre l'OCDE et les pays d'Europe centrale et orientale. Les activités du Centre ont été étendues aux nouveaux États indépendants issus de l'ex-Union soviétique en 1991 et à la Mongolie l'année suivante. En 1993, l'appellation du CCEET a été modifiée pour tenir compte du fait que les activités du Centre couvrent désormais une aire géographique plus large : le CCEET est devenu le Centre pour la Coopération avec les Économies en Transition (CCET). Depuis 1991, le Centre met en œuvre un Programme «Partenaires pour la transition» qui est destiné à apporter une aide ciblée aux pays qui sont les plus avancés dans la voie des réformes axées sur le marché et qui souhaiteraient devenir Membres de l'OCDE. Actuellement, les pays «Partenaires» sont la Hongrie, la Pologne et la République slovaque.

FOREWORD

This publication provides information on the sources and definitions underlying the indicators published quarterly by the OECD in *Short-term Economic Indicators: Transition Economies*.

A number of Central and Eastern European countries and New Independent States (NIS) of the Former Soviet Union compile their statistics in ways that are different from those followed in OECD Member countries. By providing information on these methodological and presentational differences, this publication is an essential reference for all those involved in the interpretation and analysis of the statistics found in *Short-term Economic Indicators: Transition Economies*.

This document is published under the responsibility of the Secretary-General of the OECD.

Salvatore Zecchini
OECD Deputy Secretary-General
Director of the CCET

OECD
OCDE
SHORT-TERM ECONOMIC INDICATORS, SOURCES AND DEFINITIONS
OECD/CCET © April 1996

4

INDICATEURS ÉCONOMIQUES A COURT TERME, SOURCES ET DÉFINITIONS
OCDE/CCET © avril 1996

AVANT-PROPOS

Cette publication fournit des informations sur les sources et définitions sous-jacentes aux indicateurs publiés chaque trimestre par l'OCDE dans *Indicateurs économiques à court terme : Économies en transition*.

Certains pays de l'Europe centrale et orientale et des nouveaux États indépendants (NEI) de l'ex-Union soviétique compilent leurs statistiques d'une manière différente de celles utilisées dans les pays Membres de l'OCDE. En fournissant des informations sur les différences dans la présentation et dans la méthodologie, cette publication est une référence essentielle pour ceux qui interprètent et analysent les statistiques contenues dans *Indicateurs économiques à court terme : Économies en transition*.

Ce document est publié sous la responsabilité du Secrétaire général de l'OCDE.

Salvatore Zecchini
Secrétaire général adjoint de l'OCDE
Directeur du CCET

TABLE OF CONTENTS

New Independent States

> **The Czech Republic became the 26th Member country of the OECD, formally joining the Organisation on 21 December 1995. Sources and definitions for the Czech Republic will be incorporated in statistical publications for OECD countries over the coming months.**

TABLE DES MATIÈRES

Nouveaux états indépendants

La République tchèque est devenue le 26e pays Membre de l'OCDE, en adhérant formellement à l'Organisation le 21 décembre 1995. Les sources et définitions relatives à la République tchèque seront intégrées dans les publications statistiques des pays de l'OCDE dans les prochains mois.

GENERAL METHODOLOGICAL ISSUES

Traditionally, the statistics compiled in Central and Eastern European countries (CEECs) and the New Independent States (NIS) of the former Soviet Union have differed in content, classification and methodology from similar data available in OECD Member countries. Without an understanding of the basic approaches that have been used, analysis based on available data is likely to be misleading because they do not conform to the underlying conventions that an analyst expects when working with apparently similar data for developed market economies. This introductory section reviews some of the general methodological differences that should be borne in mind when reading subsequent sections concerning individual countries.

Historically, statistical offices in CEECs and the NIS were closely integrated into the central planning system. Problems due to the close links between statistics and central planning have now disappeared but, as explained below, the transition process has introduced a number of new problems for statisticians in CEECs and the NIS.

The private sector

In the past, statistics for CEECs and the NIS covered state enterprises and co-operatives only, as until relatively recently this accounted for the whole of legal production. At varying dates from 1989 onwards, the establishment of private enterprises became legal and the number of enterprises registered has grown dramatically in many countries. Some of these are large international companies that gain world-wide attention, but many more are small private businesses.

Recording private sector activity is proving to be one of the biggest stumbling blocks that statistical offices in CEECs and the NIS are facing. In the past the register of legal enterprises was relatively small and clearly specified. Statistical inquiries tended to be censuses with mandatory reporting requirements. The explosion in the number of enterprises now means that establishing and updating the business register is a major task and one that has been unfamiliar to the national statistical offices. As the register expands, it is necessary to devise sampling procedures in order to collect data on a sample rather than a census basis, using returns that are voluntary rather than compulsory.

It is also necessary to introduce methods of estimation for non-response for those who should be on the register and are not, for those who should have replied to the survey and did not, as well as those who were deliberately not covered by the survey. These considerations are made more difficult by the fact that often an enterprise is registered but no activity takes place, or the activity that does result is very small scale and does not represent the main source of income to the entrepreneur concerned. Deleting such enterprises from the register is more difficult than the initial registration.

OECD OCDE *SHORT-TERM ECONOMIC INDICATORS, SOURCES AND DEFINITIONS* 11 *INDICATEURS ÉCONOMIQUES A COURT TERME, SOURCES ET DÉFINITIONS*

OECD/CCET © April 1996 OCDE/CCET © avril 1996

These are major innovations which will take time to implement fully and effectively. In the meantime, therefore, some series still cover only the state and co-operative sectors; the private sector is simply missing. The extent of omission varies over time, from country to country and from sector to sector.

Classifications

The classifications used in OECD publications are those developed by the United Nations for use in market economies. In particular, industrial statistics are given according to the International Standard Industrial Classification (ISIC), foreign trade is classified according to the Standard Industrial Trade Classification (SITC), and national accounts according to the System of National Accounts (SNA).

In the past, all CEECs and the NIS used the Classification of Branches of the National Economy developed by the Council for Mutual Economic Assistance (CMEA). While the type of disaggregation was broadly similar to that used for market economies, there are many differences at the more detailed level. A classic example is the difference between the mining and manufacturing industries in the two systems. Suppose a country has a deposit of iron ore which is extracted and refined into sheet metal. Under ISIC the extraction process is classified as mining while the process of refining is classified as manufacturing. Under the CMEA classification the activity is regarded as a whole and classified under manufacturing. This means that mining under the CMEA classification is usually confined to coal and low value items such as sand and stone.

These types of differences reflect not only philosophically different view points but also pragmatic considerations. Since often in CEECs and the NIS a single enterprise extracts the ore and refines the metal, a separation between the two activities at the accounting level could only have been artificial.

United Nations classifications are incorporated into this publication as soon as they introduced into regular use in the country concerned.

Secondary production

As most manufacturing enterprises make more than one product, a basic choice has to be made as to whether one is measuring the output of the entire enterprise, or only of its main product. In OECD Member countries, it is often assumed that the output of the main product is representative of the output of the entire enterprise. In the manufacturing industry, non-principal production of other manufactured products should still be included in the total output of manufactured goods. It is also not uncommon for manufacturing enterprises to produce goods that are not manufactured products, such as construction output or transport services.

Under a United Nations classification, such activity may still be included in the manufacturing heading; under the CMEA classification, this activity should always appear under construction, transportation, etc. In practice this secondary activity is typically covered in longer period statistics but not in the shorter-term statistics.

OECD
OCDE
SHORT-TERM ECONOMIC INDICATORS, SOURCES AND DEFINITIONS
OECD/CCET © April 1996
12
INDICATEURS ÉCONOMIQUES A COURT TERME, SOURCES ET DÉFINITIONS
OCDE/CCET © avril 1996
CCET

Services

Traditionally the CEECs and the NIS paid less attention to services than OECD Member countries. Under the System of Material Balances, a distinction was made between material and non-material services. Material services were seen as an extension of the production process and included, for example, repairs to, and transportation of goods. Services such as health, education, cultural activities, defence and government were classified as non-material and excluded from the measurement of production. In many areas, therefore, the coverage of production extends only to agriculture, mining, manufacturing, gas, water, electricity and construction. However, it should be noted that a similar emphasis on production of goods prevailed in OECD Member countries for many years and it is only recently that the importance of services, and the difficulty of measuring their performance accurately, have emerged as major statistical issues.

Time of recording

It is common practice in OECD Member countries to ask firms to report sales or output, for example, in the preceding month. Very often, in the former CMEA the practice was to ask for sales or output for the year to date, and monthly data were derived by subtracting the previously reported figure. Sometimes this led to errors in the time at which the activity was recorded because errors in previous reports would not be corrected explicitly but simply incorporated in a new cumulative total.

This practice introduced a distortion, at least in production statistics, because the data were used for monitoring production targets. These targets were expressed in quarterly and annual terms and many series show a larger than usual entry in March, June and September, and an exceptionally large one in December. One cause is that reporting lagged behind schedule in intervening months but was brought up to date for these key dates resulting in a seemingly large seasonal component in some series.

Price and volume indices

Historically, prices in the CEECs and NIS were fixed by the central authorities. In practice, transaction prices may have been higher due to the operation of black markets and other informal channels. The prices used in compiling the official price indices, however, were the centrally fixed prices.

One problem common to the compilation of price indices in all countries is the treatment of quality change. If a new version of a good appears with extra features and a higher price, some of the price increase can be attributed to the extra features, meaning that the real increase in the price index is less than the apparent price increase. In the past, more of the increase in prices in the CEECs and NIS was attributed to quality change than may have been justified in terms of the product improvements concerned. When volume measures such as production indices were derived by dividing current volume data by price indices, under-stated prices led to an over-statement of volume. Because most of the evidence of this practice is anecdotal, no quantification of this distortion is available and the data have not been adjusted on this account.

Index numbers on volume are compiled using both price and volume information. It is theoretically possible to calculate two types of index. The differences between the two types of index on volume can be illustrated using, as an example, the calculation of a volume index of production. The first index is base-weighted (Laspeyres) and shows the ratio of current production at base-year prices to base-year production valued at base-year prices. The other, a Paasche index, shows the ratio of current production at current prices to base-year production valued at current prices. The disadvantage of the Paasche index is that while the index number for each period can be compared with the base period, comparisons between two other periods do not accurately reflect the change between the two periods. Because inter-period comparisons are valid with base-weighted indices, these indices are most often used in OECD Member countries and publications. Many CEECs and NIS are increasingly calculating base-weighted indices that can therefore be compared within different periods in the year.

Unemployment

In centrally planned economies, unemployment was not measured. At the beginning of the transition period, the necessity of labour offices and unemployment bureaus became apparent. Unlike most OECD Member countries, many of the CEECs and the NIS did not have labour force surveys in place. Labour offices now exist in all transition countries to provide information on the number of registered unemployed, and in some instances to distribute benefits to the unemployed. Many transition countries are also introducing household labour force surveys. As is the case in many OECD Member countries differences between the number of registered unemployed in labour offices and unemployment as measured in household surveys may be significant.

Unemployed persons may not register in labour offices for a number of reasons. In practice, labour offices may have few job vacancies. The number of unemployed persons registered may be underestimated because unemployed persons who are no longer eligible to receive benefits, or who would receive only a small benefit, often do not register and are therefore omitted from official figures. This problem is also apparent in OECD Member countries but may be aggravated in transition countries where labour offices may not yet be established, or easily accessible in all regions.

Another observed phenomenon is forced underemployment. Some enterprises undergo sporadic production schedules due to interruptions in the supply of raw materials or excessive build-up of inventories. In some cases, employees work, and are paid, less than full-time (or, in some cases, not at all) but continue to be counted on enterprise rosters as employed.

Foreign trade

Until trade liberalisation was introduced, only specially registered enterprises were permitted to import and export goods and services to and from CEECs and the NIS. Data on imports and exports, therefore, were collected by direct enquiries to these firms. At varying points in time from 1989 onwards, many CEECs and NIS started to compile data on international trade from customs declarations. Furthermore, and typically in association with the change to the use of customs data, a standard international classification system categorising trade by item was also introduced. In a number of cases, the changes in coverage and timing are so great that a major discontinuity appears in the time series.

Introduction of new currencies

In many CEECs and NIS, particularly in the countries of the former Soviet Union, a new national currency was introduced shortly after political independence. In some cases this was a temporary currency and a new currency was introduced a short time later. Often, the new currencies were issued at a fixed rate to the rouble, or to the temporary currency, during the conversion period. In some cases, this is not the same rate as a rate derived by comparing exchange rates of the new currency and the rouble to the dollar or other external currency.

For more detailed information see the chapter, *Introduction of New Currencies.*

Business surveys

Business tendency surveys ask managers for their opinions and expectations about the economic situation of their companies. The data collected by these surveys are usually termed "qualitative" to distinguish them from the quantitative data collected by conventional statistical surveys. Business tendency surveys are carried out in all OECD Member countries and have proved to be a valuable source of up-to-date information on current business conditions, and likely trends in the immediate future.

The Centre for Co-operation with the Economies in Transition has been working with Eurostat to develop a programme of business tendency surveys in most transition countries.

Seasonal adjustment

As in OECD Member countries, a significant seasonal factor may be observed in many series due to seasonal variations in demand, public holidays, changes in climate, etc. Insofar as seasonal factors can be observed, series can be adjusted for seasonality in order to compare volume levels between different periods in a year. The OECD has provided the necessary technical assistance to a number of countries to carry out seasonal adjustment calculations, and additional technical support of this nature is planned.

Series availability

The series included in *Short-Term Economic Indicators: Transition Economies* are broadly similar to those published in the OECD's *Main Economic Indicators.* As far as possible, data are shown on a monthly, quarterly, and annual basis. Some quarterly and annual data are derived directly from the monthly observations. In some cases, however, the longer period data have a wider coverage. For example, monthly data may cover firms with more than one hundred employees, quarterly data all firms with over fifty employees, while the annual data attempt to cover all enterprises. A consequence of extended coverage is that the longer period data are available progressively later.

A further implication of different survey coverage is that totals derived from monthly and quarterly data may differ from each other and from annual reports.

Sources

For the countries of Central and Eastern Europe data are supplied to the OECD by statistical offices and central banks in the countries concerned, although data are not always presented in the same form as in national publications. The Interstate Statistical Committee of the Commonwealth of Independent States (CIS) supplies the data for most of its member countries. Some countries, however, prefer to supply data directly to the OECD.

OECD
OCDE
SHORT-TERM ECONOMIC INDICATORS, SOURCES AND DEFINITIONS
OECD/CCET © April 1996

16

INDICATEURS ÉCONOMIQUES A COURT TERME, SOURCES ET DÉFINITIONS
OCDE/CCET © avril 1996

INTRODUCTION OF NEW CURRENCIES

In Estonia, Latvia, Lithuania and the NIS, new national currencies were introduced shortly after independence. In a number of cases, a temporary currency was first used and replaced by a second currency slightly later. At the time the new currencies were introduced, an internal conversion rate from old to new currency was used officially by banks and in calculating wages, for example, in new terms. These internal conversion factors are shown below.

For domestic series expressed in national currency, these conversion factors have been used by the statistical offices to combine data expressed in old and new currencies for different months into quarterly and annual data.

When the new currencies were introduced, new exchange rates for hard currency were also announced. An implicit external conversion factor can be calculated by comparing the official exchange rate of the new currency against, say, the dollar, with the rouble exchange rate. In almost all cases this implicit external rate is markedly different from the internal rate, in part because although the rouble had reached an approximate market rate in most if not all countries, a black market in most of the new currencies quickly developed. It is therefore extremely difficult to combine data for external trade (outside the former rouble zone which is usually all that is available) for different periods either side of the date the new currency was introduced, and even more difficult to convert these to and from international currencies.

The Czech and Slovak Republics also changed their currencies since becoming two independent states. Each introduced their own koruny, to replace the Czecho-slovak koruny, on 1 January 1993. Because of the date involved, there is no aggregation problem to quarters and years as described above. Further, since the new koruny were introduced at par with the old one, which had reached a market exchange rate level, no arithmetic conversion of data on the old basis was necessary. The divergence of the two currencies since January 1993 can be seen in their respective exchange rates against other currencies.

A similar situation exists in the Republic of Slovenia. When Slovenia became an independent state on 8 October 1991, a new national currency, the tolar, was introduced. At the time of introduction, the conversion factor with the Yugoslav dinar was 1:1.

In Poland, the zloty was redenominated on the 1st January 1995 with the new zloty equal to 10 000 old zlotys.

Country	Currency	Date of introduction	Conversion factors
Armenia	Dram	22 November 1993	1:200
Azerbaijan	Manat [1]	15 August 1992	1:10
Belarus	Old Belarus rouble	26 July 1993	1:1
	New Belarus rouble [2]	20 August 1994	1:10
Estonia	Kroon	20 June 1992	1:10
Kazakstan	Tenge	15 November 1993	1:500
Kyrgyz Republic	Som	10 May 1993	1:200
Latvia	Latvian rouble [3]	7 May 1992	1:1
	Lat	5 March 1993	1:200
Lithuania	Talonas [3]	1 October 1992	1:1
	Litas	25 June 1993	1:100
Republic of Moldova	Leu	29 November 1993	1:1000
Russian Federation	New rouble	26 July 1993	1:1
Tajikistan	New rouble	26 July 1993	1:1
	Tajik rouble	10 May 1995	1:100
Turkmenistan	Manat	1 November 1993	1:500
Ukraine	Karbovanets	16 November 1992	1:1
Uzbekistan	Sum-coupon	15 November 1993	1:1
	Sum	27 June 1994	1:1000

1. Only legal tender from 1 January 1994.
2. The Belarus rouble was redenominated on 20 August 1994 with the new Belarus rouble equal to 10 old Belarus roubles.
3. Temporary currency.

OECD
OCDE
SHORT-TERM ECONOMIC INDICATORS, SOURCES AND DEFINITIONS
OECD/CCET © April 1996

18

INDICATEURS ÉCONOMIQUES A COURT TERME, SOURCES ET DÉFINITIONS
OCDE/CCET © avril 1996

SUMMARY METHODOLOGICAL TABLES

The following tables summarise and compare the methodologies used in the calculation of the following short-term indicators: industrial production indices, retail sales volume, unemployment, producer price indices, consumer price indices, and foreign trade. Where information is missing, the entry is blank.

All information contained in these tables, plus additional details, are included in the country chapters.

INDEX OF TOTAL INDUSTRIAL PRODUCTION

Country	"Industry" covers Mining and quarrying plus:			Private sector coverage ?	Survey coverage
	Manufacturing	Gas, water & electricity	Other		
BULGARIA	Excluding publishing.	Except cold water production, purification and distribution.	Forestry, fishing.	In annual indices only.	Monthly and quarterly surveys cover approx. 3,000 state and co-operative enterprises accounting for 91.3% of industrial output in 1994.
ESTONIA	Yes.	Except gas distribution, thermal energy and household water.		All enterprises with > 20 employees, yearly. And all enterprises with > 50 employees, monthly.	From 1994, annual surveys cover all non-private enterprises with > 20 employees. Monthly surveys cover all enterprises with > 50 employees which represents about 85% of industrial sales.
HUNGARY	Yes.	Yes.		Since 1994, enterprises with > 10 employees are surveyed; those with < 10 employees are estimated.	From 1994, a sample for enterprises with 11-50 employees is surveyed; a census of those with > 50 employees. Estimations are made for enterprises with < 10 employees.
LATVIA	Yes.	Starting in 1995, monthly surveys include water supply.		Enterprises with > 50 employees.	From 1991, monthly surveys include 90% of production (all private enterprises with > 50 employees, plus all public sector enterprises). Annual surveys cover all production.
LITHUANIA	Yes.	Yes, from January 1994.		From January 1995, enterprises with > 20 employees.	600 enterprises are surveyed monthly, sales of over 1,100 industrial goods are noted. The coverage is estimated at 90% of total production.
POLAND	Yes.	Yes. Up to 1994, excludes water production, purification and distribution.		Yes, after 1991.	From 1991, all enterprises with > 50 employees are surveyed, and a sample of 10% is drawn from enterprises with 6 to 50 employees. 5% of enterprises with < 5 employees are surveyed annually.
REPUBLIC OF SLOVENIA	Excluding publishing.	Gas, steam and water supply are excluded.		All private enterprises with > 5 employees.	All public enterprises, and all private enterprises with > 5 employees. In 1994, equalled 1,800 enterprises.

| "Production" includes : | | | | | |
Changes in stocks of finished goods	Changes in work in progress	Non-principal production	Type of index	Type of individual product data	Aggregation weights / volume deflators
Yes.	Yes.	From 1995, only.	Laspeyres.	Volume.	The Producer price index (PPI).
No.	No.	No.		From 1994, value of sales.	Value data are deflated by the OECD Secretariat using the Producer price index in base 1993=100.
Yes.	Yes.	No.	Paasche.	Value.	The Producer Price Index (PPI).
Yes.	Yes.	Yes.	From 1995, Laspeyres.	Value.	January 1992 prices.
No.	No.	No.		Volume.	The Producer Price Index (PPI).
In annual series only.	Yes.	No.	Laspeyres.	Value.	1984 prices are used to deflate 1985-90 data; 1990 prices deflate 1991-93 data; 1992 prices from 1994.
Yes.	Yes.	Yes.	Laspeyres.	Volume expressed in quantities (tonnes, pieces, etc,).	1993 value of invoiced sales adjusted by their share of value added.

INDEX OF TOTAL INDUSTRIAL PRODUCTION

Country	"Industry" covers Mining and quarrying plus:			Private sector coverage ?	Survey coverage
	Manufacturing	Gas, water & electricity	Other		
ROMANIA	Yes.	Yes.		Yes.	1,030 products and product groups are surveyed.
SLOVAK REPUBLIC	Until end 1991, excluding publishing.	Yes (production and distribution of water from 1991).		Yes, covers enterprises on the business register.	From 1992, enterprises with > 24 employees. From 1993, enterprises with < 25 employees are surveyed quarterly and used to revised monthly estimates. Estimates of individual entrepreneurs also included from 1993.
ARMENIA, BELARUS, KYRGYZ REP., REP. OF MOLDOVA TAJIKISTAN, TURKMENISTAN, UZBEKISTAN	Excluding printing and publishing.	Yes.	Logging and fishing, cleaning services, repair and maintenance of motor vehicles and repair of personal and household goods.	Yes.	Armenia: 800 enterprises; Belarus: 1,800 enterprises; Kyrgyz Rep.: 500 enterprises; Rep. of Moldova & Tajikistan & Turkmenistan: 400 enterprises; Uzbekistan: 2,000 enterprises.
AZERBAIJAN, KAZAKSTAN, RUSSIAN FEDERATION	Excluding printing and publishing.	Yes.	Logging and fishing, cleaning services, repair and maintenance of motor vehicles and repair of personal and household goods.	Yes.	Azerbaijan: 1,000 enterprises are surveyed concerning 300 products; Kazakstan: 2,500 enterprises are surveyed concerning 400 products; and Russian Federation: 24,000 enterprises are surveyed concerning 430 products.
UKRAINE	Excluding publishing.	Yes.	Logging and fishing, cleaning services, repair and maintenance of motor vehicles and repair of personal and household goods.	Yes.	90,000 enterprises are surveyed concerning 500 products.

OECD
OCDE
SHORT-TERM ECONOMIC INDICATORS, SOURCES AND DEFINITIONS
OECD/CCET © April 1996

22

INDICATEURS ÉCONOMIQUES A COURT TERME, SOURCES ET DÉFINITIONS
OCDE/CCET © avril 1996

"Production" includes :			Type of index	Type of individual product data	Aggregation weights / volume deflators
Changes in stocks of finished goods	Changes in work in progress	Non-principal production			
No.	No.		Laspeyres.	Volume.	Gross value added in 1991.
Yes.	Yes.	No.	Laspeyres.	Value.	From 1991, the Producer Price Index (PPI).
No.	Yes, for goods with a long production cycle.	Yes.	Laspeyres.	Volume.	1 January 1982 prices for 1980-90 data, and the January prices of the current year since then. Current month for Kyrgyz Rep. and Turkmenistan from 1992.
No.	Yes, for goods with a long production cycle.	Yes.	Laspeyres.	Volume.	1 January 1982 prices for 1980-90 data, and the January prices of the current year since then. Weighted averages of changes in volume are used for Russian Federation since 1993, for Azerbaijan and Kazakstan since 1994.
No.	Yes.	Yes.	Paasche.	Value.	January 1989 whosale prices.

RETAIL SALES VOLUME

Country	Retail sales value survey coverage	Items not included	Price used as deflator	Base year prices
BULGARIA	From 1996, 30% of public sector and 1.5% of private sector outlets are surveyed, respectively corresponding to 90% and 50% of retail sales by these units.		Value data are deflated by the OECD Secretariat using the Consumer Price Index: goods.	1992 prices.
ESTONIA	Starting 1993, all retail trade enterprises with > 20 employees and all state retail trade enterprises are surveyed. A sample is drawn for all other retail enterprises (600 retail enterprises).	Public catering.	Retail Price Index.	1992 prices.
HUNGARY	Target population: all retail trade and catering outlets.	Items sold directly from producing firms to consumers.	Retail Price Index.	January 1991 prices.
LATVIA	From 1995, all public trade enterprises and enterprises with turnover in a yearly program exceeds 100,000 lats, for all other enterprises 10% are surveyed.	Public catering.	Consumer Price Index: goods.	January 1991 prices.
LITHUANIA	All public and private outlets with > 5 employees.	Market sales and sales by small enterprises.	Consumer Price Index.	May 1992 prices.
POLAND	Sales by units with less than 5 employees are included in annual data only.	Agricultural sales and trade from the public to private sector.	Value data are deflated by the OECD Secretariat using the Consumer Price Index: goods.	1992 prices.
REPUBLIC OF SLOVENIA	Main retail outlets accounting for 50% of total retail trade turnover.	Items sold in food markets by producer directly to consumers.	Retail Price Index: goods.	1992 prices.
ROMANIA	3,000 public, mixed, private and co-operative owned outlets.	Public catering; agricultural products sold by individuals; electricity and gas.	Retail Price Index.	The previous month.
SLOVAK REPUBLIC	From 1996, outlets with > 20 employees are surveyed monthly.		Value data are deflated by the OECD Secretariat using the Consumer Price Index: goods.	1 January 1989 prices.

RETAIL SALES VOLUME

Country	Retail sales value survey coverage	Items not included	Price used as deflator	Base year prices
N.I.S. EXCLUDING UKRAINE	All enterprises selling consumer goods irrespective of type of ownership. From 1995 a new series for most countries also includes estimates for non registered enterprises and private persons in informal markets.	Since 1991, services.	For Armenia, Belarus and Russian Federation: Consumer price index: "goods". For all other countries: Retail trade price index .	Prices of corresponding period of the previous year.
UKRAINE	All enterprises selling consumer goods.	Since 1991, services.	Retail Price Index.	Previous period prices.

UNEMPLOYMENT

Country	Working age population	Criteria to register as unemployed	Unemployment rate = unemployed [1] as % of:	Criteria to receive unemployment benefits.
BULGARIA	15-54 (women) 15-59 (men).	Persons who have worked for 8 months; or secondary school graduates; or those registered for post-school study for at least 1 month.	Total labour force.	Registered unemployed with no alternate source of earnings.
ESTONIA	16-56,5 (women) 16-61,5 (men)[2] .	Permanent residents who have been engaged in work or in an activity equal to work for at least 180 days during the last 12 months and who are actively seeking work.	Working age population (data of the State Labour Market Board).	Registered unemployed, whose income does not exceed a state unemployment benefit.
HUNGARY	15-54 (women) 15-59 (men).	Persons available for work and looking for a job; not students or pensioners.	Total labour force at 1st January of the previous year.	Persons who have contributed to the unemployment fund for at least 360 days in the last 4 years before becoming unemployed. Graduates having finished their degrees in the last 18 months.
LATVIA	15-54 (women) 15-59 (men).	Non-working residents in working age, who does not receive wage or other income at least to the amount of the minimum wages, actively looking for a job, not involved in entrepreneurial activity. Recent graduates or those released from confinement.	Total labour force.	Registered unemployed. Not available for persons who have left their job voluntarily or were released due to discipline reasons or for breaking their work contract.
LITHUANIA	16-55 (women) 16-60 (men).	All non-working persons who can prove they are looking for work, including recent graduates and persons who have never worked, and those who have left their jobs by choice.	Total labour force in the previous year.	Registered unemployed who have worked at least 24 months in last 3 years , recent graduates, and those returning from military service or imprisonnement.
POLAND	18-60 (women) 18-65 (men).	Persons not receiving an old age or disability pension; do not own a farm; not run any agricultural economic activity; are not temporary imprisoned; are not eligible for social insurance, including disabled persons capable of working at least half-time.	Civilian labour force in the given period.	Registered unemployed having worked for at least 180 days in the last 12 months, prior to the registration day. There is no proposal of suitable employment or training course, or appointment to communal job.

Minimum period of non-activity before receiving benefits	Maximum benefit period	A beneficiary loses the right to benefits if he/she:	Benefit amount
	1 year. For recent graduates: 3 months.	Does not re-register regularly.	Proportion of last wage.
10 days.	Not fixed, generally 180 calendar days.	Obtains an income of at least the same as the state unemployment benefit or has not re-registered in person for more than 10 workdays.	Established at 180 EEK since 1991.
For recent graduates: 3 months.	1 year for those having contributed to the unemployment fund for 4 years. For recent graduates: 6 months.	Refuses a job or training; or receives a pension.	For recent graduates: 75% of the minimum wage.
2 weeks.	6 months in any given 12 month period. This period can be extended up to 12 months following the request of local authorities.	Refuses 2 job offers or professional training courses. Does not re-register every month. Leaves the country. Loses his status of the unemployed.	90% of the minimum wage. 70% of the minimum wage if the social tax payments are not made during the last 12 months in Latvia, or they have been made for less than 6 months.
For those who have worked previously: 8 days. For persons whom have left their jobs by choice: 6 months.	6 months per year.	Does not re-register every month, refuses 3 job offers or one training programme.	For the first 2 months, former salaried persons receive 70% of their former wage, for the next 2 months: 60%; for the following 2 months: 50%. From 1996, the minimum benefit is 90 litas and the maximum is 180 litas.
For eligible graduates: 3 months.	Generally 12 months; more in cases defined in the Act.	Refuses 1 offer of suitable job, training, doing communal & intervening job without any reason. Was dismissed by his employer for disciplinary reasons. Does not re-register at the local Labour Office without good reason.	Generally, 36% of the average monthly salary in the previous quarter or as defined in the relevant Act.

UNEMPLOYMENT

Country	Working age population	Criteria to register as unemployed	Unemployment rate = unemployed [1] as % of:	Criteria to receive unemployment benefits.
REPUBLIC OF SLOVENIA	15-58 (women) 15-63 (men).	All persons not having a regular job, not self employed, who do not own property which could provide a living, who are capable and willing to work.	Total labour force in the corresponding year.	Registered unemployed who have work 9 months uninterruptedly or for a total of 12 months in the last 18 months, who lost their job against their will, and who register within 30 days of losing their job.
ROMANIA	16-57 (women) 16-62 (men).	Persons who have lost their jobs or recent graduates who have never worked and have finished school or compulsory military service.	Civilian labour force at 31 December of the previous year.	Registered persons over 18 who do not have an alternate source of revenue equalling more than 50% of the minimum wage; do not own (with their family) > 20 000 square metres of agricultural land.
SLOVAK REPUBLIC	15-54 (women) 15-59 (men).	Persons without a work contract or entrepreneurial activity, looking for suitable work.	Civilian labour force.	Registered unemployed perons who have worked at least 12 months in the last 3 years.
ARMENIA	16-55 (women) 16-60 (men).	Able-bodied non-working persons who are not engaged in entrepreneurial activity, not studying in a day-time institution and not military service persons.	Civilian labour force in the previous quarter.	Benefits are paid to persons legally considered as unemployed.
AZERBAIJAN	16-55 (women) 16-60 (men).	Able-bodied non-working persons who are ready and able to start work and who do not have a job or earnings for reasons independent of themselves.	Civilian labour force in the previous quarter.	Benefits are paid to persons legally considered as unemployed.
BELARUS	16-55 (women) 16-60 (men).	Able-bodied non-working persons who are not engaged in entrepreneurial activity, not studying in a day-time institution and not military service persons.	Civilian labour force in the previous quarter.	Registered persons who do not have an income (pension, allowance, work accident compensation, etc.) that exceeds the amount of the unemployment benefit.

Minimum period of non-activity before receiving benefits	Maximum benefit period	A beneficiary loses the right to benefits if he/she:	Benefit amount
None.	2 years for those have worked previously for over 20 years. 3 months for those who have worked only 12 of the last 18 months.	Refuses 3 job offers.	70% of the average earnings of the last 3 months of activity, for the first 3 months of the benefit period. Not less than 80% of the minimum wage.
None, if the unemployed register within 30 days of the end of their contract. Higher education graduates: 60 days. Military service persons: 30 days.	9 months. After 9 months, persons who are still unemployed receive a support allowance for up to 18 months.	Refuses an appropriate job or training programme located within 50 km of the beneficiairy's residence; does not re-register monthly.	For those who have worked > 5 years, 50% of average monthly salary over the last 3 months but not less than 75% of the minimum wage. For graduates: 60-70% of minimum wage. Support allowance: 60% of the minimum wage.
	6 months. After 6 months unemployed persons may be offered paid work for public benefit or receive social rations.	Does not re-register regularly.	For the first 3 months: 60% of the former wage (but not more 3,000 SK). For next 3 months: 50% of the former wage.
10 days.	24 weeks during 12 month period. For new job seekers: 12 weeks. For pre-pensioners: 40 weeks during 12 months.	Declines 2 suitable work offers, does not re-register twice without reason, or finds a job without notifying the employment agency.	50% of the previous average wage (but not less than the minimum wage and not more than 3 times the minimum wage). For new job seekers: the minimum wage.
10 days.	26 weeks during 12 month period.	Declines 2 suitable work offers, violates re-registration rules, finds a temporary job without notifying the employment agency, receives benefits illegally or is sentenced to imprisonment.	70-75% of the previous average wage for 13 weeks; 55-60% of the previous wage during the next 13 weeks. Never less than the minimum wage or more than the average wage. Benefit is increased by 10% for each dependent. For new job seekers: the minimum wage.
None.	26 weeks during 12 month period.	Payments are stopped or suspended for up to 3 months for refusal of 2 suitable job offers, illegal benefit receipt or violation of re-registration rules and conditions.	70 % of the previous average wage for 13 weeks; 50% during the next 13 weeks. Never less than the minimum wage or more than the twice the minimum wage. For new job seekers: 85% of the minimum wage for 13 weeks; 70% during the next 13 weeks.

UNEMPLOYMENT

Country	Working age population	Criteria to register as unemployed	Unemployment rate = unemployed [1] as % of:	Criteria to receive unemployment benefits.
KAZAKSTAN	16-55 (women) 16-60 (men).	Able-bodied non-working perons who are ready and able to start work and who do not have a job or earnings for reasons independent of themselves.	Civilian labour force in the previous quarter.	Benefits are paid to persons legally considered as unemployed.
KYRGYZ REPUBLIC	16-55 (women) 16-60 (men).	Able-bodied non-working persons who are ready and able to start work and who do not have a job or earnings for reasons independent of themselves.	Civilian labour force in the previous quarter.	Benefits are paid to persons legally considered as unemployed.
REPUBLIC OF MOLDOVA	16-55 (women) 16-60 (men).	Able-bodied non-working persons who are ready and able to start work and who do not have a job or earnings for reasons independent of themselves.	Civilian labour force in the previous quarter.	Benefits are paid to persons legally considered as unemployed.
RUSSIAN FEDERATION	16-55 (women) 16-60 (men).	Able-bodied non-working persons who are ready and able to start work and who do not have a job or earnings for reasons independent of themselves.	Civilian labour force in the previous quarter.	Benefits are paid to persons legally considered as unemployed.
TAJIKISTAN	16-55 (women) 16-60 (men).	Able-bodied non-working persons who are ready and able to start work and who do not have a job or earnings for reasons independent of themselves.	Civilian labour force in the previous quarter.	Benefits are paid to persons legally considered as unemployed.
TURKMENISTAN [3]		n.a.	n.a.	n.a.

Minimum period of non-activity before receiving benefits	Maximum benefit period	A beneficiary loses the right to benefits if he/she:	Benefit amount
7 days.	26 weeks during 12 month period. For new job seekers: 13 weeks. For pre-pensioners: 36 weeks.	Payments are reduced or suspended for up to 3 months for refusal of 2 suitable job offers, temporary employment without notification of the employment agency or violation of re-registration rules.	Not more than 50% of the former wage, and not less than the minimum living standard and not more than the average wage. For new job seekers: not < 75% of the minimum living standard. The benefit to persons with children < 14 years is increased by 10%.
10 days.	26 weeks during 12 month period. The normal 26 weeks are increased by 2 weeks for each year worked exceeding the standard working period needed to receive a pension.	Payments are stopped or suspended for up to 1 month for refusal 2 suitable job offers, illegal benefit receival or violation of re-registration rules and conditions.	From 1.1 to 1.5 times the minimum wage. For new job seekers: the minimum wage. The benefit to unemployed persons with children < 14 years is increased by 10-20%.
10 days.	9 months. For new job seekers: 6 months.	Payments are stopped or suspended for up to 5 months for refusal of 1 job offer, illegal benefit receival or violation of re-registration rules and conditions.	From 50-60% of the average wage for the last 3 months. Never less than the minimum wage and not more than the average wage. For new job seekers: 75-100% of the minimum wage. Benefits for persons with children minor than 14 years are increased by 10%.
None.	12 months during 18 month period. For pre-pensioners: 24 months during 36 months.	Payments are stopped or suspended for up to 3 months for refusal of 2 suitable job offers, illegal benefit receival or violation of re-registration rules and conditions.	From 45% to 75% of the former average wage for the last 2 months. But not less than the minimum wage and not more than the average wage. For new job seekers: the minimum wage.
1 day.	26 weeks. For new job seekers: 13 weeks during 12 month period. The normal 26 weeks are increased by 2 weeks for each year worked exceeding the standard working period needed to receive a pension.	Payments are stopped or suspended for up to 3 months for refusal of 2 suitable job offers, illegal benefit receival or violation of re-registration rules and conditions.	For those having worked previously, not less than the minimum wage. For new job seekers: not less than 75% of the minimum wage.
n.a.	n.a.	n.a.	n.a.

OECD
OCDE
SHORT-TERM ECONOMIC INDICATORS, SOURCES AND DEFINITIONS
OECD/CCET © April 1996

31

INDICATEURS ÉCONOMIQUES A COURT TERME, SOURCES ET DÉFINITIONS
OCDE/CCET © avril 1996

UNEMPLOYMENT

Country	Working age population	Criteria to register as unemployed	Unemployment rate = unemployed [1] as % of:	Criteria to receive unemployment benefits.
UKRAINE	16-54 (women) 16-59 (men).	Able-bodied non-working persons of working age who are ready and able to work and do not have a job or earnings for reasons independent of themselves.	n.a.	Persons registered as unemployed with no other source of income.
UZBEKISTAN	16-55 (women) 16-60 (men).	Able-bodied non-working persons of working age who are ready and able to work and undergo professional training and do not have a job or earnings for reasons independent of themselves.	Civilian labour force in the previous quarter.	Benefits are paid to persons legally considered as unemployed.

(1) In all countries, the number of registered unemployed is used to calculate the unemployment rate.

(2) From 1994, six months will be added to the pension age each year so that in 2003 the pension age for females will be 60 and for males, 65.

(3) No information is available as yet regarding unemployment in Turkmenistan.

Minimum period of non-activity before receiving benefits	Maximum benefit period	A beneficiary loses the right to benefits if he/she:	Benefit amount
11 days.	No more than 12 months in a period of 3 years.	Undertakes retraining; refuses 2 suitable job offers; is a first job seeker and refuses a training course or paid work; does not re-register periodically during the month.	50% of the former average wage over the last 12 months, but not < the minimum wage and not > the average wage. For new job seekers: not < 75% of the minimum wage.
10 days.	26 weeks during 12 month period. For new job seekers: 13 weeks.	Payments are stopped or suspended for up to 3 months for refusal of 2 suitable job offers, illegal benefit receival or violation of re-registration rules and conditions.	50% of the former average wage over the last 12 months, but not < the minimum wage and not > the average wage. For new job seekers: not < 75% of the minimum wage. The benefit to persons with children < 16 years, or other dependents, is increased by 10%.

PRODUCER/WHOLESALE PRICE INDICES

Country	Industrial products covered	Current price enquiry	Weights used
BULGARIA Wholesale price index	Domestic production.	Items: 1,000 manufactured goods and commodity groups. Respondents: 3,000 public sector enterprises.	Sales values.
ESTONIA Producer price index	Production for the domestic and export markets.	Items: 440 industrial goods. Respondents: 110 enterprises.	From June 1995, the 1994 production volumes.
HUNGARY Producer price index	Products sold to other producers, wholesalers or retailers, or destined for export.	Items: 800. Respondents: 800 of the largest producers.	Sales values.
LATVIA Producer price index	Production for the domestic and export markets.	Items: 709 commodities. Respondents: 166 manufacturing enterprises.	1993 year sales volumes.
LITHUANIA Producer price index	Domestic production.	Items: 890 industrial goods. Respondents: 270 enterprises.	In 1996, sales value of 1994.
POLAND Producer price index	Representative items dominating the reporting unit's sales value (75% of monthly turnover).	Items: 19,000 quotations from all reporting units. Respondents: 3,500 public and private enterprises.	From 1996 weight fixed sales value in 1994 (previously - weight fixed sales value in 1992), updated by the price and sale structure changes occuring in the current month.
REPUBLIC OF SLOVENIA Producer price index	Products sold on the domestic market.	Items: 450. Respondents: 300 of the largest producers.	Sales values in the previous year.
ROMANIA Producer price index	From 1993, products surveyed are destined for either domestic or export markets.	Items: 9,000. Respondents: 740 industrial units.	1992 value of deliveries.
SLOVAK REPUBLIC Producer price index	Products in 270 industrial branches.	Items: 1,890. Respondents: 382.	1989 value of production.
UKRAINE Wholesale price index	Industrial products intended for sale on the internal market.	Items: 6,200. Respondents: 1,500 industrial firms.	1993 structure of production.

Type of index	Treatment of quality changes	Treatment of seasonal items	Taxes included?
Paasche.			No.
Laspeyres.	None.	None.	No.
Laspeyres.	Products that have undergone quality changes are treated as new commodities.	The latest quotation is carried forward during the off-season.	No.
Laspeyres.	Survey respondents are instructed to adjust for quality changes.	The latest quotation is carried forward during the off-season.	No.
Laspeyres.	From 1996, prices are corrected for quality changes.	The latest quotation is carried forward during the off-season.	Before 1995, value added tax.
Paasche.	Products that have undergone changes in quality are treated as new commodities.	None.	Yes, before 1994. In 1994-95 excluded VAT. From 1996, excluded VAT and excise taxes.
Laspeyres.	The price is linked through the end of the year. For the following year, the item is introduced as a new item.	The latest quotation is carried through the off-season.	No.
Laspeyres.	Products that have undergone changes in quality are treated as new commodities.		Excise taxes are included. VAT excluded.
Laspeyres.	Price corrections are made when there are large quality of differences.	None.	VAT excluded; consumer taxes included.
Modified Laspeyres.	Yes (partially).	None.	No.

CONSUMER PRICE INDICES

Country	Current price enquiry	Number of quotations per month	Expenditure weights: source
BULGARIA	Items: 1604. Locations: 28 regions.	6 quotations per item.	The 1992 household budget survey.
ESTONIA	Items: 317 goods and 93 services. Locations: 10 towns.	For goods: 33 quotations per items.	The 1993 family expenditure survey is currently used. Weights of alcohol and tobacco are corrected for under-reporting.
HUNGARY	Items: 1,800. Outlets: 8,000. Locations: 86 towns.	Between 30 and 150 quotations per commodity in all outlets.	Household expenditure survey covering 12,000 sample households. Weights are changed yearly. Weights are corrected for under-reporting of alcohol, tobacco, confectionary and restaurant meals.
LATVIA	Items: 388 goods and services. Outlets: 1120. Locations: 15 regions.	4-8 quotations for agricultural products; 1-4 quotations for other items.	Household expenditure survey of mid-1992 to mid-1993. Weights are corrected for under-reporting of alcohol and tobacco.
LITHUANIA	Items: 369 goods and services. Outlets: about 1,060. Locations: 7 major cities and 9 regions.	One quotation for each commodity or service.	Household expenditure survey since May 1992. Expenditure patterns currently used are for August 1992-July 1993.
POLAND	Items: 1400-1800 goods and services. Outlets: 28,000. Locations: 307 towns or districts.	3 quotations for food, alcohol and tobacco; 1 quotation for other items.	Household budget survey since 1991. It covers total population since 1993. Previously retail turnover. Weights are corrected for under-reporting of alcoholic beverages, tobacco products and catering.
REPUBLIC OF SLOVENIA	Items: 354 goods and 91 services. Outlets:150. Locations: 4 towns and rural areas.	One quotation ; 2 quotations for agricultural products.	The 1993 Family Budget survey of 3,270 households.
ROMANIA	Items: 1,800. Outlets: 4,300. Locations: 40 county capitals plus Bucharest.	2 quotations for each good or service.	Family expenditure survey of 9,000 households covering employees, farmers and retired persons. Expenditure patterns currently used are for 1993.
SLOVAK REPUBLIC	Items: 836 goods and services. Locations: 38 districts.	3-5 quotations for commodities and selected services; one quotation for other services (e.g. transport and communications).	For goods: 1989 retail turnover. For services: 1989 household expenditure.
ARMENIA	Items: 267 goods and 63 services.	All goods & services: every 10 days.	Household consumption expenditure in the previous year.

Type of index	Treatment of seasonal items	Adjustments for changes in quality	Percent of Food in total expenditure
Modified Laspeyres.			43.4
Since January 1994, Laspeyres. Fixed weights index from 1st quarter 1990 to Dec 1993.	The average price change of the other items in a given product group is imputed for an item that is not available.	Yes.	37.9
Modified Laspeyres.	Monthly weights are variable within a fixed basket of seasonal food items.	None.	28.4
Laspeyres from June 1992; previously Paasche.	For goods not "in season", an average seasonal price is imputed.	Yes.	49.7
Modified Laspeyres from May 1992; previously, Paasche.	The price of the previous month is used for non-available items.	None.	65.8
Laspeyres.	Monthly weights are variable within a fixed basket of seasonal fruits and vegetables.	None.	39.2
Laspeyres.	Monthly weights are variable within a fixed basket of seasonal fruits and vegetables.	If a product disappears, it is replaced by a product of similar quality. If none exists, adjustments are made.	31.8
Laspeyres.	Monthly weights are variable within a fixed basket of items such as fresh fruits, vegetables and wool.	Yes.	47.1
Laspeyres.	Different baskets of fruits and vegetables are used each month.	Adjustments are made to the prices in the base period.	29.9
Laspeyres.	None.	None.	75.7

OECD
OCDE
SHORT-TERM ECONOMIC INDICATORS, SOURCES AND DEFINITIONS
OECD/CCET © April 1996

37

INDICATEURS ÉCONOMIQUES A COURT TERME, SOURCES ET DÉFINITIONS
OCDE/CCET © avril 1996

CONSUMER PRICE INDICES

Country	Current price enquiry	Number of quotations per month	Expenditure weights: source
AZERBAIJAN	Items: 268 goods and 33 services.	Foodstuffs: every 7 or 10 days, non foodstuffs & services: one quotation.	Household consumption expenditure in 1993.
BELARUS	Items: 273 goods and 43 services.	All goods & services: one quotation.	Household consumption expenditure in the previous year.
KAZAKSTAN	Items: 242 goods and 33 services.	Foodstuffs: every 7 or 10 days, non foodstuffs & services: one quotation.	Household consumption expenditure in the previous year.
KYRGYZ REPUBLIC	Items: 270 goods and 35 services.	All goods & services: one quotation.	Household consumption expenditure in the previous year.
REPUBLIC OF MOLDOVA	Items: 265 goods and 47 services.	Foodstuffs: every 7 or 10 days, non foodstuffs & services: 2 quotations.	Household consumption expenditure in the previous year.
RUSSIAN FEDERATION	Items: 215 goods and 73 services.	Foodstuffs: every 7 or 10 days, non foodstuffs & services: one quotation.	Household consumption expenditure in the previous year.
TAJIKISTAN	Items: 239 goods and 35 services.	Foodstuffs: every 7 or 10 days, non foodstuffs & services: one quotation.	Household consumption expenditure in the previous year.
TURKMENISTAN	Items: 1,200 goods and services.	Foodstuffs: every 7 or 10 days, non foodstuffs & services: one quotation.	Household consumption expenditure in the previous year.
UKRAINE	Items: 345 goods and 80 services. Locations: all cities and district centres.		From 1995 structure of consumption expenditures of the previous year.
UZBEKISTAN	Items: 233 goods and 34 services.	Foodstuffs: every 7 or 10 days, non foodstuffs & services: one quotation.	Household consumption expenditure in the previous year.

Type of index	Treatment of seasonal items	Adjustments for changes in quality	Percent of Food in total expenditure
Laspeyres.	None.	None.	72.0
Laspeyres.	None.	None.	65.4
Laspeyres.	None.	None.	59.8
Laspeyres.	None.	None.	62.6
Laspeyres.	None.	None.	47.3
Laspeyres.	None.	None.	52.5
Laspeyres.	None.	None.	74.9
Laspeyres.	None.	None.	55.0
Modified Laspeyres.	None.	None.	65.0
Laspeyres.	None.	None.	66.1

FOREIGN TRADE

Country	Classification	Documents used	Imports valued	Items not included in trade
BULGARIA	From 1992, the Harmonised System.	From 1992, customs declarations. Before 1992, survey of exporters and importers.	From 1992, CIF; previously, FOB.	Services, repairs, patents, know-how, direct re-exports, fish catching and films.
ESTONIA	CBNE [1]. From July 1992, the Harmonised System.	Customs declarations from July 1992. Previously, survey of exporters and importers.	CIF.	Services; trade with Embassies.
HUNGARY	For 1991-93, the Harmonised System. From 1994, the Combined Nomenclature System.	Prior to 1991, survey of exporters and importers. For 1991-94, customs declarations. From 1995, Single Administrative Document.	CIF.	Many services, namely construction-assembly, feature films and software. Sales/purchases by extraterritorial bodies; fuel sold to foreign vessels, aircraft, etc. or bought by Hungarian shipping firms abroad; trade in ships and aircraft.
LATVIA	CBNE [1]. Harmonised System.	From 1993, customs declarations only, with additional data from special enquiries. In 1992, customs declarations were introduced and used in parallel with surveys. For 1991, surveys of exporters and importers.	FOB.	All traded services, research and development, and foreign aid. Monthly data exclude deliveries to Russian troops formerly stationed in Latvia nor transactions of the Latvian fishing fleet outside the country.
LITHUANIA	Combined Nomenclature.	Customs declarations; imports of electrical energy from enterprise reports.	CIF.	All traded services, gold, securities, goods traded temporarily, trade with Embassies, fish catching in international waters, provisions for Lithuanian ships and aircraft abroad.
POLAND	From 1992, the Combined Nomenclature System; previously according to the Foreign Trade Commodity Nomenclature (NTHZ).	In 1980-89, trade statistics were based on importer/exporter's invoices. In 1990-91, customs declarations. From 1992, the Single Administrative Document is used.	From 1992, CIF; previously, FOB.	Services (except improvement trade), repairs, construction, patents, licences, know-how, direct re-exports to/from customs-free zones.
REPUBLIC OF SLOVENIA	For 1988-95, Harmonised System and SITC Rev. 3. From 1996, the Combined Nomenclature.	Customs declarations.	CIF.	Services, lease, supply of Slovenian diplomatic missions abroad, supply of fuel to transporters, commercial samples, luggage.

FOREIGN TRADE

Country	Classification	Documents used	Imports valued	Items not included in trade
ROMANIA	In 1991-93, the Harmonised System. From 1994, the Combined Nomenclature.	From 1991, customs declarations.	From 1991, CIF; previously, FOB.	Most services: licences, patents, know-how, design and research works, construction and assembly works, fuel and food for ships' supply, printing of books and booklets.
SLOVAK REPUBLIC	From 1991, the Harmonised System.	From 1991, national customs declarations. The Single Administrative Document from 1992.	FOB.	Service trade is excluded. Includes trade with the Czech Republic from 1993 only.
ARMENIA, AZERBAIJAN, BELARUS, KAZAKSTAN, KYRGYZ REP., REP. OF MOLDOVA, RUSSIAN FED., TAJIKISTAN, TURKMENISTAN, UZBEKISTAN	The Commodity Nomenclature of Foreign Economic Activities, elaborated based on the Harmonised System to the six-digit level.	Reports submitted by external trade organisations and customs declarations.	CIF.	Foreign trade services; receipts from tourism. For the Russian Federation: construction services, financial services, publishing, education, training and health services are included. In Uzbekistan: foreign trade in services are included from 1992.
UKRAINE	Harmonised System.	Enterprise statistical reports and customs declarations.	CIF.	Total trade including trade with the former Soviet Union is available from January 1994.

(1) Classification of Branches of the National Economy developed by the former Council for Mutual Economic Assistance (CMEA).

BUSINESS TENDENCY SURVEYS

Introduction

The OECD Centre for Co-operation with the Economies in Transition has been working with Eurostat and the Commission of the European Communities to develop a programme of business tendency surveys in transition countries since 1991. This programme is part of a larger OECD/EC-Eurostat project to assist transition countries in developing appropriate short-term indicators.

Business tendency surveys collect qualitative information from business managers on their assessment of the current economic situation and on their intentions and expectations for the immediate future. Such surveys are conducted in all OECD Member countries and they have proved a cost-effective means of generating timely information on short-term economic developments. Current economic information is of particular interest to countries in transition and a reliable system of both quantitative and qualitative short-term indicators is of prime importance.

Compared to traditional quantitative statistical surveys, business tendency surveys present many advantages as a source of short-term economic information. They collect information which is easier for enterprises to supply because the answers are not based on precise records and the returns can be submitted more quickly. Business tendency surveys cover a wide range of variables selected for their ability to monitor the business cycle and include information on variables not covered by quantitative statistics, such as capacity utilisation and views on the overall economic situation.

Member countries of the European Union have found it useful to standardise (or "harmonise") a number of the questions included in their business surveys so that the results are internationally comparable. Transition countries are being encouraged to use a number of standard questions to make their survey results internationally comparable.

Business surveys covering the industrial sector (in most cases the manufacturing industry) have been conducted on a regular basis for several years in Hungary and Poland. Regular surveys were introduced during 1991 in the former CSFR, Estonia and Romania and in January 1992 in Bulgaria. A first business survey in manufacturing was conducted in Russia in January 1992. This survey, however was restricted to enterprises in the Moscow region, but a new survey has been introduced covering the western part of the Russian Federation including Moscow. Business surveys were introduced in Latvia and Lithuania during 1993 and in Belarus in 1994.

Business surveys in the construction sector are available for Bulgaria, Estonia, Hungary, Latvia, Poland, Romania and Slovak Republic. Surveys in retail trade are available for all of the above countries with the exception of Latvia.

Selected business survey results have been included in the quarterly publication *Short-term Economic Indicators: Transition Economies* since April 1993. Business survey results in Bulgaria, Estonia, Hungary, Latvia, Lithuania, Poland, Romania, Slovak Republic, Belarus and the Russian Federation are now included on a regular basis. An annual Business Tendency Survey Annex, provides more detailed results from a wider range of surveys. The first such Annex was included in *Short-term Economic Indicators: Transition Economies*, Number 2/95.

In particular, the Annex contains the full set of results from surveys conducted in manufacturing, construction and retail trade. The complete set of questions for all three surveys corresponding to these results is included in the following pages. Departures from these harmonised questions are indicated where applicable. Summary tables describing the survey characteristics in each country are also provided.

In most countries, surveys are conducted by the Central Statistical Office in the country concerned. In some countries, however, private research institutes conduct the surveys. In Estonia, the surveys are carried out by the Estonian Institute for Market Research; in Hungary by the Institute for Economic and Market Research and Informatics, Ltd. (Kopint-Datorg); in Russia, surveys are conducted by the Institute for the Economy in Transition and in Belarus by the Economic Institute in the Ministry of the Economy. In Poland, business surveys have been conducted for a number of years both by the CSO and by the Research Institute of Economic Development in the Warsaw School of Economics. Survey results described here refer to the CSO survey for manufacturing and construction and to the Research Institute of Economic Development survey for retail trade.

The chief characteristics of business surveys is that instead of asking for exact figures, they usually ask for the respondents's assessment of the current business situation compared with the "normal" state, i.e. a question on **levels**, or they ask for an judgement on the direction of changes, i.e. a question on **tendency**. Answers are typically given as "above normal/normal/below normal" or as "up/same/down". Questions may refer either to the present situation or to expectations, i.e. questions on **future tendency** for the next three to six months.

The answers received are usually weighted according to the size of the responding firm and, for convenience, the results are usually given as one figure. This is straightforward where a single figure is requested from respondents, i.e. **percentage** of capacity utilisation. Sometimes, respondents are asked to indicate one or several choices in a nominal list of alternatives, in which case the weighted **proportion** of firms selecting the alternative is given. This latter type of question is used for information concerning limits to production or investment, limits to improvement in business situation and type of investment.

In the case of three-choice questions the data are generally presented in the form of a percent **balance**. "Normal" and "same" answers are ignored and the balance is obtained by taking the difference between the weighted percentages of respondents giving favourable and unfavourable answers. Negative balances indicate that unfavourable answers exceed favourable answers; positive balances show that favourable responses predominate. In the case of two-choice questions, i.e. do you plan fixed investment for this or next year -- "yes or no", the weighted **proportion** of firms indicating "yes" is given.

In the following section, the italicised title above each question refers to the title used in the tables in the Business Tendency Survey Annex in *Short-term Economic Indicators: Transition Economies*.

In the tables, business survey series which refer to future tendency or prospects for some future period are located in all cases at the time period of the survey, not at the time period to which the forecast refers.

Manufacturing industry survey

Harmonised questions

> ***Business situation: tendency***
> **Assessment of present business situation:**
> good (+), sufficient (=), bad (-)
>
> ***Business situation: future tendency***
> **Expected business situation six months from now:**
> better (+), same (=), worse(-)
>
> ***Order books / Demand Total: level***
> **Assessment of total demand/order books (present level):**
> above normal (+), normal (=), below normal (-)
>
> ***Order books / Demand Export: level***
> **Assessment of demand from abroad/export order books (present level):**
> above normal (+), normal (=), below normal (-)
>
> ***Order books / Demand Total: future tendency***
> **Expected total demand in the next 3-4 months:**
> up (+), unchanged (=), down (-)
>
> ***Order books / Demand Export: future tendency***
> **Export expectations for the next 3-4 months:**
> up (+), unchanged (=), down (-)
>
> ***Production: tendency***
> **Assessment of production activities in the last month (quarter):**
> up (+), unchanged (=), down (-)
>
> ***Production: future tendency***
> **Production activities for the next 3-4 months:**
> up (+), unchanged (=), down (-)
>
> ***Production: current capacity***
> **Assessment of current production capacity (with regard to expected demand in the next 12 months):**
> more than sufficient (+), sufficient (=), not sufficient (-)
>
> **Production: rate of capacity utilisation**
> **Current level of capacity utilisation (in per cent of normal capacity utilisation).**

Limits to production
Limits to production (present situation):
-- none
-- insufficient domestic demand
-- insufficient foreign demand
-- competitive imports
-- shortage of labour
-- shortage of skilled labour
-- lack of appropriate equipment
-- shortage of semi-finished goods
-- shortage of raw materials
-- shortage of energy
-- financial problems (e.g. insolvency, credits)
-- unclear economic laws
-- uncertainty of the economic environment
-- others, please specify

Stocks Finished goods: level
Assessment of stocks of finished goods (present level):
above normal (+), normal (=), below normal (-)

Selling prices: future tendency
Selling price expectations for the next 3-4 months:
increase (+), remain stable (=), decrease (-);

Selling prices Rate of increase: future tendency
if increase:
increase at a higher rate (+)
increase at about the same rate (=)
increase at a lower rate (-)

Employment: future tendency
Employment expectations for the next 3-4 months:
up (+), unchanged (=), down (-)

Fixed investment: intentions
Do you plan fixed investment for this year (next year):
yes (+1), no (0)

Fixed investment: future tendency
If fixed investment (machinery, buildings etc.) is planned will investment for this year (next year) compared to last year (current year) be:
higher (+), about the same (=), lower (-)

Type of fixed investment

If fixed investment is planned for next year, what type of investment will it be primarily:

-- replacement of old equipment
-- investment aimed at extending production capacity
    . with an unchanged product range
    . so as to extend the product range
-- rationalisation investment
    . mechanisation/automation of existing production process
    . introduction of new production techniques
    . energy saving
-- other motives
    . pollution control
    . safety measures
-- others, please specify

Limits to fixed investment

Factors limiting planned investments for the next year:

-- insufficient demand
-- cost of capital too high
-- credit guarantees insufficient
-- insufficient profits
-- fear of indebtedness
-- technical factors
-- others

Departures from harmonised questions

Estonia

The assessment of total/export demand is measured in terms of a change in demand between the current and previous quarter.

In the question on limits to production, only a subset of the alternatives is included.

Hungary

The comparison period for production: future tendency and employment expectations is six months.

Selling price expectations are measured in seven intervals expressing per cent changes transformed to a qualitative three point scale (increase/remain stable/decrease) and with a comparison period of six months.

In limits to production, the alternative "shortage of energy" is not included.

Expected total/export demand refer to the volume of sales and the comparison period is six months.

BUSINESS TENDENCY SURVEYS

Poland

The assessment of total/export demand is measured as changes between the current and previous month.

The comparison period for future production and for future selling price expectations is one month.

Investment intentions refer to the value of fixed investment expenditure in the current quarter as compared to the previous quarter.

The comparison period for the expected business situation is three months.

Romania

The comparison period for the expected business situation is three months.

Slovak Republic

The assessment of total/export demand is measured in terms of the change between the current and previous month.

Answers to limits to production are restricted to a maximum of five possibilities.

The assessment of the business situation is measured as the change between current and previous period.

The comparison period of the expected business situation is three months.

Construction survey

Harmonised questions

Business activity: tendency
Assessment of business activity compared to last month (quarter)
up (+), unchanged (=), down (-)

Business activity: duration of work in hand
With normal working hours, the work in hand and work already contracted will account for approximately .... months operating time.

Order books / Demand: level
Assessment of order books or production schedules for domestic/foreign contracts
total: above normal (+), normal (=), below normal (-)
domestic: above normal (+), normal (=), below normal (-)
foreign: above normal (+), normal (=), below normal (-)

Orders / Demand Total: future tendency
Orders (contracts) expectations for the next 3-4 months
up (+), unchanged (=), down (-)

Technical capacity with regard to expected demand: tendency
Assessment of technical capacity (amount and quality of equipment) with regard to expected demand in the next 12 months
more than sufficient (+), sufficient (=), not sufficient (-)

Limits to production
Limits to production (present situation)
-- none
-- demand
-- weather conditions
-- cost of materials
-- cost of labour
-- cost of finance (e.g. interest rates)
-- access to bank credit
-- shortage of skilled labour
-- lack of equipment
-- shortage of materials
-- competition in own sector
-- others, please specify

Price expectations: future tendency
Price expectations for next 3-4 months
increase (+), remain stable (=), decrease (-);

BUSINESS TENDENCY SURVEYS

Price expectations Rate of increase: future tendency
if increase:
increase at a higher rate (+)
increase at about the same rate (=)
increase at a lower rate (-)

Employment: future tendency
Employment expectations for the next 3-4 months
up (+), unchanged (=), down (-)

Financial situation: tendency
Assessment of financial situation compared to last month (quarter)
better (+), same (=), worse (-)

Financial situation: client delays in payment
Delays in payment by public/private clients compared to last month (quarter)
total: more widespread (+), unchanged (=), less widespread (-)
private: more widespread (+), unchanged (=), less widespread (-)
public: more widespread (+), unchanged (=), less widespread (-)

Departures from harmonised questions

Hungary

Business activity is measured in comparison with a normal situation in terms of an appreciation of the level of activity.

The employment expectations and price expectations refer to the situation in six months.

Poland

The assessment of order books is measured as the change between the current and previous quarter.

The assessment of technical capacity with regard to demand is measured in terms of the change in capacity in the form of a comparison between the last quarter and future 3-4 months.

OECD
OCDE
SHORT-TERM ECONOMIC INDICATORS, SOURCES AND DEFINITIONS
OECD/CCET © April 1996
50
INDICATEURS ÉCONOMIQUES A COURT TERME, SOURCES ET DÉFINITIONS
OCDE/CCET © avril 1996

Retail trade survey

Harmonised questions

Business situation: tendency
Assessment of present business situation
good (+), satisfactory (normal for season) (=), bad (-)

Business situation: future tendency
Expected business situation six months ahead
better (+), same (=), worse (-)

Competition in own sector: tendency
Assessment of competition in own sector compared to last month (quarter)
up (+), unchanged (=), down (-)

Limits to improvements in business situation
Factors limiting improvements to the present business situation
-- none
-- demand
-- supply
-- cost of labour
-- cost of finance (e.g. interest rates)
-- access to bank credit
-- sales surface
-- storage capacity
-- competition in own sector
-- others, please specify

Intentions of placing orders: future tendency
Expectations on orders placed with domestic/foreign suppliers in the next 3-4 months
total: up (+), unchanged (=), down (-)
domestic: up (+), unchanged (=), down (-)
foreign: up (+), unchanged (=), down (-)

Stocks: level
Assessment of stocks
too small (+), adequate (normal for season) (=), too large (-)

Selling prices: tendency
Selling prices compared with the last month (quarter)
increase (+), remain stable (=), decrease (-), in absolute terms

Selling prices Rate of increase: tendency
if increase
increase at a higher rate (+)
increase at about the same rate (=)
increase at a lower rate (-)

Selling prices: future tendency
Selling price expectations for the next 3-4 months
increase (+), remain stable (=), decrease (-), in absolute terms

Selling prices Rate of increase: future tendency
If increase
increase at a higher rate (+)
increase at about the same rate (=)
increase at a lower rate (-)

Employment: future tendency
Employment expectations for the next 3-4 months
up (+), unchanged (=), down (-)

Financial situation: tendency
Assessment of financial situation compared to last month (quarter)
better (+), same (=), worse (-)

Departures from harmonised questions

Poland

The assessment of stocks is measured as the change between the current and previous quarter.

Romania

The expected business situation refers to the situation three months in the future.

Slovak Republic

The expected business situation refers to three months in the future.

The assessment of financial situation refers to the incapacity to pay or delays in payment by the firm or company.

BUSINESS SURVEYS: MANUFACTURING

Country	Survey					
	Sample size	Coverage: % of private firms in sample	Coverage: % of employment in manufacturing	Coverage: % of turnover	Coverage: % of units-less than 500 employees	Response rate
BULGARIA	1002			71		95
ESTONIA	250	80	60	60	95	70-80
HUNGARY	1000		30	65		35-40
LATVIA	233	47	55	59	76	63-84
LITHUANIA	300	50	40	61	55	50
POLAND	3400	51	61	67	75	68
ROMANIA	600	30	49	54	38	
SLOVAK REPUBLIC	220	23	48	55	24	75-77
BELARUS	500	40	100		40-45	17-37
RUSSIAN FED.	1000	84	11			50-60

BUSINESS SURVEYS: CONSTRUCTION

Country	Survey				
	Sample size	Coverage: % of employment in construction	Coverage: % of turnover	Coverage: % of units-less than 200 employees	Response rate
BULGARIA	490		54		96
ESTONIA	50	40	50	100	60
HUNGARY	600		50		20
LATVIA	113	31	19	87	58-66
POLAND	3500	74	77	65	50-60
ROMANIA	531	80		37	70-73
SLOVAK REPUBLIC	255	49	56	64	45-62
RUSSIAN FED.	630				40-50

BUSINESS SURVEYS: RETAIL TRADE

Country	Survey				
	Sample size	Coverage: % of employment in retail trade	Coverage: % of turnover	Coverage: % of private units	Response rate
BULGARIA	500		58	0	97
ESTONIA	100	20	20	95	60
HUNGARY	600		30		20
POLAND	3500				20
ROMANIA	1760		40	79	80-82
SLOVAK REPUBLIC	300	25	23	73	36

LABOUR MARKET INDICATORS

Foreword

This section of the Sources and Definitions publication provides information on the sources and definitions for the indicators which appear in the *Labour Market Indicators* annex of *the Short-term Economic Indicators: Transition Economies* publication twice per year. The annex contains employment, unemployment and wage data for seven Central and Eastern European countries and the Russian Federation. Before using the data presented in the *Labour Market Indicators* annex, users are strongly advised to refer to these methodological notes.

METHODOLOGICAL NOTES

General issues

In order to homogenise the data and to allow greater comparability between countries, the definitions of the variables used in the *Short-term Economic Indicators: Transition Economies* publication may differ from those used by the national statistical offices. Employment and wage data may differ from those found in the main country tables of the publication, again owing to differences in definitions.

Unless otherwise stated below, the following holds true:

-- *annual establishment survey data* are averages for the year and refer to the public and private sector;

-- *quarterly establishment survey data* are averages for the quarter and refer to the public and private sector;

-- *establishment survey data* on employment include conscripts, persons on maternity leave and additional child-care leave (according to national definitions) and exclude career armed forces;

-- *labour force survey data* on employment include career armed forces and persons on maternity leave, and exclude conscripts and persons on additional child-care leave.

Annual figures for the employment and unemployment indicators are calculated as annual averages of quarterly data. When a data series contains a change in the definition or data source, a vertical line indicates a break in the series. Details on the reasons for and occurrences of the breaks are provided in the country descriptions below.

Sources

Bulgaria -- From the third quarter of 1993 (September) all data refer to the labour force survey, with the exception of data on wages and hours worked in industry which are obtained from establishment surveys. The survey data are released by the National Statistical Institute. Administrative data concerning registered unemployment and flows into and out of unemployment are released by the National Employment Service.

Hungary -- All quarterly data refer to the labour force survey, with the exception of data on wages and hours worked in industry which are obtained from establishment surveys. Data on registered unemployment and flows into and out of unemployment are obtained from administrative sources and released by the Labour Market Centre. All data are obtained from the Central Statistical Office.

Poland -- All quarterly data refer to the labour force survey, with the exception of data on wages and hours worked in industry which are obtained from establishment surveys. Data on registered unemployment and flows into and out of unemployment are obtained from administrative sources. All data are released by the Central Statistical Office.

Republic of Slovenia -- All quarterly data refer to the labour force survey, with the exception of wage data which are obtained from establishment surveys. Data on registered unemployment and flows into and out of unemployment are obtained from administrative sources and are released by the National Employment Service. All other data are released by the Slovenian Statistical Office.

Romania -- All quarterly data refer to the labour force survey, with the exception of wage data which are obtained from establishment surveys. Data on registered unemployment are obtained from administrative sources. All data are released by the National Commission for Statistics.

Slovak Republic -- From the second quarter of 1993, all quarterly data refer to the labour force survey, with the exception of data on wages and hours worked in industry which are obtained from establishment surveys. Employment data prior to the second quarter of 1993 and all wage data are obtained from establishment surveys. Data on registered unemployment and flows into and out of unemployment are obtained from administrative sources. All data are released by the Slovak Statistical Office.

Russian Federation -- Employment and unemployment data are obtained from the annual labour force survey. Wage data and hours worked in industry figures refer to establishment surveys. Data on registered unemployment, unfilled vacancies and inflows to unemployment are obtained from administrative sources. All data are obtained from the State Committee of the Russian Federation on Statistics.

Labour Force Surveys

Bulgaria -- The household labour force survey is periodically conducted in Bulgaria on a sample of the resident population in Bulgaria aged 15 years or more. The survey reference period is one week. The sample comprises 30 000 households and is based on a two-stage area sampling design using the December 1992 census as a sampling frame. The Blaise system of imputation was adopted with the March 1995 survey and, since the June 1995 survey the sample size comprises approximately 24 000 households. Excluded from the survey are persons living in institutions, such as prisons, school dormitories and hospitals. Conscripts are considered as members of their usual residence and are thus included in the survey.

Hungary -- Labour force surveys are conducted each month from Monday to Sunday during the week which includes the 12th day of the month. The sample population for the quarter was approximately 30 000 households (55 000 persons) in 1992, and about 27 000 households (47 000 persons) in 1993 and 1994. However, only a third of the total sample is interviewed each month. The survey only covers persons living in private households during the reference week. Households are interviewed a total of six consecutive times, after which time they are no longer interviewed.

LABOUR MARKET INDICATORS

Poland -- Labour force surveys are conducted on a quarterly basis; the reference week includes the 15th day of the middle month of each quarter, and the population sample comprises between 18 000 and 32 000 households. The sampling process is two-stage and excludes persons with no place of residence and persons residing in institutions, such as jails and military barracks. A rotation system, incorporated into the design in May 1993, is used whereby a household is interviewed for two consecutive quarters, excluded for the next two, interviewed again for the last two quarters, and then indefinitely excluded.

Republic of Slovenia -- In 1993, with the co-operation of the National Employment Office, the Slovenian Statistical Office conducted the first labour force survey whose results conformed to ILO conventions. The labour force survey is conducted annually during the month of May on the resident population of the Republic of Slovenia over the age of 15, based on the population register. The labour force survey sample is based on the three-stage cluster sample which was introduced in the 1991 pilot survey. The survey currently undergoes a 30 per cent rotation each year and in 1995 captured approximately 1.3 per cent of the population. The reference period is the week prior to the recording one.

Romania -- The first labour force survey was conducted on a sample population of all permanent residents of Romania over the age of 14, including those having left Romania for a period longer than six months, provided they have maintained familial contact. The survey covers those persons in military service, students on study-abroad programs, persons working abroad, convicts and prisoners and persons hospitalised or temporarily staying in a sanitarium for short-term treatment. Persons living permanently in elderly, handicap and workers hostels, and sanitariums are not included in the survey. The survey is carried out during the last week of March and the first week of April, having as a reference period the week preceding the recording one. The sampling process is two-stage and in 1994 the sample size was 15 000 households or approximately 45 000 persons. In 1995 the sample size was increased to 17 000 households or approximately 50 000 persons.

Slovak Republic -- Labour force surveys are conducted on a continuous weekly basis throughout the year on a population sample of 10 000 households throughout the Slovak Republic. There is a sample rotation of 20 per cent, whereby each household is interviewed five times. The sampling of households is a two-stage process and the quarterly surveys are represented by a thirteen week cycle of interviewing. Labour force survey quarters precede calendar quarters by one month, thus permitting parallel data processing and comparisons with enterprise survey data, i.e. surveys for the first quarter of the year are conducted in December, January and February.

Russian Federation -- The statistical office of the Russian Federation, Goskomstat, has conducted three annual nation-wide household labour force surveys since 1992. The survey is conducted from Monday to Sunday during the last week of October. The survey covered approximately 260 000 households, or 583 000 persons aged 15 to 72. In 1995 the size of the sample was reduced to 0.2 per cent of the population in the age range 15 to 72 for the switch-over to half-yearly periodicity. Excluded from the survey are persons on long-term missions (over six months); workers and students living in hostels and school children living in boarding schools; inmates of penal institutions and patients of mental institutions; military personnel (conscripts and career) living in barracks; and foreign citizens. The sample frame is based on the 1989 population census and is compiled from the lists of census enumeration districts. For the survey conducted in October 1995, the sample was restructured on the basis of the 1994 population microcensus. The sample is based on a two-stage random sampling design, whereby at the first stage the census enumeration districts are selected and in the second stage the actual household is selected. The sample population undergoes a 20 per cent rotation each year. No rotation of the sample was carried out in 1994, apart from the replacement of households whose members were more than 72 years old at the time of the survey, and the inclusion of new households including individuals who had reached 15 years of age. The following areas of the Russian Federation are not surveyed and therefore

OECD
OCDE
SHORT-TERM ECONOMIC INDICATORS, SOURCES AND DEFINITIONS
OECD/CCET © April 1996

58

INDICATEURS ÉCONOMIQUES A COURT TERME, SOURCES ET DÉFINITIONS
OCDE/CCET © avril 1996

administrative data are used as a proxy to estimate aggregate labour force data: North Ossetia, Chechnia, Inguschetia, and since 1993 the autonomous territory (okrug) of Tchukovsky.

Definitions of Labour Market Indicators

This section contains the definitions and the departures from these definitions of the indicators presented in the country tables of the *Labour Market Indicators* annex. As described above, data for the following variables are collected from administrative sources and/or labour force and establishment surveys, depending on availability.

Participation rates

The *participation rate* is defined as the ratio between the total labour force, within working age, divided by the total population for the same age group. The working age population refers to women aged 15 to 54 years and men aged 15 to 59.

Departures from definition:

Hungary -- Working age population data excludes conscripts.

Poland -- The working age population data refer to women aged 15 to 59 years and men aged 15 to 64 and do not include persons living in collective households or members of private households who temporarily stay abroad (for more than two months).

Romania -- The working age population data refer to women aged 16 to 56 and men aged 16 to 61.

Slovak Republic -- Due to the unavailability of quarterly data, working age population data are kept constant for each quarter using the year-end figures provided by the national statistical office.

Unemployment

The *unemployment rate* is defined as the number of unemployed persons as a percentage of the labour force. The labour force is defined as the sum of unemployed and employed persons.

Registered unemployment data refer to those persons who have registered as unemployed at a labour office.

i) In the labour force survey, the unemployed are those persons above a specified age who, during the reference period of one week or one day, were:

a) *without work*, i.e. were not in paid employment or self-employment, as defined in the employment data section above; and

b) *currently available for work*, i.e. were available for paid employment or self-employment during the reference period; and

OECD
OCDE
SHORT-TERM ECONOMIC INDICATORS, SOURCES AND DEFINITIONS
OECD/CCET © April 1996

59

INDICATEURS ÉCONOMIQUES A COURT TERME, SOURCES ET DÉFINITIONS
OCDE/CCET © avril 1996

c) *seeking work*, i.e. had taken specific steps in a specified recent period to seek paid employment or self-employment. The specific steps may include registration at a public or private employment exchange, application to employers; checking at worksites, farms, factory gates, market or other assembly places; placing or answering newspaper advertisements; seeking assistance of friends or relatives; looking for land, building, machinery or equipment to establish own enterprise; arranging for financial resources; applying for permits and licences, etc.

ii) Notwithstanding the criterion of seeking work embodied in the standard definition of unemployment, persons without work and currently available for work who made arrangements to take up paid employment or undertake self-employment activity at a date subsequent to the reference period should be considered as unemployed.

iii) Persons temporarily absent from their jobs with no formal job attachment who were currently available for work and seeking work should be regarded as unemployed in accordance with the standard definition of unemployment.

iv) Students, homemakers and others mainly engaged in non-economic activities during the reference period who satisfy the criteria laid down above should be regarded as unemployed on the same basis as other categories of unemployed persons and be identified separately, where possible.

Departures from definition:

Bulgaria -- Registration unemployment data refer to women aged 16 to 54 and men aged 16 to 59.

Labour force survey unemployment is defined to include those persons aged 15 years or more who: did not work at all during the survey week; were actively seeking work within the preceding four-week period; and, were available to start work within the two weeks following the reference period. Also included are persons who were not actively seeking work, but who expected to start a new job or business within 30 days; or, expected to return to a former job from which they were dismissed or put on unpaid leave (where total duration of inactivity exceeds one month), provided they have the employer's promise and agreed date of return to work.

Hungary -- For the labour force survey figures, unemployment refers to persons aged 15 to 74 years who were not employed during the reference week and who: had actively looked for work at any time in the four weeks preceding the end of the reference week; and, were available for work within the two weeks following the reference week; or, were waiting to start a job within 30 days.

Poland -- Labour force survey unemployment data refer to persons 15 years of age and older.

Republic of Slovenia -- Registered unemployment data include persons who: i) do not have a regular job or are not self-employed; are not the owners or co-owners of an operating enterprise; and not the owners or users of property which could provide a living; ii) are capable of and willing to work and are prepared to accept a job suitable to their professional attainment or working skills acquired through past work experience; iii) have registered as job-seekers with the National Employment Office.

Unemployment data include persons who: did not work for pay or profit during the reference week; have actively looked for a job during the last four weeks; and, were able to start work in the next two weeks; or had found a job to start after the reference week.

Romania -- Labour force survey unemployment refers to persons who were not employed during the reference week and who: had actively looked for work at any time in the four weeks preceding the end of the reference week; and, were available for work within the two weeks following the reference week.

Slovak Republic -- Labour force survey unemployment data include persons who: did not work for pay or profit during the reference week; have actively looked for a job during the last four weeks; and, were able to start work in the next two weeks. Data refer to persons 15 years of age and older.

Russian Federation -- Labour force survey unemployment applies to person 16 years of age and older who: did not have any work in the week of the survey or did not have any work from which they were temporarily absent; had been actively seeking work in the last four weeks; and were available for work within the next two weeks. Unemployment data include full- and part-time students seeking employment, provided they are currently available for work. If they are seeking work for some future date, such as for the summer months, they are considered inactive.

Employment data

i) *Employment* covers all persons above a specified age who during the reference period, of either one week or one day, were in one of the following categories:

Paid employment:

a) *At work*: persons who performed some work for wage or salary, in cash or in kind; or,

b) With a job but *not at work*: persons who, having already worked in their present job, were temporarily not at work during the reference period and have a formal attachment to their job. This formal job attachment should be determined in the light of national circumstances, according to the one or more of the following criteria: (1) the continued receipt of wage or salary; (2) an assurance of return to work following the end of the contingency, or an agreement as to the date of return; (3) the elapsed duration of absence from the job, which, wherever relevant, may be that duration for which workers can receive compensation benefits without an obligation to accept other jobs.

Self-employment:

a) *At work*: persons who performed some work for profit or family gain, in cash or in kind;

b) With an enterprise but *not at work*: persons with an enterprise, which may be a business, farm or service undertaking, who were temporarily not at work during the reference period for any specific reason.

ii) For operational purposes and following ILO definitions, the notion of *some work* may be interpreted as work for at least one hour.

iii) Persons temporarily not at work because of illness or injury, holiday or vacation, strike or lock-out, educational or training leave, maternity leave, reduction in economic activity, temporary disorganisation or suspension of work due to such reasons as bad weather, mechanical or electrical breakdown, or shortage of raw materials or fuels, or other temporary absence with or without leave should be considered in paid employment provided they have a formal job attachment.

OECD
OCDE
SHORT-TERM ECONOMIC INDICATORS, SOURCES AND DEFINITIONS
OECD/CCET © April 1996
61
INDICATEURS ÉCONOMIQUES A COURT TERME, SOURCES ET DÉFINITIONS
OCDE/CCET © avril 1996

iv) Employers and own account workers should be considered as in self-employment and classified as *at work* or *not at work*, as the case may be.

v) Unpaid family workers at work should be considered in self-employment irrespective of the number of hours worked during the reference period.

vi) Persons engaged in the production of economic goods and services for own and household consumption are considered in self-employment if such production comprises an important contribution to the total consumption of the household.

vii) Apprentices who received pay in cash or in kind are considered in paid employment and classified as *at work* or *not at work* on the same basis as other persons in paid employment.

viii) Students, homemakers, and other mainly engaged in non-economic activities during the reference period, who at the same time were in paid employment or self-employment as defined above are considered as employed on the same basis as other categories of employed persons and are identified separately, where possible.

Departures from definition:

Bulgaria -- With the introduction of the labour force survey in September 1993, employment data refer to persons aged 15 years or more who, during the reference week: performed some work for at least one hour for pay or other income; or, did not work but had a job from which they were temporarily absent due to illness, leave, weather, vocational training, strike, etc.

Persons on maternity leave and additional child-care leave are included in employment.

Hungary -- Employment data include persons aged 15 to 74 who, during the reference week: worked one hour or more for pay, profit or payment in kind in their job or business (including a farm); or, worked one hour or more without pay in a family business or on a farm, e.g. contributing family member; or, had a job from which they were temporarily absent during the entire survey week. Persons involved in the following activities are not considered employed: work performed without pay for another household or institute (voluntary work); building or renovating of one's own house or apartment; housework without pay; work in the garden or on one's own property if the aim of the production is strictly for self-consumption.

Poland -- Data refer to persons 15 years of age and older. Persons on maternity leave are considered employed from four to six months of leave. The monthly benefit is equal to the average remuneration from the period six months before the birth of the child, and is paid from the Social Insurance Institution.

Republic of Slovenia -- In addition to the standard ILO definition, employment also includes persons who during the reference week did not work, were still under contract with their employer and who cited a "technical surplus of workers" or "the employer could not insure them enough work" as a reason for not working. In this case, the employer is required by law to provide a remuneration equal to 70 per cent of their normal wage, defined in the collective agreement, for six months. After this six month period the person either becomes unemployed or inactive. Should the person find work during the six-month lay-off period, the payments are stopped. In the 1994 survey, 4 700 persons or approximately five per cent of the unemployed were unemployed as a result of lay-offs.

Persons on maternity leave are considered employed for the first 365 days of leave. During this period the parent may receive a remuneration equal to 100 per cent of their normal wage, as defined in their labour contract, which is indexed to the average wage for the previous year. Additional child-care leave does not exist.

Romania -- Establishment survey employment is defined to include persons who have a job, regardless of how obtained, which permits them to procure an income through a social or economic activity, i.e. paid employment and self-employment. Data are year-end, exclude conscripts and refer to persons 16 years of age and older. Estimates of the number of self-employed, unpaid family workers and persons in small enterprises were made using the Agricultural and Commerce register and data from the Ministry of Finance.

Labour force survey data include persons in military service. Although military barracks are not surveyed, conscripts are captured in the questionnaire. Labour force survey data refer to those persons 14 years of age and older. Persons on unpaid leave for a period of up to 90 days, whether for preparation for an exam, sick leave for a child, seeking medical treatment abroad or other personal interests are considered employed, given an agreement by both the employee and employer.

Persons on maternity leave are considered employed for up to one year, beginning as early as two months before the birth of the child. The maternity leave benefit is paid from the social insurance fund at between 50 to 94 per cent of the person's previous salary, depending on seniority and the number of children.

Slovak Republic -- Maternity leave represents the first 28 weeks of leave, whereas additional child-care leave represents the period from 29 weeks to three years after the birth of the child.

Russian Federation -- In addition to the standard ILO definition, employment also includes conscripts residing at home. Excluded from employment are persons whose only activity consists of unpaid work around the house (e.g. painting, housework or repair work); unpaid work for religious, charitable and similar organisations; and unpaid apprentices and trainees.

Persons on maternity leave and additional child-care leave are considered employed from approximately 72 days before and up to three years after the birth of the child. The maternity leave benefit is paid by the trade unions and represents an amount equal to 100 per cent of the worker's average salary. Additional child-care leave represents the period from 73 days to three years after the birth of the child, whereby the employee's current position may be held for him or her by the employer until the worker returns, thereby establishing an informal arrangement of job attachment.

Youth unemployment

Youth employment and *unemployment* figures refer to persons from 15 to 24 years of age.

Departures from definition:

Romania -- The youth employment and unemployment figures refer to persons 14 to 24 years of age.

LABOUR MARKET INDICATORS

Russian Federation -- Youth unemployment includes those persons 16 to 24 years of age. Fifteen year olds who are surveyed are considered inactive if they do not fall under the guidelines for employment.

Prime-age unemployment

Prime-age employment and *unemployment* figures refer to persons from 25 to 49 years of age.

Departures from definition:

Hungary -- The prime-age unemployment and employment figures refer to persons 25 to 54 years of age.

Older unemployment

Older employment and *unemployment* figures refer to women 50 to 54 years of age and men 50 to 59 years of age.

Departures from definition:

Hungary -- Older employment and unemployment data refer to persons 55 to 59 years of age. The official retirement age of women is 55.

Poland -- Older employment and unemployment data refer to women 50 to 59 years of age and men 50 to 64 years of age.

Romania -- Older employment and unemployment data refer to women 50 to 56 years of age and men 50 to 61 years of age.

Unemployment by level of education

Unemployment by level of education rate is defined as the number of unemployed as a percentage of the group specific labour force. The unemployment by level of education indicators include the number of employed and unemployed having completed one of the three following educational levels, regardless of the kind of job they perform or the educational requirements: higher, secondary, or primary (according to the ISCED classifications).

The *higher education* classification includes the number of employed and unemployed having completed a post-secondary education.

The *secondary general education* classification includes the number of employed and unemployed having completed either a secondary general or vocational education.

The *primary education or less* classification includes the number of employed and unemployed having completed a primary education or less.

OECD
OCDE
SHORT-TERM ECONOMIC INDICATORS, SOURCES AND DEFINITIONS
OECD/CCET © April 1996

64

INDICATEURS ÉCONOMIQUES A COURT TERME, SOURCES ET DÉFINITIONS
OCDE/CCET © avril 1996

Departures from definition:

Bulgaria

-- The secondary general education classification includes persons with a general education which usually lasts three years after the primary education. Persons who have attended certain vocational schools, which provide a secondary general education together with some professional qualifications, are also included. Vocational education includes only secondary education schools. The duration of education is four to five years after the primary education. The vocational school provides education for jobs in industry, agriculture, transport, trade, health, and other economic activities, and art schools.

-- The primary education classification includes persons with a compulsory education which begins from six to seven years of age and until the age of 14 to 15. Some vocational schools which provide basic general education and professional skills are also included in this group.

Hungary

-- The higher education classification includes persons who are graduates of three and four year college programs, and university graduates.

-- The secondary general education classification includes persons having completed i) grammar school, which last four years, or ii) other secondary school, which includes general and vocational training, whereby the final examination provides a general or vocational certificate (i.e. industrial, agricultural, economics, commercial, catering, transport, postal work, communication, public health, training for kindergarten teachers, and arts). Both of these programs allow students to enter into an institute of higher education. Vocational education includes apprentice school graduates, which generally requires three years, provides training of skilled workers, and requires the passing of a professional exam.

-- The primary education or less classification includes persons having completed eight grades of elementary school or less.

Poland

-- The secondary general education classification includes persons who have completed secondary vocational education. Vocational education includes those who have only completed basic vocational education.

Romania

-- The higher education classification includes person who are graduates of three year college programs and universities programs of four to six years.

-- The secondary general education classification includes persons having completed either the secondary cycle I from 14 to 16 years of age or the secondary cycle II from 16 to 18 years of age. Vocational education includes persons having completed an education in either a technical school, a post-secondary vocational school, a professional school or an apprentice school.

-- The primary education or less classification includes persons having completed a primary education from 6 to 14 years of age or less.

Slovak Republic

Educational levels are classified by the Standard Classification of Fields of Education and have the following departures:

-- The secondary general education classification includes persons who have completed grammar school. Vocational education includes person who have completed a secondary vocational education, e.g. higher pedagogical schools, enterprise institutes, secondary vocational schools, conservatoires, secondary apprentice training centres with leaving exam, secondary apprentice training centres without leaving exam.

-- The primary education or less classification refers to persons who have completed a primary education, including e.g. special schools for handicapped children, unfinished primary or secondary education or less.

With the introduction of the labour force survey in the second quarter of 1993, employment data include persons on additional child-care leave. Beginning in 1994, employment excludes persons on additional child-care leave.

Russian Federation

-- The secondary general education classification includes those persons who have completed at least two years of a higher education or have finished a 10, 11 or 12 years' course of general education. Vocational education includes persons having graduated from a secondary specialised school (technical secondary school or any other specialised secondary institution, e.g. teacher or nurse training school.) The vast majority of these persons also holds a secondary general education degree, i.e. 10 to 12 years of study.

-- The primary education or less classification includes persons having an incomplete secondary education (i.e. those who completed between 7 to 11 years of study but did not graduate), completed a primary education of 8 to 9 years of study, or had no primary education. In the Russian Federation, primary education (up to 8 to 9 years of education) is classified as basic secondary education.

Long-term unemployment

Long-term unemployment refers to persons unemployed for more than 12 months. The *long-term unemployment rate* is the number of long-term unemployed as a percentage of the total labour force. The percentage of total unemployment, or incidence of long-term unemployment, is the number of long-term unemployed as a percentage of the total number of unemployed persons. Unless otherwise noted, long-term unemployment for the youth and older groups refer to the same age breakdowns found in the sections on unemployment by age groups.

Departures from definition:

Bulgaria -- Older long-term unemployment data series cover unemployed persons aged 55 years and over.

Hungary -- Long-term unemployment data cover persons unemployed for more than 52 weeks (364 days).

 OECD
OCDE
SHORT-TERM ECONOMIC INDICATORS, SOURCES AND DEFINITIONS
OECD/CCET © April 1996
66
INDICATEURS ÉCONOMIQUES A COURT TERME, SOURCES ET DÉFINITIONS
OCDE/CCET © avril 1996

Poland -- Beginning in the fourth quarter of 1994, older long-term unemployment data series cover women 50 to 59 years of age and men aged 50 to 64.

Underemployment

Underemployment refers to persons who are working part-time and would like to be working full-time (according to ILO guidelines).

Departures from definition:

Hungary -- Underemployed persons are persons aged 15 to 74 who worked part-time during the reference week for economic reasons, i.e. slack work; because full-time work was not available; did not work due to temporary lay-off; or; usually work less than full-time due to economic reasons. Part-time work is defined as less than 40 hours per week.

Poland -- Underemployed persons are those who, during the survey week, worked 39 hours or less for economic (involuntary) reasons, (i.e. could not find full-time work, production breaks, interruptions, job started/ended within the reference week, reduction in economic activity, i.e. lack of clients, orders, finances or equipment).

Republic of Slovenia -- Underemployment data include persons who are working part-time because they cannot find a full-time job.

Romania -- Underemployment data refer to those persons who, during the survey week, worked less than the usual working time independently of their will and were looking or available for more work or a full-time job during the reference period.

Slovak Republic -- Underemployment data refer to those persons who are working part-time and cannot find suitable full-time work and persons working fewer work hours than full-time at the initiative of the employer, i.e. slack work. Prior to the first quarter of 1994, the latter were excluded from underemployment.

With the introduction of the labour force survey in the second quarter of 1993, part-time employment data include persons on additional child-care leave. Beginning in 1994, part-time employment excludes persons on additional child-care leave.

Part-time employment

Part-time employment refers to persons who normally work less than full-time (according to national definitions).

Departures from definition:

Poland -- Part-time employment includes those persons who during the survey week, either: worked 39 hours or less for non-economic (voluntary) reasons, i.e. vacation, education, illness or other personal or family responsibilities or usually work part-time; or, worked 39 hours or less for economic (involuntary) reasons, (i.e. could not find full-time work, production breaks, interruptions, job started/ended within the reference week, reduction in economic activity, i.e. lack of clients, orders, finances or equipment.)

LABOUR MARKET INDICATORS

Republic of Slovenia -- Part-time employment data refer exclusively to employees and self-employed persons.

Romania -- Part-time employment refers to those persons who normally work less than what they would consider to be full-time employment for their particular profession. If the respondent has no idea as to whether he/she works full- or part-time the interviewer suggests 30 hours per week as a reference cut-off point.

Slovak Republic -- With the introduction of the labour force survey in the second quarter of 1993, part-time employment data include persons on additional child-care leave. Beginning in 1994, part-time employment excludes persons on additional child-care leave.

Self-employment

Self-employment is defined to include employers and own-account workers, contributing family workers, and persons engaged in the production of economic goods and services for their own and/or household consumption, if such production comprises an important contribution to the total consumption of the household. Persons working in producer's co-operatives or agricultural co-operatives are not included.

Departures from definition:

Hungary -- Persons involved in the following activities are excluded: building or renovating of one's own house; housework; work in the garden or in one's own property if the aim of production is strictly self-consumption.

Poland -- Prior to the first quarter of 1995, self-employment includes members of co-operatives.

Slovak Republic -- With the introduction of the labour force survey in the second quarter of 1993, self-employment data include persons on additional child-care leave. Beginning in 1994, self-employment excludes persons on additional child-care leave.

Private sector employment

Private sector employment is defined as employment in private-owned enterprises, including co-operatives.

Departures from definition:

Poland -- Employment in the private sector covers self-employment and employees working in private domestic ownership, including partnerships, co-operatives, social organisations, associations and foundations. Also covered are private foreign-owned enterprises, including small-scale foreign enterprises and partnerships with foreign capital share.

Romania -- Employment in the private sector does not include co-operatives.

Wages

The *average wage* is defined as the average gross monthly wage of full-time workers. Gross wages are defined as basic wages and salaries including bonuses and remunerations before deduction of taxes, excluding family and other social benefits. Annual wages are calculated averages from the national statistical offices.

The *coefficient of variation of wages* is defined as the sample standard deviation of wages by sector as a percentage of the average wage. The economic activities are agriculture, mining, manufacturing, electricity, gas and water, construction, trade and catering, transport and communication, financial services and real estate, health and education, public administration and other services.

Departures from definition:

Bulgaria -- Wage data refer to the public sector only and exclude persons on maternity leave and additional child-care leave and are calculated by dividing the total wage bill for the period by the average number of employees. Fourth quarter data include annual premiums and bonuses. Mining and electricity, gas and water activities are included in the manufacturing sector. The Classification of Branches of the National Economy (CNBE) is used to classify wages by sector data and is not strictly comparable to the NACE Rev. 1.

Hungary -- Wage data cover in 1993, enterprises with more than 20 employees, and since 1994 those with more than 10 employees. Earnings consist of basic wages and salaries, supplementary wages, rewards, bonus premiums and profit-sharing schemes.

Poland -- Wage data refer to either personal wages and salaries (excluding wages and salaries of outworkers and apprentices); payments from profit for distribution and balance surpluses in co-operatives; purses from establishment premium funds; or, fees paid to selected employees groups, e.g. journalists, television and radio programme producers for their work as a result of a labour contract. Prior to the fourth quarter of 1994, electricity, gas and water activities were included in the manufacturing sector, and the national classifications of economic activities were based on the Polish Classification of the National Economy (KGN). Since the first quarter of 1994, economic activities are classified by the European Classification of Activities (EKD), which is the Polish version of NACE Rev. 1.

The zloty was redenominated on the 1st January 1995 with the new zloty equal to 10 000 old zlotys.

Republic of Slovenia -- Average wages includes, in addition to the income for work actually performed during regular working hours, all other income, which includes the following: income from overtime, supplements for annual leave, sickness pay for up to 30 days, public holidays, performing of national duties, paid leave and similar, awards, premiums, income for past work, incentive bonuses and bonuses after periodic and final balance sheets. Survey coverage includes enterprises and organisations with three or more persons in paid employment. Private enterprises and members of the armed forces were included in 1992, while the police force was included in 1993. The earnings of consultants and associates are not covered. Wages by sector are classified by the national classification of economic activities (EKD).

Romania -- Wage data refer to basic salary; supplementary and indemnity payments granted as a gross percentage of basic salary or as a fixed amount; salary adjustments accorded by law or collective labour agreements; salary fund bonuses; payments in kind. Wage data cover all enterprises with more than 500 employees and a sample of smaller firms.

Slovak Republic -- Average wages are calculated as wage costs divided by the registered number of employees. Excluded from gross wages are other personnel costs, i.e. incentive pay, sickness benefits and bonuses and wages paid to persons on maternity leave and additional child-care leave. Quarterly data on average wages exclude earnings of employees of private entrepreneurs not filed in the business register and enterprises with less than 25 employees since 1992. Agricultural co-operatives are included. The national classifications of economic activities are based on the Branch Classification of Economic Activities (OKEC), developed in the Slovak Republic on the basis of NACE Rev. 1.

Russian Federation -- Average gross wages include bonuses, remunerations and payments in kind. Wages are calculated by dividing the total wage bill for the period by the average number of employees, adjusted to take into account those persons working part-time. Wage data are obtained from monthly establishment surveys whose coverage includes large and medium size enterprises, encompassing approximately 90 per cent of t otal employment in enterprises. National classifications of economic activities are based on the All-Union Classifications of Economic Sectors (OKONH), which are not comparable to NACE Rev. 1. Due to the higher aggregation of wages across sectors, the coefficients of variation of wages are not comparable with other countries.

Labour productivity

The *labour productivity* index is displayed as a ratio: labour productivity in hours worked is the ratio between the production index in industry to the index of hours worked in industry. Labour productivity for persons is the ratio of the production index in industry to the index of the number of persons employed in industry. For definitions of the industrial production indices and employment in industry used to calculate the indices of labour productivity, refer to the main methodological notes of this volume.

Departures from definition:

Hungary -- Labour productivity per hour was derived from the average number of hours worked in manufacturing per month, which includes the hours worked by full-time employees and excludes home workers and retired persons working in incorporated enterprises. The number of hours worked includes overtime and time lost (due to machine failures, shortages, etc.) For enterprise coverage refer to the above section on *wages*.

Poland -- Prior to the second quarter of 1994, hours worked in industry was defined as the average number of hours worked during the survey week per wage earner in mining and manufacturing. Since the second quarter of 1994, only wage earners in manufacturing are included.

Republic of Slovenia -- Hours worked in industry are obtained from the labour force survey and refer to the average hours actually worked during the reference week. Employment in industry figures are obtained from the labour force survey.

Romania -- Hours worked in industry data cover time worked, paid and unpaid, including overtime work and work during weekends and holidays for a period of one year. The data cover public and mixed sector enterprises in the branches of mining, manufacturing and electricity, gas and water.

BULGARIA

Industrial production

Indices of industrial production are defined according to the Classification of Branches of the National Economy (CBNE) of the former CMEA, and are available for mining, manufacturing and gas and electricity, and construction.

Monthly and quarterly industrial production indices cover the public sector. Despite a large growth in the number of small private firms registered in industry, for example from 17 000 at end 1992 to some 36 000 at end 1993, the National Statistical Institute (NSI) estimates that the approximately 3 000 public industrial enterprises covered accounted for 95.4 per cent of industrial output in 1993 and 91.3 per cent in 1994. Estimates of industrial production in the private sector are made annually and included in the annual indices.

The monthly and quarterly series include secondary production which falls within the branch concerned but exclude subsidiary production, i.e. secondary production falling outside the branch. The annual series covers all production, including subsidiary production.

Monthly, quarterly and annual data are submitted by the enterprises to the regional statistical offices, which process and transmit the information to the NSI.

Gross output covers the output of finished intermediate and final goods, semi-finished products, and changes in stocks of finished products. Non-principal production is included from 1995 only.

Until 1990, the value of total output at constant prices was calculated by multiplying the quantities of the products produced by wholesale prices of 1 January 1982. Since 1991 constant price estimates are based on the prices of the previous year and the indices are chain linked. The indices are of type Laspeyres.

The base period for the indices has been the corresponding period in 1985. The NSI has recalculated the index to show approximate month to month variations. The new indices were obtained by applying the monthly and quarterly structure of 1985 through to the series in the original form. From January 1994 some industrial production series have a base of 1990=100.

The *total industrial production index* refers to mining, manufacturing and gas and electricity.

With the introduction of price reforms in February 1991, there were difficulties experienced in calculating a price deflator for production in 1991. Comparability of monthly and quarterly data has been ensured by eliminating the impact of price changes reported by the enterprises themselves. Since 1992, the comparability of monthly and quarterly data is ensured by estimating producer price indices by industrial sub-branches. Monthly data are therefore considered preliminary and some adjustments are made. Following adjustment to the current period data, data for earlier periods are also revised.

BULGARIA

The *industrial production index for mining* covers coal mining (extraction, dressing and briqueting of coal), the oil industry, extraction and ore-dressing of non-ferrous and ferrous metals, production of mineral raw materials, extraction of non-metalliferous and quarrying materials, the logging and fishing industry.

The *industrial production index for manufacturing* refers to manufacturing as defined by ISIC, excluding publishing. It includes subsidiary production and manufacturing in the private sector.

The *industrial production index for electricity and gas* refers to the production and distribution of electricity, steam and hot water. Cold water production, purification and distribution are excluded.

The *construction index* is calculated on the basis of production including architectural construction works and geological prospecting according to the Classification of Branches of the National Economy.

Commodity output

The output of *coal* covers black coal (hard coal and anthracite, including coal used in mines), brown coal and lignite.

Crude steel production covers crude open-hearth, oxygen-blown and electric steel, as well as steel made by other processes (ingots and steel for castings).

Cement production includes all types of cement: Portland and Portland pozzolana cements and variations thereof, Portland blast-furnace cement, etc.

Business surveys

A description of business tendency survey techniques and the list of harmonised questions is given in the chapter *Business Tendency Surveys* of this publication.

Construction

Dwellings

Dwellings refer to physically discrete and independent premises intended for habitation, consisting of one or more rooms (residential and ancillary), having an independent exit accessing a common area (staircase or landing) or having access directly to the street.

A monthly survey covering construction activity provides data on the number of *dwellings completed*. The survey data includes information for all sectors: public, co-operative, municipal and private including own-account construction by households. Information concerning dwellings completed is also available from the Commission for Building Inspections which certifies dwellings as completed when they are habitable. This certification is, however, not required for dwellings built on own-account, and survey data are therefore considered more complete.

The number of dwellings completed in February 1990 includes dwellings completed in January 1990.

OECD
OCDE
SHORT-TERM ECONOMIC INDICATORS, SOURCES AND DEFINITIONS
OECD/CCET © April 1996

72

INDICATEURS ÉCONOMIQUES A COURT TERME, SOURCES ET DÉFINITIONS
OCDE/CCET © avril 1996

Domestic trade

The *retail sales value* refers to the value of food and non-food goods sold by all types of retail and catering outlets. Retail sales include direct sales from warehouses, sales from own production and the value of services for the repair of vehicles, household electrical appliances and personal care goods. From January 1996 retail sales data do not include the value of services for reparations of motor vehicle or household goods and appliances. Information on the turnover of food and non-food goods has been available monthly since May 1991.

Until 1993 data on retail sales referred to turnover in the public sector collected monthly by means of a census. Information was obtained from all state and co-operative enterprises selling goods, food and beverages or repairing goods. Estimates of private sector turnover have also been included since January 1991.

From January 1994 to December 1995, the monthly survey covered approximately 30 per cent of units in the public sector. The share of these units in total retail sales value of public sector retail outlets approximated 90 per cent. Private outlets were surveyed every quarter. This information was used to refine monthly estimates of total value of retail sales.

From January 1996, the monthly survey also covers retail sales in the private sector. Approximately 1.5 per cent of the private sector retail outlets are surveyed. These account for approximately 50 per cent of the retail sales in the private sector.

Retail sales data include turnover taxes. A value added tax replaced these from April 1994.

Until end 1994, retail price indices were used to deflate retail sales values in national sources. From January 1995 the consumer price index for food and non-food goods is used to create *retail sales volume* series. Retail sales volume is presented with the "same period of the previous year as base 100" in national sources. The fixed base index published in *Short-term Economic Indicators: Transition Economies* has been calculated by the OECD Secretariat, using the total CPI rebased to 1992. It is presented with a base of 1993 as 100.

Labour

Employment

The series *employment in the public sector*, previously referred to as *employment total*, reflects the average number of employees in state and co-operative enterprises, i.e. excluding the private sector. It refers to civilian employment only.

Prior to 1992 data were obtained from extensive quarterly enterprise surveys. Enterprises were asked to report employment for each month of the quarter. In 1992 monthly industry surveys with some indicators concerning employment and earnings began to be used. The quarterly surveys with a larger coverage of enterprises and indicators also continued. The different coverage meant that the quarterly data was not used to revise the monthly values to get a correspondence between the two series. Differences between the monthly and quarterly data are thus apparent until the second half of 1992.

From 1993 only a quarterly survey is used in which enterprises report on employment for each month of the quarter.

BULGARIA

The averages are calculated from the number of employees on each calendar day during the reference period. For holidays and non-working days, the registered number of employees is taken as the number registered on the previous day. The registered number of employees covers all persons employed at least one day in the main enterprise activity or at least five days in another enterprise activity. Apprentices and employees on maternity or child care leave are included. Part-time employees are included as full-time equivalents.

Annual data include estimates of employment in the private sector. They cover persons employed in the state and co-operative sectors, information obtained from balance sheets (described below), data concerning the number of registered private practitioners (such as solicitors), annual data concerning the number of agricultural workers, and data concerning small enterprises with fewer than ten employees which are surveyed at 30 June and 31 December.

Balance sheets are submitted to the NSI in accordance with the accounting law which covers enterprises with ten or more employees and at least 50 000 levs monthly turnover. Only a small number of private enterprises are covered by these provisions and the semi-annual survey described above is thus used to supplement the information concerning private enterprises.

Household labour force surveys, introduced in September 1993, provide supplementary estimates of employment, in particular for unpaid family workers. This survey was held three times during 1995. For further information, see the chapter *Labour Market Indicators* earlier in this volume.

The series *employment total*, previously referred to as *employment all sectors* covers employment in the whole economy. It is estimated by the National Statistical Institute. Since the estimates of employment in the private sector are available only annually, this series is only available on an annual basis.

Employment in industry includes the extractive and manufacturing industries and gas and electricity as in industrial production described above. Estimates of employment in the private sector are included only annually.

Employment in manufacturing covers the manufacturing industry as in industrial production described above. It includes employees in manufacturing activity in non-manufacturing branches. Estimates of employment in the private sector are included only annually.

The working age population in Bulgaria refers to women aged between 15 and 54 and men aged between 15 and 59.

Unemployment

Registration of *unemployment* began in July 1990. Data are obtained through the NSI from the National Employment Office of the Ministry of Labour and Social Care and refer to the total number of registered unemployed.

To be registered with the National Employment Office a person must have worked at least eight months in any job or must be a graduate from secondary school, or have been registered in post-school study for at least one month (including military training).

Registered unemployed persons with no alternate source of earnings may be eligible to receive unemployment benefits. Beneficiaries must register as unemployed regularly in order to ensure receipt of benefits. The amount of benefit paid depends on qualifications and the type of job held previously and is a proportion of the previous wage. The duration of payment depends on the length of working experience. Recent graduates receive benefits for three months only. The maximum length of benefit receipt for other persons is one year. In general persons whose benefits terminate do not continue to register as unemployed. It is estimated that approximately 35 000 persons per month are excluded in this way. The problem of accessibility to Labour Offices for persons in small towns is also a disincentive to registration.

An *unemployment rate*, estimated by the NSI, was available annually until 1993. It refers to the ratio of the average annual number of registered unemployed to the labour force. This is defined as the average annual employment total, previously referred to as employment all sectors (described above), plus the registered unemployed.

From September 1993, the labour force survey provides information on the unemployed. For further information, see the chapter *Labour Market Indicators* earlier in this volume.

Job vacancies refer to the number of job opportunities for immediate filling, notified to the National Employment Office remaining unfilled on the day of count.

Wages

Monthly earnings

Wage data are based on the same surveys and other sources of information as the employment data (described above). However, unlike the employment series, no estimates of earnings in the private sector are included, even in the annual data.

The series *monthly earnings in the public sector*, previously referred to as *total earnings*, thus reflects the average monthly earnings in state and co-operative enterprises only.

Monthly earnings in industry also refer to the public sector and cover the extractive and manufacturing industries and gas and electricity.

These monthly earnings series are available monthly from 1992 and from this date they exclude employees on maternity leave. The previously published series (available on the historical diskette) were available only quarterly and annually and thus reflected average quarterly and average annual earnings.

Prices

Wholesale prices

The *wholesale price index* refers to prices of industrial output weighted by the value of goods sold.

Monthly series are available from 1991 and are based on a sample of 1 000 goods and commodity groups. The indices are calculated on the basis of information submitted by approximately 3 000 state and co-operative industrial enterprises concerning the impact of price changes. The prices do not include taxes.

BULGARIA

The index is expressed with the same period of the previous year as base 100 and is of the type Paasche.

Consumer prices

The monthly *consumer price index (CPI)* is derived from information collected from 28 regional statistical offices with 1 604 commodities, services and catering items identified and six quotations per item, based on the consumer basket of goods and services established by the NSI. Until end 1992 the weights for the CPI were based on the survey of retail turnover. From January 1993 the CPI weights refer to the share of expenditure of each group in the household budget survey for 1992.

The number of commodities and services included and the weights currently applied are shown by expenditure group below:

Item	Commodities	Services	Weight
Food (including catering)[1]	465	2	43.4
Spirits	24	--	2.3
Tobacco products	5	--	1.9
Housing	48	26	3.6
Household energy	9	6	4.3
Furniture and household equipment	159	23	4.7
Clothing, footwear and toiletries	366	40	8.3
Hygiene and medical care	172	13	1.9
Education and recreation	108	37	3.5
Transport and communication	39	48	7.7
Other[2]	2	12	18.4
TOTAL	1 397	207	100.0

1. Food commodities cover 265 food commodities and 200 dishes surveyed in catering.
2. The weight for the group Other shown here combines the weights of 4.6 for expenditures on household plots and 13.8 for other expenditures.

Prices for certain goods, such as transport, electricity and some rents, are determined from administrative data.

From the beginning of 1993, the CPIs for the total and each subgroup include goods as well as services associated with that group. A service price index is extracted from this information. Prior to 1993 a separate service price index was also calculated but services were not included in each subgroup.

The CPIs are of type modifed Laspeyres. Since 1991 the series have been presented as indices with the previous period as base 100. Price indices in fixed base 1992=100 are available from 1992.

Domestic finance

Domestic finance data are supplied through the NSI by the Bulgarian National Bank.

Narrow money (M1) refers to currency outside banks and demand deposits of enterprises.

Quasi money refers to all time, savings and foreign currency deposits. Time deposits cover those of households and enterprises in all financial institutions, as well as deposits of the State Insurance Company held by the Bulgarian National Bank. Savings deposits cover savings and demand deposits of households. Foreign currency deposits cover those of resident and non-resident enterprises and households.

Broad money (M2) is the sum of narrow money and quasi money. Until end 1995 broad money also included import and restricted deposits.

Personal deposits for 1991 and 1992 refer to time and savings deposits. Time deposits cover those of households and enterprises in all financial institutions, as well as deposits of the State Insurance Company held by the Bulgarian National Bank. Savings deposits cover savings and demand deposits of households. Only levs deposits are included.

From 1993 personal deposits refer to time and savings deposits of households only, in both levs and foreign currencies.

Interest rates

The *official discount rate* is based on the refinancing credit interest rate applied to commercial banks by the Bulgarian National Bank.

Foreign finance

Foreign finance data are supplied through the NSI by the Bulgarian National Bank.

The *exchange rates* with the US dollar, ECU and DM are floating rates quoted daily, and refer to the quotation on the last day of the month.

Total reserves cover gross foreign assets and include gold. Data refers to the end of the period.

Gross foreign debt covers all foreign liabilities, including non-residents' deposits in levs.

Foreign trade

1980-91

Data for *exports, imports* and *net trade* are available with a breakdown for convertible and non-convertible currency areas. Up to 1990 all trade with the former USSR was non-convertible; since then the proportion of this non-convertible trade has been shrinking.

BULGARIA

The trade data were based on surveys of exporters and importers. Registers were updated by means of information supplied by the customs department. Exports and imports were both expressed FOB and the classification used was that of the CMEA.

1992 and onwards

The Harmonised System of commodity description and coding was introduced in 1992. Customs declarations, which cover all enterprises, both state and private, were also introduced and customs tariffs created.

Foreign trade covers imports of goods for domestic consumption, exports of goods for consumption in the partner country, temporary imports and exports before and after processing, and foreign aid.

Customs declarations are not registered for state trade, for loading or provisions for ships and aeroplanes but these items are included in export and import statistics. Trade data does not cover trade in services, repairs, patents, fish-catching or films, nor goods intended for direct re-export.

Imports are expressed CIF and exports FOB.

Publications

Some of the series described above, but presented according to national practice, can be found in the following publications of the Bulgarian National Statistical Institute:

> *Current Economic Business*
> *Statistical News*
> *Export and Import*
> *Industry*
> *Foreign Trade*
> *Statistical Reference Book, Economics of Bulgaria.*

CZECH AND SLOVAK FEDERAL REPUBLIC

Introduction

From 1 January 1993 the Czech and Slovak Federal Republic (CSFR) ceased to exist and the former Czech and Slovak republics became two independent states, the Czech Republic and the Slovak Republic. The notes below refer, therefore, to aggregated data for the CSFR, available until the end of 1992.

In general, data for the Czech and Slovak Federal Republic were compiled by aggregating data for the Czech Republic compiled by the Czech Statistical Office (CSO) and for the Slovak Republic compiled by the Slovak Statistical Office (SSO).

Industrial production

The index of industrial production (IIP) covers enterprises in the extractive and manufacturing industries, including electricity, gas and water, irrespective of the type of ownership.

From 1991 production was measured as the production of goods, i.e. the final production of the enterprise, rather than gross production. Production values in 1989 prices were recorded on a cumulative basis from the beginning of each year to the current month. Monthly figures were then calculated by subtracting cumulative data for the previous period.

Historically, the index measured the change in the volume of production over the corresponding period of the previous year. If the industrial structure changed, the value of production in the same period of the preceding year was recalculated on a comparable basis and the implied rate of change linked to the index with the original basis. This meant that while comparisons for the same periods in different years were valid, strictly speaking, comparisons within a year were not. Because of this, all periods in the base year were shown as 100.

Since 1991 the coverage of enterprises varied; in 1991 enterprises with 100 or more employees were monitored, in 1992 enterprises with 25 or more employees. Differences in the coverage of organisations in previous years are not significant.

From 1992 the national index was changed to a fixed base of 1989=100.

The *total industrial production index* covers mining, manufacturing (excluding publishing) and electricity, gas and water.

The *industrial production index for mining* refers to ISIC Revision 2, Major Division 2 for the mining industry.

C S F R

The *industrial production index for manufacturing* refers to ISIC Revision 2, Major Division 3 for the manufacturing industry, excluding publishing.

The *industrial production index for electricity and gas* refers to ISIC Revision 2, Major Division 4 for electricity, gas and water, and includes production and distribution of water from 1991.

The *industrial production index for construction* refers to ISIC Revision 3, Major Division 5 for the construction industry.

Commodity output

Brown coal production figures cover brown coal and lignite. The output of brown coal refers to the output of mines less wastes removed and washed out in coal preparation plants. As lignite is not washed, the output of lignite equals gross output.

The *black coal production* series covers the net output of hard coal, which is the sum of the output of individual mining enterprises, less coal delivered to coke washeries for refining, plus output of coke washeries.

Crude steel covers ferrous materials other than direct-reduced products, which are usefully malleable and which contain 2 per cent or less of carbon by weight.

Cement production covers output of Portland cement, slag Portland cement, pozzolan cements, aluminous cements, special kinds of cement and other kinds of cement (e.g. magnesium cement and high expansion cement).

Passenger car production covers passenger cars and lorries, including separate complete undercarriages, special purpose cars and minibuses.

Construction

Dwellings

A dwelling refers to a room or set of rooms that, according to the decree of the construction authority, are designed for housing and which can serve for this purpose as independent dwelling units. Individual rooms at boarding schools, halls of residence and hostels that are not run by local administrative bodies are not included in the number of dwellings.

Dwellings completed refer to those dwellings for which the delivery record has been issued. The CSFR data on dwellings completed exclude one-family houses, dwellings built by co-operative members themselves and dwellings built by non-construction organisations.

Domestic trade

Up to the end of 1990, the monthly index of retail sales value refers to the sales of goods and services in current retail prices by the public retail trade network and the catering enterprises of the state and co-operative sectors (i.e. enterprises of the Ministries of Trade, consumer co-operatives, restaurants and fuel suppliers). These commodities were sold directly to consumers for their own use or to collective consumers and socialist organisations for intermediate consumption. Receipts for services rendered are included. The monthly figures accounted for about 85 per cent of all trade.

The quarterly and annual figures up to the end of 1990 also included trading activities of non-trading enterprises in the state and co-operative sectors.

Since the beginning of 1991, the coverage of enterprises varied; in 1991 enterprises with 100 or more employees were covered, in 1992 enterprises with 25 or more employees were covered. Since 1991 monthly data include an estimate of total sales to cover the reporting units which were not subject to the statistical survey.

Data are available in two series. The first, for the period 1980-90 has the corresponding period of 1980 as its base. The second, which begins in 1991, has the corresponding period of 1990 as its base. Although the two series represent total retail sales value, due to the change in the structure of reporting units reflected in the index started in January 1991, it is not considered possible to link the series before and after this period.

Labour

Employment

The CSFR employment data cover employment in the state and co-operative sectors excluding agricultural co-operatives and private entrepreneurs. From the beginning of 1991, the data cover employees in enterprises and organisations with 100 or more employees and from 1992 in enterprises and organisations with 25 or more employees. The data refer to the average number of employees, including those in both full- and part-time employment, excluding apprentices and employees on maternity leave.

Employment in industry covers employees of national industrial enterprises, private enterprises, joint ventures, social and professional organisations (including printing houses). It excludes enterprises managed by town and local municipal authorities, productive co-operatives and waterworks in the state and co-operative sectors. Apprentices are excluded.

In 1992 the Czechoslovak national classification was replaced by the ISIC-88.

Unemployment

Registration of the unemployed began in December 1989. It was necessary to register as unemployed in order to receive retraining and financial support; a further incentive to register was that the same office handled both registration of the unemployed and job vacancies.

The *total unemployment* refers to persons who were neither under a working contract nor performing any independent earning activity and who asked the local employment agency to find suitable work for them.

The data refer to numbers at the end of the period as provided by the Federal Ministry of Labour and Social Affairs.

The *unemployment rate* represents the proportion of job applicants in the total labour force.

CSFR

Private enterprises

Until end 1989, the data covered the number of persons rendering services permitted by the national committees according to the ordinance of the governments of the Czech Republic and the Slovak Republic. Since the beginning of 1990 the data refer to the number of entrepreneurs registered according to the Act No. 105/1990.

The interpretation of the number of private entrepreneurs is obscured by several phenomena. Many people register a private enterprise and for various reasons do not actually engage in the activity. Others might only pursue the activity on a part-time basis, especially as consultants. A further complication is, for example, in the case of a private supermarket with a staff of 100 persons, each of the staff may register as an entrepreneur if the supermarket is in fact working as a partnership.

Re-registration of enterprises was required up to the end of 1992 in accordance with the Small Business Act No. 455/1991.

Wages

Monthly earnings

Quarterly and annual data on *monthly earnings total* relate to earnings in the state and co-operative sectors, and exclude agricultural co-operatives. From the beginning of 1991, the coverage of enterprises varied; in 1991 only enterprises and organisations with 100 or more employees were covered and from 1992 only enterprises and organisations with 25 or more employees.

Earnings are defined as the average monthly wages per worker and refer to gross wages, i.e. basic wages and salaries including bonuses and remunerations, but excluding family and other social benefits.

Prices

Producer prices

The *producer price index* in industry is based on the producer prices of industrial goods manufactured in the CSFR. Up to the end of 1990 the prices referred to list prices; starting in 1991, they refer to monthly price quotations of about 6 000 representative items collected from selected industrial enterprises representing about 410 branches of the Standard Classification of Industrial Branches. The index does not cover products or branches of non-standard production of mechanical engineering and metallurgy, assembly and dismantling, industrial services, repairs and energy distribution.

The reported prices are the arithmetic mean of actual transaction prices, excluding turnover and other sales taxes, of all important contracts at the middle of the month.

Representative items were sometimes substituted by items of similar quality, but when large differences in quality arose, a price correction was made.

The index is of the Laspeyres type and is derived from simple price relatives for individual items weighted by the value of production of the relevant branch in 1989. The national base was January 1989=100.

Consumer prices

The *consumer price index (CPI)* reflects the price movements of food products, industrial goods, catering and other services bought by the population. Prices of 827 selected goods and services were observed in 1992.

Major group	Number of items
Food	191
Industrial goods	387
Public catering	63
Services (including rent, transport and communications)	186
TOTAL	827

Price collectors from statistical offices noted prices from selected retail and service outlets in all districts of the Czech Republic and the Slovak Republic on about the fifteenth of each month, excepting fruit and vegetables prices, which were collected three times a month (on the first, tenth and twentieth calendar days). A separate monthly basket of fresh fruit and vegetables was compiled comprising selected varieties currently on sale in the relevant month. The index was based on prices paid in state, co-operative and private trade for full value goods; prices of second-hand goods are not included in the index.

If the observed product disappeared, it was replaced by another product of comparable quality. If the quality of the substitute product was not directly comparable, adjustments were made. Generally prices of products which follow new fashion trends were introduced directly in the index.

The CPI is of the type Laspeyres. The prices collected from the individual reporting units were used to calculate unweighted arithmetic averages. The price indices for individual groups and aggregates were calculated as weighted arithmetical means with constant weights of the base year. The weights for goods were based on the structure of retail turnover, and for services on the structure of expenditure of the population for services in 1989. Separate indices were calculated for the Czech Republic and the Slovak Republic.

The system of monitoring and calculating price indices was changed in 1991 from quarterly to monthly and a new national base of 1 January 1989=100 introduced.

Domestic finance

Narrow money (M1) refers to national currency in circulation outside the banking sector and demand deposits, excluding those of the central government.

Quasi-money refers to time, savings and foreign currency deposits of residents, except the central government.

C S F R

Interest rates

The *official discount rate* refers to the end of period rate at which the State Bank lent to commercial banks.

Foreign finance

The *US dollar exchange rate* refers to the end of period principal rate.

Until the end of 1988, the exchange system comprised the use of an official rate, a commercial rate and a non-commercial rate. The official rate and gold parity were abolished on 1 January 1989. In January 1990 the commercial and non-commercial rates were combined into a single rate, the principal rate, based on a basket of the five currencies with the largest share of the turnover of balance of payments transactions. A tourist rate was created in 1990 based on parallel market rates for the korun in Austria and Switzerland. The principal rate and the tourist rate were unified at the end of 1990 into one exchange rate.

Data on *total reserves, excluding gold* are in accordance with the International Monetary Fund's definition.

Foreign trade

In the foreign trade statistics of the CSFR exports were recorded on an FOB basis and imports on a frontier parity basis. The latter exclude transport and insurance, so are essentially also on a FOB basis. For the period 1980-88, the transaction values were converted to Czechoslovak crowns using the exchange rate which prevailed at the end of 1988. From the beginning of 1989 onwards, current exchange rates were used.

1980-90

Until end 1990, exports, imports and net trade statistics were based on a survey of licensed exporters and importers. This implies that some services are included in these data. Work undertaken abroad by Czechoslovak construction enterprises was included in exports.

1991 and onwards

From the beginning of 1991, customs declarations were used to compile foreign trade statistics. They excluded direct re-exports and exports and imports of services.

The change in the reporting system led to a change in reporting lags. Exports of goods were then recorded on the date they crossed the Czechoslovak border. Imports of goods were then recorded at the date of their release from bonded warehouses rather than at the date they crossed the frontier. There was a processing delay of one to fifteen days in the mailing of declarations. The data were continuously updated by the Central Customs Administration.

Prices

FOB prices for exports and CIF prices for imports were observed for a sample of about 1 800 representative items selected according to their importance and relatively constant share of external trade transactions. The price information was reported on a quarterly basis by 28 selected trade organisations.

The index is of the Laspeyres type and the individual price relatives are weighted by the corresponding value of exports and imports in 1985 at the 4-digit level of the Czechoslovak trade classification.

Volume

Export and import volume indices are derived by deflating foreign trade in current values by the price indices described above.

Data from 1991 onwards are approximate since the price indices were not reweighted to reflect the changes in current price data coverage since January 1991.

ESTONIA

Industrial production

Until 1993 industrial production was classified according to the Classification of Branches of the National Economy (CBNE) of the CMEA. The United Nations International Standard Industrial Classification (ISIC) Revision 3 was introduced in 1993 and data have been recalculated on this basis for 1992.

Production values from 1985 until end 1990 are calculated using volume data valued at 1982 wholesale prices. The series are not corrected for the number of working days in the month.

From 1994 data refers to industrial sales. Annual surveys cover all non-private sector and private sector enterprises with less than 20 employees. Monthly surveys cover all enterprises with 50 or more employees which represents about 85 per cent of total industrial sales.

Referring to sales, data exclude changes in stocks of finished goods, changes in work in progress and non-principal production. The Statistical Office of Estonia publishes these industrial sales data in current values only.

The industrial sales in current values are deflated, by the OECD Secretariat, using the Producer Price Index in base 1993=100.

Total industrial production in the CBNE broadly covered the mining, manufacturing and electricity. Not included are "non-productive" services, gas distribution, thermal energy and household water (ISIC some 342 + some 4102 + some 4103 + some 4200).

The *index of industrial production for electricity* consists of 100 per cent of Estonian electricity production from oil shale burning power stations.

Commodity output

Cement refers to P400 Portland cement.

Business surveys

A description of business tendency survey techniques and the list of harmonised questions is given in the chapter *Business Tendency Surveys* of this publication.

Construction

Dwellings

Dwellings refer to physically separate and independent premises intended for habitation consisting of one or more rooms (residential and ancillary) having an independent exit with direct access to a common area (staircase, landing, passage, etc.).

Construction on a dwelling is considered to have started when the permit has been issued. *Total dwellings started* include owner-built houses.

The number of *dwellings completed* by construction enterprises is collected quarterly in construction offices in each region (15 regions and Tallinn). Dwellings are defined as completed when registered in accordance with statutory procedures (for construction offices) or, in the case of dwellings constructed by private individuals, when ready for use.

Domestic trade

Until end 1992, all retail and catering establishments were surveyed including those in the private sector. The turnover of state and state-owned co-operative retail trade, including public catering (workers canteens, etc.) as well as commerce conducted directly by transport and industrial enterprises, is included. In addition, retail sales by organisations, enterprises and institutions to their personnel (in sanatoriums, child care institutions, hospitals, etc.) are included.

The profit arising from the sale of products by social food co-operatives, selling and buying/selling co-operatives is included, as well as goods produced by individuals outside the workplace but sold through commercial enterprises. All agricultural produce is also included, other than that sold informally through city markets.

Starting in 1993 a sample survey was introduced. All retail trade enterprises with 20 or more employees are surveyed. A random stratified sample survey of private enterprises with less than 20 employees is also conducted. Until end 1994, the sample size for retail trade enterprises was 350 for a population of approximately 1 200. From 1995, the sample size for retail trade enterprises is 600 for a population of approximately 3 400.

Domestic trade statistics include only retail trade enterprises (exclude catering enterprises), all state and municipal enterprises are included.

Retail sales value is expressed in roubles until December 1991 and in kroons thereafter. For more detailed information see the section on Domestic finance below and the chapter *Introduction of New Currencies.*

Retail sales volume data have 1992 as base 100. The retail price index is used as deflator.

ESTONIA

Labour

Employment

Until end 1991, total employment comprised all persons working in the state sector, on collective farms, in private co-operatives, in private agriculture and the self-employed. Only civilian employment is included, and students are excluded. Until end 1989 part-time employees were counted as one employee and not in full-time equivalent terms. Starting in 1990, part-time employees are accounted for according to the number of hours actually worked. The number employed during this period refers to the annual average number of employees in enterprises and organisations within each sector of the economy. Employees were classified by sector according to the classification system used in the former Soviet Union. For the state sector, tabulations of the number of workers and employees on the staff rosters of each enterprise and organisation within the republics of the former Soviet Union were submitted monthly to the statistical agency. The annual averages were obtained as the average of the twelve months.

Since 1991, registered enterprises fill out quarterly questionnaires on the number of employed, their wages, and the number of job vacancies. There is no minimum size limit per enterprise -- even enterprises with one employee are required to fill in the questionnaire. Until the third quarter 1993 the survey covered all registered enterprises. From the fourth quarter 1993 a sample survey of registered enterprises is used. It is estimated that 80 per cent of employees are covered by the survey. The data are then extrapolated to estimate the total number of wage earners.

Data has been classified according to ISIC from 1991.

The data refer to all civilian employees holding a labour contract, including those temporarily not working -- employees on maternity or child care leave, those on forced vacation and those whose labour contract is on hold for any reason. Part-time employees are included in full-time equivalent terms. Employees in joint ventures and the self-employed are not yet included.

Unemployment

The number of *unemployment beneficiaries* is collected through the Labour Market Board in six major towns and 15 regions in Estonia on the first day of each month.

To be registered as unemployed a person must:

-- be a permanent resident of Estonia;

-- be between 16 years and the pension age;

-- have been engaged in work or in an activity considered equivalent for at least 180 days during the last 12 months;

-- be actively seeking work.

A registered unemployed person whose income does not exceed the state unemployment benefit has the right to receive a monthly allowance. The amount of benefit has been 180 EEK since 1991. The minimum period of non-activity before receiving benefits is 10 days; in exceptional cases it is 60 days. Generally the maximum benefit period (eligibility period for being registered as unemployed at a state employment office) is 180 calendar days; in some cases it may be continued according the "Social Protection of the Unemployed Act". Persons lose their entitlement if they do not report at a state employment office in person at least once every 10 workdays, or if they obtain an income at least equivalent to the state unemployment benefit.

The *unemployment rate* refers to the number of unemployed as a percentage of the working age population. The definition of working age population has been changing. Starting in 1994, six months are added to the pension age each year so that in 2003 the pension age for females will be 60 (56,5 in 1996) and for males will be 65 (61,5 in 1996). Data are obtained from the Labour Market Board.

Information concerning the number of *job vacancies* is collected in the enterprise survey used to collect employment data (see above).

Time worked

The normal working week constitutes 40 working hours.

Wages

Monthly earnings

Wages statistics are collected through a quarterly survey of enterprises, institutions and organisations (excluding farms and self-employment). Data by economic activities for the whole economy are based on ISIC tabulation categories. All state-owned, municipal and other ownership-type enterprises, institutions and organisations with more than 19 employees are surveyed. For enterprises, institutions and organisations with less than 20 employees (excluding enterprises and institutions in state and municipal ownership), a sample survey is used. The sampling criteria are the main economic activity of an enterprise, institution or organisation and the number of employees.

Total average gross wages include:

-- B_1: payments to employees for time actually worked including payments for both full-time and part-time employees (pay for work, premium and other regularly paid bonuses);

-- B_2: remuneration to employees for time not worked including vacation pay, compensation, one-time bonuses and pay for stoppage of work;

-- R: sickness benefits paid to employees from the social security fund;

They are calculated as:

$$B_{average} = \frac{B_1 + B_2 + R}{t_{quarter} * 3}$$

where:

-- $t_{quarter}$: average number of employees in a quarter per month;

-- $B_{average}$: average monthly gross wages per quarter.

ESTONIA

Total wages are expressed in roubles until end of 1991 and in kroons thereafter. Wages in industry and manufacturing are expressed in roubles until second quarter of 1992 and in kroons thereafter. For more detailed information see the section on Domestic finance below and the chapter *Introduction of New Currencies*.

Prices

Producer prices

"Old index"

The price data used to calculate the *index of producer prices in manufacturing* with the same period of 1990 as base 100 are collected directly from enterprises every month principally using postal questionnaires. Approximately 300 industrial products are covered in one-third of the largest enterprises. This Laspeyres type index is weighted using 1989 values of production of large enterprises in major industrial branches. Prices do not include any taxes.

The *producer price indices for industry* and *manufacturing* with the previous period as base 100 are weighted using 1992 values of production of large scale enterprises in major industrial activities.

"New index"

Since 1993, the methodology for calculating the producer price index has been changed to accord with international practice. The index is of type Laspeyres.

In calculating the producer price index, the prices of goods produced for both domestic and export markets are taken into account. Until May 1995, prices were collected directly from 100 enterprises every month principally using postal questionnaires. Approximately 350 industrial goods were covered. The 1992 average prices of the products under observation were used as base prices and the volumes of industrial output by activities in 1992 were used as weights.

From June 1995, the 1994 average prices of the products under observation are used as base prices and the volumes of industrial output by activities in 1994 are used as weights. Approximately 440 industrial goods are covered and 110 enterprises are surveyed.

Net prices, without excise and sales tax are used in the index. No treatment of quality changes nor of seasonal items are made.

Producer price indices are expressed in national publications in fixed base 1992=100 and 1994=100.

 SHORT-TERM ECONOMIC INDICATORS, SOURCES AND DEFINITIONS   90   *INDICATEURS ÉCONOMIQUES A COURT TERME, SOURCES ET DÉFINITIONS*

OECD/CCET © April 1996   OCDE/CCET © avril 1996

Weights in the PPI are as follows:

Industry branch	1992	1993	1994
Manufacturing	84.7	82.6	81.0
Mining	4.3	4.7	4.6
Energy	11.0	12.7	14.4
TOTAL	100.0	100.0	100.0

Consumer prices

The *consumer price index (CPI)* reflects the price movements of food products, manufactured goods and services purchased by the population. Price collectors note three price quotations per item from selected retail and service outlets in ten towns in Estonia. From 1994, 317 goods and 93 services are priced during the week which includes the fifteenth of the month. Thirty-three quotations are taken for each good surveyed.

From 1990 to June 1992 the series refers to a cost of living index. Starting in July 1992, a consumer price index is calculated. Some differences should be noted between the two periods (i.e. repairs and maintenance on housing are included in the housing index in the latter period only; alcohol, tobacco and motor car costs are also introduced in July 1992), but most of the main sub-indices (food, clothing and footwear, housing) are considered comparable.

Another difference between the figures for June and July 1992 was an increase in the sales tax from 10-18 per cent. As all prices include any taxes levied, this accounts for some of the price rise between the two periods.

The index was a fixed weight index from the first quarter 1990 to December 1993.

From June 1992 until December 1993, the weights used in the CPI were taken from the family expenditure survey for the period March to May 1992. Expenditure patterns from earlier months were not considered because the structure of household expenditure changed sharply in March 1992 due to a dramatic increase in housing costs. The structure of expenditure in June was not taken into account because the imminent currency reform caused a drastic change in spending patterns.

From January 1994, the index is of type Laspeyres. Weights are based on the 1993 household budget survey with adjustments to reflect recent changes in prices and tariffs. The indices are calculated on the average prices of 1993, and are presented with the base 1993=100. Alcohol and tobacco figures are revised for presumed under-reporting of these items.

When seasonal items are unavailable or rare, the average price of the other items in a given product group is used allowing the missing seasonal item to retain its expenditure weight without imputing a price.

Imported goods have received higher weights, but the majority of price quotations are for domestically produced items. Quality changes are relatively smaller on domestically produced items and only small adjustments have been made to the CPIs for changes in quality.

ESTONIA

Services are included in each of the following groups and also extracted to create a separate *CPI for services*. The total weight for services was 32.75 in 1994.

Clothing and footwear includes ready-made clothing, knitted goods, footwear, textile fabrics (excluding household textiles) and tailor and cobbler services.

The *housing* group includes housing and communal services, fuels, maintenance and repair commodities. It excludes housing construction and the purchase of dwellings, which are considered an investment in capital stock.

The *transport and communication* group can be divided into three subdivisions: private transport, a principally new group, of which the former cost-of-living index took into consideration only expenses for bicycles; public transport; communications.

Entertainment includes items as varied as radio and photographic goods, travelling and sporting goods, expenses for children's daycare, toys, seeds, plants and flowers, printed matter including periodicals, services provided by cinemas, theatres, etc.

Household expenses include furniture, household textiles, electric household appliances, kitchen utensils, dishes, washing powder, electric bulbs, etc. *Personal care and effects* includes other necessary services, hygienic commodities and public catering. *Medical care* includes medicines, medical care commodities, and professional medical services.

Product group weights in the total CPI are as follows:

Item	Weight March-May 1992 (used from June 1992- December 1993)	Weight 1993 (used from January 1994)
Food	43.46	37.85
Clothing and footwear	11.77	7.61
Housing: of which: Fuel and electricity	11.25 5.98	19.73 9.99
Transport and communications	9.84	13.04
Recreation, entertainment and printed matter	7.76	6.56
Household expenses	6.06	3.20
Alcohol and tobacco	5.12	4.33
Personal care and effects	3.99	5.67
Medical care	0.75	2.01
TOTAL	100.00	100.00

Domestic finance

Domestic finance data are calculated by the Bank of Estonia and refer to the end of the period.

A new currency, the Estonian kroon was introduced on the 20th June 1992. The conversion factor at introduction was one kroon to ten roubles. These data are thus expressed in roubles before the second quarter 1992, and in Estonian kroons after that date. For more detailed information see the chapter *Introduction of New Currencies*.

Narrow money (M1) comprises currency outside banks and demand deposits.

Quasi-money comprises time and savings deposits, and foreign convertible and non-convertible currency deposits excluding deposits of central and local governments.

Personal deposits cover demand, savings and time deposits of households.

Foreign finance

Data are calculated by the Bank of Estonia.

All *exchange rate* series are averages of the official daily rates of the Bank of Estonia.

The series *official reserves* refers to total net foreign currency holdings of the Bank of Estonia at the end of the period. The series is shown net, i.e. foreign liabilities have been subtracted from the foreign currency reserves of the Bank of Estonia. Non-convertible currency is not included in the total reserves. The series includes gold until end 1993.

Gross foreign debt comprises all government backed debt and International Monetary Fund credits. Data refer to the end of the period.

Foreign trade

The data for 1987-90 were calculated by the Goskomstat USSR. The trade classification is that used in the former Soviet Union. Goods were valued at domestic prices in current roubles. Domestic prices of exported goods were prices paid by export organisations to domestic producers; domestic prices of imported goods were actual prices paid by final domestic buyers.

Trade in *non-convertible currencies* comprises trade with all republics of the former Soviet Union, including Latvia and Lithuania. Trade in *convertible currencies* covers trade with all other countries.

Foreign trade data in 1991 and the first half of 1992 were based on statistical reports by enterprises and organisations situated on the territory of Estonia.

Since July 1992, foreign trade data has been based on customs declarations.

Exports are valued at FOB-values and *imports* at CIF-values. Trade figures exclude services as well as goods for use by Embassies. Re-exports and re-imports are included.

Foreign trade data in 1991 and the first half of 1992 were based on the Classification of Branches of the National Economy (CBNE) of the former CMEA. Foreign trade has been classified according to the Harmonised System (HS) since July 1992. Receiving and originating countries are classified to the ISO 3166.

ESTONIA

Foreign trade data are expressed in roubles until second quarter of 1992 and in kroons thereafter. For more detailed information see the section on Domestic finance above and the chapter *Introduction of New Currencies*.

Publications

Some of the series described above, but presented according to national practice, can be found in English in the following publications from the State Statistical Office of Estonia:

Estonian Statistics, Monthly Statistical Bulletin
Statistical Yearbook
Estonia in Figures
National Accounts in Estonia
Regional Statistics
Government Finance Statistics
Foreign Trade.

HUNGARY

Industrial production

The *index of industrial production* (IIP) relates to the production activities defined under Divisions 10 to 41 (Groups C, D and E) of the United Nations International Standard Industrial Classification (ISIC) Revision 3. These include the mining and quarrying, manufacturing, electricity, gas and water supply industries. The index corresponds to the major branch Industry of the Hungarian industrial classification, the Standard Industrial Classification of All Economic Activities (TEAOR).

Until end 1988, monthly data cover all enterprises possessing legal entities, i.e. excluding unincorporated enterprises. In 1989-90 the data were obtained from a census of enterprises with 50 or more employees, again excluding unincorporated enterprises. Starting in 1991, however, enterprises with 50 or fewer employees were observed using a sample survey. In 1992 industrial statistics were extended to include unincorporated enterprises and individual entrepreneurs. In 1993, enterprises with 21-50 employees were observed by a sample survey and an estimation was made concerning the output of enterprises with fewer than 20 employees. Since 1994, the sample survey covers enterprises with 11-50 employees. For the total IIP, tax returns are used in order to include an estimate of the industrial output of enterprises with ten or fewer employees. Branch, sub-branch and division indices, however, are calculated using production assessments of all enterprises with more than 20 employees (1994), or more than 10 employees (1995). Therefore, the total IIP coverage is wider than that of its components.

Production is defined as the gross output of industrial activities, covering sales of final and intermediate goods and services, excluding transactions between establishments of the same enterprise, and subsidiary production carried out by the enterprise. Adjustments are made for work in progress and for changes in stocks of finished products. Consumer and value added taxes are not included.

The values of production are deflated to constant January 1985 prices using the Producer Price Index (PPI).

The IIP is a Paasche chain index; series are weighted by gross output, and weights are changed every year.

Seasonally adjusted indices are calculated by the Hungarian Central Statistical Office using X11 Arima/88 on the basis of moving averages by indicator.

The *index of industrial production for mining* relates to Divisions 10 to 14 (Group C) of ISIC Revision 3, including the mining of building materials (stone quarrying, clay and sand-pits).

The *index of industrial production for manufacturing* refers to Divisions 15 to 37 (Group D) of ISIC Revision 3. Before 1985 publishing activities were excluded.

HUNGARY

The *index of industrial production for electricity and gas* covers Divisions 40 and 41 (Group E) of ISIC Revision 3. Before 1985, water supply and waterworks were excluded.

Commodity output

Commodity output series are based on a census which collects quantity data in enterprises with more than 50 employees.

Coal production covers all types of coal with a high or low degree of coalification, with a net calorific value of 6.2-26.4 MJ per Kg. Both hard coal (including anthracite) and brown coal (including lignite) are included.

Crude steel products are defined as those containing ferrum, produced in furnaces from crude iron, scrap iron (plus additives and slagging material) and, in the case of alloys, products containing alloying additives and a maximum carbon content of 1.7 per cent.

Cement production covers all cements whose base material contains clinker, regardless of additives and clinker contained, and irrespective of the cement's solidity.

Crude petroleum production includes shale oil, but excludes natural gas liquids.

Natural gas production represents essentially methane, but a small proportion invariably refers to other gases. The data cover non-associated gas (originating from fields producing liquid and gaseous hydrocarbons), methane stripped at casing heads or recovered in coal mines, and sewage gas. Ethane, propane, butane and other liquid yields, as far as they are separated, are excluded. Losses due to technological reasons are excluded.

The *production of passenger cars* excludes vehicles for military purposes. This series has been discontinued to protect the anonymity of producing enterprises.

Business surveys

A description of business tendency survey techniques and the list of harmonised questions is given in the chapter *Business Tendency Surveys* of this publication.

Sales

Sales volume

The *sales volume* indices refer to total industrial deliveries and its two components, domestic trade and deliveries to the export market. The sales volume is obtained by deflating current values using price indices. The price index used to derive the volume of sales is obtained from the price index of industrial sales (see Producer Price Index below).

Current values are obtained from the same survey as that used for the Index of Industrial Production (see above). Seasonally adjusted series are calculated by the HCSO.

Total sales volume refers to payments made for processed and semi-processed products delivered and services ordered (e.g. assembly, repairs and maintenance, paid work) in industry (mining, manufacturing, and gas and electricity). Payments for non-industrial activities, such as construction, the re-sale of purchased products and intra-enterprise transport services are not included.

Sales volume of export goods refers to the value of goods and services invoiced to foreign purchasers and, until 1991, to foreign trade enterprises. Since 1992, only goods and services actually invoiced to foreign purchasers are included.

Domestic trade sales volume refers to the volume of all goods to be consumed domestically.

Construction

Dwellings

The data concerning the number of dwellings are calculated using local government registrations.

Dwellings started refer to the number of dwellings with permits, where construction has actually commenced.

Dwellings completed include all dwellings that have received permission to be put to use. All dwellings built by local authorities, the central government, economic organisations with legal entity or individuals are included. Until 1995, the number of dwellings completed in the first quarter of each year is included in second quarter figures.

Domestic trade

Monthly retail sales and catering surveys are carried out in department stores, shops, fuel and building material selling points, gasoline filling stations, restaurants, bars, canteens and other catering establishments selling new and second-hand goods to the population, enterprises and institutions. The turnover is recorded at purchasers' prices, i.e. consumer prices including VAT. The target population is all retail trade and catering outlets, regardless of their size. Outlets of economic units whose main activity is not retail sales or catering, and sole proprietors are included.

Sales by agents and direct sales from producing enterprises to consumers are excluded.

The 1991-93 survey sample was taken from the population of retail trade units (shops, restaurants and catering units). The units to be sampled were selected proportionally to their size which was defined by past turnover. Sales by mail order were excluded.

Since 1994, the survey has been re-designed. A dual frame sampling design is used in which a list frame is supplemented by an area frame. All enterprises with retail trade and/or catering activity belong to one of the two sampling frames. Turnover in mail order houses is included. Units are selected for the list frame using stratified sampling. The area sample is selected through simple random sampling from each of the 200 defined geographical areas in Hungary. The area sample is updated continuously. The sampling units are enterprises for the list frame and outlets for the area frame.

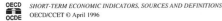

HUNGARY

Estimated turnover is classified by activity according to the Hungarian Standard Industrial Classification of All Economic Activities (TEAOR). Data from 1994 onward are therefore not comparable with those for previous periods at the detailed activity level.

The *retail sales volume* is obtained by deflating current values using retail price indices based in January 1991. Volume data are comparable between 1993 and 1994.

Foreign investment

Foreign investment data are cumulative from the beginning of the year. The series *new joint ventures* does not include existing Hungarian enterprises that become joint ventures through foreign partnership, nor foreign capital invested in capital raising ventures. Only 20-30 per cent of total foreign direct investment is therefore included.

Labour

Employment

Until end 1991 data for *total employment* include employees in all enterprises with legal entity, and all budgetary institutions. In 1992 and 1993, enterprises with less than 20 employees were not surveyed. All budgetary institutions continued to be surveyed, regardless of the number of employees. From 1994 on, employment data cover enterprises with more than ten employees. All enterprises with more than 50 employees are surveyed, and a sample is drawn from units with 11-50 employees. Although the survey coverage in 1993 was different, i.e. covering only economic units with more than 20 employees, tendencies reflected in 1993 and 1994 data are considered comparable.

Employees on long-term leave (maternity or child-care leave, active military service, sick leave lasting more than three months, etc.) are excluded. Persons who are not considered regular staff but who have been working continuously (students working during vacations, employees "on loan" from other employers, etc.) are included.

The previously published quarterly data on *employment in the material branches* refer to employees in agriculture, mining, manufacturing, gas and electricity, waterworks, construction, trade, transport, communications and data processing. Until end 1988, all economic units with legal entity are covered, and from 1989 on, only legal economic units with 50 or more employees.

Differences in coverage occur in the quarterly and annual data for *employment in industry* and *employment in manufacturing*. Quarterly data refer to all legal enterprises up to the end of 1988 and from 1989-92, enterprises with more than 50 employees. Annual data until end 1991 refer to enterprises of any size. Annual data in 1992 refer to enterprises with more than 20 employees, and all budgetary institutions.

The working age population in Hungary refers to women between 15 and 54 and men between 15 and 59.

Unemployment

The data for registered unemployment and for the number of beneficiaries are based on end of month administrative records from local labour offices which are then aggregated by region. The *registered unemployed* include, by definition:

-- those available for work and looking for a job;

-- persons not receiving a pension;

-- those not registered as students;

-- persons registered at a local Labour Office in the current month.

The unemployment register is constructed by adding:

-- persons who are entitled to receive unemployment benefits;

-- persons registered as unemployed but who are no longer entitled to unemployment benefits;

-- persons participating in active labour market programmes.

The coverage of registered unemployment changed in May 1995. From this date, job-seekers who are temporarily unable to work, for example due to child care or military obligations, are excluded from the count of registered unemployment. In May 1995, there were 27 288 persons in this category.

Beneficiaries are those persons who contributed to the unemployment insurance fund for at least 360 days in the last four years before becoming unemployed, who are not entitled to a pension and who apply for suitable job vacancies held by the Labour Office. The duration of benefits is proportional to the period of contributions paid into the unemployment insurance fund in the preceding four years. Persons who have contributed continually during the last four years receive unemployment benefits for up to one year. Those who have contributed only 12-16 months receive unemployment benefits for a maximum of three months.

Secondary or post-secondary school graduates may receive unemployment benefits if they have graduated within the last 18 months, have been registered as unemployed at a Labour Office for at least three months and are not otherwise entitled to unemployment benefits. The benefit amount for recent graduates is 75 per cent of the minimum wage; the maximum benefit period is six months.

A beneficiary loses the right to receive benefits if he/she refuses a suitable job or training possibility offered by the labour office, or if he/she is involved in gainful activity, or if he/she is eligible to receive a pension.

Payment of benefits are suspended if unemployed persons:

-- fail to co-operate with the labour centre in finding work;

-- receive maternity benefits or a child-care allowance;

-- are in confinement or imprisoned;

-- are engaged in military or civilian service;

-- are engaged in community service work proposed by the Labour Office.

HUNGARY

The *unemployment rate* refers to the number of unemployed registered in national Labour Offices on the last day of a given month divided by the total labour force on the 1 January of the previous year.

Time worked

The average number of *hours worked in manufacturing* per month refers to manual workers excluding home-workers and retired persons in enterprises in the manufacturing industry (Divisions 15 to 37 (Group D) of ISIC Revision 3). Until December 1988 all enterprises were covered. From January 1989 onwards only enterprises with more than 50 employees are included. In 1993, enterprises with more than 20 employees and in 1994, enterprises with more than ten employees, were surveyed. These data are not adjusted by the number of working days in the month.

In national statistical publications, some monthly, quarterly and annual series are published adjusted for the *number of working days*. These data may be used to assess monthly growth rates for industrial production and sales.

Wages

Monthly earnings

Total monthly earnings and earnings in *material branches* refer to average gross monthly wages earned by full-time employees and workers before subtracting personal income tax and social security and pension payments. Payments from profit-sharing schemes are included. From 1992 on, bonuses and other earnings are included, whereas previous data refer to base wages only.

Monthly earnings series are taken from the same surveys as those for employment (see Employment above for coverage).

Monthly earnings in manufacturing refer to gross average wages paid to manual workers.

Prices

Producer prices

The *producer price index (PPI) for industry* reflects price movements of industrial goods sales. Prices are obtained by a compulsory monthly mail survey and concern products sold on domestic and export markets in mining and quarrying, manufacturing, electricity, gas, steam and water supply industries. The survey is addressed to about 800 of the most important producers of the selected commodities. There are approximately 5 500 quotations of 800 items included. The varieties selected are generally produced in large quantities. The prices reported are monthly average prices of each variety sold.

The criterion used for product selection is the level of total sales. Until 1994 the PPI reflected not only changes in price levels, but also changes in the composition of domestic versus exported sales. Since 1994, the PPI has been calculated as a weighted average of domestic and export price indices, thus it is not affected by changes in the composition of domestic and export sales at the product level.

The prices refer to sales to other producers and to wholesale and retail traders, and are defined as the selling prices of goods and services sold during the month. The prices do not include the value added tax introduced in January 1988, nor the previously existing turnover tax. A price supplement based on turnover is, however, included. In the case of an exported good, the FOB price of the goods at the Hungarian border is applied.

The PPI is a Laspeyres chain index. The commodity indices are averages of relevant individual price ratios. Commodity indices are aggregated to the 4-digit branch level of the Hungarian Standard Industrial Classification of All Economic Activities (TEAOR) with weights proportional to the value of sales. The sub-branch indices are weighted by annual sales two years prior to the reference period. Commodity weights are derived from yearly industrial production statistics and revised every four years. From 1993 on, some commodity group indices are weighted by annual sales two years prior to the reference year, revised by yearly industrial production.

A systematic review of representative commodities occurs at the end of each year. For seasonal commodities the latest quotation is carried forward throughout the off-season. In the case of a quality change, the new series of price relatives is linked to the old one without adjustment.

Consumer prices

The Hungarian *consumer price index (CPI)* is compiled monthly and refers to all socio-economic groups in the entire country. Consumption expenditure includes most goods and services purchased by households. Notably, imputed rent for owner-occupied dwellings, repairs and television licences are included. Consumption in kind from own account production or goods and services received free of charge, passenger car licences, consumer credit charges, life insurance, direct taxes, free health services and second-hand transactions (with the exception of second-hand cars) are excluded.

Weights of selected items are derived from a household expenditure survey with some adjustments for conformity with national accounts estimates and are revised yearly. The survey covers a sample of 12 000 households. Each household keeps an expenditure diary providing detailed information on expenditures.

The household expenditure survey weights are corrected using consumption figures for under-reporting of items such as alcohol and tobacco, and for the under-representation of low income households by re-weighting the sub-sample of low-income households using a breakdown of population figures.

In 1996, the weights used to calculate the CPI are derived from the 1994 household expenditure survey; in 1995 weights used were taken from the 1993 survey; in 1994 the weights used were taken from the 1992 survey. Until end 1993 they were derived from the 1990 survey.

Weights and composition of the index are as follows:

HUNGARY

Major groups	Weights 1990 (used until end 1993)	Weights 1992 (used in 1994)	Weights 1993 (used in 1995)	Weights 1994 (used from 1996)
Food	28	26.6	27.4	28.4
Beverages and tobacco	12	10.3	9.6	9.6
Fuel and power	5	8.5	6.9	6.5
Clothing	8	7.8	7.8	7.5
Consumer durables	10	7.7	8.1	7.4
Other industrial articles	17	17.5	17.5	17.2
Services	20	21.6	22.7	23.4
TOTAL	100	100.0	100.0	100.0

Prices are collected for approximately 1 800 representative items. The prices are collected by 145 collectors from selected outlets in 86 towns. Fruit and vegetable prices are also obtained from selected markets. Over 100 000 price quotations are obtained per month (between 30-150 quotations per commodity) from 8 000 outlets. For seasonal food items, monthly weights are variable within a fixed basket of goods.

The CPI is a modified Laspeyres index. The monthly price of a given item refers to the arithmetic mean of all prices collected for the item in the given month. The index is compiled using relatives of mean prices calculated for each item specified, omitting any missing observations.

Domestic finance

Broad money (M2) is comprised of narrow money (M1) and quasi-money. In recent periods, M1 and quasi-money cannot be identified separately because the Hungarian National Bank does not distinguish between demand deposits and time/savings deposits.

The *narrow money* supply (M1) refers to currency outside banks plus demand deposits other than those of the central government. This series has been discontinued.

Quasi-money refers to time, savings, and foreign currency deposits, excluding foreign exchange deposits held by non-residents. This series has been discontinued.

Personal deposits refer to deposits of households excluding savings notes and foreign deposits held by non-residents. Data include the accounts registered by the National Bank of Hungary, commercial banks and specialised financial institutions.

Interest rates

The *discount rate* refers to the basic rate on refinancing credit maturing over one year that the National Bank lends to financial institutions. This rate, according to 1993 monetary policy, will be adjusted quarterly to the level of medium-term yields on the capital market.

The *call money rate* refers to the interbank money market rate on credit for two days or less. It is a monthly average of daily rates.

The *short-term interest rate* refers to the yield on 90-day Treasury bills. It is an average of the yields at the bi-monthly auctions of 90-day Treasury bills.

Foreign finance

Exchange rates: the forint is on an adjustable pegged regime to a basket of currencies made up of the US dollar (50 per cent) and the ECU (50 per cent).

Official reserves excluding gold include end of period holdings of convertible currencies.

Foreign trade

1980-90

Exports, imports and *net trade* for the period 1980-90 are expressed in current prices. The data for this period were in principle based on customs statistics, but in practice they were based on information from a survey of licensed importers and exporters. The data cover direct trade, i.e. goods imported for consumption or further processing and goods exported from Hungary.

Trade was defined as:

-- the payment for goods of foreign origin as well as goods obtained as a payment (barter trade);

-- payment for equipment, including projecting and assembling costs;

-- the value of feature films, including performance licenses;

-- the value of purchases made in foreign currencies by foreign agencies in Hungary and by Hungarian bodies abroad for their own use;

-- the value of fuels sold either to foreign vessels, aircraft, etc., on the territory of Hungary or bought abroad by Hungarian firms;

-- government aid in kind on the basis of an inter-governmental treaty;

-- the value of completed investments and the net value of construction and assembly work (excluding the value of raw materials);

-- the value of non-monetary gold, silver and platinum.

Direct trade did not include:

-- payment related to intellectual goods (manufacturing licenses, royalties, etc.);

-- personal luggage;

-- aid in kind by international organisations, such as the Red Cross;

-- the value of monetary gold.

Imports were valued CIF and exports FOB at the Hungarian border in Hungarian forints.

HUNGARY

1991 and onwards

Export, import and *net trade* information, based on customs returns according to the Harmonised System, is supplied from 1 January 1991 by customs agencies. From 1994 the Combined Nomenclature System has been used. Exports and imports refer to merchandise trade to/from all destinations as defined below.

From 1991 trade data coverage was changed to include the following items:

-- sales and purchases of goods denominated in Hungarian forints;

-- all forms of aid in kind received or granted;

-- material and products exported or imported in order to be processed at duty free values;

-- leased goods;

-- improvement and repair trade: from 1995, the value of transport goods temporarily imported for repairs which are valued at over five million dollars, such as aircraft and ships, is excluded from trade statistics. For comparability, a chain index has been calculated using 1994 data recalculated on the basis of methodology adopted in 1995.

The following items were excluded:

-- sales and purchases by foreign extraterritorial bodies;

-- the value of fuels sold either to foreign vessels, aircraft, etc. on the territory of Hungary or bought abroad by Hungarian firms;

-- trade in marine vessels and aircraft.

From 1991, the following items are classified as foreign trade in services instead of merchandise trade:

-- construction-assembly (excluding the value of raw materials);

-- the value of feature films (exported or imported) including performance licences;

-- the value of software (except its physical support which is included in merchandise trade).

To provide some comparability over time, the HCSO has adjusted the 1990 foreign trade data, which was based on information from a survey of licensed importers and exporters, according to the new definitions. It should however be noted that no new statistical sources were available and exact comparability cannot be guaranteed.

From 1995, the value of the repairs made to temporarily imported transport goods which are valued at over five million dollars, such as aircraft and ships, is included in service trade figures.

Imports are valued CIF and exports FOB in current prices at the Hungarian border. Transactions in foreign currencies are re-calculated to Hungarian forints using official exchange rates.

Prices

Export and import price indices for foreign trade are calculated from unit values derived from customs declarations. Export and import price indices reflect not only changes in actual prices paid, but also changes in the structure of individual commodities and commodity groups traded.

The unit values refer to export and import prices at frontier parity, equivalent to CIF values for imports and FOB values for exports at the Hungarian border. Transactions in foreign currencies are re-calculated to Hungarian forints using official exchange rates.

The quarterly foreign trade price indices are of a Paasche type, and yearly indices are Fischer indices.

Volume

Quarterly *export and import volume indices* of foreign trade have been derived using the unit value index described above. To obtain data comparability over time, HCSO has linked 1990 data, converted to new definitions and content, to the volume index based on the previous definition and observed data, using the ratio of first quarter 1990 (observed) to first quarter 1990 (converted) as a link.

Gross fixed capital formation

The main component of gross fixed capital formation (GFCF) is the purchase of new tangible assets. Since 1991, major renovations of existing capital assets are also included. Investment data are obtained from quarterly and annual surveys in corporations and institutions with over ten million Hungarian forints annual investment. Estimates are then made for total investment using other statistics, including VAT declarations and estimates by experts.

Publications

Some of the series described above, but presented according to national practice, can be found in the following HCSO publications:

Statisztikai Havi Közlemények (Monthly Statistical Bulletin)

Main Economic Indicators

Fogyasztói árindex füzetek (Consumer Price Index Bulletin)

Munkaeröpiaci Helyzetkép (Labour Force Statistics)

Statisztikai Evkönyv (Statistical Yearbook)

and also the

Monthly Report from the National Bank of Hungary.

LATVIA

Industrial production

Industrial production refers to commodity production destined for sales of ready-made products, semi-finished products, plus services rendered to other enterprises and non-paying services rendered within a given enterprise. Industrial production includes changes in stocks of finished goods and non-principal production.

From 1985, industrial production is classified according to the United Nations International Standard Industrial Classification (ISIC). From 1995, water supply is included in monthly surveys.

Beginning in 1991, monthly surveys cover 90 per cent of production. All state and local government organisations are surveyed, irrespective of the number of employees; all other enterprises are surveyed if they employ more than 50 persons. Annual surveys, however, cover 100 per cent of production.

Until 1994, values were deflated by the enterprises themselves and the series linked between years using the chain index method. From 1995, the index of industrial production is a Laspeyres index. It is calculated using January 1992 constant prices.

Commodity output

Cement production refers to Portland cement.

The output of *textiles* includes all cotton, silk, linen and wool, woven and non-woven fabrics.

Business Surveys

A description of business tendency survey techniques and the list of harmonised questions is given in the chapter *Business Tendency Surveys* of this publication.

Construction

Dwellings

A dwelling is defined as a living space with a separate exit to the street, yard, staircase or common corridor. Hostels with a common kitchen and facilities are not considered separate dwellings.

Completed dwellings include construction by state and local government enterprises, co-operatives, share-holding companies, consumer organisations and own construction by individuals. Private sector enterprises are not included.

A dwelling is considered complete when the statutory document certifying completion has been filed.

Domestic trade

Until end 1992, a census was carried out of all retail outlets, catering establishments, markets and kiosks. On 1 January 1992, retail outlets numbered about 7 200 and catering establishments numbered 3 500. As new outlets were appearing, a new survey was started at the end of 1992. Data are collected each month from all state and local government trade outlets irrespective of their size and specialisation. Entrepreneurial companies, joint capital enterprises, leased and private enterprises with a planned yearly retail turnover of more than 10 000 lats are surveyed quarterly. Enterprises with a planned yearly turnover below 10 000 lats are surveyed annually. Retail turnover in markets is covered using survey results in Latvia's four largest markets.

From January 1995 the survey coverage has been changed. All central and local government trade enterprises, as well as enterprises with yearly turnover exceeding 100 000 lats, are surveyed; for all other enterprises 10 per cent are surveyed and the total turnover is estimated. The retail trade turnover excludes public catering.

Monthly data are adjusted after processing of quarterly data; quarterly data are adjusted after processing of annual data.

Retail sales value is expressed in latvian roubles until second quarter 1993 and in lats thereafter. For more detailed information see the section on Domestic finance below and the chapter *Introduction of New Currencies.*

Retail sales volume is expressed in constant prices of January 1991. Retail sales volume is calculated by deflating the value data by the consumer price index "all goods". The series is presented in *Short-term Economic Indicators: Transition Economies* with a reference base of 1993 as 100.

Labour

Employment

Total employment comprises employees in the state sector, entrepreneurial companies including agricultural statutory companies, private enterprises (peasant farms, household plots and private auxiliary farms and the self-employed). Enterprises and organisations of any size are included.

Prior to 1992, the number employed refers to the annual average number of employees in enterprises and organisations within each sector of the economy. Employees were classified by sector according to the classification system of the former Soviet Union. For the state sector, tabulations of the number of workers and employees on the staff rosters of each enterprise and organisation within the republics of the former Soviet Union were submitted to the statistical agency. The annual averages were obtained as the average of 12 months.

LATVIA

From 1992, branch classifications accord with ISIC. Statistical surveys have been sent to state and mixed state/private units both monthly and quarterly, and to private enterprises once per year. Private sector data in 1992, however, is estimated.

Professional military staff and servicepersons as well as employees on maternity and child-care leave are included in employment figures. Part-time workers are included as full-time equivalents. Students of working age who are also doing paid work are included.

Unemployment

According to the law on Employment, passed in December 1991, and subsequent legislation, a person is defined as unemployed if he/she:

-- is not working;

-- is a Latvian citizen or any foreigner (non-citizen), having received permission for permanent residence;

-- is between 15 and 54 years of age (women) or 15 and 59 years of age (men);

-- is not involved in any entrepreneurial activity;

-- earns less than the minimum wage;

-- is actively searching for a job;

-- is registered with the state employment service at the place of his/her permanent residence and re-registers at least once a month.

In order to register as unemployed, applicants must present their work history certificate and passport. The decision concerning a person's status as unemployed is made by the head of the local state employment agency not later than two weeks after the registration day.

A registered unemployed person has the right to receive *unemployment benefits,* or stipends if they undertake professional training. Beneficiaries receive their first benefits 14 days after registration. The duration of these benefits can not exceed six months in any 12-month period. The duration of unemployment benefit entitlement can be extended up to 12 months following the request of local authorities. Unemployment benefits equal 90 per cent of the minimum wage for individuals who have paid social taxes for six out of the last 12 months. Benefit levels drop to 70 per cent of the minimum wage if social taxes have not been paid, and if, during this period, the individual:

-- has graduated from an educational establishment;

-- was released from imprisonment;

-- is a woman with children between 3-3.5 years old;

-- is no longer under full state care, or following retirement from the active army service;

-- was previously an invalid, but is now fit for work.

Beneficiaries must re-register once per month to continue receiving benefits.

Benefits are not available to persons who have voluntarily interrupted their work, or who were released from the previous job due to violation of regulations of the job contract or discipline problems.

A beneficiary loses the right to unemployment benefits if he/she:

-- refuses two appropriate job offers or refuses professional training or requalification courses when an appropriate job is not available;

-- without due reason, does not attend professional training or requalification courses, or does not fulfil the job contract, or undertakes temporary social work;

-- leaves for permanent residence outside Latvia;

-- loses his/her status of unemployed (as defined above).

The *unemployment rate* is the ratio of the number of registered unemployed to the labour force (employed plus registered non-working persons).

State employment agencies also register the number of *job vacancies*. All employers, irrespective of the form of ownership, provide information about vacancies. All unemployment and job vacancy monthly data refer to the end of the period, quarterly and yearly data are monthly averages.

Wages

Monthly earnings

Monthly earnings are determined by dividing the estimated payroll, including regular or one-time bonuses, premiums, and other payments from the material stimulation fund, by the average number of workers and employees for the given period (month, quarter, year). Premiums from the social security fund are not included. Monthly data are collected from state enterprises only.

Data refer to gross wages, i.e. before income tax and social security deductions. Payments in kind -- health care, free meals or transportation -- are excluded. Quarterly bonuses are included in quarterly and annual figures while annual bonuses are included both in annual figures and either in the fourth quarter or the following first quarter depending on the period of their calculation.

Wage data are expressed in Latvian roubles until second quarter 1993 and in Lats thereafter. For more detailed information see the section on Domestic finance below and the chapter *Introduction of New Currencies.*

Monthly earnings in industry refer to state and mixed state/private units.

Prices

Producer prices

In 1993 and 1994, the survey used to calculate the *producer price index (PPI) for manufactured goods* covers price quotations in 90 manufacturing enterprises in 57 ISIC branches including 469 commodities and commodity groups. Some private sector enterprises are surveyed. Prior to 1993, the survey covered 274 commodities.

LATVIA

From January 1995, the *producer price index* has been calculated according to a new weighting pattern. It covers 709 selected commodities from 166 manufacturing enterprises and 69 ISIC branches. The price base used is December of the previous year.

Producer prices are recorded only for products manufactured in Latvia. However imported raw materials, semi-manufactured goods, assembling parts and energy resources can also be used in manufacturing of these products. Industrial products destined for export are included. All taxes are excluded.

The choice of products is made by the Central Statistical Bureau of Latvia in conjunction with individual enterprises. Participating firms are instructed to adjust prices for changes in quality.

For seasonal goods, prices of the last month of production are carried forward during the months of non-production.

Prior to 1995, individual commodities were weighted by previous year sales volumes. From 1995, they are weighted by 1993 year sales volume.

The PPI is a chain Laspeyres index.

Consumer Prices

The monthly *consumer price index (CPI)* was introduced in January 1991.

Until June 1992, these indices were calculated as Paasche indices from price reports obtained in 150 retail outlets in 15 regions throughout Latvia for 950 goods (300 food items and 650 non-food items) and 150 services.

In June 1992, a Laspeyres type index was introduced. In 1993 price quotations for 388 goods and services (379 in 1992) were collected in 775 outlets in 15 out of 26 Latvian regions. Outlets include 257 state stores, 243 municipal stores, 212 co-operatives (including 155 consumer co-operatives), 49 private stores, four trade union units and ten markets.

At the end of 1995 more private outlets were included in the survey due to privatisation. The share of state and municipal outlets declined to 32 per cent, while the share of private outlets increased to 48 per cent. Prices were obtained from a total of 1120 outlets.

Four to eight price quotations are recorded per month for agricultural produce and one to four quotations for other goods.

Some goods and services were re-classified in December 1993 according to internationally accepted expenditure classifications.

The figures for January to June 1992 were recalculated on a basis consistent with the new Laspeyres index. For 1991 only the indices for *food* and *alcohol and tobacco* are viewed as comparable with the later figures.

For seasonal goods that are not "in season" in a given month, the average seasonal price is used in that month, although a few prices may be available in that month. This applies particularly to imported food goods in the winter period.

Some adjustments have been made to the CPIs for changes in quality.

The indices are calculated on the basis of the ratio of average prices. All prices include any taxes levied.

Weights are elaborated on the basis of household expenditures; from 1994 the CPI is weighted using the expenditure patterns from mid-1992 to mid-1993. Previously the CPI was weighted by the 1991 household survey. Adjustments are made for under-reporting of alcohol and tobacco expenditures by households.

The household survey weights are shown below:

Item	Weights 1991 (used in 1992-1993)	Weights 1992-93 (used from 1994)
Food	48.72	49.67
Clothing and footwear	11.12	8.68
Household operation	4.23	2.67
Alcohol and tobacco	9.54	7.37
Transport and communications	6.39	7.18
Leisure, cultural activities, education	5.09	4.32
Miscellaneous goods and services	8.72	4.93
Health care	0.92	1.09
Housing	5.27	14.09
TOTAL	100.00	100.00

The total weight for Services in the 1992/93 survey is 23.65.

All CPIs are expressed in fixed base December 1993=100 and as monthly rates of change in national publications.

The *CPI for housing* includes rent and building materials.

Domestic finance

The Latvian rouble was introduced as legal tender on 7 May 1992. It was introduced at par with the former Soviet Union rouble which continued to be legal tender. On 20 July 1992 the Latvian rouble became the only legal tender. From 5 March 1993 lats were gradually put into circulation, the conversion rate having been 1 lat to 200 Latvian roubles. From 18 October 1993 the Latvian rouble ceased to be legal tender and was completely withdrawn on 1 July 1994.

Domestic finance data is expressed in roubles and in latvian roubles until second quarter 1993 and in lats thereafter. For more information see also the chapter *Introduction of New Currencies*.

LATVIA

Broad money (M2) includes currency outside banks, personal deposits and foreign currency deposits. It refers to the end of the period.

Interest rates

The *discount rate* refers to the rate at which the Central Bank lends to commercial banks.

Foreign finance

The *exchange rate* series refer to the Latvian currency, the lat, with respect to the US dollar, the Deutsche mark and the ECU.

The lat is on a freely adjustable peg to the Special Drawing Right (SDR -- currency unit of the International Monetary Fund), and a basket of currencies which includes the US dollar, the Deutsche mark, the Japanese yen, the French franc and the British pound.

Official reserves, excluding gold comprise foreign currency holdings in Latvia and abroad and are recorded at the end of the period.

Foreign trade

Until end 1990, trade data was compiled by the Goskomstat and Soviet foreign trade organisations in current domestic prices in roubles. The trade classification was that used by republics of the former Soviet Union. The data for 1988-90 are estimates based on the 1987 input-output tables of 120 sectors.

Until 1990, exported goods were valued at the prices paid by export organisations to domestic producers; imported goods were valued at the actual prices paid by final domestic buyers. Prices of imported goods were calculated on the basis of foreign trade import prices adjusted by means of special conversion coefficients set by pricing authorities for groups of products.

From 1991, quarterly surveys of trading enterprises have been held. Approximately 80 per cent of trade was covered by these surveys in 1991. Trade in electrical energy and gas are reported, while research and development are not reported. In 1992 customs declarations were introduced according to the Harmonised System. Starting in 1993, all data are collected through customs declarations with additional data from special enquiries on trade in electrical energy, natural gas and fish sold abroad from national fishing vessels. Prior to 1995, quarterly data include goods sold to and bought from Russian army staff stationed in the territory of Latvia and an adjustment for mineral fuel imports.

The coverage of monthly data for *exports*, *imports* and *net trade* is different from the quarterly data. Monthly data do not include deliveries to Russian troops formerly stationed in Latvia nor transactions of the Latvian fishing fleet outside the country, nor any adjustment for mineral fuel imports.

Traded services and foreign aid are not included.

Both exports and imports are reported on a FOB basis.

Data are presented in latvian roubles until second quarter of 1993, and in lats thereafter. For more detailed information see the section concerning Domestic finance above and the chapter *Introduction of New Currencies*.

Concerning *exports and imports to and from the NIS*, Lithuania and Estonia are considered in the rouble zone until 1992, after which time they are calculated in the non-rouble zone. Trade with all countries outside the former Soviet Union is included in *trade to and from countries other than the NIS*.

Publications

Some of the series described above, but presented according to national practice, can be found in the following publications of the Central Statistical Bureau of Latvia:

Bulletin of Latvian Economic Statistics
Statistical Yearbook of Latvia.

LITHUANIA

Industrial production

The *index of industrial production (IIP) in manufacturing* refers to the sales of industrial goods unadjusted for changes in stocks of finished goods and excluding non-principal production. Sales volumes are reported monthly by surveyed enterprises. If an enterprise produces goods from raw materials provided by the consumer, the value of the raw materials is <u>not</u> deducted from the final value. Sales volumes of the current month are weighted by the corresponding Producer Price Index (see below), and expressed as a rate of change to the previous month. The fixed base index is calculated directly from the monthly rates of change. Annual and quarterly series are calculated from the monthly series.

Approximately 600 enterprises are surveyed and sales of 1 100 industrial goods are recorded. Until end 1994, all state-owned, private and mixed capital enterprises with more than 100 employees were included in the survey. Starting in January 1995 enterprises with more than 20 employees are surveyed. The coverage in terms of industrial output is estimated at 90 per cent.

From January 1994, industrial production has been classified according to the International Standard Industrial Classification (ISIC, Revision 3) and includes mining, quarrying, manufacturing and energy generation and distribution, and the distribution of water and gas.

Commodity output

Cement production includes all types of cement.

Business surveys

An explanation of business tendency survey techniques and the list of harmonised questions is given in the chapter *Business Tendency Surveys* of this publication.

Construction

Dwellings

A dwelling is defined according to a Council for Mutual Economic Assistance (CMEA) definition, elaborated in 1980, which includes all apartments and one-family houses. Communal housing such as sanatoria, students' and workers' hostels, etc., is excluded.

Upon completion of construction, a legal document is issued by the local building commission which is comprised of enterprise contractors, architects and representatives of utilities enterprises. This

 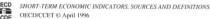

document states the characteristics of the dwelling, and confirms that it has been completed in due form. Upon registration of this document a dwelling is considered completed. For dwellings built directly by individuals, information concerning their completion is submitted to the Department of Statistics by architectural agencies in local governments. All contractors, whether in the private or public sector, must certify completion of a dwelling.

Total *dwellings completed* include dwellings built by construction enterprises in all sectors, i.e. including the private sector, plus dwellings built by individuals.

Dwellings completed in enterprises exclude dwellings, usually one-family houses, built by individuals.

Domestic trade

Retail trade data are collected using monthly statistical surveys sent to enterprises; survey responses are then aggregated by type of ownership (public, mixed capital, etc.). All state and co-operative enterprises are included in the survey regardless of their size. Sales by collective farms are, however, excluded prior to 1992. The agricultural partnerships that began to replace collective farms in 1992 are included in surveys.

Starting in 1992, a part of the private sector was included; privatised state enterprises were surveyed, but newly-established private enterprises continued to be excluded. In 1993, newly-established private enterprises with more than 20 employees began to be surveyed. It is estimated that in 1993 approximately 55-70 per cent of retail trade was covered in the survey. Another 30 per cent of retail goods were traded in outdoor markets and in private outlets with fewer than 20 employees (not covered by the survey). Since April 1994, private enterprises with five and more employees have been surveyed. Retail trade taking place in market places began to be included, as well as estimates of the "shadow" economy, using declared income of individuals minus personal deposits and savings, expenditure on rent, fuel and power, taxes and official estimates of retail trade. Since January 1995, retail trade turnover in all private enterprises, as well as in market places, is included.

Quarterly figures for the *retail sales value* are adjusted for reporting delays etc., and are therefore not the sum of the monthly series. There is, however, no difference in coverage of enterprises between the monthly and quarterly series.

All taxes are included in the value of retail trade.

Retail sales value is expressed in roubles or talonas until the end of 1992 and in litas thereafter. For more information see the section on Domestic finance below and the chapter *Introduction of New Currencies*.

The *volume of retail trade* is derived by deflating the retail trade value in current prices by a consumer price index based in May 1992 which is recalculated to correspond with items included in domestic trade data. While retail trade value includes retail trade in market places and small private enterprises from January 1995, the retail trade volume does not include this trade. The same coverage as prior to January 1995 has been kept in the volume series for reasons of historical comparability.

LITHUANIA

Labour

Employment

Total employment refers to all persons working in the state sector, in co-operatives, in private enterprises, plus the self-employed. All enterprises are surveyed, regardless of the number of employees. In both the state and private sectors, the number of workers and employees are reported quarterly to the Statistical Office. The number of employees in small enterprises (those with less than four employees) are obtained from tax returns; the number of private farmers is obtained from the farm register. In 1995, the estimated non-response rate for surveyed enterprises was 15 per cent.

Before 1992, enterprises and organisations were classified by sector according to the classification system of the ex-CMEA. In 1992, the General Industrial Classification of Economic Activities (NACE) was introduced.

Employees on maternity and child care leave and military personnel are included in employment figures. Part-time workers are included in employment figures on a full-time equivalent basis. Persons outside the working age (16-55 for women; 16 to 60 for men) who continue to hold remunerated employment are included.

Total employment includes all sectors of the economy, and notably agriculture and non-enterprise sectors (health services, government, cultural branches, etc.).

Employment in industry includes the manufacturing, mining, electricity, gas and water, agricultural processing, construction, transport and communications sectors.

Unemployment

Unemployment data have been collected since March 1991 when the Unemployment Law was introduced. Labour Exchange Bureaus register the unemployed, distribute unemployment benefits and fill job vacancies. Also registered are those job seekers who have left their jobs of their own accord, but who are not considered as "registered unemployed for economic reasons". In 1994 and 1995, two pilot labour force surveys per year were conducted. According to the findings of these surveys, the number of unemployed persons is about twice as high as the number registered at Labour Exchange Bureaus.

Total unemployment refers to the registered unemployed, as well as those who have left their job of their own accord, who do not currently have a paid job or their own business and who are available for work.

Registered unemployment refers to the number of persons who have lost their job not of their own accord and recent graduates who have registered in a Labour Exchange Bureau. Registration at Labour Exchange Bureaus is obligatory periodically during each month to continue to be considered as unemployed.

Registered unemployed persons who have worked for at least 24 months in the last three years, recent graduates and persons returning from military service may be eligible to receive unemployment benefits. The minimum period of non-activity before receiving benefits is 8 days for those who have worked previously. The minimum period is 6 months for registered persons who left a job voluntarily.

Unemployment beneficiaries receive benefits for up to six months. The maximum benefit amount does not exceed twice the minimum living standard. In 1994, the minimum benefit was approximately 20 litas, the maximum benefit was 100 litas and the average benefit was 50 litas. On January 1st 1995, a minimum benefit of 75 litas was introduced. On January 1st 1996, the minimum benefit was changed to 90 litas and the maximum benefit to 180 litas. The actual benefit amount is determined as a percentage of an individual's previous salary. For the first two months, a formerly-salaried unemployed person receives 70 per cent of her/his former wage, provided it does not exceed twice the minimum living standard. For the following two months the benefit amount drops to 60 per cent of the former salary; for the last two months of the benefit period, the unemployment benefit equals 50 per cent of the former salary. Persons who have never worked receive the minimum benefit.

A beneficiary loses the right to benefits if he/she does not re-register every month, refuses three job offers, or refuses a training course offered by the Labour Exchange Bureau to acquire new qualifications needed to find gainful employment.

The *total unemployment rate* refers to the number of total unemployed as a proportion of the average annual labour force (employed plus unemployed) in the previous year.

The *registered unemployment rate* refers to the number of registered unemployed as a proportion of the average annual labour force (employed plus unemployed) in the previous year.

The number of *job vacancies* refers to vacancies in the public and private sectors registered in Labour Exchange Bureaus.

Time worked

In national statistical publications, some monthly, quarterly and annual series are published adjusted for the *number of working days* in the period. These data may be used to assess growth rates for industrial sales and production.

Wages

Monthly earnings

Data on monthly earnings are collected in the same survey as those for Employment (see above). Monthly, quarterly and annual data include information for private sector enterprises. Estimations for sole proprietors are only included in the quarterly and annual data.

Monthly earnings represent gross wages perceived by employees before income tax payments. Overtime payments, paid vacations and all bonuses, including profit-related bonuses, are included. Monthly data are adjusted for quarterly and annual bonus payments in order that these payments be distributed equally over all months in the quarter or year. Few payments in kind exist, but these are estimated at current prices and included in monthly earnings. Social payments are not included in earnings, nor are disaster payments made by enterprises to employees for, for example a fire or a death in the family.

Wages are expressed in roubles or talonas until the end of 1992, and in litas thereafter. For more detailed information see the section on Domestic finance below and the chapter *Introduction of New Currencies.*

LITHUANIA

Prices

Producer prices

The *producer price index* (PPI) is constructed using survey responses from 270 enterprises, covering 890 industrial goods and commodity groups. Prices exclude value added tax from January 1995 on; previously, prices were quoted including VAT. In 1993, 82 per cent of industrial output was produced by enterprises included in the sample survey. In 1994-95, prices of industrial commodities are weighted by their 1993 sales values. Until 1996, products that have undergone changes in quality have been treated as new products. From 1996, prices are weighted by 1994 sales values; and prices are corrected for quality changes. For goods with a seasonal production cycle, the most recent quotation is carried forward during the off-season.

The producer price index is a Laspeyres type.

The ISIC classification has been used until end 1995. Starting in 1996, the NACE classification system has been adopted.

Consumer prices

A new *consumer price index* (CPI) was introduced in May 1992. The new index is of a modified Laspeyres type, and sub-groups are weighted using the Household Budget Survey. The previous index, in effect before May 1992, was a Paasche index and was weighted by the turnover of goods in state and co-operative retail outlets.

The new CPI is constructed from price quotations of 369 goods and services in seven major cities and nine regions in Lithuania. Sample outlets are selected by price collectors in co-operation with the Department of Statistics. About 1 060 state, co-operative and private outlets are sampled, encompassing retail outlets, canteens, restaurants and cafés as well as kiosks and open air markets. Price quotations of food and non-food goods are also collected in market places. Outlets are chosen to constitute a geographical mix, and to include large, medium-sized as well as small, specialised outlets. No registers of retail outlets are available to mathematically select the sample.

One price quotation per month is noted for all items. Food commodity prices are noted on the twenty-first to twenty-third day of the month; non-food goods are quoted on the seventeenth to twentieth of each month; and services on the fifteenth or sixteenth of the month.

The prices recorded are actual prices paid by customers, i.e. including turnover and excise taxes. Some prices continue to be fixed by the government, namely electricity, gas, postal and telecommunications services, pharmaceuticals and transportation (excluding public passenger transport within cities). Prices of housing and public passenger transport within cities are regulated by local authorities.

If a seasonal item is not available in a retail outlet, the price collected during the previous month is carried forward, or the average price in the commodity sub-group is imputed in order that the missing price does not affect the sub-group. No adjustments are made for quality changes in commodities.

The Household Expenditure Survey of August 1992 to July 1993 is used to weight the 1994 CPI. The 1991 Household Expenditure Survey was used to weight the CPI in 1992 and 1993.

Household survey weights are shown below:

Item	Weights 1991 (used in 1992 and 1993)	Weights 1992-93 (used from 1994)
Food, alcohol and tobacco	53.81	65.82
Clothing and footwear	15.38	9.61
Household operations	6.48	3.15
Transport and communications	5.70	5.91
Housing and fuel	4.93	8.07
Leisure, culture, education, miscellaneous	13.22	6.57
Medical and health care	0.48	0.87
TOTAL	100.00	100.00

Expenditure patterns are adjusted for under-reporting of alcohol and tobacco consumption using the retail turnover of these commodities.

From January 1994 on, the *CPI for food* excludes catering.

The *CPI for household operation* includes furniture, floor covering and repairs, bedding, kitchenware, detergents and other utilities and services.

The *CPI for housing* includes rent, repairs and maintenance of dwellings, energy and fuel.

The *CPI for services* includes components of most of the major sub-groups of the Household Survey, comprising repairs of footwear, household operation, health care services, etc.

Domestic finance

All monetary and financial data are prepared by the National Bank of Lithuania.

The Lithuanian talonas was introduced as a separate temporary currency to replace the former Soviet Union rouble on 1 October 1992. The talonas was replaced by the litas on 25 June 1993 on a floating exchange rate regime. The conversion rate at introduction was 1 litas to 100 talonas. Exchange rate data for 1992 refer to the exchange rate of the talonas; from 1993 on, to the exchange rate of the litas. (See also the chapter *Introduction of New Currencies*).

Monetary series are expressed in roubles or talonas until the end of 1992 and in litas thereafter.

The supply of *narrow money* (M1) refers to currency in circulation plus demand deposits of individuals, state and co-operative enterprises and non-banking financial institutions such as insurance companies.

Quasi-money covers time deposits and foreign currency deposits held by individuals and enterprises. Foreign currency deposits are converted to litas using the official exchange rate.

LITHUANIA

Personal deposits refer to demand, time and foreign currency deposits of individuals and of those private sector enterprises that do not maintain enterprise accounts. Foreign currency deposits are converted to litas using the official exchange rate. Personal deposits are held in the 25 commercial banks and the one savings bank in Lithuania.

Interest rates

The *official discount rate* is the rate at which the Central Bank lends to commercial banks and refers to the end of the period.

Foreign finance

The *litas/US dollar exchange rate* refers to the official exchange rate offered by the Central Bank. It corresponds approximately to the mid-rate between buying and selling US dollars offered by commercial banks.

Foreign trade

Foreign trade data have been compiled from customs declarations since 1993. Data relating to the imports of electrical energy, however, continue to be submitted by the importing enterprises. In 1992, invoices from trade enterprises were used to compile all trade data. All state enterprises were covered, and an estimated 20-30 per cent of private sector enterprises were included. Private sector enterprises involved in foreign trade were identified from the enterprise register.

Approximately 480 products and product groups are covered in foreign trade statistics. The Harmonised System was introduced in 1993; previously, trade was classified according to the ex-CMEA system. Foreign trade was valued at the prices paid by export organisations to domestic producers for exported goods; and at the actual prices paid by final domestic buyers for imported goods.

Some goods are excluded from trade statistics, as follows:

-- goods consigned by the Lithuanian government to armed forces and diplomatic representation abroad; goods imported by foreign Embassies in Lithuania;

-- monetary gold, securities and bank notes;

-- goods imported/exported for temporary use or for a limited period such as goods for a display, demonstration or use at exhibitions; tourism advertising material; machines, equipment and tools sent for inspection and demonstration, etc.

-- fish caught outside territorial waters;

-- repairs;

-- provisions for Lithuanian ships or air craft engaged in international transport.

Imports for re-export are included.

Imports are valued CIF; exports are valued FOB.

OECD
OCDE
SHORT-TERM ECONOMIC INDICATORS, SOURCES AND DEFINITIONS
OECD/CCET © April 1996

120

INDICATEURS ÉCONOMIQUES A COURT TERME, SOURCES ET DÉFINITIONS
OCDE/CCET © avril 1996

Total exports, imports and net trade balance are expressed in roubles or talonas until the end of 1992 and in litas thereafter. For more detailed information see the section on domestic finance above and the chapter *Introduction of New Currencies*. Total trade series are also available in US dollars.

The formerly published series for *trade with non-NIS countries* was valued in US dollars, and includes all trade transacted in convertible currencies. The Estonian kroon and the Latvian lat are treated as convertible currencies from the fourth quarter 1992.

The formerly published series for *trade with the NIS* referred to all trade effected in currencies such as the Russian rouble and the Ukrainian karbovanets.

Publications

Some of the series described above, but presented according to national practice, can be found in the following publications from the Lithuanian Department of Statistics:

Gyventoju Idarbinimas Ir Bedarbyste (Employment and Unemployment)

Lietuvos Uzsienio Prekyba (Foreign Trade of Lithuania)

Lietuvos Ekonomine ir Socialine Raida (Economic and Social Development in Lithuania)

Lietuvos Statistikos metrastis (Lithuanian Statistical Yearbook)

Main Economic Indicators of Lithuania.

POLAND

Industrial production

The indices of industrial production (IIP) refer to volume indices relating to all activities, both industrial and non-industrial, of domestic industrial enterprises.

Prior to 1994, the information was reported by enterprises classified as Industry in the National Economy Classification (KGN). Starting in January 1994, the General Industrial Classification of Economic Activities (NACE) was introduced. Data for 1993 were calculated using both NACE and KGN classifications. In accordance with NACE, units are classified according to their basic activity.

Until the end of 1990, the monthly and quarterly series refer to the production by industrial enterprises of the former socialised sector of the economy, i.e. state enterprises, co-operatives, social organisations, and enterprises with mixed capital. In 1988, for example, these enterprises accounted for 98 per cent of production. Although the growing private sector was not wholly covered before 1991, the amount of production omitted was not significant. For this reason, the discontinuity between the old and new coverage is not thought to be very important. The annual data refer to both the public and private sectors.

Since January 1991 both the monthly and quarterly series cover public and private industrial enterprises with six or more employees. Monthly reporting is obligatory for all large enterprises (more than 50 employees) and a sample of 10 per cent is drawn from medium size enterprises (between six and 50 employees). All medium-sized enterprises are surveyed once per year, and at the same time 5 per cent of small enterprises are surveyed. Results of these surveys are used to calculate annual production figures. Enterprises in the construction, trade and service branches, producing industrial goods, are only counted, however, if they have six or more employees.

Enterprises report monthly receipts from sales in current prices in cumulative terms from the beginning of the year. The current values are converted to constant prices by the Central Statistical Office using the Price Index of Industrial Production, described below under the heading Producer Prices. The Price Index of Industrial Production is used to deflate industrial production by branch before aggregation to higher-level classification. Flows on a monthly basis are derived by subtraction of the cumulated values.

These sales data cover all finished and semi-finished goods, spare parts and goods and services whether industrial or non-industrial. Non-principal production is excluded. The monthly sales data, contrary to annual data, are not adjusted for changes in stocks. The indices are of type Laspeyres.

For the period 1985-90, 1984 constant prices are used to derive volume measures; from 1991-93, 1990 constant prices are used. Starting in 1994, volume data are calculated using 1992 deflators.

OECD
OCDE
SHORT-TERM ECONOMIC INDICATORS, SOURCES AND DEFINITIONS
OECD/CCET © April 1996
122
INDICATEURS ÉCONOMIQUES A COURT TERME, SOURCES ET DÉFINITIONS
OCDE/CCET © avril 1996

For 1986-90, the volume of each month or quarter is expressed in relation to the monthly or quarterly average sales volume in 1985. For 1991, the monthly and quarterly indices have been chained to the corresponding period in 1990.

The volume indices are not adjusted for effective working time.

Total industrial production refers to the sales of mining and manufacturing products and electricity and gas. Construction is not included. Starting in 1994, total production refers to NACE branches C, D and E.

The *IIP for mining* for 1980-93 includes all branches of industry defined by the KGN as being connected with the mining of natural resources, as below:

-- Coal mining: hard coal and anthracite mining, and hard coal briquette production (branch 011), lignite mining and lignite briquette production (branch 014);

-- Fuel industry: oil and natural gas mining (branch 023), peat mining and processing, slate and rock-oil mining and processing (branch 028);

-- Ferrous metallurgical industry: iron ore mining and dressing (branch 041);

-- Non-ferrous ores: mining and dressing of non-ferrous ores (branch 051), and mining and dressing of copper ores (branch 052);

-- Chemical industry: salt and other chemical minerals mining without sulphur-bearing raw materials (branch 121), sulphur-bearing raw materials mining (branch 138);

-- Mineral industry: mining of aggregates, mineral raw materials and quarrying and processing (branch 141).

From 1994, activities are classified according to NACE branch C.

The *IIP for electricity and gas* covers the power generating industry (branch 03), and the gas producing industry (branch 022), both included in the manufacturing industry according to the KGN. The KGN classification does not include a branch connected with water production, purification and distribution.

Starting in 1994, all activities classified under NACE branch E are included.

The remaining branches of industry in the KGN classification, mostly manufacturing industries, are included in the *IIP for manufacturing*. Starting in 1994, activities are classified according to NACE branch D.

The *IIP for construction* refers to the production of building and construction enterprises covering building and construction work, repair and maintenance, drilling and excavation carried out during deep mining.

Prior to 1994, construction was defined as follows:

-- general construction (KGN, section 31, branches 311-314);

-- construction for production and services (section 32, branches 321-328);

POLAND

-- special construction (section 34, branches 341-348);

-- other (branches 381-388).

In 1994, NACE classifications were introduced. The IIP for construction conforms to NACE branch F.

Until end 1990, monthly, quarterly and annual data refer to building and construction enterprises of the former socialised sector of the economy, i.e. state enterprises, co-operatives, municipal enterprises, social organisations and enterprises with mixed capital. Since January 1991 the monthly and quarterly data refer to all building and construction enterprises in the public and private sectors (state enterprises, co-operatives, municipal enterprises, legal and natural persons) with six or more employees.

Enterprises classified as belonging to the construction industry report monthly on their income in current prices from building and construction activities. Conversion to constant prices is made by the Statistical Office using price indices for building and construction work.

Since 1990, the price indices of building and construction activities are based on a representative survey of changes in the prices of building and construction activities of approximately 500 building and construction enterprises. Before 1990, the series were based on representative surveys of changes in prices of building materials and labour in about 100 building and construction enterprises.

Commodity output

Commodity output data are collected monthly in separate surveys. Quarterly and yearly data are calculated from the monthly figures. Monthly data are obtained from units which employ 50 or more workers.

Brown coal production refers to total production extracted from surface and underground workings. Brown coal briquettes are excluded.

The *production of black coal* refers to total production of all grades of anthracite and bituminous coal extracted from underground workings, excluding waste removed at mines, coal briquettes and dust-coal.

The *production of natural gas* covers output from petroleum gas fields, from pure gas fields and from the processes of demethanelation of high-methane beds.

Crude steel production includes production in open-hearth furnaces, electric furnaces and in converters, as well as crude steel obtained in secondary processing.

The *cement production* data include all hydraulic cements used in construction: portland, metallurgic, aluminous and natural cement.

The *crude petroleum production* includes the mining of crude petroleum in its entirety, including that used in the production process.

The *production of passenger cars* includes production for general use. Special vehicles -- ambulances, police cars, special military vehicles -- are not included.

 SHORT-TERM ECONOMIC INDICATORS, SOURCES AND DEFINITIONS   124   INDICATEURS ÉCONOMIQUES A COURT TERME, SOURCES ET DÉFINITIONS

OECD/CCET © April 1996   OCDE/CCET © avril 1996

The *production of plastics* includes all crude plastic material, whether in liquid or granular form. It does not include the transformation of plastic products.

Business surveys

A description of business tendency survey techniques and the list of harmonised questions is given in the chapter *Business Tendency Surveys* of this publication.

Construction

Dwellings

A dwelling is defined as a structurally separate place for habitation, composed of a group of rooms or a single room with additional ancillary areas (e.g. entrance hall, bathroom, toilet). It must have an independent entrance from a staircase, from a common corridor, or directly from a back yard or street.

Areas in attics and basements designated for and used as habitation are treated as dwellings provided they conform to the above definition. The number of dwellings includes reconstructed existing dwellings as well as those obtained by converting buildings not designed for habitation.

Habitation areas in buildings designed for group accommodation (workers' hotels, student dormitories, old peoples' homes, etc.) are not considered to be dwellings.

A dwelling-and-utility building is a combination of a dwelling and an economic area (stable, barn) under one roof. In statistical reporting, this type of building is found only in reference to individual houses.

Information on co-operative, municipal and enterprise construction is provided by investors who report the start and completion of dwelling construction. Regarding individual houses, investors report to local government administrations who prepare monthly reports on completed houses.

Data on *dwellings started in the public sector* relate to co-operative, municipal and institutional housing only. The laying of the foundation is considered as the start of a dwelling or a dwelling-and-utility building.

Data on *dwellings under construction in the public sector* refer to dwellings in co-operative, municipal and institutional apartment buildings only.

Total dwellings under construction, however, cover the whole economy, i.e. co-operative, municipal and enterprise housing, as well as individual houses; and both apartments and dwelling-and-utility buildings.

Total dwellings completed also refer to the entire economy, i.e. co-operative, municipal and enterprise housing, as well as individual houses. Private construction enterprises came into existence in 1993. From January 1984, monthly, quarterly and annual data on completed apartments also cover apartments located in non-dwelling buildings as well as apartments acquired through the transformation of attics and re-construction of existing dwellings. Prior to 1984, this information was included only in the annual data.

POLAND

      Dwellings completed in the public sector refer to co-operative, municipal and institutional housing. The monthly and quarterly data for 1981-83 do not include apartments in non-dwelling buildings.

      A dwelling is considered complete when:

-- the investor (co-operative, municipality or enterprise) accepts by a protocol of completion that the building is ready to use; or

-- the user (or owner, in the case of individual houses) settles in the dwelling or part thereof, regardless of its state of completion.

Domestic trade

      Retail sales and sales on commission are defined as sales by retail shops, department stores, catering establishments and other retail units. The *value of retail sales* is obtained from monthly reports on turnover provided by these units and is given in current prices.

      There is a discontinuity in the value of monthly and quarterly retail sales between the end of 1990 and the beginning of 1991 for two reasons.

      Firstly, the survey for the earlier period covered only retail sales units of the former socialised sector (retail outlets owned by the state, co-operatives, municipalities, community and social organisations). Since the beginning of 1991, the monthly reporting obligation was extended to cover all retail units regardless of their ownership, with 20 or more employees, supplemented with a 10 per cent random sample drawn from units with 6-20 employees, on which the estimate for the whole of this group is based.

      The annual series covers the whole economy (private sector included) for the entire period. From 1991 onwards the sales by units with five or fewer employees are estimated once a year based on the average turnover per employee obtained from a representative survey and the number of employees.

      Secondly, since January 1991 the definition of sales has been limited because sales reported by public retail outlets no longer include sales to private units such as private traders, trading companies and craftsmen, and does not cover retail sales of units in the agricultural sector.

      Thus, monthly and quarterly retail sales data for 1980-90 refer to units of the former socialised sector, while the annual data for the same period cover the entire national economy (private sector included). The data from 1991 refer to retail sales according to the altered definition and coverage.

      The *volume of retail sales* refers to the value of retail sales at 1992 prices. This series has been calculated by the OECD Secretariat using the consumer price index for goods. It is presented in *Short-term Economic Indicators: Transition Economies* with a reference base of 1993 as 100.

Labour

Employment

      Data refer to the average number of employees, defined as the number of persons employed full- and part-time for a given period on the basis of employment evidence or a working agreement. Employment figures refer to persons employed on the basis of labour contracts, and do not include

OECD
OCDE
SHORT-TERM ECONOMIC INDICATORS, SOURCES AND DEFINITIONS
OECD/CCET © April 1996
126
INDICATEURS ÉCONOMIQUES A COURT TERME, SOURCES ET DÉFINITIONS
OCDE/CCET © avril 1996

outworkers, commission agents, members of agricultural production co-operatives, owners and co-owners of establishments and units employing wage earners, the self-employed and owners of individual agricultural farms. Data concerning persons employed in the above categories are only available annually in national sources.

Non-seasonal part-time workers are converted to full-time equivalents based on the ratio of hours worked by part-time employees to hours worked by full-time employees on an enterprise by enterprise basis. A full-time basis refers to the nominal hours required for full-time employees by the enterprise. A part-time basis refers to any working time shorter than the nominal full-time basis as defined by the enterprise.

Data for the average number of employees are provided in monthly, quarterly and annual reports by economic units.

Until the end of 1990, the information concerning the average number of employees covered only units of the former socialised sector, i.e. units owned by the state, co-operatives, social and political organisations and trade unions. From January 1991, however, monthly and quarterly data cover all units with six or more employees regardless of ownership; annual data cover all units regardless of the number of employees.

To provide a comparison between the previous and the new series, data for 1990 are available according to both the previous and the new coverage.

In 1994, employment was classified according to branches of the economy in the NACE classification. Data for 1993 were calculated using both NACE and the former KGN classifications.

The quarterly series for *employment total* covers all organisational units in the national economy with six or more persons regardless of ownership. Excluded are units of National Defence and Internal Affairs financed from the central budget. The quarterly series excludes persons employed abroad, in budgetary units of the material production sphere, and those employed in statutory activities of political or social organisations and trade unions. The annual series covers all units.

The series *employment in material branches*, *employment in industry* and *employment in manufacturing*, refer to employment in the enterprise sector, i.e. excluding employees in education, culture, government, etc.

Employment covers average employment in all units with six or more employees in six key branches of the economy:

-- industry

-- construction

-- transport

-- communication

-- trade

-- since 1991, collective services of municipalities.

The employment in material branches series has been discontinued from 1993.

POLAND

Employment in industry refers to employees in units with six or more employees mining and quarrying, manufacturing and electricity, gas and water supply.

Employment in manufacturing covers all employees in manufacturing enterprises with six or more employees. Averages derived from the quarterly and monthly series may not equal annual totals as the latter may be corrected without revision to the monthly or quarterly data.

Unemployment

Unemployment has been registered since January 1990. According to the Act of Employment of 16 October 1991 (with further amendments), in force since December 1991, a person is considered unemployed if he/she is capable of work and prepared to take up full-time employment in the framework of an employment relationship, is not currently employed, and is not attending school (except as specified in the Act).

Since 1st January 1995 the "New Act of Employment and Counteract Unemployment" of 14 December 1994, has been in force. According to the Act the term "the unemployed" means a person having no employment, not attending any day school, ready and able to take up full-time employment and registered in a local labour office. Persons may be registered if:

-- he/she is over 18 years of age, with the exception of adolescent school graduates;

-- a woman under 60 years, a man under 65 years;

-- he/she has not acquired the right to an old-age pension or disability pension or has finished work and does not receive sick benefits, maternity allowance, child care allowance or other benefits;

-- he/she is not an owner nor a possessor of agricultural real estate (according to the definition found in the above- mentioned Act);

-- he/she is not eligible to the benefits of social security system, nor working on a household farm of over 2 ha.;

-- he/she does not begin non agricultural economic activity and does not receive benefits under the social insurance and pension system;

-- he/she is the disabled and his/her state of health makes it possible to be employed at least half-time;

-- he/she is not temporarily arrested nor imprisoned.

Unemployment data refer to the end of the period and cover persons registered as looking for a job in local Labour Offices in the area in which they live.

Unemployment beneficiaries are persons who:

-- are registered as unemployed according to the above conditions;

-- have no proposal of appropriate work, training, retraining, or work of a public nature;

-- have worked for at least 180 days in the 12 month period prior to the registration day.

The minimum period of non-activity before receiving benefits is 3 months in the case of recent graduates.

A beneficiary loses the right to unemployment benefits if he/she:

-- does not re-register at the local Labour Office without good reason;

-- refuses to take an offer of suitable employment, training or communal work without good reason;

-- was dismissed by the employer for disciplinary reasons;

-- received an amount as determined in the Labour Agreement for mine employees or a miner's social benefit.

Since December 1992, the maximum benefit period has been limited to 12 months. This period may be prolonged in the cases specified in the relevant Act.

The unemployment benefit is equal to 36 per cent of the average monthly salary in the previous quarter (excepting special cases provided for in the relevant Act).

The *unemployment rate* is calculated as the number of registered unemployed at the end of the period as a percentage of the civilian labour force, which:

-- in 1990 refers to the end of 1989;

-- for 1991 onward refers to the end of the same period assumed as the constant for the whole year.

The number of *job vacancies* refers to offers in Labour Offices, including job openings both in the public and private sector.

Wages

Monthly earnings

Monthly earnings refer to average net monthly wages and salaries in various sectors of the Polish economy consistent with the employment data (see the Employment section above for coverage of sectors and branches). Quarterly data covers all sectors of the economy while monthly data covers only the enterprise sector.

Wages and salaries are defined as payments due to employees for work according to their working agreement.

Average monthly wages and salaries per employee were computed assuming the following:

-- personal wages and salaries (excluding wages and salaries of outworkers and apprentices);

-- payments from profit for distribution and balance surplus in co-operatives;

-- amounts from establishment premium funds;

-- fees paid to selected employees groups, for example, journalists, film and radio programme producers for work resulting from labour contracts.

For 1992-94, monthly earnings are net of income tax deductions for individuals.

POLAND

From 1995, seires refer to gross monthly earnings.

Wage data are expressed in old zlotys until end of 1994 and in new zlotys thereafter. For more detailed information see the section on Domestic finance below.

Prices

Producer prices

Representative surveys of *producer prices in industry* have been undertaken monthly in enterprises since 1982. Until end 1984, they refer to factory prices equal for all customers and from beginning 1985 to actually negociated sales prices. Until 1994 sales prices include taxes on commodities. In 1994-95 prices excluding VAT were observed. From 1996 prices excluding both VAT and excise taxes are collected. Representative producers of goods and services to be surveyed are chosen using statistical information on their sales value and product mix. The survey covers approximately 3 500 enterprises in both the public and private sectors of the economy.

The enterprises choose the goods and services for reporting according to indications provided by the Statistical Office. Representative goods and services are chosen from those dominating the reporting unit's sales value, i.e. accounting for about 75 per cent of monthly turnover. The average number of representative items per month from all reporting units is about 19 000. The reporting units provide monthly information on price levels and sales value for the representative items chosen.

This information is used to calculate a monthly price relative for a representative item with the previous month as the base. A monthly Paasche price index is then derived for the enterprise. Price indices at the enterprise level are calculated as averages of individual price indices of representative items weighted by their sales value in the given month. Weights are therefore changed monthly. Monthly aggregate price indices are averages of aggregate indices at lower levels weighted by their sales value in the month under consideration. The producer price indices are calculated using a weighted pattern derived from the sale value in 1992, updated by the price and sale structure changes occurring in the current month. In 1996 the sales structure of 1994 began to be used for weighting.

When a commodity undergoes a significant quality change it is treated as a new commodity. Its price is not recorded in the first month of its appearance. The price change is calculated starting with the second month. However, in such cases, when reporting the price of a new product, reporting units are also asked to give an estimated price of the product for the previous month, and then the price indice is calculated for the first month of its appearance in the survey. No special treatment is made for goods with a seasonal production cycle.

Consumer prices

The *consumer price index (CPI)* expresses monthly rates of change of prices of consumer goods and services, weighted since 1991 by the Household Budget Survey, which covers the total population since 1993. Before 1991, the CPI refers to the sale of retail goods and services for final consumption.

Data on price changes and their levels are collected from 28 000 retail outlets, catering and service centres, located in 307 price survey regions, i.e. towns and parts of cities. Prices are collected by price officers employed by the regional statistical offices. Price collection outlets are chosen by price officers themselves under supervision of regional staff. Supplementary sources of price information are price-lists and national regulations on price changes concerning:

-- gas and electricity;

-- central heating and hot water;

-- rent of community and state-owned dwellings;

-- some types of medicine;

-- transport fares (Polish State Railways and Polish Motor Transport);

-- postal and telecommunications services;

-- radio and television subscriptions;

-- alcohol (containing 30° of pure alcohol or above).

The price survey covers 1 400-1 800 representative goods and services and this list is reviewed every year. Price quotations for food products including catering, alcoholic beverages and tobacco products are collected three times a month; those for other goods and services are collected once a month.

Since 1991, the weights are obtained from Household Budget Surveys, with adjustments made, i.e. for under-reporting of alcoholic beverages, tobacco products and catering, and refer to the annual structure of expenditures in the previous year; the weights are changed every January. There are more than 200 elementary groups in the weighting system.

The weights used for major groups, in computing the CPI were the following:

Major group	1990	1991	1992	1993	1994
Total goods	88.4	85.6	79.9	72.5	73.4
Food	37.0	48.0	41.8	38.9	39.2
Alcohol	10.6	6.4	5.9	4.6	4.2
Other goods	40.8	31.2	32.2	29.0	30.0
Services	11.6	14.4	20.1	27.5	26.6
TOTAL	100.0	100.0	100.0	100.0	100.0

Separate adjustments are made for seasonal items, such as fruit and vegetables. The weight for the group including those goods is kept constant throughout the year, but weights within the group are changed monthly to reflect seasonal changes in consumption patterns.

The CPI is an index of the rate of change of prices rather than of absolute price levels. It is derived in the following way: the average price level for a representative item k in a region r is calculated as the arithmetic mean of the price quotations. For the monthly CPI, the individual price relative is the average price of a representative item k in survey region r for month t in relation to its average price in the previous year. Yearly price indices are derived as an arithmetic mean of the twelve monthly prices.

The individual representative price index at national level is computed as a geometric mean of individual representative price indexes from all the regions. The aggregate price index for a commodity group at a higher level is the weighted average of expenditure according to the Laspeyres formula.

POLAND

The CPI is expressed as a rate of change over the previous period, or over the same period of the previous year, or in relation to December of the previous year in national sources. The fixed-base calculation is made by the OECD Secretariat.

The *CPI for services* includes rent (excluding private rent), electricity and gas, fees for health services, cultural expenses, monthly fees for television, postal and telecommunication services, personal transport expenses, shoe and clothing repairs, hairdresser, laundry services, etc.

The *CPI for catering* includes workers' canteens, cafeterias and restaurants.

Domestic finance

The information on the money supply is prepared by the National Bank of Poland (NBP).

Narrow money (M1) covers money in circulation (i.e. excluding cash held by banks) in zlotys, and zloty demand deposits of the non-financial sector (including insurance companies) comprising state enterprises and private sector (households and private enterprises).

Starting in 1992, data are presented on the basis of a new plan of accounts and are thus not comparable with data for previous years. For December, fourth quarter and year 1991, the figure comparable with the old methodology is 127 006 billion old zlotys.

Quasi-money refers to time and saving zloty deposits and foreign currency deposits of the non-financial sector (comprising state enterprises, private enterprises including insurance companies and households) as well as savings bonds.

Starting in 1992, data are presented on the basis of a new plan of accounts and are thus not comparable with data for previous years. For December, fourth quarter and year 1991, the figure comparable with the old methodology is 160 175 billion old zlotys.

Personal deposits cover zloty and foreign currency deposits (both demand, saving and time deposits, and saving bonds, excluding counted interest) held by households. Before December 1991, zloty and foreign currency deposits of private enterprises are also included. Foreign currency deposits are converted to zlotys using the official end of month exchange rate of the National Bank of Poland (NBP).

Starting in 1992, data are presented on the basis of a new plan of accounts and are thus not comparable with data for previous years. For December, fourth quarter and year 1991, the figure comparable with the old methodology is 129 829 billion old zlotys.

The domestic finance series are expressed in old zlotys until end of 1994 and in new zlotys thereafter. The zloty was redenominated on the 1st January 1995 with the new zloty equal to 10 000 old zlotys.

Interest rates

The *official discount rate* refers to the end of period refinancing rate. It is the annual rate offered to commercial banks by the National Bank of Poland.

Foreign finance

In addition to the *zloty/US dollar exchange rate*, the National Bank of Poland quotes exchange rates for the ECU, SDR and the currencies of 28 market economies. Until the end of 1990 exchange rates were published by the National Bank of Poland on a weekly basis. Since the beginning of 1991, they are published daily. The zloty is on a crawling peg regime to a basket of five currencies -- the US dollar, Deutsche mark, pound sterling, French franc and Swiss franc.

The exchange rate series are expressed in old zlotys until end of 1994 and in new zlotys thereafter. For more detailed information see the section on Domestic finance above.

Total reserves excluding gold covers foreign exchange reserves of the monetary authorities.

Total gross foreign debt includes external debt in convertible currencies and in transferable roubles.

Gross foreign debt in convertible currencies covers the external debt denominated in US dollars and other convertible currencies converted into US dollars.

Gross foreign debt in non-convertible currencies refers to all foreign debt which is denominated in transferable roubles.

Foreign trade

Exports, imports and *net trade* cover the current value of goods and services purchased and sold abroad.

1980-91

Exports and imports were classified in national sources according to the trading partner country. With regard to imports, the partner country is the country of purchase, i.e. country of supplier. For exports the partner country refers to the country of sale, i.e. country of the buyer. Supplier and buyer are defined as the units with whom the transaction is realised according to a previously signed international agreement. Where no such agreement exists, the countries of purchase and sale are defined as the countries where each party in the contract has its legally registered office.

Goods were classified according to the Foreign Trade Commodity Nomenclature (NTHZ). Approximately 12 000 items were included. Approximately 1 700 exported items and 2 100 imported items were observed in price surveys.

Trade includes, notably, scientific and technical documentation, technical services (know-how) and licences. Trade data excluded government, social and private aid, gifts and donations, private parcels and luggage, and goods brought by passengers.

For the period 1980-89 only designated public (state and co-operative) enterprises could engage in foreign trade. During this period, foreign trade statistics were based on statistical forms (called FE and FI invoices) completed for each shipment of goods by these enterprises and processed by the Statistical Office. Concerning imports, these forms were the customs documents proving that goods had crossed the home border; for exports of goods these forms were certificates of acceptance for transportation by an international carrier.

POLAND

In 1990-91 when units other than designated public sector enterprises started to trade internationally, customs declarations were adopted as the main source for foreign trade statistics. They cover transactions carried out by chartered companies (excluding companies which emerged as a result of restructured state enterprises), small scale foreign manufacturers, foundations and natural persons. These customs declarations were supplemented by invoice forms. Data for 1990 are, however, estimated. In 1991, 50 per cent of trade turnover was generated by private enterprises. At that time, there were 60 000 exporting units as opposed to 100 units in 1989.

Export and import values were recorded FOB. Historically, the time of recording was generally the date of submission of appropriate documents and not the date at which the goods crossed the border. In December 1991, notably, many customs declarations were submitted before the introduction of the Single Administrative Document. The December 1991 trade figure is therefore considered to be overstated.

The series *trade in convertible and non-convertible currencies* are classified by type of currency used in the transaction, and not by geographical zone.

1992 and onwards

In January 1992, the Single Administrative Document was introduced for customs declarations. Exports are recorded FOB and imports are recorded CIF.

Also starting in 1992, country and regional trade groups are based on the countries of origin or destination of the traded goods, and no longer by the location of the buyer or supplier.

The system used to classify traded goods is the Combined Nomenclature (CN) system including approximately 9 500 items. Over 2 000 exported items and over 3 000 imported items are observed in price surveys.

In accordance with UN methodology, foreign trade commodity turnover in Poland is based on the "special trade" formula which encompasses import and export of all commodities - irrespective of the form of payment - which passed through a final customs clearance or a conditional customs clearance (in the case of improvement trade) according to the Single Administrative Document, SAD, including:

-- indirect re-exports and imports for indirect re-export;

-- donations from social organisations;

-- benevolent aid;

-- import and export of commodities which are the subject of material apports of foreign units;

-- purchases in foreign ports of chandlers' goods such as bunker;

-- trade in the products of sea fishing;

-- commodities imported or exported according to a leasing agreement or transaction, where the exploitation period is more than one year;

-- improvement trade calculated according to the gross method.

Current foreign trade turnover according to "special trade" formula does not include:

-- Turnover of custom-free zones and customs-bonded warehouses;

-- direct re-exports and imports for direct re-export;

-- services (except improvement trade calculated according to the gross method);

-- repairs;

-- construction;

-- patents, licences, know-how.

From 1992 onwards, all trade has been conducted in convertible currencies. The sole exception concerns gas imports from the Russian Federation, whereby the contract is payable in part in roubles until the year 2005.

Foreign trade data are expressed in old zlotys until end of 1994 and in new zlotys thereafter. For more detailed information see the section on Domestic finance above.

Prices

Until end 1991 prices are recorded in relation to average prices of the previous period. They refer to transaction prices in 1991, and are based on "unit values" for earlier years.

Starting in 1992, prices refer to unit values calculated by dividing total value by commodity weight at the lowest level of CN classification of goods. These unit values are cumulated from the beginning of the recording year. They are weighted by cumulative quantities (expressed by weight) and are expressed with respect to the average monthly price of the previous year. Price indices for the lowest CN levels are aggregated by branch according to the Uniform Commodities List (SWW) in cumulative monthly periods. For higher levels of commodity aggregation, the weights used are the cumulative values of traded goods from the beginning of the year.

The prices refer to exports FOB and imports CIF and are expressed in zlotys.

The price index is of the Paasche type using current year weights.

Volume

The price information obtained in the survey and unit values for earlier years are used to calculate the constant price *export and import volume indices*. The monthly and quarterly data in constant prices are calculated as differences in cumulative values. For the period 1980-90 the constant prices refer to 1984, and from 1991 to constant prices of 1990.

In 1991, re-exports and re-imports were not included in trade volumes, with the exception of improvement trade. Traded services were excluded, with the exception of printing services. In 1992, trade without payment (gifts, etc.) was excluded from the total trade volume.

Additional differences in the coverage of trade between 1991 and 1992 are outlined above (see section "1980-91" and section "1992 and onwards").

POLAND

Gross fixed capital formation

Gross fixed capital formation refers to the outlays for the purchase and modernisation of buildings, machinery and equipment, and all methods of transport. Agricultural buildings and machinery are included, but the purchase of livestock is excluded. Expenditure for repairs and maintenance is not included.

Starting in 1991, all units with more than 50 employees are included in the manufacturing sector; all units with more than 20 employees are covered in all other branches.

Publications

Some of the series described above, but presented according to national practice, can be found in the following Polish Central Statistical Office publications:

Biuletyn Statystyczny (Statistical Bulletin)

Concise Statistical Yearbook of Poland

Information on the Social and Economic Situation in Poland

Kwartalnik Statystyki Miedzynarodowej (International Quarterly Statistics)

Monitoring Rynku Pracy (Monitoring of the Labour Market)

and also the:

Monthly Report of the National Bank of Poland.

OECD
OCDE
SHORT-TERM ECONOMIC INDICATORS, SOURCES AND DEFINITIONS
OECD/CCET © April 1996

136

INDICATEURS ÉCONOMIQUES A COURT TERME, SOURCES ET DÉFINITIONS
OCDE/CCET © avril 1996

REPUBLIC OF SLOVENIA

Industrial production

The *index of total industrial production* is classified by branch according to the National Classification of Activities in Industry (formerly the Yugoslav Unified Classification of Activities in Industry), covering mining, manufacturing (excluding publishing) and the supply of electricity. Gas, steam and water supply are excluded.

Industrial products are classified according to the National Nomenclature of Industrial Products, which comprises about 3 400 finished and semi-finished products. Non-principal production is included.

Until 1990, the industrial survey covered all industrial enterprises. Since 1992, surveys have been conducted monthly in public enterprises and in all private enterprises with five employees or more, as listed in the Business Register of Slovenia. In 1994, these numbered 1 800 enterprises in Slovenia.

Enterprises report the volume of output in quantity terms (tons, pieces, etc.). Quantities are weighted by their 1993 value of their invoiced sales, corrected by the share of value added at the branch level in 1993. Branch indices are aggregated to the total industrial production index using the shares of value added of industrial activities in the previous year as weights. Weights of products and of branches change every year according to the changes in the share of value added by branch in the previous two years. Both branch and total indices are of type Laspeyres.

Commodity output

Coal production includes brown coal and lignite.

Natural gas includes associated and non-associated gas.

Crude petroleum represents mineral oil consisting of a mixture of hydrocarbons of natural origin.

Crude steel refers to steel used for casting and ingots.

Cement covers Portland cement only.

Electrical energy includes hydro, conventional thermal and nuclear electricity.

Textile production includes cotton, wool and artificial silk fabrics.

Production of refrigerators includes refrigerators and freezers for household use only.

REPUBLIC OF SLOVENIA

Construction

The index of the *number of hours worked in construction* measures construction activity in enterprises with 10 or more employees. Surveyed enterprises are those which are registered in the Business Register of Slovenia under construction activity. The monthly survey covers 160 enterprises, reflecting an estimated 90 per cent of total construction production.

Dwellings

A dwelling is any structurally unified whole intended for residence, with one or more rooms, with or without appropriate utility spaces (kitchen, hallway, bathroom, toilet) and with at least one distinct entrance. Students' and workers' dormitories, senior citizens' homes, etc. are not included in the number of dwellings.

The number of *dwellings completed* refers to dwellings that have been certified by local authorities as ready for habitation, in which all designed construction, installation and finishing works in all interiors have been completed.

The number of *dwellings completed by enterprises* excludes all dwellings built for private individuals. Data are obtained from the same survey as that used for hours worked in construction (see above).

Domestic trade

Retail trade refers to the sale of goods in both public and private sales outlets, including chemist's, commission shops, kiosks, petrol stations and retail trade carried out directly from a warehouse. Trade in food markets between private producers and consumers is not included.

Retail trade is measured using a quarterly cut-off sample survey of the largest retail outlets which account for 50 per cent of turnover. The response rate to the survey has been 100 per cent. Enterprises are classified by type and branch according to the National Classification of Activities. Changes occurring within enterprises and other organisations during the year are not taken into account until the beginning of the following year.

The *retail sales volume* index refers to the retail sales value deflated by the retail price index. The retail price index is constructed from the prices of goods, excluding services, and is weighted by retail turnover (see Retail prices, below).

Labour

Employment

Persons in paid employment in enterprises and other organisations refer to persons who have signed a work contract for a fixed or unspecified period of time, irrespective of whether they work in the enterprise or other organisation full time or less than full time, including trainees. Persons performing temporary or occasional contract work are not included, nor are Slovenian citizens working abroad. The working age population refers to women between 15 and 58 and men between 15 and 63.

Until end 1991, the statistical surveys on persons in paid employment in enterprises and other organisations covered all non-private enterprises and organisations and their constituent units. From 1992 coverage has included private enterprises with three or more employees, plus staff of the armed forces. Since 1993, staff in internal affairs administrations have also been included. The self-employed and their employees are not included in the monthly employment survey. Data concerning self-employed persons and their employees are estimated based on records from the Register of Health Insurance and the 1991 population census. Part-time workers are included on the same basis as full-time workers; part-time workers are estimated to represent less than two per cent of employees.

Administrative records on retirement and disability insurance and health insurance are used to cross-check employment figures.

Branch classifications based on the General Industrial Classification of Economic Activities (NACE) were introduced in January 1995.

Unemployment

Data concerning *registered unemployed* persons and *job vacancies* are forwarded to the CSO by the National Employment Office (NEO).

Registered unemployed covers persons who:

-- do not have a regular job and are not self-employed, do not own or co-own an operating enterprise, and do not own or use property which could provide an income;

-- are capable of and willing to work and are prepared to accept a job suitable to their professional attainment or working skills;

-- have registered as job-seekers with the NEO.

According to the Law on Employment and Insurance Against Unemployment, registered unemployed persons who have lost their job against their will and through no fault of their own, have the right to unemployment benefits if they register with the NEO within 30 days of losing their job.

Unemployment benefits may be paid to unemployed persons who have worked uninterruptedly for at least nine months or for 12 months, with interruptions during the last 18 months. The benefit amount is calculated as a percentage of the unemployed persons' average earnings of the last three working months. During the first three months of the benefit period, beneficiaries receive 70 per cent of their average earnings of the last three months of work. Afterwards, the percentage decreases, but the amount is never less than 80 per cent of the minimum wage.

The duration of benefits is, for example, three months for those who have worked only 12 months out of the last 18 months; nine months for those who have worked 5-10 years; and 18 months for those who have been employed 15-20 years. Upon expiry of the benefit period, an unemployed person may claim supplementary benefits within 30 days if their total income, together with the total earnings of their family members, in the three months prior to the claim for supplementary benefit did not exceed 80 per cent of the guaranteed earnings per person. Persons lose the right to benefits if they refuse three job offers by the NEO.

REPUBLIC OF SLOVENIA

The *unemployment rate* represents unemployed persons as a percentage of the total labour force (employed plus unemployed) in the corresponding period.

Wages

Monthly earnings

Wage information is collected in the same survey as employment (see above). Wages of external associates and consultants are not included. In addition to income earned for work actually done during regular working hours, the following other types of income are counted: income from overtime, supplements for annual leave, sickness pay for up to 30 days, slowdown through no fault of employees, public holidays, performing of national duties, paid leave, awards, premiums, income for past work, incentive and other bonuses.

Before 1992, only net official earnings (gross earnings minus contributions for social security and income tax) are available. From 1992 on, wages are gross. Monthly earnings series are therefore not comparable between 1991 and 1992.

The quarterly and annual figures do not always equal the average of monthly wages due to different coverage in the basic data.

Prices

Producer prices

Producer prices are collected monthly using postal questionnaires. Prices are selected for about 450 products sold domestically in approximately 300 of the biggest producing enterprises. The list of products is harmonised with the nomenclature of industrial statistics (see Industrial Production above). To create the Laspeyres *producer price index*, individual product prices, excluding taxes, are weighted by their share of production. Each of 30 industrial groups of products is weighted by its share in the value of sales in the previous year to obtain the total producer price index. For goods with a seasonal production cycle, the most recent quotation is carried forward during the off-season.

Consumer prices

Consumer prices are collected for 354 goods and 91 services in 150 retail outlets, fixed market areas and service establishments in four major cities and rural areas. One price quotation is noted per month and per outlet for all goods and services, between the third and the twenty-fifth day of each month. Two quotations are noted for agricultural produce. Prices used in the calculation of the index are the prices paid by consumers, i.e. taxes are included. Sales and discounted prices are not taken into account.

Rent quotations are obtained monthly from a sample of 64 rented dwellings. These dwellings are divided into eight groups by age of building. Calculations are based on one square metre. Owner occupied dwellings are excluded from the index.

If an item undergoes a quality change, it is either replaced by a similar item, assuming there is no price change, or a linking method is used. When a product is no longer available, it is (1) replaced at the beginning of the year by the new product, or (2) the weight is added to another item, or (3) its weight is distributed within the subgroup. New items are introduced when their sales become significant.

The prices of seasonal items such as fresh fruit and vegetables are collected only when they are available. During the off season, their weights are subtracted within a fixed basket of seasonal fruit and vegetables.

The CPI is a Laspeyres index. Average prices in each urban centre are calculated as simple arithmetic averages; these average prices are then weighted by retail turnover in the respective urban centre to obtain the average national price per item. Consumer price indices per product group are calculated by dividing the average prices in the current period by the average prices in the base period. The national total CPI is aggregated using the Family Budget Survey expenditure patterns as weights.

The weights currently used to calculate the CPI are derived from the 1993 Family Budget Survey. This survey was carried out on 3 270 households chosen by simple random sampling. Weights are corrected at the beginning of each year by the price change in the product group in the previous year.

The weights obtained from the Family Budget Surveys are as follows:

Major groups	1990 survey		1993 survey	
	Number of items	Weight	Number of items	Weight
Food	121	34.0	132	31.8
Clothing and footwear	82	15.0	82	9.8
Transport and communication	38	12.3	38	18.5
Education and recreation	48	8.2	47	8.3
Beverages and tobacco	17	6.6	17	5.3
Personal and medical care	30	6.5	30	8.4
Household equipment	61	6.2	66	5.7
Fuel and electricity	17	6.1	14	7.5
Rent	19	5.1	19	4.7
TOTAL	433	100.0	445	100.0

Retail prices

The average prices used to calculate the *retail price index* are the same as those used for the CPI (see section Consumer prices, above). Some goods are only included, however, in the retail price index, e.g. building materials. The *retail price index* includes selected services including crafts, housing and community services, cultural services, social care and personal services, transport and communication services, and financial and other services. The main difference between the CPI and the RPI is the weighting system used. Weights used for the calculation of the RPI refer to the structure of retail turnover of goods and services.

REPUBLIC OF SLOVENIA

The retail price index is used to calculate the official inflation rate. It is also used to calculate monthly adjustments to interest rates by the banking sector. The consumer price index is used to index-link allowances and re-value wages, including the minimum wage.

Domestic finance

Narrow money (M1) includes currency in circulation, sight deposits (current accounts) of non-banking sectors including government institutions at banks, and deposits of enterprises and non-monetary financial institutions at the Bank of Slovenia. The latter include for the most part savings banks' and co-operatives' reserves at the Bank of Slovenia; they are statistically not treated as bank reserves, as the definitions do not include these institutions among deposit money banks.

Quasi-money includes all savings and time deposits of non-banking sectors at banks, including foreign currency deposits, mostly of individuals. Foreign currency deposits are calculated in tolars using end of month official exchange rates.

Personal deposits include all demand, savings and time deposits of individuals at banks, including foreign currency deposits. Foreign currency deposits are calculated in tolars using end of month official exchange rates.

Interest rates

The *official discount rate* is not used directly in any Central Bank transactions. It may be regarded as an implicit indicator of central bank policy aspirations.

The *call money* rate refers to the period average interest rate on the interbank money market for one-day and overnight loans.

Foreign finance

The Slovenian tolar was introduced on 8 October 1991. At the time of its introduction, the conversion factor of the tolar to the Yugoslav dinar was 1:1. *Exchange rates* with the US dollar, the Deutschemark and the ECU are expressed at the end of the period. They are official Bank of Slovenia exchange rates.

Total reserves, excluding gold include foreign currencies, deposits at foreign banks and securities held as official reserves by the Bank of Slovenia, denominated in convertible currencies. Special Drawing Rights and the reserve position with the IMF are excluded, as well as liquid foreign exchange reserves held by commercial banks.

Gross foreign debt includes all long and medium term debt in convertible currencies, official and private, including obligations to the IMF. The allocation of a part of the foreign debt of former Yugoslavia is still in the process of negotiation among successor states.

Foreign trade

The source for all foreign trade statistics is customs declarations. The Harmonised System and Standard International Trade Classification, Rev. 3 were introduced in 1988. The Combined Nomenclature was introduced in 1996.

Exports cover all goods exported from Slovenia, originating from production or free circulation in the internal market. Imports represent all goods which are released for consumption upon arrival in Slovenia or on leaving warehouses. Trade without payment is included. Temporary export and import (except temporary export and import for processing), lease, supply of Slovenian diplomatic missions abroad, supply of fuel abroad to Slovenian transporters and domestically to foreign transporters, commercial samples and travellers' luggage are not included. Trade in services is excluded.

Traded goods are valued based on the original documents (contracts, invoices) of the exporting and importing enterprises. They refer to invoiced values stipulated at the moment of the contract. These values are re-calculated at Slovenian border parity -- exports are valued FOB and imports, CIF. Values in different foreign currencies are recalculated to tolars and to US dollars according to the exchange rates valid on the day of customs clearance. Trade before 1987, however, was calculated using yearly exchange rates to the Yugoslav dinar.

Some methodological changes were introduced for calculations of trade statistics between 1991 and 1992. Data before 1992 were calculated for each republic of the former Yugoslavia separately. Trade was attributed to the republic that produced exported goods or consumed imported goods. Trade between the republics of the former Yugoslavia, however, was excluded.

From 1992 the coverage of exports and imports also include processing trade and trade with the countries on the territory of the former Yugoslavia. Additionally, before 1992, trade was registered in the month reported, whether the goods had been cleared in the reporting month or in previous months. From 1992 on, trade is recorded in the month of customs clearance. The annual 1992 figures which are calculated according to 1991 methodology are: exports -- 4 181 million US dollars; imports -- 4 133 million US dollars.

Publications

Some of the series described above, but presented according to national practice, can be found in the following Slovenian Statistical Office publications:

Statistical Yearbook

Mesicni Statisticni Pregled (Monthly Statistical Bulletin)

various issues of *Statisticne Informacije* (Statistical Information)

as well as the

Monthly Bulletin of the Bank of Slovenia.

ROMANIA

Industrial production

The *Index of Industrial Production* (IIP) relates to the physical production activities under Divisions 10 to 41 (Groups C, D and E) of the United Nations International Standard Industrial Classification (ISIC) Revision 3 (mining and quarrying, manufacturing, electricity, gas and water supply). The detailed branch classification is based on the General Industrial Classification of Economic Activities (NACE) introduced in February 1991.

A new method of calculation was introduced in February 1991. Volume data is collected for a basket of 1030 products and product groups. Private enterprises, although relatively insignificant (7 per cent of production in 1993), are included. Value data deflated by price indices are, however, used for a few products. The new index is of the Laspeyres type. For data starting in 1993, the weights used are 1991 gross value added and, at the individual product level, the average price for the period 1981-93. Before 1993, however, volume measures of individual product series were obtained using the average prices of products in 1989 as weights. This was due to the fact that these are the only prices available and that this period was fairly stable in terms of price fluctuations. Indices of previous years have been recalculated to the present base year using the chain index method.

Industrial production indices include own consumption within a given enterprise, and exclude changes in stocks of finished goods and in work in progress.

Indices from 1990-93 were formerly published corrected for the number of working days in the month, taking into account continuous shift work. The adjustment for working days is not only an adjustment within each year but also between years, as the number of working days varies slightly between years. All indices of industrial production are now published non-adjusted for the number of working days in the period.

The *index of total industrial production* relates to Divisions 10 to 41 (Groups C, D and E) of ISIC Revision 3. These series are physical production indices and are not comparable with the previously published commodity production index for 1981-90, which represents value data expressed in comparable producers' prices according to the old method of calculation. Annual figures for 1981-90, however, have been re-calculated by the Romanian Statistical Office according to the new methodology.

The *index of industrial production for manufacturing* relates to Divisions 15 to 37 (Group D) of ISIC, Revision 3.

The *index of industrial production for mining* relates to Divisions 10 to 14 (Group C) of ISIC Revision 3. A yearly and half-yearly series is also available before 1990 based on the old method of calculation.

OECD
OCDE
SHORT-TERM ECONOMIC INDICATORS, SOURCES AND DEFINITIONS
OECD/CCET © April 1996

144

INDICATEURS ÉCONOMIQUES A COURT TERME, SOURCES ET DÉFINITIONS
OCDE/CCET © avril 1996

The *index of industrial production for electricity* relates to Divisions 40 to 41 (Group E) of ISIC Revision 3. A yearly and half-yearly series is also available before 1990 based on the old method of calculation.

The *index of industrial production for construction* relates to Division 45 (Group F) of ISIC Revision 3. The series is based on the old method of calculation (using value data). It refers to the deflated value of new construction works, capital and current repairs and maintenance to existing structures carried out by economic agents, administrative units and individual persons. The quarterly data for 1993 and 1994 refer to the index of construction works, including services, on the basis of a sample of 1 633 units for which the main activity is construction work. This sample also covers units that carry out construction works under state supervision as well as units performing construction works on own account.

Commodity output

Commodity output data are obtained from surveys completed by all producing enterprises with more than 50 employees. Data for a representative sample of units with less than 50 employees are also included. Data are revised annually to include commodity output in enterprises having their main activity outside Divisions 10 to 41 (Groups C, D and E) of ISIC Revision 3.

Coal production relates to net (prepared) coal, i.e. sorted anthracite, net pitcoal, net lignite and sorted brown coal.

Natural gas production refers to extracted natural gas (15°C and 770 mm Hg) including methane gas, oil well gas and free gas.

Production of crude petroleum refers to the total production, excluding liquid petroleum gas.

Crude steel production refers to the total production of ingots, continuous and in cast steel pieces. Wrought (puddled) iron is excluded.

Cement production covers all sorts of cement including cement containing 80 per cent of clinker as base material.

Business surveys

A description of business tendency survey techniques and the list of harmonised questions is given in the chapter *Business Tendency Surveys* of this publication.

Construction

Dwellings

All series concerning the number of dwellings refer to dwellings constructed by public sector enterprises only. A dwelling is a unit of construction composed of one or more rooms, placed on the same floor, or on different floors of the same building, generally equipped with a kitchen, bathroom, etc., which is functionally independent, with a distinct entrance from a staircase, hall, courtyard, or street and which has been built, transformed or arranged in order to be used by a single household.

ROMANIA

Dwellings started refer to residential constructions that have received construction permits and for which work on the foundation has been started.

The figures for *dwellings under construction* refer to the number of dwellings registered at the end of the period.

Dwellings completed refer to completely finished residential constructions, whose structural elements, including the foundation, did not exist previously.

The three series, *dwellings started, dwellings completed,* and *dwellings under construction,* do not equate over corresponding periods for a number of reasons. Dwellings under construction that are transferred, bought or sold between the public and private sectors are included; those dwellings that are transferred from the public to the private sector therefore disappear from official statistics. Additionally, omissions to series are often added in subsequent periods; therefore the number of dwellings under construction is calculated using a revised figure for dwellings started and completed.

Domestic trade

Retail trade represents the reselling activity of new or used goods, principally to the population, through shops, kiosks, by mail order, commercial travellers, consumer co-operatives, sales by auction and retail sales by own shops of producing enterprises. Data is collected using statistical surveys carried out in units whose main activity is retail trade and in producing enterprises that sell their products in their own shops.

The *value of retail trade* is recorded in standard state prices until April 1990. Starting in 1990, public catering is omitted from the calculation of the retail sales value.

The value of retail sales is now recorded in current retail prices including value added tax. Retail sales include food and non-food goods sold in 3 000 public, mixed and co-operative trade units and, from 1990 on, in private retail trade units. Starting in 1993, family associations and independent persons whose main activity is retail trade (e.g. producers of household items, furniture, handicraft, jewellery, fabrics, wearing apparel, knitwear, footwear, leather goods) are included. Estimates are made for activity in the hidden economy. Sales of agricultural goods by individuals in outdoor markets are not included, nor are sales of electric or thermal energy and natural gas.

Monthly data collections are complemented with a quarterly statistical survey carried out in private retail trade outlets. The sample comprises 722 outlets which were selected from a population of 60 000 economic agents on the basis of income. Sample outlets were chosen so that different income categories are represented in the same proportions in the sample as in the total population.

The *retail sales volume* series refers to the retail sales value deflated by the prices in the corresponding month in 1989, or by those in the previous month.

Foreign investment

The data concerning *foreign investors* and *foreign capital* are compiled by the Romanian Agency for Development. They aim to register all foreign investors in all branches of the economy, regardless of their size.

Labour

Employment

The employment series refer to employees in state units, units with mixed state and private capital, domestic or foreign, and co-operative units, but exclude private sector employment until 1994. Considered as employed are persons of 14 years and over who have carried out an economic activity for at least one hour during the reference period. Persons temporarily absent from work, i.e. due to accident or illness, holiday or strike, are counted as employed.

Annual and monthly average numbers of employees differ because annual data include commissioners, seasonal and occasional workers and those working abroad, for which information is not collected monthly. In 1990, for example, these categories represented about 110 000 employees.

Total employment refers to the average number of employees and covers all branches of the economy.

The figures for *employment in industry* refer to the average number of employees, covering industries in Divisions 10 to 41 (Groups C, D and E) of ISIC Revision 3 and the forestry industry from Division 2.

Employment in manufacturing refers to the average number of employees, covering Divisions 15 to 37 (Group D) of ISIC Revision 3.

Unemployment

Unemployment figures are prepared by the Ministry of Labour and Social Protection.

Registered unemployment refers to the number of persons registered by labour offices including persons receiving unemployment benefits, those receiving a support allowance and persons not eligible or no longer eligible for unemployment benefits according to the unemployment Law 1/1991.

The data for *unemployment beneficiaries* refer to the number of persons entitled to unemployment benefits under the Law 1/1991 concerning the social protection of the unemployed and their professional reintegration.

Unemployment benefits are accorded to registered persons over 18 years of age who have lost their job, or who have never worked (i.e. persons having recently finished their studies or compulsory military service), who do not have an alternative source of revenue equalling more than 50 per cent of the gross minimum wage, whose family does not own over 20 000 square metres of agricultural land (40 000 square metres in mountainous areas) and who are physically fit to work. Persons who have left their jobs voluntarily or who have been dismissed for displinary reasons do not receive benefits. The maximum benefit period is 270 days.

Any beneficiary who does not accept a job corresponding with their professional and educational experience or a training programme located at a distance of not more than 50 km. from their residence proposed by the Unemployment office loses their right to unemployment benefits. Beneficiaries are required to re-register monthly.

ROMANIA

The benefit amount for persons having worked for five years, for example, is equal to 50 per cent of their average salary over the last three months, but not less than 75 per cent of the minimum wage, minus taxes. Secondary school graduates receive 60 per cent of the monthly minimum wage (70 per cent for university graduates).

Non-beneficiaries refer to persons <u>not</u> eligible for unemployment benefits, plus those no longer receiving benefits due to the expiration of the benefit period. Since April 1992, due to new provisions of the Unemployment Law 1/1991, persons who no longer receive unemployment benefits after expiration of the 270 day period and have not found employment receive a support allowance representing 60 per cent of the national minimum wage, subject to indexation and taxes, for a period of 18 months. Persons receiving the support allowance are required to re-register at employment offices monthly.

The *unemployment rate* refers to the total number of registered unemployed as a proportion of the civilian labour force (employed plus registered unemployed) on 31 December of the previous year.

Wages

Monthly earnings

The data refer to monthly net earnings, i.e. gross earnings minus tax payments. From 1993 onward, premiums paid from the wage fund, profit fund and other funds are included. Until end 1993, data cover earnings in the public and co-operative sectors only; from 1994 earnings in the private sector are included.

The figures for *monthly earnings total* refer to the average monthly nominal net earnings as above.

Monthly earnings in industry refer to the average monthly nominal net earnings as above. The coverage relates to Divisions 10 to 41 (Groups C, D and E) of ISIC Revision 3. Electric and thermal energy, and gas and water production industries are excluded before 1994.

The figures for *monthly earnings in manufacturing* refer to the average monthly nominal net earnings as above. The coverage relates to Divisions 15 to 37 (Group D) of ISIC Revision 3.

Prices

Producer prices

The *producer price index* (PPI) does not include arms, uranium or rare metals production, industrial production with long fabrication cycles, unique engineering products, repairs of industrial works, or production consumed within the producing enterprise. The producer price is composed of production costs, profits and some fees and excise duties (consumption tax applied to some imported and domestically-produced goods). Prices for exported goods refer to the price negociated and paid valued at the exchange rate in effect at the time the transaction was concluded. The producer prices exclude value added tax.

The monthly PPI from 1993 onward is not compatible with that previously published. Annual data for 1990-92 are Paasche indices. Starting in 1993, all data are Laspeyres indices using 1992 average prices as a base. Commodity prices are weighted by the value of deliveries in 1992.

In 1993, approximately 840 industrial units and 1 753 commodities comprising 9 000 domestically produced items, were represented. In 1994, the sample covered 1030 representative industrial units, 2 450 products and product groups and about 12 000 items. In 1995, approximately 740 units and 1 700 product groups representing 9 000 items were sampled. Included are products destined for both the domestic and export markets.

The previously published industrial *wholesale price index* was composed of production costs, profits and taxes on commodity circulation. The calculated index was of the Laspeyres type and was computed by successive aggregations: by item, commodity, class of commodity, division, and the whole industry, in accordance with the Classification of Activities in the National Economy (CAEN).

Consumer prices

All *consumer price indices (CPI)* are derived from the official Romanian Consumer Price Index. Annual data for the period 1980-90 are based on the "comparable price" methodology with 1980 as reference base year. These price indices do not reflect the most common form of price inflation, i.e. quality changes over the period, and are not comparable with the monthly data published from October 1990.

The new CPI, a Laspeyres index introduced in October 1990, is compiled monthly. The new method uses the standard OECD approach for dealing with quality changes, i.e. price changes due to improvements in functionally relevant features of a new product model are not treated as price increases.

The prices measured are "transaction prices", i.e. including trade margins and a VAT of 18 per cent (from 1 July 1993).

Prices of 1 800 goods and services are collected from a sample of more than 4 300 different selling and service outlets including markets, retail outlets, co-operatives and service establishments. Prices are collected in all 40 counties plus the municipality of Bucharest. Price quotations are collected twice per month, for all goods and services. A prior problem, common in a shortage economy, was that items included in the list of representative goods and services were not available in all periods. To account for this, many goods were previously priced every week, increasing the chances of obtaining at least one observation per month. The number of items in the list was also larger than usual. The list included several varieties of the same item so that if some of the types were missing in a month it was still possible to calculate a price relative from the varieties available.

Prices for transport, telecommunication tariffs, public housing rent, electricity, gas, water and postal services, set by governmental agencies, are collected directly from those agencies. Housing costs are represented by rents in both state-owned and private-owned dwellings. Owner-occupied dwellings are not included. Seasonal items such as fresh fruit and vegetables and wool are grouped in a monthly basket whose overall weight remains constant.

October 1990 is used as the reference base period, being prior to price liberalisation. All remaining subsidies on consumer goods and key services were removed during 1993.

All major elements of household consumption are included in the CPI. Some elements excluded are consumption of goods and services resulting from own household production, taxes, charges, fines, gambling, interest on credit, insurance, interest on savings deposits, household expenditure for agricultural workers as well as expenditure for construction materials used to build new dwellings.

ROMANIA

The CPI uses weights from a nationwide family expenditure survey conducted in 9 000 households in which the head of household was an employee, farmer or a retired person. The CPI from 1990-93 uses weights from the 1990 expenditure survey; from 1994 on, from the 1993 expenditure survey.

The weights used in the computation of the CPI are as follows:

Major Groups	Weights 1990 (used from 1990-93)	Weights 1993 (used from 1994)
Food	40.5	47.1
Other goods	43.7	40.9
Services	15.8	12.0
TOTAL	100.0	100.0

Domestic finance

All data are prepared by the National Bank of Romania and refer to the end of the period. Since January 1993, all money supply aggregates include deposits in foreign banks in Romania.

The *narrow money supply (M1)* covers currency outside banks and demand deposits.

Quasi-money includes sight and time deposits of households, time deposits of economic agents, plus foreign currency deposits of residents.

The figures for *personal deposits* refer to sight and term deposits of households.

Interest rates

The *official discount rate* refers to the rate charged by the National Bank of Romania for re-financing loan lines granted. Rates are weighted by the volume of loans granted in the corresponding month.

Foreign finance

Until January 1990 the *leu/US dollar exchange rate* refers to the commercial rate applicable to all trade and capital transactions in convertible currencies. In February 1990 the commercial and non-commercial rates were unified into an official rate. Since November 1991 the data reflect the floating exchange rate established on the inter-bank market.

Total reserves, excluding gold cover foreign exchange reserves held in the National Bank of Romania, and in all commercial banks.

OECD
OCDE
SHORT-TERM ECONOMIC INDICATORS, SOURCES AND DEFINITIONS
OECD/CCET © April 1996

150

INDICATEURS ÉCONOMIQUES A COURT TERME, SOURCES ET DÉFINITIONS
OCDE/CCET © avril 1996

Foreign trade

Exports, imports, and net trade data for the period 1980-89 have been revised using the commercial exchange rates in effect. From 1990, trade data have been calculated using the official exchange rate of the National Bank of Romania.

Export data are valued FOB; imports are FOB until end 1990. Starting in 1991, imports are valued CIF.

The procedures for collection of foreign trade data were changed in January 1991. Information based on customs returns according to the Harmonised System (at the six digit level) began to be used for statistical registration. In 1994, the Combined Nomenclature (CN) classification was introduced at the eight digit level of detail. SITC Revision 3 conversion keys are used to equate the two classification systems.

Goods which are transported by cable or pipe (electrical energy or natural gas, for example), are recorded directly by importing/exporting enterprises.

Trade refers to traded goods, imports destined for re-export, and goods entering Romania from customs-free zones and warehouses. Productive services such as patents, know-how licences, design and research works, montage and construction works, food and fuel destined to supply ships, printing of books, booklets, advertising material, etc. are not included in trade.

In national sources, exports are classified with respect to countries of destination, which refer to the country in which a good is finally consumed. Imports are classified according to countries of origin, which are the country in which the good was produced, or had undergone its latest transformation.

Gross fixed capital formation

Quarterly statistical surveys are submitted by a sample of public, mixed capital and co-operative enterprises, socio-cultural units, public administrations, political and community organisations.

Total gross fixed capital formation includes investment in equipment and means of transport, construction, installation and assembly and all other investment in new fixed assets, including the purchase of livestock, as well as development and modernisation of existing assets. The value of imported fixed assets is included; the value of land is excluded from the gross fixed capital. The value of services provided for the transfer of ownership of existing fixed assets or land, however, is included.

Investment in *equipment* includes the purchase of all machines and equipment, computers, electric machines and equipment, radio, television and communications equipment, medical and optical equipment, watches and clocks, and all means of transportation.

ROMANIA

Publications

Some of the series described above, but presented according to national practice, can be found in the following publications of the National Commission for Statistics:

Buletin Statistic Trimestrial (Quarterly Statistical Bulletin)

Situation Sociale et Economique de la Roumanie (Social and Economic Situation of Romania)

Monthly Statistical Bulletin

Statistical Bulletin - Prices

Statistical Bulletin - Industry

Statistical Bulletin - Foreign Trade

as well as many issues by subject matter of:

Informatii Statistice Operative (Quick Statistical Information).

OECD
OCDE
SHORT-TERM ECONOMIC INDICATORS, SOURCES AND DEFINITIONS
OECD/CCET © April 1996

152

INDICATEURS ÉCONOMIQUES A COURT TERME, SOURCES ET DÉFINITIONS
OCDE/CCET © avril 1996

SLOVAK REPUBLIC

Introduction

The Slovak Republic became an independent state on 1 January 1993. Prior to that date it was part of the Czech and Slovak Federal Republic (CSFR).

In general, data for the Czech and Slovak Federal Republic were compiled by aggregating data for the two separate republics, thus historical data for many series are available for the Slovak Republic.

Value data are expressed in CSFR koruny until end 1992 and in Slovak koruny from January 1993, when separate currencies were introduced in both the Czech Republic and the Slovak Republic. The two currencies were at parity until the Slovak koruny was devalued by 10 per cent on 9 July 1993.

Industrial production

The indices of industrial production cover enterprises in the mining and manufacturing industries, including electricity, gas and water, irrespective of the type of ownership.

The industrial branch structure for 1990 accords with the Uniform Czecho-Slovak Classification of the Branches of the National Economy. From 1992 the branch structure is based on the General Industry Classification of Economic Activities (NACE), Revision 1 which corresponds to ISIC Revision 3 at the Division level. Data for 1991 have been recalculated on this basis.

Until end 1990 a census of all industrial enterprises was undertaken. Since 1991 the coverage of enterprises has varied. In 1991 enterprises with 100 or more employees were surveyed. In 1992 and 1993 quarterly surveys were made of enterprises with 25 or more employees. From 1993 the monthly figure for total industrial production includes estimates of industrial production of enterprises with fewer than 25 employees and estimates of production of individual entrepreneurs. The enterprises with fewer than 25 employees are surveyed each quarter and the data used to refine the monthly estimates of total industrial production. All data from 1991 have been revised to include estimates for these units.

Industrial production indices for branches, however, cover only enterprises with more than 25 employees.

Since 1991 production has been measured as the final production of the enterprise. Production includes changes in stocks of finished goods and changes in work in progress, but excludes non-principal production.

Historically, the indices measured the change in the volume of production over the corresponding period of the previous year. If the industrial structure changed, the value of production in the same period of the preceding year was recalculated on a comparable basis and the implied rate of

SLOVAK REPUBLIC

change linked to the index with the original basis. This meant that while comparisons for the same periods in different years were valid, strictly speaking, comparisons within a year were not.

Production values in 1989 prices were recorded on a cumulative basis from the beginning of each year to the current month. Monthly figures were then calculated by subtracting cumulative data for the previous period. From 1993 monthly data on the value of production is obtained directly. The Producer Price Index is used to deflate the data. The indices are of type Laspeyres.

From 1992 the indices were changed to a price base of 1 January 1989=100. The series are expressed in *Short-term Economic Indicators: Transition Economies* with a reference base of 1990 as 100.

The *total industrial production index* covers mining, manufacturing (excluding publishing before 1992) and electricity, gas and water.

The *industrial production index for mining* refers to NACE, Revision 1 section mining and quarrying.

The *industrial production index for manufacturing* for 1991 refers to NACE, Revision 1 section the manufacturing industry, excluding publishing. From 1992 publishing is included.

The *industrial production index for electricity and gas* refers to NACE, Revision 1 section for electricity, gas and water supply, and includes production and distribution of water from 1991.

The *industrial production index for construction* refers to NACE, Revision 1 section concerning the construction industry, covering construction companies registered in the Slovak Republic.

Commodity output

Brown coal production figures cover brown coal and lignite. The output of brown coal refers to the output of mines less wastes removed and washed out in coal preparation plants. As lignite is not washed, the output of lignite equals gross output. This series has been discontinued.

Crude steel covers ferrous materials other than direct-reduced products, which are usefully malleable and which contain 2 per cent or less of carbon by weight.

Cement production covers output of Portland cement, slag Portland cement, pozzolan cements, aluminous cements, special kinds of cement and other kinds of cement (e.g. magnesium cement and high expansion cement).

Natural gas production refers to the output of mines.

Passenger car production covers primarily the production of pick-up vans.

Business surveys

A description of business tendency survey techniques and the list of harmonised questions is given in the chapter *Business Tendency Surveys* of this publication.

Construction

Dwellings

A dwelling is considered a room or set of rooms that, according to the decision of the construction authority, are designed for housing and which can serve for this purpose as independent dwelling units. Individual rooms at boarding schools, halls of residence and dwellings run by local administrative bodies are not included in the number of dwellings.

The number of *dwellings started* is determined from the number of permits authorising construction issued by District Offices of the Environment Ministry.

Dwellings completed are those dwellings for which the approval, certifying the building fit for habitation, has been issued. While delivery records are only compulsory for construction organisations and companies, the data include estimates from investment surveys in order to cover all dwellings built within the scope of capital construction, including individual housing.

The differences in the source of these data mean that they cannot be used to directly ascertain the number of *dwellings under construction.* Estimates, including information from investment surveys, were however made in the past and the series referred to all dwellings begun in the survey period and those unfinished at the end of the survey period.

From 1993 only the number of dwellings completed are monitored by the Statistical Office. Data are collected half-yearly.

Domestic trade

Up to the end of 1990, the *retail sales value* covered the sales of goods and services in current retail prices by the public retail trade network and the catering enterprises of the state and co-operative sectors (i.e. enterprises of the Ministries of Trade, consumer co-operatives, restaurants and fuel suppliers). They also included trading activities of non-trading enterprises in the state and co-operative sectors.

These commodities were sold directly to consumers for their own use or for collective consumption and to public sector organisations for intermediate consumption. Receipts for services rendered are included. The monthly figures accounted for about 85 per cent of all trade.

From 1991 retail sales include sales and receipts for accommodation and catering, and services including motor vehicle repairs. The data refer to sales value of goods and services sold directly to consumers for their own use. A VAT was introduced on 1 January 1993 and the data cover total sales value including taxes.

Until 1990 a census was undertaken of all trading units. Since the beginning of 1991, the coverage of enterprises has varied; in 1991 enterprises with 100 or more employees were surveyed, from 1992 to 1995 enterprises with 25 or more employees were surveyed monthly and quarterly. Small enterprises of up to 24 employees were surveyed quarterly; these data were used to refine the monthly estimates. From 1996, enterprises with 20 or more employees are surveyed monthly. Adjustments have been made to the data from 1991 in order to include an estimate of total sales by units which were not subject to the surveys.

SLOVAK REPUBLIC

A *retail sales volume* series has been estimated by the OECD Secretariat. It is calculated using the value of retail sales and the consumer price index and is expressed with base 1993 as 100.

Labour

Employment

Employment data for the *total* economy, and for *industry*, are obtained quarterly through the enterprise surveys used for industrial production. The same enterprise coverage therefore applies. Adjustments have also been made to the total employment data from 1991 in order to include estimates for small units and individual entrepreneurs (e.g. using data on the number of small tradepersons licences issued).

The data thus cover employment in the state, co-operative (for historical data) and private sectors including an estimate of private entrepreneurs and persons employed by them. Data refer to the average number of civilian employees, including those in both full- and part-time employment. Apprentices and employees on maternity or child care leave are excluded.

A labour force survey of 10 000 households was introduced in December 1992. These data are now collected quarterly. They are used for comparative purposes and to widen the scope of employment indicators to cover employment by education, under-employment etc.. For further information concerning this survey, see the chapter *Labour Market Indicators* earlier in this volume.

The working age population refers to women between 15 and 54 and men between 15 and 59.

Unemployment

Registration of the unemployed began in February 1990 through the then newly created Labour Office of the Ministry of Labour, Social Affairs and the Family. The *total unemployment* refers to persons who are neither under a working contract nor perform any independent earning activity and who have asked the local employment agency to find suitable work for them.

It is necessary to register as unemployed in order to receive retraining and financial support; a further incentive to register is that the same office handles both registration of the unemployed and job vacancies. However, persons working part-time or wishing to change jobs may not register as unemployed.

Data concerning unemployment *beneficiaries* refer to all persons currently receiving benefits from the Labour Office. To receive benefits persons must have been employed for at least 12 months during the last three years. Persons who do not register regularly lose their entitlements. Persons registered may receive benefits for a maximum of six months. For the first three months the payment is equivalent to 60 per cent of the average wage in the last job, to a maximum of 3 000 Slovak koruny. For the next three months the rate is 50 per cent of the average wage in the last job. Persons may earn up to 800 Slovak koruny without this influencing the level of benefit.

After six months persons may be offered community work for public benefit. They continue to receive 50 per cent of the average wage in the last job as well as a supplementary payment of 800 Slovak koruny. If work for public benefit is not available, persons in need may be entitled to social allowances which are available through a different government agency.

The *unemployment rate* refers to the proportion of registered unemployed to the civilian labour force (i.e. unemployed plus employed referring to persons who worked more than one hour a week during the survey period, excluding defence forces and including persons on maternity or child care leave).

Job vacancies refer to job opportunities for immediate filling notified to the employment offices remaining unfilled on the day of count.

The labour force survey referred to above, and described in the chapter *Labour Market Indicators* earlier in this volume, provides further information on the unemployed (e.g. age and sex structure, duration of unemployment etc.).

Private enterprises

Until end 1989, the data covered the number of persons providing services permitted by the national committees according to the ordinance of the governments of both the Czech Republic and the Slovak Republic. Since the beginning of 1990 the data refer to the number of entrepreneurs registered according to the Act No. 105/1990.

Data for private *entrepreneurs registered* in 1990 and 1991 were obtained from the Slovak Ministry of the Interior. Since 1992 data have been taken from the Register of Statistical units of the Statistical Office of the Slovak Republic. Entrepreneurs registered also covers trades persons, and independent farmers. An estimate is also made for individual entrepreneurs not covered by the register.

The interpretation of the number of private entrepreneurs is obscured by several phenomena. Many people register a private enterprise and for various reasons do not actually engage in the activity. Others might only pursue the activity on a part-time basis.

Re-registration of entrepreneurs was required up to the end of 1992 in accordance with the Small Business Act No. 455/1991 in order to ascertain the active or non-active status of registered private entrepreneurs. New laws were introduced at end 1992 requiring the payment of social security contributions and insurance for rent of premises by private entrepreneurs. This resulted in a decrease in the number registered as only active private entrepreneurs able to meet these charges remained registered.

Wages

Monthly earnings

The data on average *monthly total earnings* are obtained from the same enterprise surveys used for industrial production and employment and thus the same coverage applies. The Statistical Office of the Slovak Republic has also adjusted these data since 1991 to include estimates of monthly earnings in the small private sector (enterprises with between 1 and 24 employees). No adjustments are made to include the wages of small tradespersons engaged in individual activity and not registered on the business register. Through the labour force survey, estimates exist of the earnings of individual entrepreneurs since 1993, but these data are not currently published nor included directly in earnings data.

Data relate to employees only (i.e. excluding managers). Earnings are defined as the average monthly wages per worker and refer to gross wages, i.e. basic wages and salaries including bonuses and remunerations, but excluding family and other social benefits.

OECD
OCDE
SHORT-TERM ECONOMIC INDICATORS, SOURCES AND DEFINITIONS
OECD/CCET © April 1996

157

INDICATEURS ÉCONOMIQUES A COURT TERME, SOURCES ET DÉFINITIONS
OCDE/CCET © avril 1996

SLOVAK REPUBLIC

Earnings in *industry* and earnings in *manufacturing* are based only on data for enterprises with 25 and more employees.

Prices

Producer prices

The *producer price index* in industry (PPI) is based on the producer prices of industrial goods manufactured in the Slovak Republic. Up to the end of 1990 the prices referred to list prices and were collected quarterly. Starting in 1991, they refer to monthly price quotations of approximately 1 890 representative items collected from 382 producers in 270 industrial branches. Non-standard production in the mechanical engineering industry, in metallurgy, assembling and dismantling, industrial services, repairs and transmission of electric power are excluded.

The reported prices are the arithmetic mean of actual transaction prices of all important contracts at the middle of the month. Up to 1993 they exclude the turnover tax.

Selected items may be substituted by items of similar quality, but when large differences in quality arise, a price correction is made. No special treatment is made for goods with a seasonal production cycle. The index excludes VAT, which was introduced on 1 January 1993, but includes consumption tax on certain products.

The index is of type Laspeyres and is derived from simple price relatives for individual items weighted by the value of production of the relevant branch in 1989. The national base is 1 January 1989=100 and monthly data are available on this basis from 1991.

Consumer prices

The *consumer price index (CPI)* reflects the price movements of food products, industrial goods, catering and other services bought by the population. Prices of 836 selected goods and services are observed, as shown in the folllowing table.

Major groups	Number of items	Weight
Food	160	29.9
Industrial goods	423	44.6
Public catering	59	11.5
Services (including rent, transport and communications)	194	14.0
TOTAL	836	100.0

Price collectors from statistical offices note prices from selected retail and service outlets in 38 districts of the Slovak Republic during the first 20 days of each month, excepting fruit and vegetable prices, which are collected three times a month (on the first, tenth and twentieth calendar days). A separate monthly basket of fresh fruit and vegetables is compiled comprising selected varieties currently on sale in the relevant month. Between three and five quotations are taken for food and non-food items and selected services. For other services such as transport and communications one price is quoted. The index is based on prices paid in shops and salesrooms of state, co-operative and private trade for full value goods; prices of second-hand goods are not included in the index.

If the observed product disappears, it is replaced by another product of comparable quality. If the quality of the substitute product is not directly comparable, adjustments are made. Generally prices of products which follow new fashion trends are introduced directly in the index.

The CPI is of the Laspeyres type. The prices collected from the individual reporting units are used to calculate unweighted arithmetic averages. The price indices for individual groups and aggregates are calculated as weighted arithmetical means with constant weights of the base year.

The weights for goods are based on the structure of retail turnover in 1989, and for services on the structure of expenditure of the population for services in 1989.

The system of monitoring and calculating price indices was changed in 1991 from quarterly to monthly and a new national base of January 1989=100 introduced. The series are expressed in *Short-term Economic Indicators: Transition Economies* with a reference base of 1990 as 100.

Domestic finance

Narrow money (M1) covers national currency in circulation outside the banking sector and demand deposits, excluding those of the central government.

Quasi-money covers time, savings and foreign currency deposits of residents, except the central government.

Personal deposits refers to all savings deposits of resident households in all financial institutions, including banks and insurance organisations, on Slovak territory.

Interest rates

The *official discount rate* refers to the end of period rate at which the National Bank lends to commercial banks. There is a maximum limit on the amount that may be lent at this rate and over this limit, money may be lent by the National Bank at the market rate.

Foreign finance

The *US dollar exchange rate* refers to the period average rate. To end 1992 it refers to the exchange rate of the CSFR koruny. From January 1993 it refers to the exchange rate of the Slovak koruny.

Foreign trade

Until 1990 foreign trade data were based on a survey of licensed exporters and importers. Since the beginning of 1991 foreign trade statistics have been based on customs declarations and the Harmonised System used. The Unitary Customs Declaration was introduced in the Slovak Republic on 1 January 1992. The returns are processed by the Central Customs Administration, established separately in the Slovak Republic in early 1993.

SLOVAK REPUBLIC

Since 1 January 1991 exports of goods have been recorded on the date they cross the border. Imports of goods are recorded at the date of their release from bonded warehouses rather than at the date they cross the frontier. Revisions to the data are made retrospectively as returns are processed.

Data include re-exports and re-imports but exclude exports and imports of services. From 1993, imports and exports include trade with the Czech Republic.

From 1991 imports and exports are both valued FOB.

The breakdown of foreign trade into *convertible* and *non-convertible currencies* is based on the receiver or destination country status as "market" or "non-market". The sum of the two may not equal the total value of trade due to difficulties in identifying source or destination countries / currencies on some returns.

Gross capital formation (Capital Investment)

Data concerning *gross capital formation (capital investment)* are collected quarterly. Until 1991, data concerned only fixed investment, primarily machinery and equipment. From 1992 other investment (on research, software etc.) has been monitored. A new survey was introduced in 1994. All types of units in the business register are surveyed, including private entrepreneurs.

Construction works include work by budgetary and government organisations, construction by private enterprises and own-account construction. All construction is covered, whether it be as a primary or secondary activity of the unit.

The Slovak definition of *other gross capital formation* includes the value of sales and purchases of land following changes in ownership, which is the main item in this category.

Publications

Some of the series described above, but presented according to national practice, can be found in the following publications of the Statistical Office of the Slovak Republic:

Slovak Economic Monitor
Slovak Statistical Review.

TEN NEW INDEPENDENT STATES

The following chapter contains the methodological notes and definitions of the data for ten New Independent States (NIS): Armenia, Azerbaijan, Belarus, Kazakstan, Kyrgyz Republic, Republic of Moldova, Russian Federation, Tajikistan, Turkmenistan and Uzbekistan.

This information is supplied to the OECD by the Interstate Statistical Committee of the Commonwealth of Independent States.

Industrial production

Total industrial output and the output of individual branches of industry represent the gross output of industrial establishments as reported regularly from their statistical records. The gross output of an industrial establishment covers the value of products manufactured by the establishment during the accounting period including the value of semi-finished products sold, or intended for sale, to other entities. Also included is the value of industrial services rendered to other entities on a contractual basis, as well as services rendered to units in the non-material sector and establishments within an enterprise. The value of the establishment's output used in the production process, unfinished products, as well as changes in stocks and inventories are excluded. Changes in work in progress are taken into account in industrial branches with long production cycles.

Monthly and quarterly series cover public sector industrial establishments, those which are owned collectively and joint stock companies. Enterprises of other forms of ownership are generally included only in annual series.

Annual series also include subsidiary production, e.g. industrial production of collective farms, state farms and construction enterprises. The share of subsidiary production in total output is estimated at 6-7 per cent.

Annual and quarterly figures do not always correspond to the average of the quarters and the months, due to differences in coverage of enterprises.

The *index of industrial production* (IIP) is based on the total value of production expressed in "comparable" prices. Industrial output in "comparable" prices is calculated by enterprises by multiplying output in physical units by "comparable" producer prices which exclude turnover tax, VAT and excise taxes.

Prices of 1 January 1982 were used during the period 1980-90. From 1991, prices of January of each year have been used and the indices chain linked.

Departures from definition:

-- *Russian Federation from 1993, Azerbaijan and Kazakstan from 1994:* the index of industrial production (IIP) is calculated as a weighted average of the changes in production volume. The indices are calculated from a fixed set of representative commodities with subsequent aggregation up to branch and total indices. The number of goods used for index calculation in Azerbaijan, Kazakstan and Russian Federation is 300, 400 and 430 respectively.

-- *Kyrgyz Republic* and *Turkmenistan*: From 1992, in the Kyrgyz Republic and Turkmenistan value series are deflated by the prices of the current month.

The classification of industrial production is based on the Classification of Branches of the National Economy (CBNE) which was developed by the former Council for Mutual Economic Assistance (CMEA).

The *IIP total* covers broadly the mining and quarrying, manufacturing and electricity, gas and water divisions (Divisions 2, 3 and 4) of the International Standard Industrial Classification (ISIC Rev. 2). In addition, it includes logging and fishing divisions, cleaning services, repair and maintenance of motor vehicles and repair of personal and household goods. It excludes printing and publishing.

The *IIP for mining and quarrying* covers establishments engaged in extracting minerals, ferrous and non-ferrous metal ores as well as non-ore raw materials used in the metallurgical industry, crude petroleum extraction, mining for non-metal ore extraction, gas, coal, peat, slate, salt as well as non-ore construction materials, light filling substances and lime.

Drilling, mineral prospecting and on-site crude petroleum and natural gas refining are excluded.

The *IIP for manufacturing* covers establishments engaged in the processing of mining products and of products previously processed, as well as the processing of agricultural produce. This NIS classification differs from Division 3 of ISIC Rev. 2 in that it includes the production of electricity (except hydro-electricity) and the repair of motor vehicles, furniture and household appliances but excludes printing and publishing.

In the *IIP for construction*, the definition of output is restricted to the value of investments in new construction, expansion and reconstruction. This comprises installation, drilling, architectural, design and drafting activities and other major construction jobs, plus capital repair of buildings and structures. The value of unfinished constructions is included. The value of machines and equipment and plantations are excluded.

The construction data are collected from state and co-operative enterprises, private enterprises, joint ventures, agricultural housing and individual housing projects, irrespective of methods of financing.

Data from 1980-84 are expressed in 1973 constant prices; for 1985-88, in constant 1983 prices; from 1989, in prices of the previous year.

Commodity output

Coal production covers black coal and brown coal, gross of losses due to briquette production, sorting, cleaning, etc.

Black coal includes coking coal, anthracite and coal used in power stations. Peat, coke and semi-coke made from coal are excluded.

Brown coal includes lignite but excludes coke and semi-coke made from lignite or peat.

Natural gas production covers natural gas obtained from gas wells and petroleum gas obtained from petroleum wells (casinhead).

According to the methodology adopted in the NIS, gas production is registered at 20 degrees Celsius at a pressure of 760 mm mercury.

The output of *crude petroleum* covers crude petroleum obtained by all methods excluding gas condensate production.

Crude steel production covers all types of steel (open-hearth, electric steel, steel converters, bessemer steel, etc.), steel in ingots for rolling, forging and punching by the enterprise and shipped elsewhere; steel ingots obtained by continuous casting, ingots for recasting (excluding the steel for duplex processes at own enterprise). Liquid steel used for steel casting is included.

Departures from definition:

-- *Tajikistan* and *Kyrgyz Republic*: Since 1992, all steel has been produced by auxiliary industrial establishments, which report only annually.

All types of *cement production* are covered excluding local viscous materials obtained from slags and shale. Cement produced as subsidiary output in industrial branches not specialised in construction materials is included.

The *production of electricity* measures all types of electricity production including hydro-electric, hydraulic, conventional, thermal, nuclear, geothermal, solar and tidal. The gross output of electric power stations includes independent electric nets and electric heating systems.

Metal cutting machine production includes all types of lathes, planing, drilling, milling, grinding and broaching machines and other types of metal cutting machines, including ultrasonic and electro-erosion (but excluding hand driven and portable metal cutting machines).

The *production of lorries* covers all types of lorries and semi-lorries (excluding special purpose motor vehicles) as well as lorries manufactured on the basis of passenger car chassis.

Mineral fertiliser production includes all types of mineral fertilisers containing nitrogen, phosphorous, potassium, boron and boron-magnesium.

The *production of refrigerators* covers only household type refrigerators and food freezers as well as automobile refrigerators and freezers.

Passenger car output includes all types of cars excluding lorries manufactured on the basis of passenger car chassis.

There may be some differences in the coverage of enterprises between quarterly and annual commodity output series.

Business surveys

Results of business surveys are available for the Russian Federation from the first quarter of 1992 and for Belarus from the second quarter of 1994. A description of business tendency survey techniques and the list of harmonised questions is given in the chapter *Business Tendency Surveys* of this publication.

Construction

Dwellings

Included are all *dwellings completed*, regardless of the type of enterprise responsible for their construction. Dwellings completed include constructions by state enterprises, dwelling-building co-operatives, social organisations and trade unions, kolkhozian and other agricultural housing, private enterprises and dwellings built by individuals, regardless of the source of financing. There may be some differences in enterprise coverage between quarterly and annual data.

Dwellings refer to premises intended for permanent habitation, physically independent of other premises and having an independent, direct access to a staircase, common place, hall or street. A dwelling may comprise, under one roof, one or several rooms, a corridor, kitchen, utility, a hall and a closet.

Two dwelling series are presented: one represents the number of dwellings completed, the other represents the total area of dwellings completed including apartments and hotel-type accommodation, as well as dormitories. Total dwelling area comprises the living area and any ancillary premises such as the kitchen, corridor, closet, utility areas. In the case of hostels, ancillary premises may also include medical and cultural spaces. Verandas, loggias, terraces and balconies may be included in part, using a coefficient determined by the technical and economic indicators of the dwelling project. Dwelling area excludes entrance halls, staircases and common corridors.

Domestic trade

The *value of retail sales* is defined as the total value of consumer goods sold, by retail trade and public catering establishments and shipped directly by industrial, transport and other enterprises. Outlets of all forms of ownership are included. Retail trade turnover includes sales of foodstuffs as well as non-food commodities to sanatoria, hospitals, childrens' and other institutions.

Retail trade data are collected directly from all enterprises selling consumer goods through officially licensed trade outlets, irrespective of the type of administration or ownership. Urban markets are excluded.

Prior to 1990 retail trade turnover included the revenues from some services rendered to households such as individual apparel manufacturing, repair of clothing and footwear or the repair of consumer durables. The share of these services in total turnover was approximately 2 per cent but since 1991, no services have been included in retail trade turnover.

The total annual trade turnover might exceed the sum of the revenue in the corresponding months and quarters due to a wider coverage of trade enterprises.

OECD
OCDE
SHORT-TERM ECONOMIC INDICATORS, SOURCES AND DEFINITIONS
OECD/CCET © April 1996

164

INDICATEURS ÉCONOMIQUES A COURT TERME, SOURCES ET DÉFINITIONS
OCDE/CCET © avril 1996

The value of retail sales is expressed in new national currencies where these have been introduced. For more detailed information see the chapter *Introduction of New Currencies*.

From 1995, a new series concerning *retail sales value total* is available for all countries except the Republic of Moldova and Tajikistan. This series covers total retail trade turnover through all outlets, including estimates of sales by non-registered enterprises and private persons in informal markets.

The *retail sales volume* index is calculated by deflating retail trade turnover to constant prices. The value of retail turnover has been deflated by the consumer price index for total goods in Armenia, Belarus and Russian Federation and by the retail trade price index in other countries (see Prices below).

Labour

Employment

Total employment refers to the average number of persons employed in enterprises and organisations owned or controlled by the state, co-operative and social institutions, joint ventures as well as the self-employed such as private farmers, persons engaged in home agricultural production and in individual labour activity. Military personnel are excluded. Social institutions include, for example sports clubs, trade unions, writers' and journalists' unions, the Red Cross and Crescent organisation, the Peace Fund, the Children's Fund. Starting in 1991 persons engaged in private enterprises are also included.

The data are based on quarterly and annual reports concerning the labour force in enterprises, organisations and institutions. All units, regardless of their type of ownership, are required to report on their labour force. This information is generally compared with similar data collected by tax agencies and state banks. The number of persons engaged in home agricultural production is estimated.

All branches of the national economy are included, whether involved in material or non-material activity.

Part-time workers, including persons placed by labour offices as part-time workers, are recorded as full-time equivalents. Persons holding more than one job are recorded at their main place of work. Civil employees in military industrial complexes, persons on sick leave, apprentices, home contract workers and casual employees are included.

Employment in material branches covers the following branches of the national economy.

-- industry;

-- agriculture;

-- forestry;

-- transport and communications, insofar as they service material branch activity;

-- trade, public catering, material supply, procurement;

-- information and computing services;

-- other branches of material production including publishing and film production and distribution, waste and scrap processing, fishing, hunting, etc.

This series has been discontinued from the second quarter of 1993.

Employment in industry covers all employees engaged in industrial establishments in industrial enterprises as well as industrial establishments of enterprises included in other branches. Employees in non-industrial establishments of industrial enterprises are included in the branch of activity to which the establishment belongs. The branch coverage is the same as that for the total IIP (see section on Industrial production above).

Employment in manufacturing represents the average number of workers and employees directly involved in the production process in manufacturing enterprises as recorded on payrolls. The branch coverage is the same as that for the IIP for manufacturing (see section on Industrial production above).

Unemployment

Total *registered unemployment* represents the number of persons registered as unemployed by state employment offices at the end of the month, in accordance with employment legislation in effect in each of the New Independent States.

Able-bodied persons of working age (from 16 to 60 for men and from 16 to 55 for women) are considered as unemployed, irrespective of the reasons for their not having gainful employment, provided they have been duly recorded by a state employment office as seeking employment, are able and ready for any gainful activity and have not received an appropriate employment proposal.

The registration of persons as unemployed by state employment offices began from the following dates:

-- 1 July 1991 in Belarus, Kazakstan, Kyrgyz Republic, Republic of Moldova, Russian Federation;

-- 1 October 1991 in Azerbaijan;

-- 1 March 1992 in Armenia;

-- 16 April 1992 in Tajikistan;

-- 1 July 1992 in Uzbekistan;

In accordance with the legislation in the various countries, the employment offices take decisions concerning the registration of an individual not more than ten days after his/her application. Persons previously employed must present a passport, professional record book and earnings records of their last employer. New job seekers must present a passport and education certificates. Once registered, an individual remains registered until he/she finds work.

It is not compulsory for persons who have lost their jobs to register as unemployed. Persons seeking to change jobs, or part-time workers seeking full-time work are not considered as unemployed, but may register in the employment offices as seeking work. In all countries, once registered as unemployed, unemployed persons are obliged to re-register periodically at state employment offices. Persons are required to re-register:

-- four times a month in Kazakstan and Tajikistan;

-- twice a month in Armenia, Kyrgyz Republic, the Republic of Moldova, the Russian Federation and Uzbekistan;

-- once a month in Belarus.

Unemployment *beneficiaries* receive benefits when they are registered as unemployed from:

-- the first day in Belarus and the Russian Federation;

-- the second day in Tajikistan;

-- the eighth day in Kazakstan;

-- the eleventh day in Armenia, Azerbaijan, Kyrgyz Republic, the Republic of Moldova and Uzbekistan.

The amount and duration of benefits varies widely between the countries and according to the category of recipient. In general the amount paid to a new job seeker is at least 70 per cent of the legally established minimum wage and is paid to beneficiaries for periods ranging from 12 weeks in Armenia to 12 months in the Russian Federation. For formerly employed persons the amount paid is generally at least 50 per cent of the average wage paid by the former employer and is paid for periods ranging from 24 weeks in Armenia to 12 months in the Russian Federation.

Non-beneficiaries are those persons registered as unemployed who are not entitled to receive benefits and those for whom benefit entitlements have been stopped or suspended for refusing two suitable job offers (one in the Republic of Moldova), not re-registering regularly, receiving illegal benefits or working without legal declaration.

The *unemployment rate* reflects the number of registered unemployed as a percentage of the civilian labour force (i.e. employed plus unemployed). Monthly estimates of employment, used to calculate the labour force, are derived from quarterly employment data.

Wages

Monthly earnings

Monthly earnings are not based on the same records as those related to employment (see above): earnings of private farmers, persons engaged in home agricultural production and other self-employed are excluded.

Data relate to the average gross wage per employed person, calculated by dividing the total wage fund by the total number of employees. For calculation of the average wage, part-time workers are recorded as full-time equivalents, employees on maternity or child care leave are excluded. The wage fund includes payments such as health, food and travel allowances, payments in kind, profit-related bonuses, payments for overtime and paid leave. Social security payments, however, are excluded.

The series *monthly earnings in material branches* have been discontinued from the second quarter of 1993.

Monthly earnings are expressed in new national currencies where these have been introduced. For more detailed information see the chapter *Introduction of New Currencies*.

Prices

"Old" Consumer Price Index

Monthly *Consumer Price Indices* (CPI) were introduced in January 1991.

Until December 1993 for all countries (except the Russian Federation from 1991 and the Republic of Moldova: see below), prices were observed for 1030 representative goods selected from all commodity groups included in retail turnover. With regard to the CPI *for services*, prices were noted for 72 items, representative of the structure of sales of paid services to households in more than 250 towns.

In the Russian Federation, the CPI was calculated from price quotations of a set of 409 enlarged groups of goods and services. In the Republic of Moldova, prices of 1585 goods and services were included in the CPI.

Price quotations included taxes and were recorded each month in about 5 000 outlets throughout the NIS, ranging from large outlets selling a wide variety of commodities to small specialised outlets (bookstores or children's goods, etc.). The indices reflected changes in prices in state, co-operative and private trade outlets, as well as in the prices of goods produced by co-operatives and individual working activity.

There was no estimation included for the informal sector. Urban outdoor markets were excluded from the calculation of CPI sub-groups, but are taken into account in the total CPI.

Seasonal food items, received different weights in aggregated indices according to whether they are grown in a greenhouse and sold as early produce, or sold "in season". With regard to services, some enterprises provide discounts for selected services during seasonal decline in demand. These discounts were reflected in price registration.

In all countries, except for the Russian Federation, Uzbekistan and the Kyrgyz Republic, the CPI for consumer goods was a Paasche index up to December 1992 and a Laspeyres index from January 1993. In Uzbekistan and Kyrgyz Republic the CPI was calculated as a Paasche index over all periods.

For all countries, except the Russian Federation and the Republic of Moldova, the weights used for regional and group aggregations were based on the structure of retail turnover in the current year. The CPI for services was a Laspeyres index with weights based on sales of services to households in the base period.

In the Russian Federation the CPI is a Laspeyres type from January 1991 (see also the section below "New Consumer Price Index"). The weights used are derived from the structure of actual consumer expenditures of the Russian population in the previous year. The elementary indices are aggregated in three main sub-group: Food, non Food and Services. The total CPI is calculated as average weighted of elementary indices.

In the Republic of Moldova, the CPI is of type Laspeyres from January 1993, with weights based on the structure of consumption expenditure by households, in the previous year (see also the section below "New Consumer Price Index").

An annual index showing the rate of change over the previous year is also available. Given the conditions of price liberalisation and the dramatic increase in prices, together with the changes that have

OECD
OCDE
SHORT-TERM ECONOMIC INDICATORS, SOURCES AND DEFINITIONS
OECD/CCET © April 1996

168

INDICATEURS ÉCONOMIQUES À COURT TERME, SOURCES ET DÉFINITIONS
OCDE/CCET © avril 1996

occurred in the structure of production and sales, the monthly and annual indices of the CPI were not consistent, with the exception of those for the Russian Federation.

In the Russian Federation, the 409 enlarged groups of goods and services were chosen to take into account structural changes related to very large price increases in the monthly indices, so that yearly figures calculated by direct comparison of the prices of December with December of the previous year would be consistent with the monthly figures.

"New" Consumer Price Index

New monthly CPIs were introduced in 1991 in the Russian Federation, 1993 in the Republic of Moldova and during 1994 in all other NIS.

The indices are of type Laspeyres.

The CPIs are calculated on the basis of retail prices and tariffs of representative goods and services.

The baskets used for the compilation of the CPIs have been set up on the basis of the structure of consumer expenditure. The baskets of goods and services, comprising 300 to 400 items, include foodstuffs, non food commodities, and services purchased by households.

Departure from definition:

-- *Uzbekistan*: excludes jewellery and delicacies.

The total population residing on the country's territory is taken into account to calculate consumer expenditures.

For each region the total prices are calculated as arithmetic averages. At the national level each region is weighted by the share of its population.

The weights used to calculate the aggregated indices are derived from the household consumer expenditure survey of the previous year.

Departure from definition:

-- *Azerbaijan:* household consumer expenditure survey of 1993.

Prices of services are observed in trade and service outlets and organisations regardless of their ownership: public sector, private sector, informal markets.

The prices are observed for foodstuffs every seven or ten days; for non-foodstuffs and services once per month.

Departures from definition:

-- *Armenia*: prices for non-foodstuffs and services are observed every ten days;

-- *Belarus, Kyrgyz Republic:* prices for foodstuffs are observed each month;

-- *Republic of Moldova:* prices for non-foodstuffs and services are observed twice per month.

 SHORT-TERM ECONOMIC INDICATORS, SOURCES AND DEFINITIONS   169   INDICATEURS ÉCONOMIQUES A COURT TERME, SOURCES ET DÉFINITIONS

OECD/CCET © April 1996   OCDE/CCET © avril 1996

Domestic finance

Personal deposits cover time and savings deposits, held in savings banks and are shown at the end of the period. Annual interest payments are included in the December, fourth quarter and yearly figures.

Starting on 1 September 1991 in all countries, personal deposits include a 40 per cent compensation payment for massive price rises. Compensation of up to 200 roubles was credited to the main deposit account. Where these compensation payments exceeded 200 roubles, the additional amount was deposited in a special account. The deposits in these special accounts have been included in the data concerning personal deposits.

Departure from definition:

-- *Kazakstan:* data on personnel deposits do not include compensation payments.

Persons have been able to withdraw these compensatioon payments in Armenia since 1 March 1994, in Moldova and Uzbekistan since April 1994, in Russian Federation and Turkmenistan from 1992 and in Belarus from 1993.

Personal deposits are expressed in new national currencies where these have been introduced. For more detailed information see the chapter *Introduction of New Currencies.*

Foreign finance

Exchange rates between the national currency, US dollar and/or <u>new</u> rouble are published for the NIS. These rates are fixed by the national banks in each country and refer to the end of the period, or to the period average for the rouble exchange rate. For more information concerning the introduction of new currencies, see the chapter *Introduction of New Currencies.*

Foreign trade

Exports and *imports* data are obtained from reports submitted by external trade organisations as well as from commodity customs declarations. Exports and imports are recorded on the date they cross the border. Exports are valued FOB; imports are valued CIF. Bartered goods are valued at world market prices for similar goods.

Foreign trade data exclude services, except in the Russian Federation where construction services, financial services, publishing, education, training and health services are included until 1994. Foreign trade data for Uzbekistan until 1992 included material services. Receipts from tourism are excluded in all NIS countries. Exports of gold, silver and other precious metals and diamonds are in principle included, but are in practice not fully covered.

Re-exports and re-imports are registered only when goods enter the country.

Recording of exports and imports started in 1991, except those for the Russian Federation where recording started in 1988.

Until 1994 only data for trade with countries other than NIS are available. From 1994 total trade data are available, broken into trade with NIS and trade with countries other than NIS.

Trade with NIS refers to trade with countries of the former Soviet Union, excluding Estonia, Latvia and Lithuania, which are included in trade with countries other than NIS.

Concerning trade with countries other than NIS, annual data include certain customs data not allocated in the quarterly data for 1993 and 1994 for Kazakstan, and 1993 for Belarus. Annual data are therefore not the sum of the quarterly and the monthly data in these countries.

Russian Federation exports and imports from 1988-90 are expressed in US dollars based on the following average annual official exchange rates:

-- 1988 at 0.61 roubles/dollar;

-- 1989 at 0.63 roubles/dollar;

-- 1990 at 0.58 roubles/dollar.

Russian Federation exports and imports in 1991 were revalued to US dollars using the average of the official and commercial exchange rates, 1.26 roubles/dollar.

For other NIS, foreign trade transactions have been estimated in US dollars since 1992. For all NIS, exchange rates determined by the national banks are used.

Gross capital formation

Total gross capital formation represents expenditure on new capital goods, as well as extensions, reconstruction and renovation of fixed assets in operation. The value of capital investments represents the cost of construction and installation, the purchase of equipment and tools, and expenditure on capital works.

Capital investment is valued at its original cost, i.e. the price at which it was purchased before deductions for fixed capital depreciation. Unfinished buildings and structures that have been paid for by contractors are included in capital investment; capital repair is excluded.

Projects are included, regardless of their financing: investment expenditures of state-owned enterprises and institutions, leased enterprises, consumer co-operatives and public organisations, co-operatives, collective farms, dwelling construction co-operatives and self-financed individual construction.

Data on investment expenditures are recorded at current prices and converted to 1984 constant prices, either based on data supplied by the enterprises or on the basis of price indices. The series for 1984-90 are based on data supplied by enterprises.

Gross capital formation in construction and installation includes work related to construction, expansion and reconstruction of buildings and structures, whether permanent or temporary, as well as installations of construction blocks and equipment.

Since 1991 volume indices of capital investment in most of the NIS are calculated as the ratio of values at constant prices derived by deflating the value of capital investment in current prices by a price index of capital investment. This price index is derived on the basis of data on price changes for the main elements of capital investment (construction and installation works, equipment and tools, major repairs, other capital expenditures).

Gross capital formation is expressed in new national currencies where these have been introduced. For more detailed information see the chapter *Introduction of New Currencies*.

Publications

Some of the series described above, but presented according to national practice, can be found in various publications of the Interstate Statistical Committee of the Commonwealth of Independent States or in publications of the national statistical offices of the individual countries.

UKRAINE

Industrial production

Total industrial production and the production of individual branches of industry represent the gross production of industrial establishments as reported regularly from their statistical records. The gross output of an industrial establishment covers the value of products manufactured by the establishment during the accounting period including the value of semi-finished products sold, or intended for sale, to other entities. Also included is the value of industrial services rendered to other entities on a contractual basis, as well as services rendered to units in the non-material sector and establishments within an enterprise. The value of the establishment's output used in the production process, unfinished products, as well as changes in stocks and inventories are excluded. Changes in work in progress are taken into account in industrial branches with long production cycles.

Annual indices of industrial production are compiled from figures for total industrial output produced by enterprises operating on an independent accounting basis, by manufacturing units, joint ventures with foreign capital shareholdings, small firms and co-operatives, subsidiary industrial enterprises -- without financial autonomy -- of non-industrial organisations, by collective and state farms and by multi-sectoral organisations under all forms and types of ownership (state, private, collective and mixed).

Monthly and quarterly industrial production series are compiled from returns for total industrial output produced by firms operating on an independent basis, and by units under all forms of ownership including output from subsidiaries of manufacturing units.

The classification of industrial production is based on the Classification of Branches of the National Economy of the former Soviet Union (CBNE) developed by the former Council for Mutual Economic Assistance (CMEA).

Industrial production indices are of type Paasche.

The *index of industrial production (IIP) total* covers broadly the mining and quarrying, manufacturing and electricity, gas and water divisions of the International Standard Industrial Classification (ISIC Divisions 2, 3 and 4). In addition, it includes logging and fishing divisions, cleaning services, repair and maintenance of motor vehicles and repair of personal and household goods. It excludes publishing.

The IIP total is based on the total value of production expressed in constant prices of January 1989. Industrial output in constant prices is evaluated directly by enterprises. Enterprises deflate the value of production using wholesale prices excluding turnover taxes, value added taxes and excise taxes.

Approximately 90 000 enterprises are surveyed and 500 items are included in the total index.

UKRAINE

All indices of industrial output by branch are deflated by the January prices of the previous year.

The *IIP for mining and quarrying* covers establishments engaged in extracting minerals, ferrous and non-ferrous metal ores as well as non-ore raw materials used in the metallurgical industry, crude petroleum extraction, mining for non-metal ore extraction, gas, coal, peat, slate, salt as well as non-ore construction materials, light filling substances and lime. Drilling, mineral prospecting and on-site crude petroleum and natural gas refining are excluded.

The *IIP for manufacturing* covers establishments engaged in the processing of mining products and of products previously processed, as well as the processing of agricultural produce. It excludes the production of electricity; the repair of motor vehicles, furniture and household appliances, and publishing.

The *IIP for electricity* measures all types of electricity production including hydro-electric, hydraulic, conventional, thermal, nuclear, geothermal, solar and tidal. The gross output of electric power stations includes independent electric nets and electric heating systems.

The *IIP for construction* includes cement, asbestos cement, rolled roofing materials and waterproof materials, precast ferroconcrete and concrete structures and products, wall construction material, building ceramics, polymer construction materials and products, quarrying and dressing of natural stone facing slabs, porous aggregates, lime gypsum, locally-procurable binders and products and thermal insulating materials. It also includes other construction materials such as ready-mix concrete and mortar and asphalt concrete.

The construction data are collected from state and co-operative enterprises, private enterprises, joint ventures, agricultural housing and storage facilities and individual housing projects, irrespective of methods of financing.

Commodity output

Coal production covers black coal and brown coal, gross losses due to briquette production, sorting, cleaning, etc.

Black coal includes coking coal, anthracite and coal used in power stations. Peat, coke and semi-coke made from coal are excluded.

Brown coal includes lignite but excludes coke and semi-coke made from lignite or peat.

Natural gas production covers natural gas obtained from gas wells and petroleum gas obtained from petroleum wells. According to the methodology adopted in Ukraine, gas production is registered at 20 degrees Celsius at a pressure of 760 mm mercury. Data have been recalculated according to international practice, using a coefficient of 1 073 to correct to zero degrees Celsius and 760 mm of mercury.

The output of *crude petroleum* covers crude petroleum obtained by all methods including gas condensate production.

Crude steel production covers all types of steel (open-hearth, electric steel, steel converters, bessemer steel, etc.), steel in ingots for rolling, forging and punching either by the enterprise or for shipping elsewhere; steel ingots obtained by continuous casting, ingots for recasting (excluding the steel for duplex processes at own enterprise). Liquid steel used during the production of steel castings is included.

All types of *cement production* are covered excluding local viscous materials obtained from slags and shale. Cement produced as subsidiary output in industrial branches not specialised in construction materials is included.

Passenger car output includes all types of cars excluding lorries manufactured on the basis of passenger car chassis. Passenger cars produced by military enterprises are excluded.

Construction

Dwellings

Several series are presented for *dwellings completed*: the area of dwellings completed in the public sector and the number of dwellings completed and their area regardless of the type of enterprise responsible for their construction.

Total dwellings completed includes constructions by state enterprises, dwelling-building co-operatives, social organisations and trade unions, kolkhozian and other agricultural housing, private enterprises, sub-contractors and dwellings built by individuals, regardless of the source of financing. Dwellings refer to premises intended for permanent habitation, physically independent of other premises and having an independent, direct access to a staircase, common place, hall or street. A dwelling may comprise, under one roof, one or several rooms, a corridor, kitchen, utility, a hall and a closet.

Total area of dwellings completed includes apartments and hotel-type accommodation, as well as dormitories. Total dwelling area comprises the living area and any ancillary premises such as the kitchen, corridor, closet, utility areas; in the case of hostels, ancillary premises may also include medical and cultural spaces. Verandas, loggias, terraces and balconies may be included in part, using a coefficient determined by the technical and economic indicators of the dwelling project. Dwelling area excludes entrance halls, staircases and common corridors.

Domestic trade

The value of *retail sales* is defined as the total value of consumer goods sold, including sales taxes, by retail trade and catering establishments or sold directly by industrial, transport and other enterprises. Both public and private outlets are included. Retail trade turnover includes sales of foodstuffs as well as non-food commodities to sanatoria, hospitals, childrens' and other institutions. The retail sales turnover also includes the revenue resulting from the sale of goods by catering co-operatives and commodities produced by individual work activity and sold through the general distribution network.

Retail trade data are collected directly from all enterprises selling consumer goods through specially established and officially licensed trade outlets, irrespective of the type of administration or ownership. Complete reporting by all retail outlets, kiosks and markets are taken into account every quarter.

 SHORT-TERM ECONOMIC INDICATORS, SOURCES AND DEFINITIONS   175   *INDICATEURS ÉCONOMIQUES A COURT TERME, SOURCES ET DÉFINITIONS*

OECD/CCET © April 1996   OCDE/CCET © avril 1996

UKRAINE

Until 1990 retail trade turnover included the revenues from some services rendered to households such as individual apparel manufacturing, repair of clothing and footwear or the repair of consumer durables. The share of these services in total turnover was approximately 2 per cent. Since 1991, these services have not been included in retail trade turnover.

Annual and quarterly retail trade turnover in some cases exceed the sum of the revenue in the corresponding quarters and months due to a wider coverage of trade enterprises.

Retail sales refer to the month and quarter during which goods are delivered, not when they are paid.

Retail sales value is expressed in roubles until November 1992 and in karbovanets thereafter. For more detailed information see the section on Domestic finance below and the chapter *Introduction of New Currencies*.

The index of *retail sales volume* is calculated by deflating retail trade turnover to constant prices. The value of retail turnover has been deflated by the retail price index (see Prices below). Until 1990, all price changes were regulated by the government. Since 1991, price indices are based on a sample of retail trade outlets.

Labour

Employment

Starting 1991, annual data for all *employment* series, except that for industry, include public sector, small business, co-operatives, joint ventures, kolkhoz, persons engaged in own-account agricultural production, and the semi-public/semi-co-operative sector. The quarterly data include only employees in the public sector and kolkhoz.

For *employment in industry*, data cover only the public sector which accounts for approximately 95 per cent of employment in this branch.

All branches of the national economy are included, whether involved in material or non-material activity.

The data are based on quarterly and annual reports concerning the labour force of enterprises, organisations and institutions. All enterprises, regardless of their type of ownership, are required to report on their labour force. This information is generally compared with similar data collected by tax agencies and state banks. The number of persons engaged in own-account agricultural production is estimated.

Part-time workers are recorded as full-time equivalents. Persons holding more than one job are recorded at their main place of work. Civil employees in military industrial complexes, persons on sick leave, apprentices, home contract workers and casual employees are included. Employees on maternity or child care leave are excluded.

Employment in material branches covers the following branches of the national economy:

-- industry;

-- agriculture, including own-account agricultural production;

-- forestry;

-- transport and communications, insofar as they service material branch activity;

-- trade, catering, material supply, procurement;

-- information and computing services;

-- other branches of material production including publishing and film production and distribution, waste and scrap processing, fishing, hunting, etc.

Employment in industry covers all employees engaged in industrial establishments in industrial enterprises as well as industrial establishments of enterprises included in other branches. Employees in non-industrial establishments of industrial enterprises are included in the branch to which the establishment belongs. The branch coverage is the same as that for the total IIP (see section on Industrial production above).

Employment in manufacturing represents the average number of workers and employees directly involved in the production process in manufacturing establishments. The branch coverage is the same as that for the IIP for manufacturing (see section on Industrial production above).

Unemployment

Total *registered unemployment* represents the number of persons registered as unemployed by state employment offices at the end of the month, in accordance with the legislation in Ukraine.

The legislation concerning unemployment came into force on 1 June 1991. In accordance with the legislation the state employment office takes decisions concerning the registration of an individual not more than eleven days after his/her application. Persons previously employed must present a passport, professional record book and earnings records of their last employer. New job seekers must present a passport and education certificates. Once registered, an individual remains registered until he/she finds work.

Able-bodied persons of working age (16-54 for women; 16-59 for men) are considered as unemployed, irrespective of the reasons for their not having gainful employment, provided they have no income from activity; have been duly recorded by a state employment office as seeking employment; are able and ready for any gainful activity; and have not received an appropriate employment proposal.

It is not compulsory for persons who have lost their jobs to register as unemployed. Persons seeking to change jobs, or part-time workers seeking full-time work are not considered as unemployed, but may register in the employment offices as seeking work.

Once registered as unemployed, unemployed persons are obliged to re-register periodically with the state employment office.

UKRAINE

Unemployment beneficiaries refer to those registered as unemployed and who have no other source of income. According to the Ukrainian legislation unemployed persons not eligible to be unemployment beneficiaries are:

-- those under the age of 16, except for persons who have already been employed and who have been dismissed owing to changes in the organisation of production and labour, the reorganisation or closure of a firm, institution or organisation, or the reduction in the number of employees.

-- those seeking work for the first time who are without a recognised vocational qualification, including school leavers, if they have refused to undergo a vocational training course or to take paid work, including temporary work.

-- those who have refused two suitable job offers since registering with the employment service as persons seeking work. In this case they lose the right to be designated unemployed for three months after they re-register.

-- persons who receive a pension under Ukrainian law.

Unemployment beneficiaries receive benefits from the eleventh day they are registered as unemployed. The maximum benefit period is one year.

For formerly employed persons unemployment benefits are no less than the minimum wage and at least 50 per cent of the average wage or salary paid by the former employer during the last 12 months of employment, up to a maximum equivalent to the average annual wage. For graduates who have registered as unemployed within one month of graduation, and for persons who have completed national service and registered within three months thereafter, unemployment benefits paid are not less than the minimum wage. For persons who lost their job due to work-place accidents or diseases and who require re-training, unemployment benefits represent 75 per cent of the average wage of the last job held for at least 6 months. For other persons, including those who are seeking a job for the first time or after a break of more than a year, unemployment benefits paid are not less than 75 per cent of the minimum wage.

Wages

Monthly earnings

The coverage of the data is the same as that for the quarterly employment data (see above).

Data relate to the average gross wage per employed person, calculated by dividing the total wage fund by the total number of employees. The wage fund includes payments such as health, food and travel allowances, payments in kind, efficiency-related bonuses, wage-indexation payments, payments for overtime and paid leave. Social security payments, however, are excluded.

Monthly earnings are expressed in roubles until November 1992 and in karbovanets thereafter. For more detailed information see the section on Domestic finance below and the chapter *Introduction of New Currencies*.

OECD
OCDE
SHORT-TERM ECONOMIC INDICATORS, SOURCES AND DEFINITIONS
OECD/CCET © April 1996

178

INDICATEURS ÉCONOMIQUES A COURT TERME, SOURCES ET DÉFINITIONS
OCDE/CCET © avril 1996

Prices

Wholesale prices

The *wholesale price index* (WPI) is calculated from prices of goods intended for the internal market collected by survey from 1 500 industrial firms for 6 200 representative items. Each month, firms supply the current prices and the prices of the previous month.

The WPI is a modified Laspeyres index. The weighting system used to calculate the total index between 1991 and 1993 is derived from the value of output for 1991, aggregated from data concerning industrial output by branches and sub-branches. For 1994 the weights are based on the total value of output in 1993.

The prices do not include taxes.

Owing to high inflation and very important structural changes in sales and production, some categories of products are replaced by others. Therefore, the annual figures cannot be recalculated by chaining the monthly prices. The Ministry of Statistics of Ukraine is presently composing a new basket of representative goods.

Consumer prices

1990-93

A monthly *retail price index* (RPI) was introduced in January 1991. Prices are observed for 1 200 representative commodities selected from all commodity groups included in retail trade data. Price quotations include taxes and were recorded each month in about 10 000 outlets throughout Ukraine, ranging from some of the biggest outlets selling a wide variety of commodities to small specialised outlets (bookstores, children's goods, etc.).

The indices reflect changes in prices in state, co-operative and private trade outlets, as well as in the prices of goods produced by co-operatives and individual working activity.

New products or services may be introduced into the index. The price of a new product or service in the previous month is estimated on the basis of the price of a similar product with similar characteristics. No adjustments are made for changes in product quality or for the scarcity of goods.

Prices of non-food goods are observed throughout the year, whether or not they follow a seasonal pattern. Seasonal food items, however, receive different weights in aggregated indices according to whether they are grown in a greenhouse and sold as early produce, or sold in season. With regard to services, some enterprises provide discounts for selected services during seasonal declines in demand. These discounts are reflected in price registration.

With regard to the *RPI for services*, price ratios were noted for 72 items, representative of the structure of sales of paid services to households.

UKRAINE

The RPI was a Paasche index with weights for regional and group aggregates based on the structure of retail trade in the current year. The published annual indices show the rate of change over the previous year. These figures cannot be derived from the monthly figures because Paasche indices are not transitive over a year. A chain of 12 monthly Paasche price indices ending in the current month does not generally equal the Paasche index for the current month against the same month of the previous year.

1994

Consumer price indices (CPI) are available from January 1994. These differ from the Retail price index for earlier periods.

The CPIs express monthly rates of change of goods and services prices, weighted by the structure of consumption expenditures of the population in 1993. The index is of the type modified Laspeyres. The following table shows the weights used:

Major groups	Weights
Goods	93
Food	47
Non-food	46
Services	7
TOTAL	100

Prices are collected between the tenth and the twenty-fifth day of each month for 300 items in 29 towns and 54 000 outlets covering all forms of ownership. The selection of outlets has been made by experts in the regional offices.

1995 and onwards

Starting from January 1995, the CPI is calculated using price observations for 345 goods and 80 services. Prices are observed between the first and twenty-fifth of each month in all cities and district centres in Ukraine.

The CPI is calculated as a modified Laspeyres index, using the structure of consumption expenditure of the population in the previous year as weights. The following table shows the weights of major groups according to the consumption structure of 1994:

Major groups	Weights
Goods	88
Food	65
Non-food	23
Services	12
TOTAL	100

Domestic finance

Personal deposits cover time and demand deposits, in karbovanets only, held in savings banks and are shown at the end of the period. Annual interest payments are included in the December, fourth quarter and yearly figures. From 1994, the series includes deposits with all commercial banks including the State commercial bank of Ukraine.

Personal deposits represent more than 99 per cent of the deposits in Ukraine.

Starting on 1 July 1993 personal deposits include a 40 per cent compensation payment for massive price rises. This payment was credited to the main deposit account.

Personal deposits are expressed in roubles until November 1992 and in karbovanets thereafter. For more information see the chapter *Introduction of New Currencies*.

Foreign finance

The official *US dollar exchange rate* of the karbovanets is quoted by the Ukrainian National Bank. This exchange rate refers to the end of the period.

Foreign trade

1990-91

Recording of *imports and exports* started in 1991. Foreign trade statistics for this period do not include trade with countries of the former Soviet Union.

Exports and imports were obtained from reports submitted by external trade organisations as well as from commodity customs declarations. Exports and imports were recorded on the date they crossed the border. Exports were valued FOB; imports were valued CIF. Bartered goods were valued at world market prices for similar goods.

Foreign trade data exclude material and non-material services and receipts from tourism. Exports of gold, silver and other precious metals and diamonds are in principle included, but are in practice not fully covered.

Re-exports and re-imports are registered only when goods enter the country.

1992-93

The foreign trade statistics were based on company accounts, harmonised with declared customs consignments. Foreign trade data did not include trade with countries of the former Soviet Union. Traded goods were classified according to the Harmonised System.

From the 12 January 1993, by Ministerial decree, foreign trade data excluded 200 products deemed necessities and which were considered non exportable (such as sugar, oil, petroleum). Transactions were included in the month in which the goods cross the border. Re-imports and re-exports were excluded.

UKRAINE

The statistics were converted into US dollars by the Ministry of Statistics of Ukraine.

1994 and onwards

From 1994, trade data broken into trade with countries of the former Soviet Union and trade with countries other than those of the former Soviet Union are available. Data are based on monthly reports from enterprises irrespective of type of ownership harmonised with declared customs consignments.

Export of the following goods was restricted from 1 November 1994:

-- cereals;

-- pig-iron;

-- coal:

-- waste and scrap of precious and semi-precious metals;

-- waste and scrap of ferrous and non-ferrous metals;

-- iron ores and concentrates of precious metals;

-- precious and semi-precious stones and metals, and products derived from them.

In 1995 the export restrictions were imposed only on exports of precious and semi-precious metals and their scrap.

Trade for 1994, including that with countries of the former Soviet Union, is estimated by type of good according to the classification of goods, based on the Harmonised System, introduced on the 1 January 1994. This covers approximately 5 000 items.

Exports are valued FOB; imports CIF.

Exported and imported goods are valued at the prices actually paid. Bartered goods are valued at world market prices for similar goods. Since 1 January 1995, the value of raw materials supplied by the customer for processing has been included in trade data.

Data are converted into US dollars by the Ministry of Statistics of Ukraine using the average monthly exchange rates calculated by the National Bank of Ukraine.

Trade in services is measured through reports from enterprises, organisations and institutions collected on a quarterly basis. Data are converted into US dollars by the Ministry of Statistics of Ukraine using the average quaretrly exchange rates calculated by the National Bank of Ukraine.

Gross capital formation

Total gross capital formation represents expenditure on new capital goods, as well as extensions, reconstruction and renovation of fixed assets in operation. The value of capital investments represents the cost of construction and installation, the purchase of equipment and tools, and expenditure on capital works.

Capital investment is valued at its original cost, i.e. the price at which it was purchased before deductions for fixed capital depreciation. Unfinished buildings and structures that have been paid for by contractors are included in capital investment; capital repair is excluded.

Projects are included, regardless of their financing: investment expenditures of state-owned enterprises and institutions, lease enterprises, consumer co-operatives and public organisations, co-operatives, collective farms, dwelling construction co-operatives and self-financed individual construction.

Data on investment expenditures are recorded at current prices and converted to 1984 constant prices, either based on data supplied by the enterprises or on the basis of price indices. The series for 1984-90 are based on data supplied by enterprises.

Gross capital formation in construction and installation includes work related to construction, expansion and reconstruction of buildings and structures, whether permanent or temporary, as well as installations of construction blocks and equipment.

Gross capital formation is expressed in the national currency, karbovanets.

Publications

Some of the series described above, but presented according to national practice, can be found in the Statistical Yearbooks and other publications of the Ministry of Statistics of Ukraine.

ASPECTS MÉTHODOLOGIQUES GÉNÉRAUX

Les statistiques établies par les pays d'Europe centrale et orientale (PECO) et les nouveaux États indépendants (NEI) nés de l'ex-Union soviétique ont toujours différé par leur contenu, leur mode de classification et leur méthodologie des données analogues disponibles dans les pays Membres de l'OCDE. Sauf à bien appréhender les approches de base utilisées, on risque de mal interpréter les données en question, car celles-ci ne se conforment pas aux schémas implicites qu'un analyste s'attend à rencontrer après avoir travaillé sur des données apparemment semblables en économie de marché développée. Dans cette section d'introduction, nous examinerons certaines des différences méthodologiques générales qu'il convient d'avoir à l'esprit lorsque l'on aborde les sections suivantes, consacrées aux différents pays.

Dans le passé, les offices statistiques des PECO et des NEI étaient étroitement intégrés au système de planification centrale. Les problèmes soulevés par l'étroite relation entre les statistiques et la planification centrale ont désormais disparu, mais, comme on le verra ci-dessous, le processus de transition a fait naître pour les statisticiens de ces pays un certain nombre de difficultés nouvelles.

Le secteur privé

Dans le passé, les statistiques des PECO et des NEI ne couvraient que les entreprises d'État et les coopératives, lesquelles représentaient, jusqu'à une période assez récente, l'ensemble de la production autorisée. A des dates diverses à partir de 1989, la création d'entreprises privées est devenue légale et le nombre des entreprises enregistrées a augmenté de façon spectaculaire dans de nombreux pays ; on y compte quelques grandes sociétés internationales qui se sont attirées une audience internationale, mais surtout de nombreuses petites entreprises privées.

L'observation de l'activité du secteur privé se révèle l'une des tâches les plus difficiles pour les offices statistiques des PECO et des NEI. Autrefois, le registre des entreprises autorisées était relativement petit, avec des spécifications claires. Les enquêtes statistiques étaient généralement des recensements à caractère obligatoire. Avec l'explosion du nombre des entreprises, la création et la mise à jour du registre des entreprises sont devenues des tâches de grande ampleur, avec lesquelles les offices statistiques de ces pays sont peu familiarisés. A mesure que le registre grossit, il faut mettre au point des procédures d'échantillonnage afin de collecter les données par sondage et non plus par recensement, les déclarations étant volontaires et non plus obligatoires.

Il faut aussi concevoir des méthodes d'estimation pour les non réponses afin de couvrir les entreprises qui devraient se trouver sur le registre mais ne s'y trouvent pas, celles qui auraient dû répondre au questionnaire mais ne l'ont pas fait et celles qui ont été délibérément exclues de l'enquête. Ces problèmes sont d'autant plus complexes qu'il arrive souvent qu'une entreprise soit enregistrée, mais qu'aucune activité ne s'y exerce ou que l'activité qui se met effectivement en place soit très limitée et ne constitue pas la principale source de revenu de l'entrepreneur concerné. Il est plus difficile de rayer ces entreprises du registre que de les y inscrire.

Il faudra du temps pour mettre en oeuvre de façon complète et efficace ces innovations importantes. C'est pourquoi, en attendant, certaines séries ne couvrent encore que le secteur étatique et coopératif, le secteur privé étant tout simplement omis. L'étendue des omissions varie suivant la période, le pays et le secteur.

Classifications

Les classifications utilisées dans les publications de l'OCDE sont celles qui ont été mises au point par les Nations Unies à l'intention des économies de marché. En particulier, les statistiques industrielles se conforment à la Classification internationale type, par industrie, de toutes les branches d'activité économique (CITI), le commerce extérieur est classé selon la Classification type pour le commerce international (CTCI) et les comptes nationaux suivent le Système de comptabilité nationale (SCN).

Tous les PECO et les NEI utilisaient, par le passé, la Classification des branches de l'économie nationale élaborée par le Conseil d'assistance économique mutuelle (CAEM). Si le mode de ventilation était à peu près semblable à celui des économies de marché, il n'y en avait pas moins de nombreuses différences au niveau plus détaillé. On en a une illustration classique avec la distinction entre industries minières ou extractives et industries manufacturières dans l'un et l'autre systèmes. Supposons qu'un pays ait un gisement de minerai de fer qui est extrait et transformé en feuilles de métal. Dans la CITI, le processus d'extraction est classé comme une activité minière et le processus de transformation comme une activité manufacturière. Dans la classification du CAEM, les deux processus sont considérés comme un tout et classés ensemble comme activité manufacturière. Cela signifie que, dans la classification du CAEM, les activités minières se réduisent généralement à l'exploitation du charbon et de matériaux de faible valeur comme le sable et la pierre.

Des différences comme celles-là relèvent non seulement de divergences philosophiques mais aussi de considérations pragmatiques. Étant donné que, souvent, dans les PECO et les NEI, la même entreprise assure l'extraction et la transformation du minerai, une distinction entre ces deux activités au niveau comptable n'aurait pu être qu'artificielle.

Les classifications des Nations Unies sont introduites dans cette publication dès qu'elles sont mises régulièrement en oeuvre dans le pays concerné.

Production secondaire

La plupart des entreprises manufacturières fabriquent plus d'un produit, ce qui nécessite un choix de base : mesurer la production de l'ensemble de l'entreprise ou seulement de son principal produit. Dans les pays Membres de l'OCDE, on considère souvent que la production du produit principal est représentative de la production de l'ensemble de l'entreprise. Dans les industries manufacturières, la production secondaire d'autres produits manufacturés devrait quand même être intégrée à la production de produits manufacturés. Par ailleurs, il n'est pas rare que des industries manufacturières produisent des produits non manufacturés, par exemple des constructions ou des services de transport.

Selon la classification des Nations Unies, ces activités sont quand même comptées dans les industries manufacturières ; dans la classification du CAEM, elles figureront toujours en tant que construction, transports, etc. Dans la pratique, cette production est généralement couverte dans les statistiques de longue période mais pas dans les statistiques à court terme.

Services

Les PECO et les NEI ne se sont jamais autant intéressés aux services que les pays Membres de l'OCDE. Dans le système de comptabilité du produit matériel, on faisait une distinction entre les services dits matériels et les services dits immatériels. Les premiers étaient considérés comme une extension du processus de production et englobaient, par exemple, la réparation et le transport des biens. Des services tels que la santé, l'enseignement, les activités culturelles, la défense et les administrations étaient classés comme services immatériels et exclus de la mesure de la production. Par conséquent, dans beaucoup de domaines, la production ne couvre que l'agriculture, les industries extractives, les industries manufacturières, l'électricité, le gaz, l'eau et la construction. On notera toutefois que les pays Membres de l'OCDE ont eux aussi, pendant bien longtemps, mis l'accent sur la production de biens et que ce n'est que récemment que l'importance des services, et la difficulté d'en mesurer avec précision les performances, sont apparues au premier rang de leurs préoccupations en matière statistique.

Période de référence

Il est d'usage dans les pays Membres de l'OCDE de demander aux entreprises d'indiquer leur chiffre de vente ou de production concernant, par exemple, le mois précédent. Très souvent, dans les anciens pays du CAEM, la pratique était de demander les chiffres concernant les douze mois écoulés, puis de calculer les données mensuelles par soustraction des chiffres déclarés précédemment. Il en découlait parfois des erreurs pour la période de déclaration de l'activité, du fait que les erreurs précédentes n'étaient pas explicitement corrigées mais que les corrections étaient simplement incorporées au nouveau total cumulé.

Cette pratique introduisait un biais, au moins dans les statistiques de production, du fait que les données étaient utilisées pour suivre les objectifs de production. Ces objectifs étaient exprimés en chiffres trimestriels et annuels, et de nombreuses séries font apparaître un gonflement en mars, juin et septembre et surtout en décembre. Une des explications données est que, pendant les mois intermédiaires, les déclarations accumulaient un retard que l'on se dépêchait de rattraper avant la fin du trimestre, d'où la présence d'une composante saisonnière apparemment importante dans un certain nombre de séries.

Indices de prix et de volume

Dans le passé, les prix dans les PECO et les NEI étaient officiellement fixés par les autorités centrales. En fait, les prix de transaction étaient sans doute plus élevés en raison de l'existence du marché noir et d'autres canaux informels. Cependant, les prix utilisés pour l'établissement des indices de prix officiels étaient les prix fixés par les autorités centrales.

Un problème soulevé par le calcul de ces indices et commun à tous les pays est celui du traitement des changements de qualité. Si une nouvelle version d'un produit apparaît, avec des caractéristiques supplémentaires et un prix plus élevé, une partie de l'augmentation de prix peut être attribuée aux caractéristiques nouvelles, de sorte que l'augmentation réelle intégrée dans l'indice des prix est inférieure au renchérissement apparent. Dans le passé, les PECO et les NEI attribuaient au changement de qualité une part de l'augmentation de prix plus grande que ne le justifiait l'amélioration du produit. Quand des mesures en volume, telles que les indices de production, étaient calculées en divisant les chiffres de volume courants par les indices de prix, la sous-estimation des prix entraînait une surestimation des volumes. Étant donné que l'on n'a que des observations ponctuelles de cette pratique, il n'est pas possible de quantifier cette distorsion et les données ne sont donc pas corrigées sur ce point.

Les indices de volume sont calculés en utilisant des informations sur les prix et les volumes. Il est théoriquement possible de calculer deux types d'indices. Les différences entre les deux types d'indice de volume peuvent être décrites en utilisant par exemple, le calcul d'un indice de volume de production. Le premier indice, pondéré par les données de la période de base (indice de Laspeyres), rapporte la production courante aux prix de l'année de base, à la production de l'année de base, aux prix de l'année de base. Le deuxième indice, qui est un indice de Paasche, rapporte la production de la période courante aux prix courants, à la production de l'année de base, évaluée aux prix courants. L'inconvénient de l'indice de Paasche, est que, si l'on peut comparer le chiffre de chaque période à celui de la période de base, les comparaisons entre deux autres périodes ne reflètent pas avec exactitude la variation entre les deux périodes. Les indices de Laspeyres permettant des comparaisons valides entre deux périodes quelconques, ce sont ceux qui sont le plus souvent utilisés dans les pays Membres de l'OCDE et dans les publications de l'OCDE. Les PECO et les NEI sont de plus en plus nombreux à en faire autant et les comparaisons entre différentes périodes de l'année deviennent donc possibles.

Chômage

Dans les économies à planification centrale, on ne mesurait pas le chômage. Au début de la période de transition, il est apparu nécessaire de mettre en place des services de l'emploi et des bureaux de chômage. Contrairement à la plupart des pays Membres de l'OCDE, de nombreux PECO et NEI ne procédaient pas à des enquêtes de population active. Il existe maintenant dans tous les pays en transition des services de l'emploi qui réunissent des informations sur le nombre de chômeurs inscrits et dans certaines circonstances, distribuent les prestations de chômage. Beaucoup de ces pays mettent aussi en place des enquêtes de population active réalisées auprès des ménages. Comme c'est le cas dans nombre de pays Membres de l'OCDE, l'écart entre le nombre des chômeurs inscrits auprès des services de l'emploi et le chômage mesuré par les enquêtes auprès des ménages peut être important.

Nombreux sont les chômeurs qui ne se font pas enregistrer, et ce pour de nombreuses raisons. Dans la pratique, les services de l'emploi ont souvent peu d'offres d'emploi à proposer. Le nombre des chômeurs inscrits sous-estime sans doute le chômage car les personnes qui n'ont plus droit à des allocations ou celles qui ne percevraient qu'une très faible indemnisation omettent souvent de s'inscrire et ne figurent donc pas dans les chiffres officiels. Ce problème, que connaissent aussi les pays Membres de l'OCDE, est probablement aggravé dans les pays en transition, où il se peut que les services de l'emploi n'aient pas encore été mis en place ou ne soient pas facilement accessibles en toutes régions.

On observe aussi le phénomène du sous-emploi "forcé". Certaines entreprises ont une production sporadique liée à des interruptions d'approvisionnement en matières premières ou à l'accumulation de stocks trop importants. Dans certains cas, les salariés travaillent et sont payés, moins qu'un temps plein (ou, dans certains cas, pas du tout), mais continuent à figurer sur les registres de l'entreprise.

Commerce extérieur

Jusqu'à la libéralisation des échanges, seules des entreprises ayant reçu une autorisation spéciale pouvaient importer et exporter des biens et des services dans les PECO et les NEI. Les données sur ces transactions étaient donc recueillies directement auprès des entreprises en question. A des dates diverses à partir de 1989, de nombreux PECO et NEI ont commencé à établir des statistiques du commerce extérieur à partir des déclarations douanières. De plus, et généralement en parallèle avec le passage à l'exploitation des données douanières, un système de classification internationale type catégorisant les échanges par article a été introduit. Dans un certain nombre de cas, les changements dans la couverture et le calendrier sont tels que les séries temporelles sont affectées de ruptures très importantes.

L'introduction de nouvelles monnaies nationales

Dans de nombreux PECO et NEI, notamment dans les pays de l'ex-Union soviétique, une nouvelle monnaie nationale a été créée peu après l'accession à l'indépendance politique. Dans certains cas, une monnaie provisoire a été introduite, avant d'être remplacée quelques temps plus tard par la nouvelle monnaie. La nouvelle monnaie était souvent émise à parité fixe avec le rouble, ou la monnaie provisoire, durant la période de conversion. Dans certains cas, cette parité diffère de celle que l'on obtient en comparant les taux de change de la nouvelle monnaie et du rouble par rapport au dollar ou à d'autres devises extérieures.

Pour plus de précisions, voir le chapitre *Introduction de nouvelles monnaies.*

Enquêtes de conjoncture

Les enquêtes de conjoncture permettent de recueillir les opinions des dirigeants d'entreprises sur la situation économique présente et future de leur société. Les données collectées à cette occasion sont généralement considérées comme "qualitatives" par opposition aux données quantitatives recueillies lors des enquêtes statistiques classiques. Ce type d'enquête, qui existe dans tous les pays Membres de l'OCDE, s'avère être un précieux outil d'information sur la situation présente des entreprises et leur évolution probable dans le proche avenir.

Le Centre pour la coopération avec les économies en transition s'est associé avec Eurostat pour mettre au point un programme d'enquêtes de conjoncture dans la plupart des pays en transition.

Correction des variations saisonnières

Comme dans les pays Membres de l'OCDE, on peut observer dans de nombreuses séries un important élément saisonnier lié aux variations saisonnières de la demande, aux jours fériés, aux variations climatiques, etc. Dans la mesure où l'on observe ces facteurs de saisonnalité, on peut désaisonnaliser les séries pour comparer les volumes d'une période de l'année à l'autre. L'OCDE a fourni, à un certain nombre de pays, l'assistance technique nécessaire pour effectuer ces ajustements, et d'autres aides techniques de cette nature sont envisagées.

Séries disponibles

Les séries publiées dans les *Indicateurs économiques à court terme : Économies en transition* sont à peu près semblables à celles des *Principaux indicateurs économiques* de l'OCDE. Pour le plus grand nombre de séries possible, les données sont présentées sur une base mensuelle, trimestrielle et annuelle. Dans certains cas, les données trimestrielles et annuelles sont dérivées directement des observations mensuelles. Dans d'autres, cependant, les données relatives aux périodes plus longues ont une couverture plus étendue. Par exemple, les données mensuelles peuvent couvrir les entreprises de plus de cent salariés, les données trimestrielles celles de plus de cinquante salariés, alors que les données annuelles s'efforcent de couvrir toutes les entreprises. La conséquence de cet élargissement de la couverture est que les données à longue périodicité ne sont disponibles que plus tard.

Une autre implication de la couverture différente des enquêtes est que le total dérivé des données mensuelles et trimestrielles peut différer de celui des relevés annuels.

Sources

En ce qui concerne les pays d'Europe centrale et orientale, les données sont fournies à l'OCDE par les offices statistiques et les banques centrales des pays concernés, bien qu'elles ne soient pas toujours présentées sous la même forme que dans les publications nationales. La Commission statistique inter-états de la Communauté des états indépendants fournit les données pour la plupart de ses pays membres. Certains pays toutefois, préfèrent fournir directement leurs données à l'OCDE.

OECD
OCDE
SHORT-TERM ECONOMIC INDICATORS, SOURCES AND DEFINITIONS
OECD/CCET © April 1996

190

INDICATEURS ÉCONOMIQUES A COURT TERME, SOURCES ET DÉFINITIONS
OCDE/CCET © avril 1996

INTRODUCTION DE NOUVELLES MONNAIES

De nouvelles monnaies ont été introduites en Estonie, en Lettonie, en Lituanie ainsi que dans les NEI, peu de temps après leur accession à l'indépendance politique. Dans un certain nombre de cas, une monnaie provisoire a d'abord été utilisée pour être remplacée peu de temps après par une seconde monnaie. Lors de l'introduction de ces nouvelles monnaies, un facteur de conversion interne entre la nouvelle et l'ancienne monnaie a été utilisé officiellement par les banques pour le calcul, par exemple, des salaires dans la nouvelle monnaie. Ces facteurs de conversion internes sont indiqués ci-après.

Pour les séries exprimées en monnaie nationale, ces facteurs de conversion ont également été utilisés par les instituts statistiques pour recalculer les chiffres mensuels et/ou trimestriels pour l'année au cours de laquelle est intervenu le changement de monnaie.

Quand les nouvelles monnaies ont été introduites, de nouveaux taux de change pour les monnaies ont été publiés. Un facteur de conversion implicite peut être calculé en comparant le taux de change officiel de la nouvelle monnaie contre le dollar, avec le taux de change du rouble. Dans la plupart des cas ce taux implicite est nettement différent du taux interne, parce que, bien que le rouble soit coté à un niveau proche de celui du marché dans la plupart, sinon dans tous les pays, un marché noir se développe pour la majorité des nouvelles monnaies. Il est alors très difficile de combiner les données du commerce extérieur (en dehors de l'ancienne zone rouble, souvent les seules données disponibles) pour des périodes différentes de part et d'autre de la date d'introduction de la nouvelle monnaie et encore plus difficile de convertir ces données en ou depuis des monnaies internationales.

La République tchèque et la République slovaque ont également changé leur monnaie depuis qu'ils sont devebus deux États indépendants. Chacun a introduit sa propre couronne, qui a remplacé la couronne tchécoslovaque le 1er janvier 1993. Grâce à cette date d'introduction, il n'y a aucun problème d'agrégation pour les trimestres et les années. D'autre part, comme la nouvelle couronne a été introduite à un taux de 1:1 avec l'ancienne couronne, et que celle-ci a atteint un niveau proche de celui du marché, aucun facteur arithmétique de conversion de données sur l'ancienne base n'est nécessaire. La différence entre les deux monnaies depuis janvier 1993 est reflétée dans leur taux de change respectif avec les autres monnaies.

Une situation similaire existe en République de Slovénie. Quand la Slovénie est devenue un État indépendant le 8 Octobre 1991, une nouvelle monnaie, le tolar, a été introduite. Cette monnaie a été introduite à un taux de conversion de 1:1 avec le dinar yougoslave.

En Pologne, une nouvelle dénomination du zloty a été introduite le 1er janvier 1995, le nouveau zloty équivalant à 10 000 anciens zlotys.

OECD
OCDE *SHORT-TERM ECONOMIC INDICATORS, SOURCES AND DEFINITIONS*
OECD/CCET © April 1996

191

INDICATEURS ÉCONOMIQUES A COURT TERME, SOURCES ET DÉFINITIONS
OCDE/CCET © avril 1996

Pays	Monnaie	Date d'introduction	Facteur de conversion
Arménie	Dram	22 novembre 1993	1:200
Azerbaïdjan	Manat [1]	15 août 1992	1:10
Bélarus	Ancien rouble bélarus	26 juillet 1993	1:1
	Nouveau rouble bélarus [2]	20 août 1994	1:10
Estonie	Couronne	20 juin 1992	1:10
Kazakstan	Tenge	15 novembre 1993	1:500
République kirghize	Som	10 mai 1993	1:200
Lettonie	Rouble letton [3]	7 mai 1992	1:1
	Lat	5 mars 1993	1:200
Lituanie	Talonas [3]	1er octobre 1992	1:1
	Litas	25 juin 1993	1:100
République de Moldova	Leu	29 novembre 1993	1:1000
Fédération de Russie	Nouveau rouble	26 juillet 1993	1:1
Tadjikistan	Nouveau rouble	26 juillet 1993	1:1
	Rouble tadjik	10 mai 1995	1:100
Turkménistan	Manat	1er novembre 1993	1:500
Ukraine	Karbovanets	16 novembre 1992	1:1
Ouzbékistan	Sum-coupon	15 novembre 1993	1:1
	Sum	27 juin 1994	1:1000

1. Seul moyen de paiement depuis le 1er janvier 1994.
2. Une nouvelle dénomination du rouble bélarus a été introduite le 20 août 1994, le nouveau rouble bélarus équivalant à 10 anciens roubles bélarus.
3. Monnaie provisoire.

TABLEAUX MÉTHODOLOGIQUES RÉCAPITULATIFS

On trouvera dans les tableaux qui suivent un résumé comparatif des méthodes utilisées pour le calcul des indicateurs à court terme suivants : les indices de production industrielle, les ventes de détail en volume, le chômage, les indices de prix à la production, les indices de prix à la consommation et le commerce extérieur. Une case vide indique l'absence d'information et non pas une réponse négative.

Toutes les informations contenues dans ces tableaux ainsi que des précisions complémentaires, figurent dans les chapitres par pays.

OECD
OCDE
SHORT-TERM ECONOMIC INDICATORS, SOURCES AND DEFINITIONS
OECD/CCET © April 1996

193

INDICATEURS ÉCONOMIQUES A COURT TERME, SOURCES ET DÉFINITIONS
OCDE/CCET © avril 1996

INDICE DE LA PRODUCTION INDUSTRIELLE TOTALE

Pays	L'"industrie" couvre les industries extractives, plus :			Couverture du secteur privé?	Couverture de l'enquête
	Industries manufacturières	Gaz, eau, électricité	Autres		
BULGARIE	Sauf édition.	Sauf la production, l'assainissement et la distribution d'eau froide.	Sylviculture et pêche.	En indice annuel uniquement.	Les enquêtes mensuelles et trimestrielles couvrent environ 3.000 entreprises d'État et coopératives représentant 91,3% de la production industrielle en 1994.
ESTONIE	Oui.	Sauf distribution de gaz, énergie thermique et eau à usage domestique.		Toutes les entreprises de plus de 20 salariés, annuellement. Et, toutes les entreprises de plus de 50 salariés, mensuellement.	Depuis 1994, les enquêtes annuelles couvrent toutes les entreprises du secteur non privé de plus de 20 salariés. Les enquêtes mensuelles couvrent toutes les entreprises de plus de 50 salariés, représentant environ 85% des ventes industrielles.
HONGRIE	Oui.	Oui.		Depuis 1994, les entreprises de plus de 10 salariés sont couvertes; les autres sont estimées.	A partir de 1994, l'enquête par sondage couvre les entreprises de 11 à 50 salariés; pour les entreprises de plus de 50 salariés, il s'agit d'un recensement. Des estimations sont effectuées pour les entreprises de moins de 10 salariés.
LETTONIE	Oui.	La distribution d'eau est incluse depuis 1995 dans les enquêtes mensuelles.		Entreprises de plus de 50 salariés.	Depuis 1991, les enquêtes mensuelles couvrent 90% de la production (toutes les entreprises privées de plus de 50 salariés, plus toutes les entreprises publiques). Les enquêtes annuelles couvrent l'ensemble de la production.
LITUANIE	Oui.	Oui, depuis janvier 1994.		Depuis janvier 1995, entreprises de plus de 20 salariés.	L'enquête mensuelle couvre 600 entreprises et les ventes de plus de 1.100 produits industriels. On estime que la production totale est couverte à 90%.

La "production" couvre :					
Variations des stocks de produits finis	Variations de productions en cours	Production autre que principale	Type d'indice	Type de données sur les produits	Pondération / déflateurs utilisés
Oui.	Oui.	Depuis 1995, uniquement.	Laspeyres.	En volume.	Indice des prix à la production (IPP).
Non.	Non.	Non.		Valeur des ventes depuis 1994.	Les données en valeur sont déflatées par le Secrétariat de l'OCDE à l'aide de l'indice des prix à la production en base 1993=100.
Oui.	Oui.	Non.	Paasche.	En valeur.	L'indice des prix à la production (IPP).
Oui.	Oui.	Oui.	Laspeyres, à partir de 1995.	En valeur.	Prix de janvier 1992.
Non.	Non.	Non.		En volume.	L'indice des prix à la production (IPP).

INDICE DE LA PRODUCTION INDUSTRIELLE TOTALE

Pays	L'"industrie" couvre les industries extractives, plus :			Couverture du secteur privé?	Couverture de l'enquête
	Industries manufacturières	Gaz, eau, électricité	Autres		
POLOGNE	Oui.	Oui. Avant 1994, la production, l'épuration et la distribution d'eau sont exclues.		Oui, après 1991.	Depuis 1991, toutes les entreprises de plus de 50 salariés sont couvertes et un échantillon de 10% est tiré pour les entreprises de 6 à 50 salariés. 5% des entreprises de moins de 5 salariés sont couvertes dans l'enquête annuelle.
RÉPUBLIQUE DE SLOVÉNIE	Excepté l'édition.	La distribution de gaz, de vapeur et d'eau est exclue.		Toutes les entreprises privées de plus de 5 salariés.	Toutes les entreprises publiques et toutes les entreprises privées de plus de 5 salariés, représentant 1.800 entreprises en 1994.
ROUMANIE	Oui.	Oui.		Oui.	L'enquête couvre 1.030 produits et groupes de produits.
RÉPUBLIQUE SLOVAQUE	A l'exception de l'édition jusqu'à la fin de 1991.	Oui (y compris la production et la distribution d'eau à partir de 1991).		Oui, sont couvertes les entreprises figurant au registre du commerce.	Depuis 1992, les entreprises > 24 salariés. Depuis 1993, les entreprises < 25 salariés sont enquêtées chaque trimestre, et servent à réviser les estimations mensuelles; des estimations sont aussi incluses pour les entrepreneurs individuels depuis 1993.
ARMÉNIE, BÉLARUS, RÉPUBLIQUE KIRGHIZE, RÉPUBLIQUE DE MOLDOVA, TADJIKISTAN, TURKMÉNISTAN, OUZBÉKISTAN	Excepté l'imprimerie et l'édition.	Oui.	Y compris l'exploitation forestière et la pêche, les services de nettoyage, la réparation et l'entretien des véhicules à moteur et la réparation des biens personnels et domestiques.	Oui.	Arménie: 800 entreprises; Bélarus: 1.800 entreprises; Rép. Kirghize: 500 entreprises; Rép. de Moldova & Tadjikistan & Turkménistan: 400 entreprises; et Ouzbékistan: 2.000 entreprises.

La "production" couvre :					
Variations des stocks de produits finis	Variations de productions en cours	Production autre que principale	Type d'indice	Type de données sur les produits	Pondération / déflateurs utilisés
Uniquement dans les séries annuelles.	Oui.	Non.	Laspeyres.	En valeur.	Les prix de 1984 sont utilisés comme déflateur des données de 1985-90; les prix de 1990 pour déflater les données de 1991-93; les prix de 1992 pour déflater les données depuis 1994.
Oui.	Oui.	Oui.	Laspeyres.	Volume exprimé en quantités (tonnes, nombre de pièces, etc.).	Valeur des ventes facturées en 1993 pondérées par leur part dans la valeur ajoutée.
Non.	Non.		Laspeyres.	En volume.	Valeur ajoutée brute de 1991.
Oui.	Oui.	Non.	Laspeyres.	En valeur.	L'indice des prix à la production (IPP), depuis 1991.
Non.	Oui, pour les produits ayant un cycle de production long.	Oui.	Laspeyres.	En volume.	Prix au 1er janvier 1982 pour les données de 1980-1990 et prix de janvier de l'année en cours par la suite. Prix du mois en cours pour la République Kirghize et le Turkménistan depuis 1992.

SHORT-TERM ECONOMIC INDICATORS, SOURCES AND DEFINITIONS
OECD/CCET © April 1996

197

INDICATEURS ÉCONOMIQUES A COURT TERME, SOURCES ET DÉFINITIONS
OCDE/CCET © avril 1996

OECD
OCDE

INDICE DE LA PRODUCTION INDUSTRIELLE TOTALE

Pays	L'"industrie" couvre les industries extractives, plus :			Couverture du secteur privé?	Couverture de l'enquête
	Industries manufacturières	**Gaz, eau, électricité**	**Autres**		
AZERBAÏDJAN, KAZAKSTAN, FÉDÉRATION DE RUSSIE	Excepté l'imprimerie et l'édition.	Oui.	Y compris l'exploitation forestière et la pêche, les services de nettoyage, la réparation et l'entretien des véhicules à moteur et la réparation des biens personnels et domestiques.	Oui.	Azerbaïdjan: 1.000 entreprises couvertes concernant 300 produits; Kazakstan: 2.500 entreprises couvertes concernant 400 produits; Fédération de Russie: 24.000 entreprises couvertes concernant 430 produits.
UKRAINE	Excepté l'édition.	Oui.	Y compris l'exploitation forestière et la pêche, les services de nettoyage, la réparation et l'entretien des véhicules à moteur et la réparation des biens personnels et domestiques.	Oui.	L'enquête couvre 90.000 entreprises concernant 500 produits.

| La "production" couvre : | | | Type d'indice | Type de données sur les produits | Pondération / déflateurs utilisés |
Variations des stocks de produits finis	Variations de productions en cours	Production autre que principale			
Non.	Oui, pour les produits ayant un cycle de production long.	Oui.	Laspeyres.	En volume.	Prix au 1er janvier 1982 pour les données de 1980-1990 et prix de janvier de l'année en cours par la suite. Moyenne pondérée des variations en volume pour la Fédération de Russie depuis 1993 et pour l'Azerbaïdjan et le Kazakstan depuis 1994.
Non.	Oui.	Oui.	Paasche.	En valeur.	Prix de gros de janvier 1989.

VENTES DE DÉTAIL EN VOLUME

Pays	Couverture de l'enquête des ventes de détail	Groupes ou articles non inclus	Prix utilisé comme déflateur	Année de base des prix
BULGARIE	Depuis 1996, l'enquête couvre 30% des points de vente du secteur public et 1,5% du secteur privé, ce qui correspond à 90% et 50% respectivement des ventes de ces unités.		Les données en valeur sont déflatées par le Secrétariat de l'OCDE à l'aide de l'indice des prix à la consommation: biens.	Prix de 1992.
ESTONIE	Depuis 1993, commerces de détail de plus de 20 salariés et commerces de détail d'État sont enquêtés. Pour tous les autres commerces, un échantillon est utilisé (600 commerces de détail).	Restauration publique.	Indice des prix de détail.	Prix de 1992.
HONGRIE	Population visée: tous les commerces de détail et les établissements de restauration.	Articles vendus directement aux consommateurs par les entreprises productrices.	Indice des prix de détail.	Prix de janvier 1991.
LETTONIE	Depuis 1995, toutes les entreprises commerciales du secteur public et les entreprises dont le chiffre d'affaires annuel dépasse 100.000 lats, et 10% des autres entreprises sont couvertes par l'enquête.	Restauration publique.	Prix à la consommation: biens.	Prix de janvier 1991.
LITUANIE	Tous les points de vente du secteur public et du secteur privé de plus de 5 salariés.	Ventes sur les marchés et ventes des petites entreprises.	Prix à la consommation.	Prix de mai 1992.
POLOGNE	Les ventes des entreprises de moins de 5 salariés sont comprises dans les données annuelles uniquement.	Ventes du secteur agricole et ventes du secteur public au secteur privé.	Les données en valeur sont déflatées par le Secrétariat de l'OCDE à l'aide de l'indice des prix à la consommation: biens.	Prix de 1992.
RÉPUBLIQUE DE SLOVÉNIE	Les principaux points de vente de détail couvrant 50% du chiffre d'affaires total des ventes de détail.	Produits vendus directement par les producteurs aux consommateurs sur les marchés alimentaires.	Indice des prix de détail: biens.	Prix de 1992.
ROUMANIE	3.000 points de vente des secteurs public, privé, coopératif et d'économie mixte.	Restauration publique; produits agricoles vendus par les particuliers; electricité et gaz.	Indice des prix de détail.	Le mois précédent.

VENTES DE DÉTAIL EN VOLUME

Pays	Couverture de l'enquête des ventes de détail	Groupes ou articles non inclus	Prix utilisé comme déflateur	Année de base des prix
RÉPUBLIQUE SLOVAQUE	Depuis 1996, les points de vente de plus de 20 salariés sont enquêtés mensuellement.		Les données en valeur sont déflatées par le Secrétariat de l'OCDE à l'aide de l'indice des prix à la consommation: biens.	Prix du 1er janvier 1989.
N.E.I. SAUF L'UKRAINE	Entreprises vendant des biens de consommation quel que soit le type de propriété. Depuis 1995, une nouvelle série est disponible pour la plupart des pays couvrant les ventes par les entreprises non inscrites et par les personnes sur les marchés informels.	Depuis 1991, les services.	Pour l'Arménie, le Bélarus et la Fédération de Russie: Indice des prix à la consommation: "biens". Pour tous les autres pays: Indice des prix de détail.	Prix de la période correspondante de l'année précédente.
UKRAINE	Toutes les entreprises vendant des biens de consommation.	Depuis 1991, les services.	Indice des prix de détail.	Prix de la période précédente.

OECD
OCDE   *SHORT-TERM ECONOMIC INDICATORS, SOURCES AND DEFINITIONS*
        OECD/CCET © April 1996

201

INDICATEURS ÉCONOMIQUES A COURT TERME, SOURCES ET DÉFINITIONS
OCDE/CCET © avril 1996

CHÔMAGE

Pays	Âge actif	Conditions d'inscription au chômage	Taux de chômage = nb de chômeurs [1] en % de :	Conditions d'ouverture des droits à allocation
BULGARIE	15-54 ans (femmes) 15-59 (hommes).	Personnes ayant travaillé pendant 8 mois, ou diplômés de l'enseignement secondaire, ou personnes inscrites dans un établissement post-scolaire pendant au moins un mois.	Population active totale.	Chômeurs inscrits sans autre source de gains.
ESTONIE	16-56,5 ans (femmes) 16-61,5 (hommes)[2]	Résidents permanents ayant travaillé ou eu une activité équivalant à un travail pendant au moins 180 jours au cours des 12 derniers mois et qui cherche activement du travail.	Population d'âge actif (données de l'Office national du travail).	Chômeurs inscrits dont les revenus sont inférieurs aux indemnités de chômage versées par l'État.
HONGRIE	15-54 ans (femmes) 15-59 (hommes).	Personnes disponibles pour travailler et cherchant un emploi; les étudiants et les retraités ne peuvent être inscrits comme chômeurs.	Population active totale au 1er janvier de l'année précédente.	Personnes ayant cotisé aux caisses de chômage pendant au moins 360 jours au cours des 4 années précédant la période de chômage. Étudiants ayant obtenu leur diplôme au cours des 18 derniers mois.
LETTONIE	15-54 ans (femmes) 15-59 (hommes).	Résidents sans travail en âge de travailler qui ne reçoivent pas de revenus au moins égal au salaire minimum et recherchant activement un emploi, n'exerçant pas d'activité d'entrepreneur indépendant. Nouveaux diplômés ou personnes libérées de prison.	Population active totale.	Tout chômeur inscrit. Non accordée aux personnes ayant volontairement quitté leur travail ou ayant été licenciées pour raisons disciplinaires ou pour rupture de contrat.
LITUANIE	16-55 ans (femmes) 16-60 (hommes).	Toutes les personnes sans travail, qui peuvent prouver qu'elles en cherchent, y compris les nouveaux diplômés et les personnes qui n'ont jamais travaillé ou ont volontairement quitté leur emploi.	Population active totale de l'année précédente.	Chômeurs inscrits ayant travaillé au moins 24 mois au cours des 3 dernières années, nouveaux diplômés et personnes revenant du service militaire ou sortant de prison.
POLOGNE	18-60 ans (femmes) 18-65 (hommes).	Ne reçoit pas de pension vieillesse ou invalidité, ne possède pas de ferme, n'a pas d'activité économique agricole, n'est pas en prison, n'a pas droit aux assurances sociales, y compris les personnes handicapées pouvant travailler au moins à mi-temps.	Population active civile durant la période courante.	Chômeur inscrit ayant travaillé au moins 180 jours au cours des 12 derniers mois, à compter du jour d'enregistrement. N'ayant pas eu de proposition d'offre d'emploi convenable, de formation, de travail d'utilité collective, d'emploi temporaire.

Période minimale d'inactivité avant versement des allocations	Période maximale d'indemnisation	L'allocataire perd ses droits si :	Montant des allocations
	1 an. Pour les nouveaux diplômés: 3 mois.	Il ne pointe pas régulièrement.	Proportionnel au dernier salaire.
10 jours.	Variable, 180 jours civils en général.	Il obtient des revenus au moins égaux aux indemnités de chômage versées par l'État; ou n'a pas pointé en personne depuis plus de 10 jours ouvrables.	Fixé à 180 couronnes estoniennes depuis 1991.
Pour les nouveaux diplômés: 3 mois.	1 an pour ceux qui ont cotisé pendant les 4 dernières années. Pour les nouveaux diplômés: 6 mois.	Il refuse une offre d'emploi ou une formation; ou reçoit une retraite.	Pour les nouveaux diplômés: 75% du salaire minimum.
2 semaines.	6 mois sur toute période de 12 mois donnée. Cette période peut être portée à 12 mois à la demande des autorités locales.	Il refuse 2 offres d'emploi ou de stage de formation professionnelle; il ne pointe pas chaque mois. Il quitte le pays. Il perd son statut de chômeur.	90 % du salaire minimum. 70% du salaire minimum si les cotisations sociales n'ont pas été acquittées au cours des 12 derniers mois en Lettonie, ou si elles l'ont été pendant moins de 6 mois.
Pour ceux ayant précédemment travaillé: 8 jours. Pour les personnes ayant volontairement quitté leur emploi: 6 mois.	6 mois par an.	Il ne pointe pas chaque mois, refuse 3 offres d'emploi ou un programme de formation.	Les personnes précédemment salariées reçoivent 70% de leur salaire antérieur pendant les 2 premiers mois, 60% les deux mois suivants, et 50% les deux derniers mois. Depuis 1996, le minimum est de 90 litas et le maximum de 180 litas.
Pour les diplômés remplissant les conditions nécessaires: 3 mois.	En général, 12 mois; davantage dans les cas définis dans la Loi en vigueur.	Sans raison: refuse 1 offre d'emploi convenable, une formation, un travail d'intérêt collectif, un emploi temporaire; ou n'a pas pointé. A été licencié pour raisons disciplinaires.	En général, 36% du salaire mensuel moyen du trimestre précédent, sous réserve des dispositions de la Loi en vigueur.

CHÔMAGE

Pays	Âge actif	Conditions d'inscription au chômage	Taux de chômage = nb de chômeurs [1] en % de :	Conditions d'ouverture des droits à allocation
RÉPUBLIQUE DE SLOVÉNIE	15-58 ans (femmes) 15-63 (hommes).	Toutes les personnes qui n'ont pas d'emploi régulier, ne sont pas des travailleurs indépendants, ne possèdent pas de biens susceptibles de leur assurer des moyens d'existence, et sont capables et désireuses de travailler.	Population active totale de l'année correspondante.	Chômeurs qui ont perdu un travail contre leur gré; qui se sont inscrits dans les 30 jours et qui ont travaillé 9 mois sans interruption ou 12 mois au total au cours des derniers 18 mois.
ROUMANIE	16-57 ans (femmes) 16-62 (hommes).	Personnes qui ont perdu leur emploi ou nouveaux diplômés qui n'ont jamais travaillé, ont fini leurs études et ont effectué le service militaire obligatoire.	Population active civile au 31 décembre de l'année précédente.	Chômeurs inscrits de plus de 18 ans qui n'ont pas d'autre source de revenus d'un montant supérieur à la moitié du salaire minimum; qui ne possèdent pas (avec leur famille) plus de 20.000 m^2 de terres agricoles.
RÉPUBLIQUE SLOVAQUE	15-54 ans (femmes) 15-59 (hommes).	Personnes n'ayant pas de contrat de travail et n'exerçant pas d'activité à titre d'entrepreneur indépendant, cherchant un emploi susceptible de leur convenir.	Population active civile.	Chômeurs inscrits ayant travaillé au moins 12 mois au cours des 3 dernières années.
ARMÉNIE	16-55 ans (femmes) 16-60 (hommes).	Personnes en âge et en état de travailler, n'ayant pas d'emploi et n'exerçant pas d'activité d'entrepreneur indépendant, n'étudiant pas dans un établissement de jour et n'effectuant pas leur service militaire.	Population active civile du trimestre précédent.	Les allocations sont versées à toute personne officiellement au chômage.
AZERBAÏDJAN	16-55 ans (femmes) 16-60 (hommes).	Personnes en âge et en état de travailler, sans emploi qui peuvent commencer à travailler et y sont disposées et qui n'ont pas d'emploi ou de gains pour des raisons indépendantes de leur volonté.	Population active civile du trimestre précédent.	Les allocations sont versées à toute personne officiellement au chômage.

Période minimale d'inactivité avant versement des allocations	Période maximale d'indemnisation	L'allocataire perd ses droits si :	Montant des allocations
Aucune.	2 ans pour ceux qui ont travaillé plus de 20 ans. 3 mois pour ceux qui n'ont travaillé que 12 mois au cours des 18 derniers mois.	Il refuse 3 offres d'emploi.	Pendant les 3 premiers mois: 70% du salaire moyen des 3 derniers mois d'activité. Ne peut être inférieur à 80% du salaire minimum.
Aucune, si le chômeur s'inscrit dans les 30 jours qui suivent la fin de son contrat. Pour les diplômés de l'enseignement supérieur: 60 jours. Pour les appelés du contingent: 30 jours.	9 mois. Après cela, les personnes qui sont toujours au chômage perçoivent une allocation d'aide pendant une période de 18 mois.	Il refuse 1 emploi correspondant à ses qualifications ou une formation à une distance ne dépassant pas 50Km de son domicile; il ne pointe pas chaque mois.	Pour ceux qui ont travaillé plus de 5 ans, 50% du salaire mensuel moyen des 3 derniers mois, mais au moins 75% du salaire minimum. Pour les diplômés: 60-70% du salaire minimum. Allocation d'aide: 60% du salaire minimum.
	6 mois. Après cela, les chômeurs peuvent se voir proposer un travail rémunéré d'intérêt public ou recevoir des aides sociales.	Il ne pointe pas régulièrement.	Pour les 3 premiers mois: 60% du salaire précédent (sans dépasser 3.000 couronnes slovaques). Pendant les 3 mois suivants: 50% du dernier salaire.
10 jours.	24 semaines sur une période de 12 mois. Pour les primo-demandeurs d'emploi: 12 semaines. Pour les pré-retraités: 40 semaines sur 12 mois.	Il refuse 2 offres d'emploi convenables, ne pointe pas 2 fois sans justification ou trouve un emploi sans en avertir l'agence pour l'emploi.	50% du salaire moyen précédent (mais pas < au salaire minimum et pas > à 3 fois le salaire minimum). Pour les primo-demandeurs d'emploi: le salaire minimum.
10 jours.	26 semaines sur une période de 12 mois.	Il refuse 2 offres d'emploi convenables, ne respecte pas les règles de pointage, trouve un emploi temporaire sans en avertir l'agence pour l'emploi, perçoit des prestations de façon illégale ou est condamné à une peine de prison.	70 à 75% du salaire moyen précédent pendant 13 semaines; 55 à 60% durant les 13 semaines suivantes. Jamais < au salaire minimum ni > au salaire moyen. Prestations majorées de 10% par personne à charge. Primo-demandeurs d'emploi: le salaire minimum.

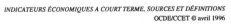

CHÔMAGE

Pays	Âge actif	Conditions d'inscription au chômage	Taux de chômage = nb de chômeurs [1] en % de :	Conditions d'ouverture des droits à allocation
BÉLARUS	16-55 ans (femmes) 16-60 (hommes).	Personnes en âge et en état de travailler, n'ayant pas d'emploi et n'exerçant pas d'activité d'entrepreneur indépendant, n'étudiant pas dans un établissement de jour et n'effectuant pas leur service militaire.	Population active civile du trimestre précédent.	Personnes inscrites n'ayant pas de revenus (pensions, allocations, indemnisations d'accidents du travail, etc.) supérieurs au montant des prestations de chômage.
KAZAKSTAN	16-55 ans (femmes) 16-60 (hommes).	Personnes en âge et en état de travailler, sans emploi qui peuvent commencer à travailler et y sont disposées et qui n'ont pas d'emploi ou de gains pour des raisons indépendantes de leur volonté.	Population active civile du trimestre précédent.	Les allocations sont versées à toute personne officiellement au chômage.
RÉPUBLIQUE KIRGHIZE	16-55 ans (femmes) 16-60 (hommes).	Personnes en âge et en état de travailler, sans emploi qui peuvent commencer à travailler et y sont disposées et qui n'ont pas d'emploi ou de gains pour des raisons indépendantes de leur volonté.	Population active civile du trimestre précédent.	Les allocations sont versées à toute personne officiellement au chômage.
RÉPUBLIQUE DE MOLDOVA	16-55 ans (femmes) 16-60 (hommes).	Personnes en âge et en état de travailler, sans emploi qui peuvent commencer à travailler et y sont disposées et qui n'ont pas d'emploi ou de gains pour des raisons indépendantes de leur volonté.	Population active civile du trimestre précédent.	Les allocations sont versées à toute personne officiellement au chômage.
FÉDÉRATION DE RUSSIE	16-55 ans (femmes) 16-60 (hommes).	Personnes en âge et en état de travailler, sans emploi qui peuvent commencer à travailler et y sont disposées et qui n'ont pas d'emploi ou de gains pour des raisons indépendantes de leur volonté.	Population active civile du trimestre précédent.	Les allocations sont versées à toute personne officiellement au chômage.

Période minimale d'inactivité avant versement des allocations	Période maximale d'indemnisation	L'allocataire perd ses droits si :	Montant des allocations
Aucune.	26 semaines sur une période de 12 mois.	Les versements sont supprimés ou interrompus pendant une période maximum de 3 mois s'il refuse 2 offres d'emploi convenables, reçoit des prestations de façon illégale ou ne respecte pas les règles et conditions de pointage.	70% du salaire moyen précédent pendant 13 semaines; 50% durant les 13 semaines suivantes. Mais pas < au salaire minimum ni > à 2 fois le salaire minimum. Primo-demandeurs d'emploi: 85% du salaire minimum pendant 13 semaines; 70% les 13 semaines suivantes.
7 jours.	26 semaines sur une période de 12 mois. Pour les primo-demandeurs d'emploi: 13 semaines. Pour les pré-retraités: 36 semaines.	Les versements sont réduits ou interrompus pendant une période maximale de 3 mois s'il refuse 2 offres d'emploi convenables, prend un emploi temporaire sans en avertir l'agence pour l'emploi ou ne respecte pas les règles de pointage.	Pas plus de 50 % du salaire précédent, dans une fourchette allant du minimum vital au salaire moyen. Pour les primo-demandeurs d'emploi: pas < à 75% du minimum vital. Prestations majorées de 10% pour les personnes ayant des enfants < 14 ans.
10 jours.	26 semaines sur une période de 12 mois. Les 26 semaines maximum sont prolongées de 2 semaines pour chaque année travaillée en sus de la période de travail nécessaire à l'ouverture des droits.	Les versements sont supprimés ou interrompus pendant une période maximale de 1 mois s'il refuse 2 offres d'emploi convenables, reçoit des prestations de façon illégale ou ne respecte pas les règles et conditions de pointage.	De 1,1 à 1,5 fois le salaire minimum. Pour les primo-demandeurs d'emploi: le salaire minimum. Prestations majorées de 10 à 20% pour les personnes ayant des enfants < 14 ans.
10 jours.	9 mois. Pour les primo-demandeurs: 6 mois.	Les versements sont supprimés ou interrompus pendant une période maximale de 5 mois s'il refuse 1 offre d'emploi, reçoit des prestations de façon illégale ou ne respecte pas les règles et conditions de pointage.	Entre 50 et 60% du salaire moyen des 3 derniers mois, mais pas < au salaire minimum et pas > au salaire moyen. Pour les primo-demandeurs d'emploi: 75-100% du salaire minimum. Prestations plus 10% pour les personnes ayant des enfants < 14 ans.
Aucune.	12 mois sur une période de 18 mois. Pour les pré-retraités: 24 mois sur une période de 36 mois.	Les versements sont supprimés ou interrompus pendant une période maximale de 3 mois s'il refuse 2 offres d'emploi convenables, reçoit des prestations de façon illégale ou ne respecte pas les règles et conditions de pointage.	Entre 45 et 75% du salaire moyen précédent des deux derniers mois, mais avec un plancher égal au salaire minimum et un plafond égal au salaire moyen. Pour les primo-demandeurs d'emploi: le salaire minimum.

CHÔMAGE

Pays	Âge actif	Conditions d'inscription au chômage	Taux de chômage = nb de chômeurs [1] en % de :	Conditions d'ouverture des droits à allocation
TADJIKISTAN	16-55 ans (femmes) 16-60 (hommes).	Personnes en âge et en état de travailler, sans emploi qui peuvent commencer à travailler et y sont disposées et qui n'ont pas d'emploi ou de gains pour des raisons indépendantes de leur volonté.	Population active civile du trimestre précédent.	Les allocations sont versées à toute personne officiellement au chômage.
TURKMÉNISTAN[3]	n.d.	n.d.	n.d.	n.d.
UKRAINE	16-54 ans (femmes) 16-59 (hommes).	Personnes en âge et en état de travailler, sans emploi qui peuvent commencer à travailler et y sont disposées et qui n'ont pas d'emploi ou de gains pour des raisons indépendantes de leur volonté.	n.d.	Personnes inscrites comme chômeurs, sans autre source de revenus.
OUZBÉKISTAN	16-55 ans (femmes) 16-60 (hommes).	Personnes en âge et en état de travailler, sans emploi qui peuvent commencer à travailler et y sont disposées et qui n'ont pas d'emploi ou de gains pour des raisons indépendantes de leur volonté.	Population active civile du trimestre précédent.	Les allocations sont versées à toute personne officiellement au chômage.

(1) Dans tous les pays, c'est le nombre de chômeurs inscrits qui sert à calculer le taux de chômage.

(2) A partir de 1994, l'âge de départ à la retraite sera reculé de six mois chaque année, de sorte qu'en 2003 il sera de 60 ans pour les femmes et de 65 ans pour les hommes.

(3) Aucune information concernant le chômage n'est encore disponible au Turkménistan.

Période minimale d'inactivité avant versement des allocations	Période maximale d'indemnisation	L'allocataire perd ses droits si :	Montant des allocations
1 jour.	26 semaines. Pour les primo-demandeurs d'emploi: 13 semaines sur 12 mois. Les 26 semaines maximum sont prolongées de 2 semaines pour chaque année travaillée en sus de la période de travail nécessaire à l'ouverture des droits.	Les versements sont supprimés ou interrompus pendant une période maximale de 3 mois s'il refuse 2 offres d'emploi convenables, reçoit des prestations de façon illégale ou ne respecte pas les règles et conditions de pointage.	Pour les personnes ayant déjà occupé un emploi, pas moins du salaire minimum. Pour les primo-demandeurs d'emploi: au moins 75% du salaire minimum.
n.d.	n.d.	n.d.	n.d.
11 jours.	Pas plu de 12 mois dans une période de 3 ans.	Il commence une formation. Il refuse 2 offres d'emploi convenables, est un primo-demandeur d'emploi et refuse un emploi rémunéré ou une formation, ne pointe pas régulièrement durant le mois.	50% du salaire moyen des 12 derniers mois, jamais < au salaire minimum et pas > au salaire moyen. Primo-demandeurs d'emploi: au moins 75% du salaire minimum.
10 jours.	26 semaines sur une période de 12 mois. Pour les primo-demandeurs d'emploi: 13 semaines.	Les versements sont supprimés ou interrompus pendant une période maximale de 3 mois s'il refuse 2 offres d'emploi convenables, reçoit des prestations de façon illégale ou ne respecte pas les règles et conditions de pointage.	50% du salaire moyen des 12 derniers mois, jamais < au salaire minimum et pas > au salaire moyen. Primo-demandeurs d'emploi: au moins 75% du salaire minimum. Prestations majorées de 10% pour ceux ayant des enfants < 16 ans ou autre personne à charge.

INDICES DES PRIX À LA PRODUCTION / DE GROS

Pays	Produits industriels couverts	Enquête sur les prix	Pondération utilisée
BULGARIE Indice des prix de gros	Production intérieure.	1.000 produits et groupes de produits manufacturés, 3.000 entreprises publiques couvertes.	Valeur des ventes.
ESTONIE Indice des prix à la production	Production destinée aux marchés intérieur et à l'exportation.	440 biens industriels, 110 entreprises couvertes.	Depuis juin 1995, volume de la production de 1994.
HONGRIE Indice des prix à la production	Produits vendus à d'autres producteurs, grossistes ou détaillants, ou destinés à l'exportation.	800 articles, 800 des principaux producteurs couverts.	Valeur des ventes.
LETTONIE Indice des prix à la production	Production destinée aux marchés intérieur et à l'exportation.	709 produits ou groupes de produits. 166 entreprises manufacturières couvertes.	Volume des ventes de 1993.
LITUANIE Indice des prix à la production	Production intérieure.	890 biens industriels, 270 entreprises couvertes.	En 1996, valeur des ventes de 1994.
POLOGNE Indice des prix à la production	Articles les plus représentatifs de la valeur des ventes de l'unité déclarante (75% du chiffre d'affaires mensuel).	19.000 relevés de prix provenant de toutes les unités déclarantes; 3.500 entreprises publiques et privées couvertes.	Depuis 1996, valeur des ventes de 1994 (auparavant, valeur des ventes de 1992). Les coefficients de pondération sont modifiés chaque mois en fonction des changements de la structure des ventes.
RÉPUBLIQUE DE SLOVÉNIE Indice des prix à la production	Produits destinés à la vente sur le marché intérieur.	450 articles, 300 des principaux producteurs couverts.	Valeur des ventes de l'année précédente.
ROUMANIE Indice des prix à la production	Depuis 1993, les produits couverts sont destinés aux marchés intérieurs ou à l'exportation.	9.000 articles, 740 unités industrielles couvertes.	Valeur des livraisons de 1992.
RÉPUBLIQUE SLOVAQUE Indice des prix à la production	Produits de 270 branches industrielles.	1.890 articles, 382 entreprises couvertes.	Valeur de la production de 1989.

Type d'indice	Traitement des changements de qualité	Traitement des articles saisonniers	Taxes comprises ?
Paasche.			Non.
Laspeyres.	Aucun.	Aucun.	Non.
Laspeyres.	Les produits ayant subi des changements de qualité sont traités comme de nouveaux produits.	Le dernier relevé est reconduit durant la période hors saison.	Non.
Laspeyres.	Les déclarants sont invités à corriger les prix pour tenir compte des changements de qualité.	Le dernier relevé est reconduit durant la période hors saison.	Non.
Laspeyres.	Depuis 1996, les prix sont corrigés pour tenir compte des changements de qualité.	Le dernier relevé est reconduit durant la période hors saison.	Avant 1995, la taxe sur la valeur ajoutée.
Paasche.	Les produits qui ont subi des changements de qualité sont traités comme de nouveaux produits.	Aucun.	Oui, avant 1994. En 1994-95, hors TVA. Depuis 1996, hors TVA et droits d'accise.
Laspeyres.	On procède à un raccordement des prix jusqu'à la fin de l'année. L'année suivante, l'article est traité comme un nouvel article.	Le dernier relevé est reconduit durant la période hors saison.	Non.
Laspeyres.	Les produits qui ont subi des changements de qualité sont traités comme de nouveaux produits.		Les taxes d'accise sont incluses. TVA exclue.
Laspeyres.	Les prix sont corrigés lorsque les écarts de qualité observés sont importants.	Aucun.	TVA exclue; taxe à la consommation incluse.

INDICES DES PRIX À LA PRODUCTION / DE GROS

Pays	Produits industriels couverts	Enquête sur les prix	Pondération utilisée
UKRAINE Indice des prix de gros	Produits industriels destinés à la vente sur le marché intérieur.	6.200 articles, 1.500 entreprises industrielles couvertes.	Structure de la production de 1993.

Type d'indice	Traitement des changements de qualité	Traitement des articles saisonniers	Taxes comprises ?
Laspeyres modifié.	Oui (partiellement).	Aucun.	Non.

OECD
OCDE
SHORT-TERM ECONOMIC INDICATORS, SOURCES AND DEFINITIONS
OECD/CCET © April 1996

213

INDICATEURS ÉCONOMIQUES A COURT TERME, SOURCES ET DÉFINITIONS
OCDE/CCET © avril 1996

INDICE DES PRIX À LA CONSOMMATION

Pays	Enquête sur les prix	Nombre de relevés par mois	Pondération des dépenses : source
BULGARIE	1.604 articles, 28 régions.	6 relevés par article.	Enquête sur le budget des ménages de 1992.
ESTONIE	317 biens et 93 services, 10 villes.	Biens: 33 relevés.	L'enquête sur les dépenses familiales de 1993 est actuellement utilisée. Les coefficients de pondération sont corrigés pour tenir compte des sous-déclarations des tabacs et alcools.
HONGRIE	1.800 articles, 8.000 points de vente, 86 villes.	Entre 30 et 150 relevés par produit dans tous les points de vente.	Enquête sur les dépenses des ménages effectuée auprès de 12.000 ménages. Les coefficients de pondération sont modifiés chaque année et corrigés pour tenir compte de la sous-déclaration des tabacs, alcools, confiseries et repas pris au restaurant.
LETTONIE	388 biens et services, 1120 points de vente, 15 régions.	4-8 relevés pour les produits agricoles; 1-4 relevés pour les autres articles.	L'enquête sur les dépenses des ménages de mi-1992 à mi-1993. Les coefficients de pondération sont corrigés pour tenir compte de la sous-déclaration des tabacs et alcools.
LITUANIE	369 biens et services, environ 1.060 points de vente, 7 grandes villes et 9 régions.	Un relevé pour tous les produits et services.	Enquête sur les dépenses des ménages depuis mai 1992. L'enquête utilisée actuellement est celle d'août 1992 à juillet 1993.
POLOGNE	Entre 1400 et 1800 biens et services, 28.000 points de vente, 307 villes ou chefs-lieux.	3 relevés pour les produits alimentaires, l'alcool et le tabac; 1 relevé pour les autres articles.	Enquête sur le budget des ménages depuis 1991. Elle couvre toute la population depuis 1993. Auparavant, volume des ventes de détail. Les coefficients de pondération sont corrigés pour tenir compte de la sous-déclaration des alcools, tabac et restauration.
RÉPUBLIQUE DE SLOVÉNIE	354 biens et 91 services. 150 points de ventes dans 4 villes et zones rurales.	2 relevés pour les produits agricoles. Un relevé pour les autres biens et services.	Enquête des dépenses des familles couvrant 3.270 ménages en 1993.
ROUMANIE	1.800 articles, 4.300 points de vente, 40 chefs-lieux plus Bucarest.	2 relevés pour chaque bien ou service.	Enquête sur les dépenses familiales de 9.000 ménages comprenant des salariés, des agriculteurs et des retraités. L'enquête utilisée actuellement est celle de 1993.

Type d'indice	Traitement des articles saisonniers	Traitement des changements de qualité	Part (en %) de l'alimentation dans les dépenses totales
Laspeyres modifié.			43,4
Depuis janvier 1994, Laspeyres. Indice à pondération fixe du 1er trimestre 1990 à décembre 1993.	La variation moyenne des prix des autres articles du groupe de produits correspondant est imputée au produit indisponible.	Oui.	37,9
Laspeyres modifié.	Les pondérations mensuelles varient à l'intérieur d'un panier fixe de produits alimentaires saisonniers.	Aucun.	28,4
Indice de Laspeyres depuis juin 1992, auparavant, indice de Paasche.	Pour les produits hors saison, on impute un prix saisonnier moyen.	Oui.	49,7
Indice de Laspeyres modifié depuis mai 1992; auparavant, indice de Paasche.	Le prix du mois précédent est utilisé pour les articles indisponibles.	Aucun.	65,8
Laspeyres.	Les pondérations mensuelles varient à l'intérieur d'un panier fixe de fruits et de légumes saisonniers.	Aucun.	39,2
Laspeyres.	Les pondérations mensuelles varient à l'intérieur d'un panier fixe de fruits et de légumes saisonniers.	Si un produit disparaît, il est remplacé par un autre de qualité similaire. S'il n'en existe aucun, un ajustement est fait.	31,8
Laspeyres.	Les pondérations mensuelles varient à l'intérieur d'un panier fixe d'articles tels que fruits frais, légumes et laine.	Oui.	47,1

OECD
OCDE
SHORT-TERM ECONOMIC INDICATORS, SOURCES AND DEFINITIONS
OECD/CCET © April 1996

215

INDICATEURS ÉCONOMIQUES A COURT TERME, SOURCES ET DÉFINITIONS
OCDE/CCET © avril 1996

INDICE DES PRIX À LA CONSOMMATION

Pays	Enquête sur les prix	Nombre de relevés par mois	Pondération des dépenses : source
RÉPUBLIQUE SLOVAQUE	836 biens et services. 38 chefs-lieux.	3 à 5 relevés pour les biens et certains services; un relevé pour les autres services (par exemple transports et communications).	Pour les biens: chiffre d'affaires de 1989. Pour les services: dépenses des ménages de 1989.
ARMÉNIE	267 biens et 63 services.	Ensemble des biens et services: tous les 10 jours.	Enquête des dépenses de consommation des ménages de l'année précédente.
AZERBAÏDJAN	268 biens et 33 services.	Produits alimentaires: tous les 7 ou 10 jours; autres produits et services: un relevé.	Enquête des dépenses de consommation des ménages de 1993.
BÉLARUS	273 biens et 43 services.	Ensemble des biens et services: un relevé.	Enquête des dépenses de consommation des ménages de l'année précédente.
KAZAKSTAN	242 biens et 33 services.	Produits alimentaires: tous les 7 ou 10 jours; autres produits et services: un relevé.	Enquête des dépenses de consommation des ménages de l'année précédente.
RÉPUBLIQUE KIRGHIZE	270 biens et 35 services.	Ensemble des biens et services: un relevé.	Enquête des dépenses de consommation des ménages de l'année précédente.
RÉPUBLIQUE DE MOLDOVA	265 biens et 47 services.	Produits alimentaires: tous les 7 ou 10 jours; autres produits et services: 2 relevés.	Enquête des dépenses de consommation des ménages de l'année précédente.
FÉDÉRATION DE RUSSIE	215 biens et 73 services.	Produits alimentaires: tous les 7 ou 10 jours; autres produits et services: un relevé.	Enquête des dépenses de consommation des ménages de l'année précédente.
TADJIKISTAN	239 biens et 35 services.	Produits alimentaires: tous les 7 ou 10 jours; autres produits et services: un relevé.	Enquête des dépenses de consommation des ménages de l'année précédente.
TURKMÉNISTAN	1.200 biens et services.	Produits alimentaires: tous les 7 ou 10 jours; autres produits et services: un relevé.	Enquête des dépenses de consommation des ménages de l'année précédente.
UKRAINE	345 biens et 80 services. Toutes les villes et chefs-lieux.		Depuis 1995, structure de la consommation de l'année précédente.
OUZBÉKISTAN	233 biens et 34 services.	Produits alimentaires: tous les 7 ou 10 jours; autres produits et services: un relevé.	Enquête des dépenses de consommation des ménages de l'année précédente.

Type d'indice	Traitement des articles saisonniers	Traitement des changements de qualité	Part (en %) de l'alimentation dans les dépenses totales
Laspeyres.	Des paniers de fruits et légumes différents sont utilisés chaque mois.	On corrige les prix de la période de référence.	29,9
Laspeyres.	Aucun.	Aucun.	75,7
Laspeyres.	Aucun.	Aucun.	72,0
Laspeyres.	Aucun.	Aucun.	65,4
Laspeyres.	Aucun.	Aucun.	59,8
Laspeyres.	Aucun.	Aucun.	62,6
Laspeyres.	Aucun.	Aucun.	47,3
Laspeyres.	Aucun.	Aucun.	52,5
Laspeyres.	Aucun.	Aucun.	74,9
Laspeyres.	Aucun.	Aucun.	55,0
Laspeyres modifé.	Aucun.	Aucun.	65,0
Laspeyres.	Aucun.	Aucun.	66,1

COMMERCE EXTÉRIEUR

Pays	Classification	Documents utilisés	Evaluation des importations	Articles non compris dans le commerce extérieur
BULGARIE	Depuis 1992, Système harmonisé.	Depuis 1992, déclarations douanières. Avant 1992, enquêtes auprès des exportateurs et importateurs.	Depuis 1992, caf; auparavant, fab.	Services, réparations, brevets, savoir-faire, réexportations directes, produits de la pêche et films.
ESTONIE	NBEN [1]. Depuis juillet 1992, Système Harmonisé.	Depuis juillet 1992, déclarations douanières. Auparavant, enquêtes auprès des exportateurs et importateurs.	caf.	Services; biens destinés aux ambassades.
HONGRIE	Pour 1991-1993, Système harmonisé. Depuis 1994, Nomenclature combinée.	Avant 1991, enquêtes auprès des exportateurs et importateurs. Pour 1991-1994, déclarations douanières. Depuis 1995, Document administratif unique.	caf.	Nombreux services: opérations de construction, de montage, films et logiciels. Achats-ventes des organismes extraterritoriaux; carburant vendu/acheté à/par des bateaux, avions, etc. étrangers/hongrois; transactions effectuées à bord de bateaux, avions.
LETTONIE	NBEN[1] Système harmonisé.	Depuis 1993, déclarations douanières seules, complétées par des données tirées d'enquêtes spéciales. En 1992, déclarations douanières utilisées parallèlement aux enquêtes. En 1991, enquêtes auprès des exportateurs et importateurs.	fab.	Tous les services exportables, recherche et développement, aide étrangère. Les chiffres mensuels excluent les biens échangés avec les militaires russes stationnés en Lettonie, ainsi que les ventes de poisson à l'étranger par les bateaux de pêches lettons.
LITUANIE	Nomenclature combinée.	Déclarations douanières; sauf pour les importations d'énergie électrique: notifications des entreprises.	caf.	Tous les services échangés, l'or, les valeurs mobilières, les biens échangés à titre temporaire, les échanges avec les ambassades, le poisson pêché dans les eaux internationales, l'approvisionnement des navires et des avions lituaniens à l'étranger.
POLOGNE	Depuis 1992, Nomenclature combinée. Auparavant, Nomenclature des produits du commerce extérieur (NTHZ).	Pour 1980-89, les statistiques du commerce extérieur étaient établies sur la base des factures des importateurs et exportateurs. Pour 1990-91, déclarations douanières. Depuis 1992, le Document administratif unique est utilisé.	Depuis 1992, caf; auparavant, fab.	Services (sauf finitions), réparations, construction, brevets, licences, savoir-faire, réexportations directes depuis/vers les zones franches.

COMMERCE EXTÉRIEUR

Pays	Classification	Documents utilisés	Evaluation des importations	Articles non compris dans le commerce extérieur
RÉPUBLIQUE DE SLOVÉNIE	Pour 1988-1995, Système harmonisé et CTCI Rév. 3. Depuis 1996, la Nomenclature combinée.	Déclarations douanières.	caf.	Services, locations, approvisionnement des missions slovènes à l'étranger, approvisionnement des transporteurs en carburant, échantillons commerciaux et bagages.
ROUMANIE	Pour 1991-1993, Système harmonisé. Depuis 1994, Nomenclature combinée.	Depuis 1991, déclarations douanières.	Depuis 1991, caf; auparavant, fab.	La plupart des services: licences, brevets, savoir-faire, travaux de conception et de recherche, travaux de construction et de montage; carburant et produits alimentaires destinés à l'approvisionnement des bateaux; impression de livres et brochures.
RÉPUBLIQUE SLOVAQUE	Depuis 1991, Système harmonisé.	Depuis 1991, déclarations douanières nationales. Document administratif unique depuis 1992.	fab.	Les échanges de service sont exclus. Le commerce avec la République tchèque n'est inclus que depuis 1993.
ARMÉNIE, AZERBAÏDJAN, BÉLARUS, KAZAKSTAN, RÉP. KIRGHIZE, RÉP. DE MOLDOVA, FÉD. DE RUSSIE, TADJIKISTAN, TURKMÉNISTAN, OUZBÉKISTAN	Nomenclature des produits des activités économiques extérieures élaborée sur la base du Système harmonisé jusqu'au niveau de détail à six chiffres.	Rapports soumis par les organismes de commerce extérieur et déclarations douanières.	caf.	Services faisant l'objet d' échanges internationaux (inclus en Ouzbékistan depuis 1992); recettes du tourisme. Fédération de Russie: services de construction, de santé et financiers, édition, enseignement et formation sont inclus.
UKRAINE	Système harmonisé.	rapports statistiques des entreprises et déclarations douanières.	caf.	Le commerce avec l'ex-Union soviétique est disponible depuis janvier 1994.

(1) Nomenclature des branches de l'économie nationale élaborée par l'ex-Conseil d'Assistance Économique Mutuelle (CAEM).

ENQUÊTES DE CONJONCTURE

Introduction

Le Centre pour la coopération avec les économies en transition de l'OCDE travaille depuis 1991 avec Eurostat et la Commission des Communautés européennes à mettre au point un programme d'enquêtes de conjoncture dans les pays en transition. Ce programme fait partie d'un projet commun de plus grande ampleur destiné à aider les pays en transition à élaborer des indicateurs à court terme appropriés.

Les enquêtes de conjoncture servent à recueillir auprès des chefs d'entreprise des informations qualitatives sur leur appréciation de la situation économique du moment, ainsi que sur leurs intentions et prévisions pour l'avenir immédiat. Ce type d'enquête, qui existe dans tous les pays Membres de l'OCDE, s'avère constituer un moyen rentable de disposer en temps utile de renseignements sur l'évolution économique à court terme. L'information économique sur la période courante présente un intérêt particulier pour les pays en transition et l'existence d'un système fiable d'indicateurs à court terme quantitatifs et qualitatifs est primordiale.

Par rapport aux enquêtes statistiques quantitatives classiques, les enquêtes de conjoncture présentent maints avantages en tant qu'outil d'information économique à court terme. Les renseignements qui y sont demandés sont plus faciles à fournir pour les entreprises car elles n'ont pas besoin pour répondre de s'appuyer sur des données chiffrées précises et les questionnaires remplis peuvent être renvoyés plus rapidement. Les enquêtes de conjoncture renseignent sur toute une série de variables choisies parce qu'elles permettent de suivre le cycle conjoncturel, y compris des variables dont les statistiques quantitatives ne rendent pas compte, comme l'utilisation des capacités et les opinions sur la situation économique générale.

Les pays membres de l'Union européenne ont jugé utile de normaliser (ou "harmoniser") un certain nombre des questions posées dans leurs enquêtes de conjoncture, de sorte que les résultats sont comparables au plan international. Les pays en transition sont encouragés à en faire autant pour que les résultats de leurs enquêtes se prêtent aussi à des comparaisons internationales.

Des enquêtes de conjoncture couvrant le secteur industriel (dans la plupart des cas, les industries manufacturières) sont effectuées périodiquement depuis plusieurs années en Hongrie et en Pologne, tandis que des enquêtes périodiques ont été instituées dans le courant de 1991 dans l'ex-République fédérative tchèque et slovaque, en Estonie et en Roumanie, puis en janvier 1992 en Bulgarie. En Russie, une première enquête de conjoncture a été menée dans l'industrie manufacturière en janvier 1992. Elle s'est toutefois limitée aux entreprises de la région de Moscou, mais une nouvelle enquête a été introduite et couvre en outre la partie ouest de la Russie. En Lettonie et en Lituanie, les enquêtes de conjoncture ont été mises en place pendant l'année 1993, et il en a été de même au Bélarus en 1994.

Pour le secteur de la construction, on dispose d'enquêtes de conjoncture pour la Bulgarie, l'Estonie, la Hongrie, la Lettonie, la Pologne, la Roumanie et la République slovaque. Pour le commerce de détail, il en existe dans tous les pays précités sauf la Lettonie.

Depuis avril 1993, une sélection de résultats des enquêtes de conjoncture est publiée dans les *Indicateurs économiques à court terme : Économies en transition* chaque trimestre. Les résultats des enquêtes de conjoncture des pays suivants : Bulgarie, Estonie, Hongrie, Lettonie, Lituanie, Pologne, Roumanie, République slovaque, Bélarus et Fédération de Russie sont maintenant inclus régulièrement.

Une annexe annuelle consacrée aux enquêtes de conjoncture présente dans leur intégralité les résultats d'enquêtes menées dans l'industrie, la construction et le commerce de détail. Cette annexe a été publiée pour la première fois dans *Indicateurs économiques à court terme : Économies en transition*, numéro 2/95.

L'annexe contient, en particulier, les résultats complets des enquêtes conduites dans le secteur manufacturier, la construction et le commerce de détail. On trouvera dans la présente section le jeu complet des questions posées dans le cadre de ces trois enquêtes, ainsi que les différences qui existent par rapport aux questions harmonisées. Des tableaux récapitulatifs décrivant les caractéristiques des enquêtes dans chaque pays sont également inclus.

Dans la plupart des pays, les enquêtes sont réalisées par l'Office central de statistique du pays concerné. Cependant, dans quelques pays, ce sont des instituts de recherche privés qui réalisent les enquêtes. En Estonie, les enquêtes sont réalisées par l'Institut estonien d'études de marché ; en Hongrie par l'Institut de recherche économique, d'études de marché et d'informatique (Kopint-Datorg) ; en Russie les enquêtes sont conduites par l'Institut des économies en transition et au Bélarus par l'Institut d'études économiques du Ministère de l'économie. En Pologne, les enquêtes de conjoncture ont été réalisées pendant un certain nombre d'années aussi bien par l'Office central de statistique que par l'Institut de recherche sur le développement économique de la Faculté des sciences économiques de Varsovie. Les résultats dont il est fait état ici proviennent des enquêtes de l'Office central de statistique pour ce qui est de l'industrie manufacturière et du secteur de la construction et de celles menées à bien par l'Institut de recherche sur le développement économique pour ce qui est du commerce de détail.

Les enquêtes de conjoncture ont ceci de caractéristique, qu'elles visent à recueillir non pas des chiffres précis mais l'opinion des intéressés sur la situation présente, en comparaison avec la "normale", i.e. une question sur les **niveaux**, ou sur le sens dans lequel ce climat évolue, i.e. une question sur les **tendances**. Les réponses sont généralement "supérieur/égal/inférieur à la normale" ou "en augmentation/sans changement/en baisse". Les questions peuvent se référer soit à la situation présente soit aux anticipations, i.e. une question sur les **perspectives** sur les trois à six prochains mois.

Les réponses reçues sont généralement pondérées par rapport à la taille de l'entreprise qui répond, et par conséquent, les résultats sont généralement présentés en un seul chiffre. Il est beaucoup plus simple de traiter les réponses quand un seul chiffre est demandé, i.e. **taux** d'utilisation des capacités. Cependant, quelquefois, on demande aux enquêtés de choisir une ou plusieurs réponses dans une liste qui leur est proposée, dans ce cas on calcule la **proportion** pondérée des entreprises ayant donné telle ou telle réponse. Ce dernier type de question est utilisé pour recueillir les informations concernant les limites de la production ou de l'investissement, les limites de l'amélioration de la situation économique et le type d'investissement.

Dans le cas de question à choix multiple, les données sont généralement présentées sous la forme de **solde** des réponses obtenues pour les questions à triple choix. Les réponses "normale" ou "sans changement" ne sont pas prises en compte et l'on obtient le solde en calculant la différence entre les pourcentages de réponses favorables et de réponses défavorables. Un solde négatif indique que les réponses défavorables l'ont emporté, un solde positif que les réponses favorables sont les plus nombreuses. Pour les questions à double choix du type "pensez-vous réaliser des investissements cette année ou l'an prochain : oui -- non ?" le **pourcentage** pondéré d'entreprises ayant répondu "oui" est donné.

Dans la section suivante, les titres en italique, au-dessus de chaque question se rapportent aux titres des séries dans les tableaux de l'annexe consacrée aux enquêtes de conjoncture de la publication *Indicateurs économiques à cour -terme : Économies en transition*.

Dans les tableaux, quand les séries des enquêtes de conjoncture se réfèrent aux perspectives, c'est dans tous les cas par rapport à la date de l'enquête et non à la période où la prévision doit être réalisée.

OECD
OCDE
SHORT-TERM ECONOMIC INDICATORS, SOURCES AND DEFINITIONS
OECD/CCET © April 1996
221
INDICATEURS ÉCONOMIQUES A COURT TERME, SOURCES ET DÉFINITIONS
OCDE/CCET © avril 1996

ENQUÊTES DE CONJONCTURE

Enquête sur l'industrie manufacturière

Questions harmonisées

État des affaires : tendance
Appréciation portée sur la situation actuelle des affaires :
bonne (+), passable (=), mauvaise (-)

État des affaires : perspectives
Perspectives sur la situation des affaires dans six mois :
meilleures (+), identiques (=), pires (-)

Carnets de commandes / Demande totale : niveau
Appréciation portée sur la demande totale/les carnets de commandes (niveau actuel) :
supérieur (+), égal (=), inférieur (-), à la normale

Carnets de commandes / Demande d'exportations : niveau
Appréciation portée sur la demande de l'étranger/les carnets de commandes d'exportations (niveau actuel) :
supérieur (+), égal (=), inférieur (-), à la normale

Carnets de commandes / Demande totale : perspectives
Demande totale prévue pour les 3 ou 4 prochains mois :
en hausse (+), sans changement (=), en baisse (-)

Carnets de commandes / Demande d'exportations : perspectives
Exportations : pronostics pour les 3 ou 4 prochains mois :
en hausse (+), sans changement (=), en baisse (-)

Production : tendance
Appréciation portée sur les activités de production du mois (trimestre) écoulé :
en hausse (+), sans changement (=), en baisse (-)

Production : perspectives
Activités de production prévues pour les 3 ou 4 prochains mois :
en hausse (+), sans changement (=), en baisse (-)

Production : capacité actuelle
Appréciation portée sur la capacité de production actuelle (compte tenu de la demande prévue pour les 12 prochains mois) :
plus que suffisante (+), suffisante (=), insuffisante (-)

Production : taux d'utilisation des capacités
Niveau actuel de l'utilisation des capacités (en pourcentage de leur utilisation normale).

OECD
OCDE
SHORT-TERM ECONOMIC INDICATORS, SOURCES AND DEFINITIONS
OECD/CCET © April 1996

222

INDICATEURS ÉCONOMIQUES A COURT TERME, SOURCES ET DÉFINITIONS
OCDE/CCET © avril 1996

Limitations à la production

Limitations à la production (situation actuelle) :

-- aucune
-- demande intérieure insuffisante
-- demande extérieure insuffisante
-- importations compétitives
-- pénurie de main-d'oeuvre
-- pénurie de main-d'oeuvre qualifiée
-- manque d'équipement approprié
-- pénurie de produits semi-finis
-- pénurie de matières premières
-- pénurie d'énergie
-- problèmes financiers (par exemple insolvabilité, crédits)
-- législation économique peu claire
-- environnement économique incertain
-- autres (veuillez préciser)

Stocks de produits finis : niveau

Appréciation portée sur les stocks de produits finis (niveau actuel) :

supérieur (+), égal (=), inférieur (-), à la normale

Prix de vente : perspectives

Prix de vente : perspectives pour les 3 ou 4 prochains mois, ils :

augmenteront (+), resteront stables (=), baisseront (-)

Prix de vente taux d'augmentation : perspectives

En cas d'augmentation, ils :

augmenteront à un taux plus élevé (+)
augmenteront à peu près au même taux (=)
augmenteront à un taux plus faible (-)

Emploi : perspectives

Emploi : perspectives pour les 3 ou 4 prochains mois :

en hausse (+), sans changement (=), en baisse (-)

Investissements fixes : intentions

Projetez-vous des investissements fixes pour cette année (pour l'an prochain) :

oui (+1), non (0)

Investissements fixes : perspectives

Si des investissements fixes (machines, bâtiments, etc.) sont prévus, les investissements seront-ils cette année (l'an prochain), par rapport à l'an dernier (l'année en cours) :

supérieurs (+), à peu près les mêmes (=), inférieurs (-)

ENQUÊTES DE CONJONCTURE

Type d'investissement fixe

Si des investissements fixes sont prévus pour l'an prochain, de quel type d'investissement s'agira-t-il principalement :

-- remplacement d'équipements anciens
-- investissements de capacité
    . avec une gamme de produits inchangée
    . afin d'élargir la gamme de produits
-- investissements de rationalisation
    . mécanisation/automatisation du procédé de production existant
    . introduction de nouvelles techniques de production
    . économies d'énergie
-- autres motifs
    . lutte contre la pollution
    . mesures de sécurité
-- autres (veuillez préciser)

Limitations à l'investissement

Facteurs limitant les investissements prévus pour l'an prochain :

-- demande insuffisante
-- coût du capital trop élevé
-- garanties insuffisantes pour les crédits
-- profits insuffisants
-- peur de l'endettement
-- facteurs techniques
-- autres

Différences par rapport aux questions harmonisées

Estonie

L'appréciation concernant le niveau actuel de la demande totale et celui de la demande étrangère est donnée sous la forme d'une variation par rapport au trimestre précédent.

La question sur les limitations à la production ne prévoit qu'un sous-ensemble des choix énumérés dans la question harmonisée.

Hongrie

La période de prévision applicable aux perspectives en matière de production et à l'évolution de l'emploi est de six mois.

Les prévisions relatives aux prix de vente sont d'abord exprimées au moyen de sept fourchettes de pourcentages de variation, puis reportées sur une échelle qualitative à trois degrés (ils augmenteront/resteront stables/baisseront), la période de prévision étant de six mois.

Parmi les limitations à la production, la réponse "pénurie d'énergie" ne figure pas.

Les questions sur l'évolution probable de la demande totale et de la demande d'exportations s'appliquent au volume des ventes et la période de prévision est de six mois.

Pologne

L'appréciation concernant le niveau actuel de la demande totale et celui de la demande d'exportation est donnée sous la forme d'une variation par rapport au mois précédent.

La période de prévision applicable aux perspectives en matière de production et aux prix de vente futurs est d'un mois.

Les intentions d'investissement sont exprimées sous la forme d'une comparaison de la valeur des dépenses d'immobilisation pour le trimestre en cours à celle du trimestre précédent.

La période de prévision applicable à l'état des affaires est de trois mois.

Roumanie

La période de prévision applicable à l'état des affaires est de trois mois.

République slovaque

L'appréciation relative au niveau actuel de la demande totale et de la demande d'exportations est donnée sous la forme d'une variation par rapport au mois précédent.

Le nombre des réponses possibles quant aux limitations à la production sont réduites à cinq au maximum.

L'appréciation portée sur l'état des affaires est donnée sous la forme d'une variation par rapport à la période précédente.

La période de prévision applicable à l'état des affaires est de trois mois.

ENQUÊTES DE CONJONCTURE

Enquête sur le secteur de la construction

Questions harmonisées

Activité de l'entreprise : tendance
Appréciation portée sur l'activité de l'entreprise par rapport au mois (trimestre) écoulé :
en hausse (+), sans changement (=), en baisse (-)

Activité de l'entreprise : durée des travaux commandés
Avec des horaires de travail normaux, les travaux en cours, y compris ceux déjà commandés représenteront approximativement ... mois d'exploitation.

Carnets de commandes / Demande : niveau
Appréciation portée sur les carnets de commandes ou le programme d'exécution des travaux concernant les marchés intérieurs/étrangers :
totaux : supérieurs (+), égaux (=), inférieurs (-), à la normale
intérieurs : supérieurs (+), égaux (=), inférieurs (-), à la normale
étrangers : supérieurs (+), égaux (=), inférieurs (-), à la normale

Carnets de commandes / Demande totale : perspectives
Commandes (marchés conclus) : pronostics pour les 3 ou 4 prochains mois :
en hausse (+), sans changement (=), en baisse (-)

Capacité technique par rapport à la demande prévue : tendance
Appréciation portée sur la capacité technique (volume et qualité de l'équipement) compte tenu de la demande prévue pour les 12 prochains mois :
plus que suffisante (+), suffisante (=), insuffisante (-)

Limitations à la production
Limitations à la production (situation actuelle) :
-- aucune
-- demande
-- intempéries
-- coût des matériaux
-- coût de la main-d'oeuvre
-- coût du financement (par exemple taux d'intérêt)
-- accès au crédit bancaire
-- pénurie de main-d'oeuvre qualifiée
-- manque d'équipement
-- pénurie de matériaux
-- concurrence dans le secteur
-- autres (veuillez préciser)

Pronostics sur les prix : perspectives
Prix : pronostics pour les 3 ou 4 prochains mois, ils :
augmenteront (+), resteront stables (=), baisseront (-) ;

Pronostics sur le taux d'augmentation des prix : perspectives
En cas d'augmentation, ils :
augmenteront à un taux plus élevé (+)
augmenteront à peu près au même taux (=)
augmenteront à un taux plus faible (-)

Emploi : perspectives
Emploi : perspectives pour les 3 ou 4 prochains mois :
en hausse (+), sans changement (=), en baisse (-)

Situation financière : tendance
Appréciation portée sur la situation financière par rapport au mois (trimestre) écoulé :
meilleure (+), identique (=), pire (-)

Situation financière : retards de paiement de la clientèle
Retards de paiement de la clientèle publique/privée par rapport au mois (trimestre) écoulé :
totale : plus fréquents (+), sans changement (=), moins fréquents (-)
privée : plus fréquents (+), sans changement (=), moins fréquents (-)
publique : plus fréquents (+), sans changement (=), moins fréquents (-)

Différences par rapport aux questions harmonisées

Hongrie

Le niveau d'activité de l'entreprise est apprécié par rapport à une situation normale.

Les prévisions relatives à l'emploi et aux prix ont trait à la situation six mois plus tard.

Pologne

L'appréciation portée sur l'état actuel des carnets de commandes est donnée sous la forme d'une variation par rapport au trimestre précédent.

L'appréciation portée sur la capacité technique compte tenu de la demande est exprimée sous la forme d'une variation, entre le trimestre écoulé et les 3 ou 4 mois à venir.

ENQUÊTES DE CONJONCTURE

Enquête sur le commerce de détail

Questions harmonisées

État des affaires : tendance
Appréciation portée sur l'état actuel des affaires :
bon (+), satisfaisant (normal pour la saison) (=), mauvais (-)

État des affaires : perspectives
Situation probable de l'état des affaires dans six mois :
meilleure (+), identique (=), pire (-)

Concurrence dans le secteur : tendance
Appréciation portée sur la concurrence dans le secteur par rapport au mois (trimestre) écoulé :
en hausse (+), sans changement (=), en baisse (-)

Limitations à l'amélioration de l'état des affaires
Facteurs limitant l'amélioration de l'état actuel des affaires :
-- aucun
-- demande
-- approvisionnement
-- coût de la main-d'oeuvre
-- coût du financement (par exemple taux d'intérêt)
-- accès au crédit bancaire
-- surface de vente
-- capacité d'entreposage
-- concurrence dans le secteur
-- autres (veuillez préciser)

Intentions de commandes placées : perspectives
Évolution prévue des commandes placées auprès des fournisseurs nationaux/étrangers au cours des 3 ou 4 prochains mois :
totaux : en hausse (+), sans changement (=), en baisse (-)
intérieurs : en hausse (+), sans changement (=), en baisse (-)
étrangers : en hausse (+), sans changement (=), en baisse (-)

Stocks : niveau
Appréciation portée sur les stocks :
trop faibles (+), satisfaisants (normaux pour la saison) (=), trop importants (-)

Prix de vente : tendance
Prix de vente par rapport au mois (trimestre) écoulé, ils :
augmenteront (+), resteront stables (=), baisseront (-), en valeur absolue

Prix de vente taux d'augmentation : tendance
En cas d'augmentation, ils :
augmenteront à un taux plus élevé (+)
augmenteront à peu près au même taux (=)
augmenteront à un taux plus faible (-)

Prix de vente : perspectives
Prix de vente pour les 3 ou 4 prochains mois, ils :
augmenteront (+), resteront stables (=), baisseront (-), en valeur absolue

Prix de vente taux d'augmentation : perspectives
En cas d'augmentation, ils :
augmenteront à un taux plus élevé (+)
augmenteront à peu près au même taux (=)
augmenteront à un taux plus faible (-)

Emploi : perspectives
Emploi : pronostic pour les 3 ou 4 prochains mois :
en hausse (+), sans changement (=), en baisse (-)

Situation financière : tendance
Appréciation portée sur la situation financière par rapport au mois (trimestre) écoulé :
meilleure (+), identique (=), pire (-)

Différences par rapport aux questions harmonisées

Pologne

L'appréciation portée sur le niveau actuel des stocks est exprimée sous la forme d'une variation par rapport au trimestre précédent.

Roumanie

L'état probable des affaires est celui qui est prévu pour trois mois plus tard.

République slovaque

L'état actuel des affaires se réfère à un horizon de trois mois.

L'appréciation portée sur la situation financière concerne l'incapacité de paiement ou les retards de paiement de l'entreprise ou de la société.

ENQUÊTES DE CONJONCTURE : INDUSTRIES MANUFACTURIÈRES

Pays	Enquête					
	Taille de l'échantillon	Champ couvert : % des entreprises privées dans l'échantillon	Champ couvert : % de l'emploi dans l'industrie manufacturière	Champ couvert : % du chiffre d'affaires	Champ couvert : % des unités de moins de 500 salariés	Taux de réponse
BULGARIE	1002			71		95
ESTONIE	250	80	60	60	95	70-80
HONGRIE	1000		30	65		35-40
LETTONIE	233	47	55	59	76	63-84
LITUANIE	300	50	40	61	55	50
POLOGNE	3400	51	61	67	75	68
ROUMANIE	600	30	49	54	38	
RÉP SLOVAQUE	220	23	48	55	24	75-77
BÉLARUS	500	40	100		40-45	17-37
FÉD DE RUSSIE	1000	84	11			50-60

ENQUÊTES DE CONJONCTURE : CONSTRUCTION

Pays	Enquête				
	Taille de l'échantillon	Champ couvert : % de l'emploi dans la construction	Champ couvert : % du chiffre d'affaires	Champ couvert : % des unités de moins de 200 salariés	Taux de réponse
BULGARIE	490		54		96
ESTONIE	50	40	50	100	60
HONGRIE	600		50		20
LETTONIE	113	31	19	87	58-66
POLOGNE	3500	74	77	65	50-60
ROUMANIE	531	80		37	70-73
RÉP SLOVAQUE	255	49	56	64	45-62
FÉD DE RUSSIE	630				40-50

ENQUÊTES DE CONJONCTURE : COMMERCE DE DÉTAIL

Pays	Enquête				
	Taille de l'échantillon	Champ couvert : % de l'emploi dans le commerce de détail	Champ couvert : % du chiffre d'affaires	Champ couvert : % des unités privées	Taux de réponse
BULGARIE	500		58	0	97
ESTONIE	100	20	20	95	60
HONGRIE	600		30		20
POLOGNE	3500				20
ROUMANIE	1760		40	79	80-82
RÉP SLOVAQUE	300	25	23	73	36

INDICATEURS DU MARCHÉ DU TRAVAIL

Avant-Propos

Cette section de la publication fournit des informations sur les sources et définitions concernant les indicateurs figurant dans l'annexe qui paraît deux fois par an sur les *Indicateurs du marché du travail* publiée dans *Indicateurs économiques à court terme : Économies en transition*. Cette annexe contient des données sur l'emploi, le chômage et les rémunérations pour sept pays d'Europe centrale et orientale et la Fédération de Russie. Il est vivement conseillé de consulter ces notes méthodologiques avant d'utiliser les données présentées dans l'annexe sur les *Indicateurs du marché du travail*.

OECD OCDE
SHORT-TERM ECONOMIC INDICATORS, SOURCES AND DEFINITIONS
OECD/CCET © April 1996

232

INDICATEURS ÉCONOMIQUES A COURT TERME, SOURCES ET DÉFINITIONS
OCDE/CCET © avril 1996

NOTES MÉTHODOLOGIQUES

Généralités

Afin d'homogénéiser les données et de permettre une plus grande comparabilité entre les pays, les définitions utilisées pour établir les indicateurs présentés dans la publication *Indicateurs économiques à court terme : Économies en transition* peuvent différer de celles employées par les offices statistiques nationaux. Les données sur l'emploi et les rémunérations peuvent ne pas être identiques à celles figurant dans les tableaux par pays du volume principal du fait, là encore, de petites différences dans les définitions.

Sauf indication contraire :

-- *les données tirées des enquêtes annuelles auprès des établissements* correspondent à la moyenne pour l'année et couvrent le secteur public et le secteur privé ;

-- *les données tirées des enquêtes trimestrielles auprès des établissements* correspondent à la moyenne pour le trimestre et couvrent le secteur public et le secteur privé ;

-- *les données sur l'emploi extraites des enquêtes auprès des établissements* englobent les appelés, les personnes en congé de maternité et en congé parental (tels qu'ils sont définis par la législation nationale) et excluent l'armée de métier ;

-- *les données sur l'emploi tirées des enquêtes sur la population active* incluent l'armée de métier ainsi que les personnes en congé de maternité et excluent les personnes en congé parental et les appelés.

Les chiffres annuels relatifs aux divers indicateurs de l'emploi et du chômage sont donnés par la moyenne annuelle des chiffres trimestriels. Lorsqu'une définition a été modifiée ou que la source des données a changé, un trait vertical signale une rupture dans la série correspondante. Des informations concernant les ruptures de séries et leurs raisons sont fournies plus loin dans les notes relatives aux divers pays.

Sources

Bulgarie -- Depuis le troisième trimestre de 1993 (septembre), les données sur l'emploi et le chômage proviennent de l'enquête sur la population active, à l'exception des données sur les salaires et sur les heures effectuées dans l'industrie, qui sont tirées des enquêtes auprès des établissements. Les données d'enquêtes sont fournies par l'Institut statistique national. Les informations administratives concernant le nombre des chômeurs inscrits et les entrées et sorties du chômage émanent du Service national de l'emploi.

Hongrie -- Toutes les données trimestrielles sont issues de l'enquête sur la population active à l'exception de celles sur les salaires et sur les heures effectuées dans l'industrie, qui proviennent des enquêtes auprès des établissements. Les informations concernant le nombre de chômeurs inscrits et les

INDICATEURS DU MARCHÉ DU TRAVAIL

entrées et sorties du chômage sont tirées de sources administratives et proviennent du Centre pour le marché du travail. Toutes les données émanent de l'Office central de statistique.

Pologne -- Toutes les données trimestrielles sont issues de l'enquête sur la population active à l'exception de celles sur les salaires et sur les heures effectuées dans l'industrie, qui proviennent des enquêtes auprès des établissements. Les informations concernant le nombre de chômeurs inscrits et les entrées et sorties du chômage proviennent de sources administratives. Toutes les données émanent de l'Office central de statistique.

République de Slovénie -- Toutes les données trimestrielles sont issues de l'enquête sur la population active, à l'exception de celles sur les salaires qui proviennent des enquêtes auprès des établissements. Les informations concernant le nombre de chômeurs inscrits et les entrées et sorties du chômage proviennent de sources administratives et émanent du Service national de l'emploi. Toutes les autres données émanent de l'Office statistique de la République de Slovénie.

Roumanie -- Toutes les données trimestrielles sont issues de l'enquête sur la population active, à l'exception de celles sur les salaires qui proviennent des enquêtes auprès des établissements. Les informations concernant le nombre de chômeurs inscrits proviennent de sources administratives. Toutes les données émanent de la Commission nationale de statistique.

République slovaque -- Depuis le deuxième trimestre de 1993, toutes les données trimestrielles proviennent de l'enquête sur la population active, à l'exception de celles sur les salaires et sur les heures effectuées dans l'industrie, qui sont issues des enquêtes auprès des établissements. Les données sur l'emploi pour la période antérieure au deuxième trimestre de 1993 et toutes les données sur les salaires sont tirées des enquêtes auprès des établissements. Les informations concernant le nombre de chômeurs inscrits et les entrées et sorties du chômage proviennent de sources administratives. Toutes les données émanent de l'Office statistique slovaque.

Fédération de Russie -- Les données sur l'emploi et le chômage sont issues de l'enquête annuelle sur la population active. Les données sur les salaires et les heures travaillées dans l'industrie proviennent d'enquêtes auprès des établissements. Les données sur les chômeurs inscrits, les postes vacants non pourvus et les entrées au chômage proviennent de sources administratives. Toutes les données émanent du Comité d'État sur les statistiques de la Fédération de Russie.

Enquêtes sur la population active

Bulgarie -- L'enquête sur la population active est régulièrement réalisée en Bulgarie auprès des ménages ; elle porte sur un échantillon de résidents âgés de 15 ans et plus. La période de référence est d'une semaine. L'échantillon comprend environ 30 000 ménages et est établi par double stratification sur la base du recensement de décembre 1992. Le système d'imputation de Blaise a été adopté lors de l'enquête de mars 1995, depuis l'enquête de juin 1995 l'échantillon est constitué d'environ 24 000 ménages. En sont exclues les personnes vivant dans des établissements du type prisons, pensionnats et hôpitaux. Les appelés sont considérés comme membres des ménages dont ils relèvent habituellement et sont donc pris en compte dans l'enquête.

OECD
OCDE
SHORT-TERM ECONOMIC INDICATORS, SOURCES AND DEFINITIONS
OECD/CCET © April 1996

234

INDICATEURS ÉCONOMIQUES À COURT TERME, SOURCES ET DÉFINITIONS
OCDE/CCET © avril 1996

Hongrie -- Une enquête sur la population active est effectuée tous les mois ; elle porte sur la semaine s'étendant du lundi au dimanche entre lesquels est compris le 12ème jour du mois. L'échantillon interrogé chaque trimestre comprenait environ 30 000 ménages (55 000 personnes) en 1992, 27 000 ménages (47 000 personnes) en 1993 et en 1994. Le tiers seulement de l'échantillon total est interrogé chaque mois. L'enquête ne concerne que les personnes qui vivaient dans des ménages privés pendant la semaine de référence. Chaque ménage est interrogé six fois de suite au total, après quoi il est retiré de l'échantillon.

Pologne -- Les enquêtes sur la population active sont réalisées sur une base trimestrielle ; la semaine de référence est celle qui inclut le 15ème jour du mois médian de chaque trimestre. L'échantillon, qui comprend entre 18 000 et 32 000 ménages, est obtenu par double stratification et exclut les personnes sans domicile fixe ainsi que la population des ménages collectifs, notamment les détenus et les appelés cantonnés dans des casernes. Un système de rotation, qui a été intégré dans le plan de sondage en mai 1993, est utilisé, de telle sorte que chaque ménage est interrogé deux trimestres de suite, exclu les deux suivants, puis à nouveau interrogé les deux derniers trimestres avant d'être retiré définitivement de l'échantillon.

République de Slovénie -- En 1993, l'Office statistique de la République de Slovénie a réalisé, en coopération avec le Service national de l'emploi, sa première enquête sur la population active en respectant les conventions du BIT. Celle-ci est effectuée annuellement au mois de mai sur la population résidente âgée de plus de 15 ans, telle qu'elle ressort des registres démographiques. L'échantillon est fondé sur l'échantillon en grappes à trois strates qui avait été utilisé pour l'enquête pilote de 1991. Le taux de rotation annuel y est actuellement de 30 pour cent et, en 1995, cet échantillon englobait approximativement 1,3 pour cent de la population. La période de référence de l'enquête est la semaine précédant celle des entretiens.

Roumanie -- La première enquête sur la population active a été réalisée sur un échantillon de la population résidente âgée de 14 ans et plus, y compris les personnes ayant quitté le territoire roumain pour plus de six mois, sous réserve qu'elles aient conservé des relations avec leur famille. Sont inclus dans l'échantillon : les appelés, les étudiants poursuivant des études à l'étranger, les personnes travaillant à l'étranger, les détenus, les personnes hospitalisées et celles qui suivent un traitement de courte durée dans un établissement de soins. En sont exclues les personnes qui résident en permanence dans un foyer pour personnes âgées, pour handicapés ou pour travailleurs, ou dans un établissement de soins. L'enquête est effectuée au cours de la dernière semaine de mars et la première semaine d'avril, la période de référence étant la semaine qui précède celle des entretiens. L'échantillon est établi par double stratification et, en 1994, il comptait 15 000 ménages, soit environ 45 000 personnes. En 1995, la taille de l'échantillon a été portée à 17 000 ménages, soit environ 50 000 personnes.

République slovaque -- Une enquête permanente sur la population active est réalisée toutes les semaines de l'année auprès d'un échantillon de 10 000 ménages sur l'ensemble du territoire de la République. L'échantillon subit une rotation de 20 pour cent, chaque ménage étant interrogé cinq fois. Il est obtenu par double stratification et les enquêtes trimestrielles suivent un cycle de 13 semaines. Les trimestres des enquêtes sur la population active précèdent d'un mois les trimestres civils afin que le traitement et l'analyse des données puissent être effectués en parallèle avec ceux des données découlant des enquêtes auprès des entreprises -- autrement dit les enquêtes concernant le premier trimestre de l'année portent sur les mois de décembre, janvier et février.

Fédération de Russie -- Le Goskomstat, l'Office statistique de la Fédération de Russie, a effectué, depuis 1992, trois enquêtes annuelles nationales sur la population active auprès des ménages. L'enquête a lieu la dernière semaine d'octobre du lundi au dimanche. Elle couvrait environ 260 000 ménages ou 583 000 personnes âgées de 15 à 72 ans. En 1995, la taille de l'échantillon a été ramenée à

OECD
OCDE
SHORT-TERM ECONOMIC INDICATORS, SOURCES AND DEFINITIONS
OECD/CCET © April 1996

235

INDICATEURS ÉCONOMIQUES A COURT TERME, SOURCES ET DÉFINITIONS
OCDE/CCET © avril 1996

0,2 pour cent de la population âgée de 15 à 72 ans à l'occasion du passage à une périodicité semestrielle. Étaient exclues de l'enquête les personnes en mission de longue durée (plus de six mois), les travailleurs ou les étudiants vivant dans des foyers et les écoliers vivant dans des pensionnats, les détenus et les patients d'hôpitaux psychiatriques, le personnel militaire (conscrits et militaires de carrière) vivant dans des casernes et les ressortissants étrangers. L'échantillon est construit sur la base du recensement de la population de 1989 et à partir des listes des districts utilisés pour le recensement. Lors de l'enquête réalisée en octobre 1995, l'échantillon a été restructuré sur la base de l'enquête par sondage de la population de 1994. Il s'agit d'un échantillon aléatoire, la procédure consistant dans un premier temps à choisir des districts, puis dans un deuxième temps, des ménages. La population de l'échantillon est renouvelée par tranche de 20 pour cent chaque année. Aucune rotation de l'échantillon n'a été effectuée en 1994, outre le remplacement des ménages dont les membres avaient plus de 72 ans au moment de l'enquête, et l'inclusion de nouveaux ménages comprenant des personnes ayant atteint l'âge de 15 ans. Les régions suivantes de la Fédération de Russie : l'Ossétie du Nord, la Tchétchénie, l'Ingouchie et depuis 1993 le district autonome (okrug) de Tchoukovsky n'entrent pas dans le cadre de l'étude. Par conséquent, l'estimation des données agrégées sur la population active est fondée sur des données administratives.

Définition des indicateurs du marché du travail

On trouvera dans la section qui suit les définitions des indicateurs présentés dans les tableaux par pays de l'annexe des *indicateurs du marché du travail* et les écarts par rapport à ces définitions. Comme il est indiqué plus haut, les données relatives aux variables énumérées ci-après proviennent de sources administratives et/ou des enquêtes sur la population active ou auprès des établissements lorsqu'elles existent.

Taux d'activité

Le *taux d'activité* est le rapport entre la population active totale d'âge actif et la population totale de la même tranche d'âge. La population d'âge actif inclut les femmes de 15 à 54 ans et les hommes de 15 à 59 ans.

Écarts par rapport à la définition :

Hongrie -- Les appelés sont exclus de la population d'âge actif.

Pologne -- La population d'âge actif englobe les femmes de 15 à 59 ans et les hommes de 15 à 64 ans ; en sont exclues les personnes vivant dans des ménages collectifs et les membres des ménages privés qui séjournent provisoirement à l'étranger (plus de deux mois).

Roumanie -- La population d'âge actif englobe les femmes de 16 à 56 ans et les hommes de 16 à 61 ans.

République slovaque -- Comme il n'existe pas de données trimestrielles, les chiffres de la population d'âge actif sont les mêmes pour les quatre trimestres et sont fondés sur les données de fin d'année, fournies par l'Office statistique national.

Chômage

Le *taux de chômage* est défini comme le nombre de chômeurs en pourcentage de la population active. Cette dernière correspond à l'effectif total des chômeurs et des personnes pourvues d'un emploi.

Les données sur le *chômage déclaré* se réfèrent aux personnes inscrites comme chômeurs auprès des services de l'emploi.

i) Dans les enquêtes sur la population active, sont considérées comme des chômeurs les personnes excédant un âge limite qui, au cours de la semaine ou du jour de référence, étaient :

  a) *sans travail*, c'est-à-dire qui n'étaient pourvues ni d'un emploi salarié ni d'un emploi non salarié, comme défini plus haut dans la section relative aux données sur l'emploi ; et

  b) *disponibles pour travailler* dans un emploi salarié ou non salarié durant la période de référence ; et

  c) *à la recherche d'un travail*, c'est-à-dire qui avaient pris des dispositions spécifiques au cours d'une période récente spécifiée pour chercher un emploi salarié ou un emploi non salarié. Ces dispositions spécifiques peuvent inclure : l'inscription à un bureau de placement public ou privé ; la candidature auprès d'employeurs ; les démarches sur les lieux de travail, dans les fermes ou à la porte des usines, sur les marchés ou dans les autres endroits où sont traditionnellement recrutés les travailleurs ; l'insertion ou la réponse à des annonces dans les journaux ; les recherches par relations personnelles ; la recherche de terrains, d'immeubles, de machines ou d'équipements pour créer une entreprise personnelle ; les démarches pour obtenir des ressources financières, des permis et licences, etc.

ii) En dépit du critère de recherche de travail incorporé dans la définition type du chômage, les personnes sans travail et disponibles pour travailler, qui ont pris des dispositions pour prendre un emploi salarié ou pour entreprendre une activité indépendante à une date ultérieure à la période de référence, devraient être considérées comme chômeurs.

iii) Les personnes temporairement absentes de leur travail et sans lien formel avec leur emploi, qui étaient disponibles pour travailler et à la recherche d'un travail, devraient être considérées comme chômeurs conformément à la définition type du chômage.

iv) Les étudiants, les personnes s'occupant du foyer et les autres personnes principalement engagées dans des activités non économiques durant la période de référence et qui satisfont aux critères exposés ci-dessus devraient être considérés comme chômeurs au même titre que les autres catégories de chômeurs et être identifiés séparément lorsque cela est possible.

Écarts par rapport à la définition :

Bulgarie -- Les données sur le chômage déclaré se réfèrent aux femmes de 16 à 54 ans et aux hommes de 16 à 59 ans.

Dans les enquêtes sur la population active, par chômeurs il faut entendre les personnes de 15 ans et plus qui ne travaillaient pas du tout pendant la semaine de référence, qui avaient activement recherché du travail pendant les quatre semaines précédentes et qui étaient disponibles pour commencer à travailler au cours des deux semaines suivant la semaine de référence. Sont également prises en compte les personnes qui ne cherchaient pas activement du travail mais, soit devaient intégrer un nouvel emploi ou s'établir à leur compte dans les 30 jours, soit attendaient de réintégrer un emploi précédent dont elles avaient été licenciées ou mises en congé sans solde (dès lors que la durée totale d'inactivité est supérieure à un mois), sous réserve d'en avoir obtenu la promesse de leur employeur et d'avoir convenu avec lui de la date de leur réintégration.

Hongrie -- Dans les enquêtes sur la population active, par chômeurs il faut entendre les personnes de 15 à 74 ans qui n'avaient pas d'emploi pendant la semaine de référence et qui avaient activement cherché du travail à un moment quelconque au cours des quatre semaines précédant la fin de la semaine de référence et étaient disponibles pour commencer à travailler au cours des deux semaines suivant la semaine de référence, ou attendaient de commencer un travail dans les 30 jours.

Pologne -- Les données sur le chômage tirées de l'enquête sur la population active portent sur les personnes de 15 ans et plus.

République de Slovénie -- Les données sur le chômage déclaré englobent les personnes qui : i) n'occupent pas d'emploi régulier ou n'exercent pas d'activité indépendante ; ne sont ni propriétaires ni copropriétaires d'une entreprise en exploitation ; et ne sont ni les propriétaires ni les utilisateurs de biens qui pourraient leur offrir un moyen de subsistance ; ii) sont capables et désireuses de travailler et sont prêtes à accepter un emploi correspondant à leur qualifications professionnelles ou à leurs compétences acquises dans le cadre d'une activité professionnelle passée ; iii) sont inscrites comme demandeurs d'emploi auprès du Service national de l'emploi.

Les données sur le chômage issues des enquêtes sur la population active englobent les personnes qui ne travaillaient pas pour un salaire ou un profit durant la semaine de référence, avaient activement cherché du travail pendant les quatre semaines précédentes et étaient disponibles pour commencer à travailler au cours des deux semaines suivantes ou avaient trouvé un emploi débutant après la semaine de référence.

Roumanie -- Par chômeurs, il faut entendre dans l'enquête sur la population active les personnes qui n'occupaient pas d'emploi durant la semaine de référence, avaient activement cherché du travail à un moment quelconque au cours des quatre semaines précédant la fin de la semaine de référence et étaient disponibles pour travailler dans les deux semaines suivant la semaine de référence.

République slovaque -- Les données sur le chômage issues des enquêtes sur la population active englobent les personnes qui ne travaillaient pas pour un salaire ou un profit au cours de la semaine de référence, avaient activement cherché du travail pendant les quatre semaines précédant la semaine de référence et étaient disponibles pour commencer à travailler au cours des deux semaines suivant la semaine de référence. Les données portent sur les personnes de 15 ans et plus.

Fédération de Russie -- Les données sur le chômage tirées de l'enquête sur la population active se réfèrent aux personnes âgées de 16 ans et plus qui : n'avaient pas de travail durant la semaine de l'enquête ou n'avaient pas de travail dont elles étaient temporairement absentes ; avaient activement cherché du travail au cours des quatre dernières semaines et étaient disponibles pour travailler dans les deux semaines suivant la semaine de référence. Les données sur le chômage englobent les étudiants à plein temps ou à temps partiel à la recherche d'un emploi à condition qu'ils soient immédiatement disponibles pour occuper un emploi. S'ils cherchent un travail pour une date ultérieure, par exemple pour les mois d'été, ils sont considérés inactifs.

Données sur la population active occupée

i) Les *personnes pourvues d'un emploi* comprennent toutes les personnes ayant dépassé un âge spécifié qui, durant la période -- semaine ou jour -- de référence, appartenaient à l'une des catégories suivantes :

Emploi salarié :

a) *Personnes au travail* : personnes qui durant la période de référence, ont effectué un travail moyennant un salaire ou un traitement en espèces ou en nature ; ou,

b) *Personnes qui ont un emploi, mais ne sont pas au travail* : personnes qui ayant déjà travaillé dans leur emploi actuel, en étaient temporairement absentes durant la période de référence et ont un lien formel avec leur emploi. Ce lien formel avec l'emploi devrait être déterminé à la lumière des circonstances nationales, par référence à l'un ou à plusieurs des critères suivants : (1) le paiement ininterrompu du salaire ou du traitement ; (2) une assurance de retour au travail à la fin de la situation d'exception ou un accord sur la date de retour ; (3) la durée de l'absence du travail qui, le cas échéant, peut être la durée pendant laquelle les travailleurs peuvent recevoir une indemnisation sans obligation d'accepter d'autres emplois.

Emploi non salarié :

a) *Personnes au travail* : personnes qui, durant la période de référence ont effectué un travail en vue d'un bénéfice ou d'un gain familial, en espèces ou en nature ;

b) *Personnes ayant une entreprise mais n'étant pas au travail* : personnes qui, durant la période de référence avaient une entreprise qui peut être une entreprise industrielle, un commerce, une exploitation agricole ou une entreprise de prestations de services, mais n'étaient temporairement pas au travail pour toute raison spécifique.

ii) Dans la pratique et selon les définitions du BIT, la notion de *travail effectué au cours de la période de référence* peut être interprétée comme étant un travail d'une durée d'une heure au moins.

iii) Les personnes temporairement absentes de leur travail pour raison de maladie ou d'accident, de congé ou de vacances, de conflit de travail ou de grève, de congé éducation ou formation, de congé maternité, de mauvaise conjoncture économique ou de désorganisation ou de suspension temporaires du travail dues à des causes telles que conditions météorologiques défavorables, incidents mécaniques ou électriques, pénurie de matières premières ou de combustibles, ou toute autre cause d'absence temporaire avec ou sans autorisation, devraient être considérées comme pourvues d'un emploi salarié, à condition qu'elles aient un lien formel avec leur emploi.

iv) Les employeurs et les personnes travaillant à leur propre compte devraient être considérés comme travailleurs non salariés et classés comme *étant au travail* ou *n'étant pas au travail*, selon les cas.

v) Les travailleurs familiaux non rémunérés devraient être considérés comme travailleurs non salariés indépendamment du nombre d'heures de travail effectué durant la période de référence.

vi) Les personnes engagées dans la production de biens et services économiques pour leur propre consommation ou celle du ménage devraient être considérées comme travailleurs non salariés si une telle production apporte une importante contribution à la consommation totale du ménage.

vii) Les apprentis qui ont reçu une rétribution en espèces ou en nature devraient être considérés comme personnes pourvues d'un emploi salarié et classés comme *étant au travail* ou *n'étant pas au travail* sur la même base que les autres catégories de personnes pourvues d'un emploi salarié.

viii) Les étudiants, les personnes s'occupant du foyer et autres personnes principalement engagées dans des activités non économiques durant la période de référence et qui étaient en même temps pourvues d'un emploi salarié ou non salarié comme défini ci-dessus devraient être considérés comme ayant un emploi, sur la même base que les autres catégories de personnes ayant un emploi et être identifiés séparément lorsque cela est possible.

Écarts par rapport à la définition :

Bulgarie -- Depuis la mise en place de l'enquête sur la population active en septembre 1993, les personnes pourvues d'un emploi sont les personnes de 15 ans et plus qui, durant la période de référence, ont effectué un travail quelconque pendant au moins une heure moyennant une rémunération ou un autre revenu ; ou qui n'ont pas travaillé, mais avaient un emploi dont elles s'étaient absentées temporairement pour cause de maladie, congé, conditions météorologiques, formation professionnelle, grève, etc.

Les personnes en congé de maternité ou en congé parental sont incluses dans les données sur l'emploi.

Hongrie -- Les données sur l'emploi couvrent les personnes âgées de 15 à 74 ans qui, durant la semaine de référence : ont travaillé au moins une heure moyennant un salaire, un bénéfice ou une rémunération en nature dans le cadre d'un emploi ou de leur propre entreprise (y compris les exploitations agricoles) ; ou ont travaillé au moins une heure dans une entreprise familiale ou une exploitation agricole, par exemple à titre de contribution familiale ; ou avaient un emploi dont elles étaient temporairement absentes durant toute la semaine de l'enquête. Les personnes ayant les activités suivantes ne sont pas considérées comme pourvues d'un emploi : travail non rémunéré au profit d'un autre ménage ou d'une organisation (bénévolat) ; construction ou rénovation de leur propre logement ; travail ménager non rémunéré ; jardinage ou travail sur un bien appartenant à l'intéressé, destinés à l'auto-consommation.

Pologne -- Les données se réfèrent aux personnes de 15 ans et plus. Les personnes en congé de maternité sont prises en compte dans les chiffres de l'emploi tant que leur absence reste comprise entre quatre et six mois. L'allocation qu'elles perçoivent tous les mois est égale à leur rémunération moyenne sur la période de six mois ayant précédé la naissance de l'enfant et leur est versée par la caisse d'assurance sociale.

République de Slovénie -- Outre les composantes de la définition type du BIT, les données sur l'emploi englobent les personnes qui, n'ayant pas travaillé durant la semaine de référence, ont conservé un lien contractuel avec leur employeur et ont motivé leur absence par un "excédent technique de main-d'oeuvre" ou le fait que "l'employeur ne pouvait leur donner assez de travail". Dans ce cas, l'employeur est tenu par la loi de verser pendant six mois une rémunération égale à 70 pour cent du salaire normal, tel qu'il est défini par la convention collective. A l'issue de cette période de six mois, l'intéressé devient soit chômeur, soit inactif. Si l'intéressé trouve un autre travail au cours de cette période de licenciement de six mois, il est mis un terme aux versements. Sur l'ensemble des chômeurs identifiés dans l'enquête de 1994, 4 700, soit environ 5 pour cent, étaient au chômage par suite de licenciements économiques.

Les personnes en congé de maternité sont considérées comme pourvues d'un emploi pendant leurs 365 premiers jours d'absence. Durant cette période, elles peuvent percevoir une rémunération égale à 100 pour cent de leur salaire normal, tel qu'il est fixé par leur contrat de travail, indexé sur le salaire moyen de l'année précédente. Le congé parental n'existe pas.

Roumanie -- Les données sur l'emploi issues des enquêtes auprès des établissements se rapportent aux personnes pourvues d'un emploi, quelle que soit la façon dont elles l'ont obtenu, qui leur procure un revenu par le biais d'une activité économique ou sociale, à savoir un emploi salarié ou non salarié. Les données sont des chiffres de fin d'année et couvrent les personnes de 16 ans et plus, à l'exclusion des appelés. Les estimations relatives au nombre de travailleurs indépendants et de travailleurs familiaux non rémunérés ainsi qu'à l'emploi dans les petites entreprises sont fondées sur les données du registre de l'agriculture et du commerce et du Ministère des finances.

Les données de l'enquête sur la population active englobent les personnes qui effectuent leur service militaire. Bien que l'enquête ne s'adresse pas aux résidents des cantonnements militaires, il est tenu compte des appelés dans le questionnaire. Les données de l'enquête sur la population active couvrent les personnes de 14 ans et plus. Les personnes en congé sans solde pour une durée n'excédant pas 90 jours, que ce soit pour préparer un examen, soigner un enfant malade, recevoir un traitement médical à l'étranger ou pour toute autre raison personnelle sont considérées comme pourvues d'un emploi, sous réserve qu'elles aient conclu un accord à cet effet avec leur employeur.

Les personnes en congé de maternité sont incluses dans les chiffres de l'emploi dès lors que leur absence n'excède pas un an à compter de deux mois avant la naissance de l'enfant. Elles reçoivent de la caisse d'assurance sociale une allocation dont le montant représente de 50 à 94 pour cent de leur salaire précédent, selon l'ancienneté et le nombre d'enfants.

République slovaque -- Le congé de maternité correspond aux 28 premières semaines d'absence, tandis que le congé parental correspond à la période comprise entre la 29ème semaine et trois ans après la naissance de l'enfant.

Fédération de Russie -- Outre la définition-type du BIT, les chiffres de l'emploi englobent également les conscrits résidant chez eux. Sont exclues les personnes dont la seule activité consiste à effectuer des travaux non rémunérés dans la maison (peinture, travaux de ménage ou de réparation, par exemple), à travailler sans rémunération pour des organisations religieuses, caritatives et analogues et les apprentis et stagiaires non rémunérés.

Les personnes en congé de maternité et en congé parental sont considérées comme étant occupées à partir d'environ 72 jours avant et jusqu'à 3 ans après la naissance de leur enfant. La prestation de congé de maternité est versée par les syndicats et équivaut à 100 pour cent du salaire moyen de l'intéressée. Le congé parental correspond à la période comprise entre le 73ème jour et trois ans après la naissance de l'enfant, le poste occupé par le salarié étant conservé par l'employeur jusqu'au retour de l'intéressé, établissant ainsi un lien informel avec l'emploi.

Chômage des jeunes

Les chiffres de l'*emploi* et du *chômage des jeunes* concernent les personnes de 15 à 24 ans.

Écarts par rapport à la définition :

OECD
OCDE
SHORT-TERM ECONOMIC INDICATORS, SOURCES AND DEFINITIONS
OECD/CCET © April 1996

241

INDICATEURS ÉCONOMIQUES A COURT TERME, SOURCES ET DÉFINITIONS
OCDE/CCET © avril 1996

INDICATEURS DU MARCHÉ DU TRAVAIL

Roumanie -- Les chiffres de l'emploi et du chômage des jeunes concernent les personnes de 14 à 24 ans.

Fédération de Russie -- Le chômage des jeunes concerne les personnes âgées de 16 à 24 ans. Les jeunes de 15 ans sur lesquels porte l'enquête sont considérés comme inactifs s'ils ne correspondent pas aux définitions de la population active occupée.

Chômage des classes d'âge de forte activité

Les chiffres de l'*emploi* et du *chômage des classes d'âge de forte activité* se réfèrent aux personnes de 25 à 49 ans.

Écarts par rapport à la définition :

Hongrie -- Les chiffres sur le chômage et l'emploi des classes d'âge de forte activité couvrent les personnes de 25 à 54 ans.

Chômage des travailleurs âgés

Les chiffres de l'*emploi* et du *chômage des travailleurs âgés* couvrent les femmes de 50 à 54 ans et les hommes de 50 à 59 ans.

Écarts par rapport à la définition :

Hongrie -- Les données sur le chômage et l'emploi des travailleurs âgés couvrent les personnes de 55 à 59 ans. L'âge officiel de la retraite pour les femmes est 55 ans.

Pologne -- Les données sur le chômage et l'emploi des travailleurs âgés concernent les femmes de 50 à 59 ans et les hommes de 50 à 64 ans.

Roumanie -- Les données sur le chômage et l'emploi des travailleurs âgés concernent les femmes de 50 à 56 ans et les hommes de 50 à 61 ans.

Chômage par niveau d'éducation

Le *taux de chômage par niveau d'éducation* est le nombre de chômeurs en pourcentage de la population active de chaque catégorie. Les indicateurs du *chômage par niveau d'éducation* incluent le nombre d'actifs occupés ou chômeurs ayant atteint, quels que soient le type d'activité exercée ou les qualifications requises, l'un des trois niveaux d'instruction suivants : supérieur, secondaire ou primaire (selon la Classification internationale type de l'éducation, CITE).

La catégorie *niveau de l'enseignement supérieur* comprend les actifs occupés ou les chômeurs qui ont fait des études post-secondaires complètes.

La catégorie *niveau des études secondaires générales* comprend les actifs occupés ou les chômeurs ayant suivi un enseignement secondaire général complet ou une formation professionnelle.

La catégorie *niveau égal ou inférieur à l'enseignement primaire* comprend les actifs occupés ou les chômeurs ayant fait des études primaires complètes ou partielles.

Écarts par rapport à la définition :

Bulgarie

-- La catégorie niveau des études secondaires générales couvre les personnes qui ont suivi un enseignement général dont la durée est d'ordinaire de trois ans après les études primaires. Sont également incluses les personnes ayant fréquenté certaines écoles professionnelles qui dispensent un enseignement général secondaire et permettent aussi d'obtenir certaines qualifications professionnelles. L'enseignement professionnel ne couvre que les personnes ayant fréquenté des écoles secondaires. La durée des études est de quatre à cinq ans après les études primaires. Les écoles professionnelles forment aux métiers de l'industrie, de l'agriculture, des transports, du commerce, de la santé et à d'autres activités économiques, ainsi qu'aux métiers d'art.

-- La catégorie niveau égal ou inférieur à l'enseignement primaire couvre les personnes ayant suivi une scolarité obligatoire qui commence à l'âge de 6 ou 7 ans et se termine à l'âge de 14 ou 15 ans. Certaines écoles professionnelles assurant un enseignement général de base et une formation professionnelle sont également incluses.

Hongrie

-- La catégorie niveau de l'enseignement supérieur couvre les diplômés des établissements d'enseignement supérieur ayant suivi un cycle de trois ou quatre ans d'études et les diplômés d'université.

-- La catégorie niveau des études secondaires générales couvre les personnes ayant fréquenté i) un établissement d'enseignement classique, dont le cycle s'étend sur quatre ans, ou ii) un autre établissement secondaire, d'enseignement général ou professionnel, dont l'examen de fin d'études débouche sur un certificat d'enseignement général ou professionnel (industrie, agriculture, économie, commerce, restauration, transports, services postaux, communications, santé publique, éducateur de jeunes enfants ou métiers d'art). Ces deux filières permettent ensuite de s'inscrire dans un établissement d'enseignement supérieur. L'enseignement professionnel englobe les diplômés des écoles d'apprentissage où la formation dure habituellement trois ans, qui forment des travailleurs qualifiés et se terminent par le passage d'un examen professionnel.

-- La catégorie niveau égal ou inférieur à l'enseignement primaire inclut les personnes qui ont suivi huit années ou moins d'enseignement élémentaire.

Pologne

-- La catégorie niveau des études secondaires générales comprend les personnes ayant suivi un enseignement professionnel secondaire. L'enseignement professionnel couvre les personnes n'ayant reçu qu'un enseignement professionnel de base.

Roumanie

-- La catégorie niveau de l'enseignement supérieur couvre les diplômés des établissements d'enseignement supérieur ayant suivi un cycle de trois ans et les diplômés d'université ayant fait quatre à six ans d'études.

-- La catégorie niveau des études secondaires générales englobe les personnes ayant achevé le premier (14 à 16 ans) ou le second (16 à 18 ans) cycle du secondaire. L'enseignement professionnel comprend les personnes ayant fréquenté une école technique, un établissement post-secondaire d'enseignement professionnel, une école professionnelle ou une école d'apprentissage.

-- La catégorie niveau égal ou inférieur à l'enseignement primaire inclut les personnes ayant achevé ou non leurs études primaires, lesquelles débutent à 6 ans pour s'achever à 14.

République slovaque

Les niveaux d'éducation sont fondés sur la classification type des domaines de formation ; les écarts par rapport à la définition sont les suivants :

-- La catégorie niveau des études secondaires générales englobe les personnes ayant fréquenté un établissement d'enseignement classique. L'enseignement professionnel comprend les personnes ayant suivi un enseignement professionnel secondaire, que ce soit dans un établissement d'études pédagogiques avancées, une école d'entreprise, un établissement secondaire d'enseignement professionnel, un conservatoire ou un centre d'apprentissage de niveau secondaire avec ou sans examen de fin d'études.

-- La catégorie niveau égal ou inférieur à l'enseignement primaire inclut les personnes ayant achevé leurs études primaires, y compris celles qui ont fréquenté un établissement spécial pour enfants handicapés, par exemple, et celles qui n'ont pas terminé leurs études primaires ou secondaires.

Lors de la mise en place de l'enquête sur la population active au deuxième trimestre de 1993, les données sur l'emploi comprenaient les personnes en congé parental. Depuis 1994, elles excluent les personnes en congé parental.

Fédération de Russie

-- La catégorie niveau des études secondaires générales comprend les personnes ayant fait au moins deux ans d'études supérieures ou ayant suivi 10, 11 ou 12 années complètes d'enseignement général. La catégorie niveau de l'enseignement professionnel comprend les personnes diplômées d'une école secondaire spécialisée (école secondaire technique ou tout autre établissement d'enseignement secondaire spécialisé, comme une école normale ou une école d'infirmières). La grande majorité de ces personnes possède également un diplôme d'études secondaires générales, c'est-à-dire qu'elles ont fait 10 à 12 ans d'études.

-- La catégorie niveau égal ou inférieur à l'enseignement primaire comprend les personnes ayant fait des études secondaires incomplètes (c'est-à-dire les personnes qui ont fait entre 7 et 11 ans d'études, mais n'ont pas obtenu de diplômes), qui ont fait des études primaires complètes, soit 8 à 9 ans d'études ou qui n'avaient pas fait d'études primaires. Dans la Fédération de Russie, l'enseignement primaire (jusqu'à 8 à 9 ans d'études) est considéré comme enseignement secondaire de base.

Chômage de longue durée

Les données relatives au *chômage de longue durée* se réfèrent aux personnes au chômage depuis plus de 12 mois. Le *taux de chômage de longue durée* correspond au pourcentage de chômeurs de longue durée dans la population active totale. La part du chômage de longue durée dans le chômage total, ou *fréquence du chômage de longue durée*, correspond au nombre de chômeurs de longue durée en pourcentage du nombre total de chômeurs. Sauf indication contraire, les données sur le chômage de longue durée des jeunes et des travailleurs âgés correspondent aux mêmes classes d'âge que celles qui sont indiquées dans les sections sur le chômage par classe d'âge.

Écarts par rapport à la définition :

Bulgarie -- Le chômage de longue durée des travailleurs âgés se réfère aux chômeurs de 55 ans et plus.

Hongrie -- Les chiffres du chômage de longue durée se réfèrent aux personnes au chômage depuis plus de 52 semaines (364 jours).

Pologne -- Depuis le quatrième trimestre de 1994, les données sur les chômeurs âgés de longue durée englobent les femmes de 50 à 59 ans et les hommes de 50 à 64 ans.

Sous-emploi

Les données relatives au *sous-emploi* se réfèrent aux personnes qui travaillent à temps partiel et souhaiteraient travailler à temps plein (conformément aux directives du BIT).

Écarts par rapport à la définition :

Hongrie -- Sont considérées comme sous-employées les personnes âgées de 15 à 74 ans qui, durant la semaine de référence ont travaillé à temps partiel pour des raisons économiques (ralentissement de l'activité) ; parce qu'il n'y avait pas d'emploi à plein temps disponible ; ou pour cause de chômage technique ; ou qui travaillent habituellement moins qu'à temps plein pour des raisons économiques. La définition du temps partiel correspond à une semaine de moins de 40 heures.

Pologne -- Sont considérées comme sous-employées les personnes qui, pendant la semaine de référence, ont effectué 39 heures ou moins pour des raisons économiques (indépendantes de leur volonté), par exemple parce qu'elles n'ont pas pu trouver de travail à temps plein, à cause d'une baisse de la production ou d'interruptions d'activité, parce que leur emploi a débuté ou pris fin durant la semaine de référence ou par suite d'un ralentissement de l'activité de l'entreprise, à cause de manque de clients, de commandes, de financement ou d'équipements.

République de Slovénie -- Les chiffres du sous-emploi couvrent les personnes qui travaillent à temps partiel parce qu'elles ne parviennent pas à trouver un emploi à plein temps.

Roumanie -- Les chiffres du sous-emploi couvrent les personnes qui, pendant la semaine de l'enquête, ont effectué un nombre d'heures inférieur à la durée habituelle du travail pour des raisons indépendantes de leur volonté et qui étaient à la recherche d'un travail supplémentaire ou d'un emploi à plein temps, ou étaient disponibles pour un tel travail ou emploi pendant la période de référence.

République slovaque -- Les données sur le sous-emploi couvrent les personnes qui travaillent à temps partiel et ne parviennent pas à trouver un travail à plein temps qui leur convienne, ainsi que celles qui travaillent pendant une durée inférieure au temps plein à l'initiative de leur employeur, en raison d'un ralentissement de l'activité. Jusqu'au premier trimestre de 1994, ces dernières étaient exclues du chiffre du sous-emploi.

INDICATEURS DU MARCHÉ DU TRAVAIL

Lors de la mise en place de l'enquête sur la population active au deuxième trimestre de 1993, les données sur le sous-emploi comprenaient les personnes en congé parental. Depuis 1994, elles excluent les personnes en congé parental.

Emploi à temps partiel

L'*emploi à temps partiel* se réfère aux personnes qui travaillent normalement pendant une durée inférieure au temps plein (selon les définitions nationales).

Écarts par rapport à la définition :

Pologne -- Sont considérées comme ayant travaillé à temps partiel les personnes qui, durant la semaine de l'enquête, ont : soit effectué 39 heures de travail ou moins, pour des raisons non économiques (c'est-à-dire volontairement), par exemple, pour cause de congés, formation, maladie ou autres responsabilités personnelles ou familiales ou parce qu'elles travaillent habituellement à temps partiel ; soit effectué 39 heures de travail ou moins pour des raisons économiques (indépendantes de leur volonté), par exemple parce qu'elles n'ont pas pu trouver de travail à temps plein, à cause d'une baisse de la production ou d'interruptions d'activité, parce que leur emploi a débuté ou pris fin durant la semaine de référence ou par suite d'un ralentissement de l'activité économique (manque de clients, de commandes, de financement ou d'équipements).

République de Slovénie -- Les données sur l'emploi à temps partiel recouvrent exclusivement l'emploi salarié et l'emploi non salarié.

Roumanie -- L'emploi à temps partiel englobe les personnes qui travaillent normalement pendant une durée inférieure à ce qu'elles estiment correspondre au temps plein dans leur profession. Lorsque la personne interrogée est incapable de juger si elle travaille à plein temps ou à temps partiel, l'enquêteur lui propose de fixer à 30 heures par semaine le seuil sur la base duquel se départager.

République slovaque -- Lors de la mise en place de l'enquête sur la population active au deuxième trimestre de 1993, les données sur l'emploi à temps partiel comprenaient les personnes en congé parental. Depuis 1994, elles excluent les personnes en congé parental.

Emploi non salarié

La définition de l'*emploi non salarié* couvre les employeurs, les personnes travaillant à leur propre compte, les travailleurs familiaux et les personnes engagées dans la production de biens et services pour leur propre consommation et/ou celle du ménage si une telle production apporte une importante contribution à la consommation totale du ménage. En sont exclus les membres des coopératives de production et des coopératives agricoles.

Écarts par rapport à la définition :

Hongrie -- Les personnes ayant comme activité la construction ou la rénovation de leur propre logement, le travail ménager, le jardinage ou le travail sur un bien leur appartenant destinés à l'auto-consommation sont exclues.

Pologne -- Avant le premier trimestre de 1995, l'emploi non salarié inclut les membres des coopératives.

République slovaque -- Lors de la mise en place de l'enquête sur la population active au deuxième trimestre de 1993, les données sur l'emploi non salarié comprenaient les personnes en congé parental. Depuis 1994, elles excluent les personnes en congé parental.

Emploi dans le secteur privé

L'*emploi dans le secteur privé* désigne l'emploi dans les entreprises privées, y compris les coopératives.

Écarts par rapport à la définition :

Pologne -- L'emploi dans le secteur privé couvre les travailleurs non salariés et les salariés des entreprises polonaises privées, qu'elles prennent la forme de partenariats, de coopératives, d'organismes sociaux, d'associations ou de fondations. L'emploi dans le secteur privé couvre également les entreprises privées à capitaux étrangers, y compris les petites entreprises étrangères et les partenariats à participation étrangère.

Roumanie -- Les coopératives sont exclues de l'emploi dans le secteur privé.

Salaires

Le *salaire moyen* correspond au salaire mensuel brut moyen des travailleurs à temps plein. Le salaire brut désigne les traitements et salaires de base, y compris les primes et gratifications, avant déduction des prélèvements, hors prestations familiales ou sociales. Les salaires annuels sont des moyennes calculées à partir des chiffres fournis par les offices nationaux de statistique.

Le *coefficient de variation des salaires* correspond à l'écart-type des salaires par secteur, exprimé en pourcentage du salaire moyen. Les secteurs sont l'agriculture, les industries extractives, les industries manufacturières, l'électricité, le gaz et l'eau, la construction, le commerce et la restauration, les transports et communications, les services financiers et l'immobilier, la santé et l'éducation, les administrations publiques et autres services.

Écarts par rapport à la définition :

Bulgarie -- Les salaires se réfèrent uniquement au secteur public, excluent les personnes en congé de maternité ou congé parental et sont obtenus en divisant la masse salariale totale de la période considérée par le nombre moyen de salariés. Les données du quatrième trimestre incluent les primes et gratifications annuelles. Les industries extractives, l'électricité, le gaz et l'eau sont inclus dans le secteur manufacturier. La Nomenclature des branches de l'économie nationale (NBEN) est utilisée pour classer les salaires par secteur et n'est pas strictement comparable à la NACE Rév. 1.

Hongrie -- Les données salariales couvrent, en 1993, les entreprises de plus de 20 salariés et depuis 1994 celles de plus de 10 salariés. Les gains comprennent les salaires et traitements de base, les salaires complémentaires, les récompenses, primes et gratifications et les participations aux bénéfices.

Pologne -- Les données salariales couvrent les traitements et salaires individuels (non compris les traitements et salaires des travailleurs à domicile et des apprentis), les versements au titre des bénéfices distribués et des excédents des coopératives, les bourses provenant des fonds d'encouragement des établissements, ou les honoraires versés à certaines catégories de travailleurs comme les rémunérations du travail effectué dans le cadre d'un contrat des journalistes ou des producteurs de radio et télévision. Avant le premier trimestre de 1994, l'électricité, le gaz et l'eau étaient inclus dans le secteur manufacturier, et la classification nationale des activités économiques était fondée sur la Classification polonaise de l'économie nationale (KGN.). Depuis le premier trimestre de 1994, les activités économiques sont classées selon la Classification européenne des activités (EKD), qui est la version polonaise de la NACE Rév. 1.

Une nouvelle dénomination du zloty a été introduite le 1er janvier 1995, le nouveau zloty équivalant à 10 000 anciens zlotys.

République de Slovénie -- Outre la rémunération du travail effectivement réalisé pendant les heures normales de travail, le salaire moyen inclut toutes les autres formes de gain et notamment la rémunération des heures supplémentaires, les suppléments pour congés annuels, les indemnités de maladie pour les absences n'excédant pas 30 jours, la rémunération des jours fériés, la rétribution des tâches d'intérêt national, les congés payés et assimilés, les gratifications et primes, la rémunération de travaux passés, les incitations financières et l'intéressement aux bénéfices après clôture des comptes de la période ou de l'exercice. L'enquête s'adresse aux entreprises et établissements de trois salariés ou plus. En 1992 elle prenait en compte les entreprises privées et les membres des forces armées et, en 1993, les membres de la police. Les gains des consultants et associés ne sont pas pris en considération. Les salaires par secteur sont classés selon la classification nationale des activités économiques (EKD).

Roumanie -- Les données salariales couvrent le salaire de base, les primes et gratifications, qu'elles prennent la forme d'un pourcentage du salaire de base ou d'un versement forfaitaire, les ajustements de salaire découlant de la législation ou des conventions collectives, les versements prélevés sur le fonds salarial et les paiements en nature. Elles portent sur toutes les entreprises de plus de 500 salariés et sur un échantillon d'entreprises plus petites.

République slovaque -- Les salaires moyens sont calculés en divisant la masse salariale par le nombre de salariés enregistrés. Sont exclus du salaire brut les paiements tels que : les primes et gratifications, les indemnités de maladie, les primes et salaires versés à des personnes en congé de maternité ou parental. Les données trimestrielles sur les salaires moyens excluent les gains des salariés d'entrepreneurs privés non inscrits au registre du commerce, et les entreprises de moins de 25 salariés depuis 1992. Les coopératives agricoles sont incluses. La classification nationale des activités économiques est fondée sur la Classification des branches d'activités économiques (OKEC) établie dans la République slovaque sur la base de la NACE Rév. 1.

Fédération de Russie -- Les salaires bruts moyens comprennent les primes, gratifications et paiements en nature. On calcule les salaires en divisant la masse salariale totale pour la période considérée par le nombre moyen de salariés, ajusté pour tenir compte des travailleurs à temps partiel. On obtient des données sur les salaires par le biais d'enquêtes mensuelles auprès des établissements qui portent sur les grandes et moyennes entreprises, lesquelles représentent près de 90 pour cent de l'emploi total dans les entreprises. La classification nationale des activités économiques est fondée sur la Classification des secteurs économiques de tous les syndicats (OKONH) qui n'est pas comparable à la NACE, Rév. 1. Les coefficients de variation des salaires ne sont pas comparables avec ceux des autres pays car les données sur les salaires n'ont pas le même niveau d'agrégation sectorielle.

OECD
OCDE
SHORT-TERM ECONOMIC INDICATORS, SOURCES AND DEFINITIONS
OECD/CCET © April 1996

248

INDICATEURS ÉCONOMIQUES A COURT TERME, SOURCES ET DÉFINITIONS
OCDE/CCET © avril 1996

Productivité du travail

Les indices de la *productivité du travail* sont présentés sous forme de rapports. La productivité du travail exprimée en heures travaillées est le rapport entre l'indice de la production de la branche d'industrie et l'indice des heures travaillées dans la branche d'industrie. La productivité du travail exprimée en personnes est le rapport entre l'indice de la production de la branche d'industrie et l'indice des effectifs employés dans la branche d'industrie. On trouvera la définition des indices de production industrielle et de l'emploi dans l'industrie utilisés pour calculer les indices de la productivité du travail dans les notes méthodologiques principales de ce volume.

Écarts par rapport à la définition :

Hongrie -- La productivité du travail horaire est calculée à partir du nombre moyen mensuel d'heures travaillées dans le secteur manufacturier, lequel inclut le nombre d'heures effectuées par les salariés à temps plein et exclut les travailleurs à domicile et les retraités des entreprises à responsabilité limitée. Le nombre d'heures travaillées inclut les heures supplémentaires et les heures perdues (pour cause de pannes, ruptures d'approvisionnement, etc.). En ce qui concerne les entreprises qui sont prises en compte, se reporter à la section consacrée aux *salaires*.

Pologne -- Avant le deuxième trimestre de 1994, les heures travaillées dans l'industrie étaient définies comme le nombre moyen d'heures travaillées durant la semaine de l'enquête pour les salariés des industries extractives et manufacturières. Depuis le deuxième trimestre de 1994, seuls les salariés du secteur manufacturier sont pris en compte.

République de Slovénie -- Les données relatives aux heures effectuées dans l'industrie émanent de l'enquête sur la population active et se réfèrent au nombre moyen d'heures effectivement travaillées durant la semaine de référence. Les données relatives à l'emploi dans l'industrie émanent de l'enquête sur la population active.

Roumanie -- Les données relatives aux heures travaillées dans l'industrie portent sur les heures effectuées, rémunérées ou non, y compris les heures supplémentaires et le travail effectué pendant les fins de semaine et les congés durant un an. Elles couvrent les entreprises publiques et les entreprises d'économie mixte des industries extractives, manufacturières et du secteur de l'électricité, du gaz et de l'eau.

BULGARIE

Production industrielle

Les indices de la production industrielle sont définis par référence à la Nomenclature des branches de l'économie nationale (NBNE) du ex-CAEM, et sont disponibles pour les industries extractives, les industries manufacturières, le gaz et l'électricité et la construction.

Les indices mensuels et trimestriels de la production industrielle couvrent le secteur public. Malgré la rapide augmentation du nombre des petites entreprises privées observée dans l'industrie, par exemple, de 17 000 à la fin de 1992 à environ quelque 36 000 à la fin de 1993, l'Institut national de statistique (INS) estime que les 3 000 (environ) entreprises industrielles publiques représentaient 95.4 pour cent de la production industrielle en 1993 et 91.3 pour cent en 1994. Des estimations de la production industrielle du secteur privé sont effectuées chaque année et incorporées dans les indices annuels.

Dans les séries mensuelles et trimestrielles, la production inclut la production secondaire qui relève de la branche concernée, et exclut la production subsidiaire, c'est-à-dire la part de la production secondaire qui ne relève pas de la branche. Les séries annuelles couvrent l'ensemble de la production, y compris la production subsidiaire.

Les données mensuelles, trimestrielles et annuelles sont fournies par les entreprises aux offices statistiques régionaux qui les transmettent, une fois traitées, à l'INS.

La production brute couvre la production de produits finis, intermédiaires et finaux, les produits semi-finis et les variations de stocks de produits finis. La production non-principale est incluse depuis 1995 seulement.

Jusqu'à 1990, on calculait la valeur de la production totale aux prix constants en multipliant les quantités produites par les prix de gros au 1er janvier 1982. Depuis 1991, les estimations de la production aux prix constants s'appuient sur les prix de l'année précédente et les indices ont été raccordés. Les indices sont de type Laspeyres.

La période de base des indices était la période correspondante de 1985. L'INS a recalculé l'indice de façon à faire apparaître des variations approximatives de mois en mois. Les nouveaux indices ont été obtenus en appliquant aux séries d'origine la structure mensuelle et trimestrielle de 1985. A partir de janvier 1994, certaines séries de la production industrielle ont 1990 pour année de base.

L'*indice de la production industrielle totale* englobe les industries extractives, les industries manufacturières et le gaz et l'électricité.

Depuis l'introduction d'une réforme des prix en février 1991, des difficultés ont été rencontrées dans le calcul d'un déflateur de prix pour la production en 1991. On assure la comparabilité des données mensuelles et trimestrielles en éliminant l'incidence des variations de prix notifiées par les entreprises elles-mêmes. Depuis 1992, l'estimation de l'indice des prix à la production au niveau des sous branches

OECD
OCDE
SHORT-TERM ECONOMIC INDICATORS, SOURCES AND DEFINITIONS
OECD/CCET © April 1996

250

INDICATEURS ÉCONOMIQUES A COURT TERME, SOURCES ET DÉFINITIONS
OCDE/CCET © avril 1996

industrielles permet la comparabilité des données mensuelles et trimestrielles. Les données mensuelles sont donc considérées comme préliminaires et certains ajustements sont faits. A la suite de ces ajustements pour la période courante, les données pour les périodes antérieures sont aussi révisées.

L'*indice de la production industrielle pour les industries extractives* couvre l'exploitation du charbon (extraction, préparation et production de briquettes), l'industrie pétrolière, l'extraction et la préparation des minerais de métaux ferreux et non ferreux, la production de matières premières minérales, l'extraction de matériaux non métallifères, l'exploitation de carrières, l'industrie du bois et la pêche.

L'*indice de la production industrielle pour les industries manufacturières* couvre les industries manufacturières définies dans la CITI, et exclut l'édition. L'indice inclut la production subsidiaire et les activités manufacturières du secteur privé.

L'*indice de la production industrielle pour l'électricité et le gaz* couvre la production et la distribution d'électricité, de vapeur et d'eau chaude. La production, l'assainissement et la distribution de l'eau froide sont exclus.

L'*indice de la construction* est calculé sur la base de la production, y compris les ouvrages architecturaux et la prospection géologique, selon la Nomenclature des branches de l'économie nationale.

Quantités produites

La *production de charbon* couvre la houille (houille anthraciteuse et anthracite, y compris le charbon utilisé dans les mines), le charbon brun et le lignite.

La *production d'acier brut* couvre l'acier brut obtenu en four Martin, par soufflage d'oxygène et en four électrique, ainsi que par d'autres procédés (lingots et acier pour moulages).

La *production de ciment* couvre tous les types de ciment : ciments Portland, ciments Portland aux pouzzolanes et assimilés, ciments Portland de haut fourneau, etc.

Enquêtes de conjoncture

On trouvera une description des techniques de réalisation de ces enquêtes et la liste des questions harmonisées dans le chapitre de cette publication consacré aux *Enquêtes de conjoncture*.

Construction

Logements

Les logements sont définis comme des locaux à usage d'habitation physiquement distincts et indépendants, comportant une ou plusieurs pièces (d'habitation et de service) et ayant une entrée indépendante donnant sur une partie commune (escalier ou palier) ou ayant directement accès à la rue.

Une enquête mensuelle couvrant les activités de construction fournit des données sur le nombre de *logements achevés*. Elle donne des informations pour tous les secteurs : public, coopératif, municipal et privé, y compris la construction pour compte propre par les ménages. On dispose aussi d'informations sur les logements achevés émanant de la Commission d'inspection du bâtiment, qui délivre un certificat de

BULGARIE

conformité lorsque le logement est jugé habitable. Ce certificat n'est toutefois pas exigé pour les logements construits pour compte propre, ces données paraissent donc moins complètes que celles de l'enquête mensuelle.

Le nombre de logements achevés en février 1990 inclut aussi les logements achevés en janvier 1990.

Commerce intérieur

Les *ventes de détail en valeur* se réfèrent à la valeur des biens alimentaires et non alimentaires vendus par tous types de points de vente de détail et de restauration. La valeur des ventes de détail englobe aussi la valeur des ventes directes des entrepôts et des ventes de production pour compte propre ainsi que les services de réparation de véhicules, d'appareils électroménagers et de biens personnels. Depuis janvier 1996, les statistiques sur les ventes de détail ne comprennent plus la valeur des services de réparation de véhicules à moteur ou d'appareils et d'équipements ménagers. On dispose depuis mai 1991 de données mensuelles sur le chiffre d'affaires de produits alimentaires et non alimentaires.

Jusqu'en 1993, les données sur les ventes de détail se référaient au chiffre d'affaires du secteur public et étaient recueillies chaque mois à l'occasion d'un recensement. Les informations provenaient de toutes les entreprises d'État et les coopératives vendant des biens, des aliments et des boissons ou réparant les biens. Depuis janvier 1991, des estimations du chiffre d'affaires du secteur privé sont également incluses.

De janvier 1994 à décembre 1995, une enquête mensuelle couvrait environ 30 pour cent des unités du secteur public. Ces unités contribuaient pour une part d'environ 90 pour cent aux ventes totales des points de vente de détail du secteur public. Les points de vente privés faisaient l'objet d'une enquête trimestrielle. L'information ainsi recueillie permettait d'affiner les estimations mensuelles de la valeur totale des ventes de détail.

Depuis janvier 1996, cette enquête mensuelle porte également sur les ventes de détail du secteur privé. Environ 1,5 pour cent des commerces de détail du secteur privé sont couverts. Ce qui représente environ 50 pour cent des ventes de détail du secteur privé.

Les données sur les ventes de détail incluent les taxes sur le chiffre d'affaires. Celles-ci sont remplacées depuis avril 1994 par une taxe à la valeur ajoutée.

Jusqu'à la fin de 1994, les indices de prix de détail étaient utilisés pour déflater les ventes de détail en valeur dans les sources nationales. Depuis janvier 1995, l'indice des prix à la consommation pour l'alimentation et les biens non alimentaires est utilisé pour calculer la série *ventes de détail en volume*. Cette série est présentée en base "même période de l'année précédente=100" dans les sources nationales. L'indice en base fixe publié dans *Indicateurs économiques à court terme : Économies en transition* a été calculé par le Secrétariat de l'OCDE, en utilisant l'indice des prix à la consommation total rebasé en 1992 = 100. Cette série est présentée en base 1993 = 100.

Main-d'oeuvre

Emploi

La série *emploi dans le secteur public*, précédemment intitulée *emploi total*, se rapporte au nombre moyen de salariés des entreprises d'État et des coopératives, i.e. à l'exclusion du secteur privé. Elle ne se réfère qu'à l'emploi civil.

Avant 1992, les données provenaient de vastes enquêtes trimestrielles auprès des entreprises. Celles-ci devaient indiquer leurs effectifs pour chaque mois du trimestre. En 1992, des enquêtes industrielles mensuelles comportant quelques indicateurs concernant l'emploi et les gains ont également été mises en place. Les enquêtes trimestrielles couvrant un nombre plus élevé d'entreprises avaient été maintenues. La couverture des enquêtes étant différente, les données trimestrielles n'ont pas été utilisées pour réviser les données mensuelles, les deux séries ne correspondaient donc pas et des différences entre les données mensuelles et trimestrielles apparaissent jusqu'au second semestre de 1992.

Depuis 1993, il n'existe plus qu'une enquête trimestrielle, au cours de laquelle les entreprises font état de leurs effectifs pour chaque mois du trimestre.

Les moyennes sont calculées à partir du nombre de salariés relevé chaque jour au cours de la période couverte. Pour les jours fériés et les jours non ouvrables, le nombre de salariés retenu est le même que pour le jour qui précède. Le nombre de salariés enregistrés couvre l'ensemble des personnes employées pendant au moins un jour à l'activité principale de l'entreprise ou au moins cinq jours à une autre activité de l'entreprise. Les apprentis et les salariés en congé de maternité ou congé parental sont inclus. Les salariés à temps partiel sont comptés, en équivalent plein temps.

Les données annuelles englobent des estimations de l'emploi dans le secteur privé. Il s'agit de données sur les personnes employées dans le secteur étatique et coopératif, d'informations tirées des bilans (voir ci-dessous), de données sur le nombre des personnes exerçant des professions à caractère libéral (comme les notaires), les données annuelles concernant le nombre de travailleurs agricoles et les données concernant les petites entreprises de moins de 10 salariés, font chaque année l'objet d'une enquête au 30 juin et au 31 décembre.

Les bilans sont communiqués à l'INS conformément à la loi comptable qui s'applique aux entreprises ayant au moins 10 salariés et un chiffre d'affaires mensuel d'au moins 50 000 levs. Seules quelques entreprises privées sont concernées par ces dispositions et l'enquête semi-annuelle évoquée plus haut permet donc de compléter les informations relatives aux entreprises privées.

Une enquête sur la population active auprès des ménages mise en place en septembre 1993, fournit des informations supplémentaires sur l'emploi, en particulier pour les travailleurs non salariés ayant une activité au sein de leur famille. Cette enquête a eu lieu trois fois en 1995. Pour plus de précisions, voir ci-dessus le chapitre *Indicateurs du marché du travail*.

La série *emploi total,* auparavant appelé *emploi tous secteurs*, couvre l'emploi dans l'ensemble de l'économie. Elle est estimée par l'Institut national de statistique. Comme on ne dispose d'estimations des effectifs du secteur privé que sur une base annuelle, cette série n'est elle-même disponible que sur une base annuelle.

BULGARIE

L'emploi dans l'industrie couvre les industries extractives et manufacturières et le gaz et l'électricité, comme définies ci-dessus à propos de la production industrielle. Les estimations relatives à l'emploi du secteur privé ne sont incluses que dans les chiffres annuels.

L'emploi dans l'industrie manufacturière couvre les industries manufacturières telles que définies ci-dessus à propos de la production industrielle. La série englobe les salariés exerçant une activité manufacturière dans les branches non manufacturières. Les estimations relatives à l'emploi du secteur privé ne sont incluses que dans les chiffres annuels.

La population d'âge actif en Bulgarie se réfère aux femmes âgées de 15 à 54 ans et aux hommes âgés de 15 à 59 ans.

Chômage

L'enregistrement du *chômage* a commencé en juillet 1990. Les données proviennent, via l'INS, de l'Office national de l'emploi du Ministère du travail et des affaires sociales et se réfèrent au nombre total de chômeurs inscrits sur les registres administratifs.

Pour être inscrit en tant que chômeur auprès de l'Office national de l'emploi, l'intéressé doit avoir travaillé au moins 8 mois dans une activité quelconque ou être diplômé de l'enseignement secondaire, ou encore avoir été inscrit dans un établissement post-scolaire pendant au moins un mois (y compris dans le cadre d'une formation militaire).

Les personnes inscrites en tant que chômeur sans autres sources de revenu peuvent recevoir des indemnités. Les allocataires doivent pointer régulièrement pour continuer à recevoir des indemnités. Le montant des indemnités versées dépend des qualifications et du type d'emploi occupé précédemment ; il est proportionnel au salaire précédent. La durée des versements dépend de celle des états de service. Les jeunes diplômés ne perçoivent des prestations que pendant trois mois. Pour les autres personnes, la durée maximum d'indemnisation est d'un an. En général, les personnes arrivant en fin de droits cessent de s'inscrire au chômage. On estime à 35 000 environ le nombre de personnes qui sont ainsi rayées chaque mois. La difficulté d'accès aux bureaux de l'emploi pour les habitants des petites villes tend également à les décourager de s'inscrire.

Le *taux de chômage*, estimé par l'INS, était disponible annuellement jusqu'en 1993. Il s'agit du rapport du nombre moyen annuel de chômeurs enregistrés à la population active, celle-ci étant définie comme la somme de l'emploi annuel moyen total auparavant appelé emploi tous secteurs (voir plus haut) et du chômage enregistré.

Depuis septembre 1993, l'enquête sur la population active fournit des informations sur le chômage. Pour plus de précisions, voir ci-dessus le chapitre *Indicateurs du marché du travail*.

Les *offres d'emploi* se réfèrent aux emplois vacants à pourvoir immédiatement, déclarés à l'Office national de l'emploi et restant vacants le jour de référence.

Salaires

Gains mensuels

Les données s'appuient sur les mêmes enquêtes et autres sources d'information que les statistiques de l'emploi (voir ci-dessus). Toutefois, contrairement à ce qui est le cas pour ces dernières, aucune estimation relative au secteur privé n'est incluse, même dans les données annuelles.

La série *gains mensuels dans le secteur public*, précédemment appelée *gains totaux*, n'indique donc que les gains mensuels moyens des entreprises étatiques et coopératives.

Les *gains mensuels dans l'industrie* se rapportent également au secteur public et couvrent les industries extractives et manufacturières, et le gaz et l'électricité.

Ces séries relatives aux gains mensuels sont disponibles sur une base mensuelle depuis 1992, et depuis cette date elles excluent les salariées en congé de maternité. Les séries publiées précédemment (disponibles sur la disquette de statistiques rétrospectives) n'étaient disponibles que sur une base trimestrielle et annuelle et indiquaient donc les gains annuels moyens et les gains trimestriels moyens.

Prix

Prix de gros

L'*indice des prix de gros* se réfère aux prix de la production industrielle pondérée par la valeur des biens vendus.

Des séries mensuelles sont disponibles depuis 1991 et s'appuient sur un échantillon de 1 000 produits et groupes de produits. Les indices sont calculés sur la base des informations fournies par environ 3 000 entreprises industrielles du secteur étatique et coopératif, concernant l'incidence des changements de prix. Les prix s'entendent hors taxes.

L'indice, de type Paasche, a pour période de base la période correspondante de l'année précédente.

Prix à la consommation

L'*indice des prix à la consommation* (IPC) mensuel est tiré des informations collectées dans 28 bureaux statistiques régionaux, pour 1 604 biens et services avec six relevés par article, sur la base d'un panier de biens et services de consommation établi par l'INS. Jusqu'à la fin de 1992, les coefficients de pondération utilisés provenaient de l'enquête sur le chiffre d'affaires du commerce de détail. Depuis janvier 1993, la pondération se réfère à la part des dépenses de chaque groupe dans l'enquête sur le budget des ménages de 1992.

Le tableau ci-dessous indique le nombre de biens et de services inclus et les coefficients de pondération actuellement appliqués, par groupe de dépenses :

BULGARIE

Poste	Produits	Services	Poids
Alimentation (y compris restauration) [1]	465	2	43.4
Spiritueux	24	--	2.3
Tabac	5	--	1.9
Logement	48	26	3.6
Consommation énergétique des ménages	9	6	4.3
Meubles et équipements ménagers	159	23	4.7
Habillement, chaussures et articles de toilette	366	40	8.3
Hygiène et soins médicaux	172	13	1.9
Education et loisirs	108	37	3.5
Transports et communications	39	48	7.7
Autres [2]	2	12	18.4
TOTAL	1 397	207	100.0

1. Le groupe Alimentation comprend 265 produits alimentaires et 200 plats de restauration.
2. Le coefficient de pondération du groupe Autres est la somme des coefficients de pondération des dépenses consacrées par les ménages à leur lopin cultivé (4.6) et des autres dépenses (13.8).

Les prix de certains produits, tels que les transports, l'électricité et certains loyers, sont déterminés à partir d'informations administratives.

Depuis le début de 1993, l'indice total et les indices des différents groupes incluent les biens ainsi que les services associés au groupe considéré. On en déduit un indice des prix des services. Avant 1993, on calculait aussi un indice des prix des services distinct, mais les services n'étaient pas inclus dans chaque groupe.

Les indices des prix à la consommation sont de type Laspeyres modifié. Depuis 1991, la période de base utilisée est la période précédente. Des indices de prix en base fixe 1992=100 sont disponibles depuis 1992.

Finances internes

Les données sont fournies, via l'INS, par la Banque nationale de Bulgarie.

La *masse monétaire au sens étroit (M1)* se réfère à la monnaie hors encaisses des banques et dépôts à vue des entreprises.

La *quasi-monnaie* englobe tous les dépôts à terme, dépôts d'épargne et dépôts en devises. Pour les dépôts à terme, il s'agit aussi bien des dépôts des entreprises et des ménages dans toutes les institutions financières que des dépôts de la Compagnie d'assurance d'État auprès de la Banque nationale de Bulgarie. Les dépôts d'épargne englobent les dépôts d'épargne et dépôts à vue des ménages. Les dépôts en devises couvrent ceux des entreprises et des ménages résidents et non résidents.

OECD
OCDE
SHORT-TERM ECONOMIC INDICATORS, SOURCES AND DEFINITIONS
OECD/CCET © April 1996

256

INDICATEURS ÉCONOMIQUES A COURT TERME, SOURCES ET DÉFINITIONS
OCDE/CCET © avril 1996

La *masse monétaire au sens large (M2)* est la somme de la masse monétaire au sens étroit et de la quasi-monnaie. Jusqu'à la fin de 1995, elle englobait également les dépôts à l'importation et les dépôts réglementés.

Pour 1991 et 1992, les *dépôts personnels* couvrent les dépôts à terme et les dépôts d'épargne. Pour les dépôts à terme, il s'agit des dépôts des entreprises et des ménages dans toutes les institutions financières, ainsi que des dépôts de la Compagnie d'assurance d'État auprès de la Banque nationale de Bulgarie. Les dépôts d'épargne englobent les dépôts d'épargne et les dépôts à vue des ménages. Seuls sont inclus les dépôts en levs.

Depuis 1993, les dépôts personnels incluent les dépôts d'épargne et les dépôts courants des ménages uniquement, en levs et en devises.

Taux d'intérêt

Le *taux d'escompte officiel* se réfère au taux d'intérêt des crédits de refinancement des banques commerciales auprès de la Banque nationale de Bulgarie.

Finances extérieures

Les données sont fournies, via l'INS, par la Banque nationale de Bulgarie.

Les *taux de change* vis-à-vis du dollar des États-Unis, de l'Écu et du deutsche mark sont des taux flottants avec des cours quotidiens. Les taux indiqués se réfèrent au dernier jour du mois.

Les *réserves officielles* englobent les créances brutes sur les pays étrangers et l'or. Les données se réfèrent au stock en fin de période.

La *dette extérieure brute* couvre toutes les exigibilités brutes envers les pays étrangers, y compris les dépôts en levs des non résidents.

Commerce extérieur

1980-1991

Des données sur les *exportations, les importations* et le *solde commercial* sont disponibles, avec une distinction suivant que les transactions sont effectuées en monnaies convertibles ou en monnaies non convertibles. Jusqu'en 1990, toutes les transactions avec l'ex-URSS étaient en monnaie non convertible, mais, depuis, la proportion du commerce en monnaie non convertible s'est réduite.

Les statistiques commerciales reposaient sur des enquêtes auprès des exportateurs et importateurs. Les registres étaient mis à jour grâce aux informations fournies par le service des douanes. Exportations et importations étaient enregistrées fab et la classification utilisée était celle du CAEM.

BULGARIE

A partir de 1992

Le Système harmonisé de description et de codage des marchandises a été introduit en 1992. Les documents de déclarations douanières qui couvrent toutes les entreprises du secteur public et du secteur privé ont également été mis en place, ainsi que les tarifs de douanes.

Le commerce extérieur couvre les importations des biens destinés à la consommation intérieure, les exportations de biens destinés à la consommation dans les pays commanditaires, les importations et exportations temporaires -- avant et après traitements --, ainsi que l'aide internationale.

Les déclarations douanières ne sont pas enregistrées pour le commerce d'État, pour le chargement ou l'approvisionnement des bateaux et des avions ; ces rubriques sont cependant incluses dans les statistiques d'importations et d'exportations. Les données du commerce extérieur ne couvrent pas le commerce des services, des réparations, des brevets, de la pêche et des films de cinéma ni les biens destinés à la réexportation directe.

Les importations sont enregistrées caf et les exportations fab.

Publications

Certaines des séries décrites ci-dessus figurent aussi, mais avec une présentation conforme à la pratique nationale, dans les publications suivantes de l'Institut national de statistique bulgare :

Current Economic Business (La conjoncture économique)

Statistical News (Actualité statistique)

Export and Import (Exportations et importations)

Industry (L'industrie)

Foreign Trade (Commerce extérieur)

Statistical Reference Book, Economics of Bulgaria (Livre de référence statistique, L'économie de la Bulgarie).

RÉPUBLIQUE FÉDÉRATIVE TCHÈQUE ET SLOVAQUE

Introduction

Le 1er janvier 1993, la République fédérative tchèque et slovaque a cessé d'exister et les ex-républiques tchèque et slovaque sont devenues deux États indépendants, la République tchèque et la République slovaque. Cependant, les notes ci-dessous se réfèrent aux données agrégées pour la RFTS, disponibles jusqu'à la fin de 1992.

En règle générale, les données relatives à la RFTS ont été obtenues par agrégation des données concernant la République tchèque, établies par l'Office statistique tchèque (OST), et des données concernant la République slovaque, établies par l'Office statistique slovaque (OSS).

Production industrielle

L'indice de la production industrielle (IPI) couvre les entreprises des industries extractives et manufacturières, y compris l'électricité, le gaz et l'eau, et ce quelle que soit la forme de propriété des entreprises.

Depuis 1991, la production était mesurée par la production de biens, c'est-à dire la production finale de l'entreprise et non la production brute. Les valeurs de la production aux prix de 1989 étaient enregistrées de façon cumulative depuis le début de l'année jusqu'au mois en cours. Les chiffres mensuels étaient calculés par soustraction des données cumulées successives.

Dans le passé, l'indice mesurait la variation du volume de production par rapport à la période correspondante de l'année précédente. Si la structure industrielle changeait, on recalculait la valeur de la production de la même période de l'année précédente sur une base comparable et on enchaînait le taux de variation obtenu à l'indice avec la base d'origine. Cela signifie que si l'on pouvait valablement comparer une même période sur différentes années, il n'en allait pas de même à strictement parler pour les comparaisons à l'intérieur d'une même année. C'est pourquoi toutes les périodes de l'année de base étaient ramenées à 100.

Depuis 1991, la couverture des entreprises avait changé : en 1991, il s'agissait des entreprises d'au moins 100 salariés ; en 1992, les entreprises d'au moins 25 salariés. Les différences par rapport à la couverture des entreprises des années précédentes ne sont pas significatives.

Depuis 1992, l'indice national a été changé en base fixe 1989=100.

L'indice de la production industrielle totale englobe les industries extractives, les industries manufacturières (sauf l'édition) et l'électricité, le gaz et l'eau.

L'indice de la production industrielle des industries extractives se réfère à la branche 2 de la CITI Révision 2, "Industries extractives".

L'indice de la production industrielle des industries manufacturières se réfère à la branche 3 de la CITI Révision 2, "Industries manufacturières", sauf l'édition.

L'indice de la production industrielle pour l'électricité et le gaz se réfère à la branche 4 de la CITI Révision 2, "Électricité, gaz et eau". Depuis 1991, il inclut la production et la distribution d'eau.

L'indice de la production industrielle pour la construction se réfère à la branche 5 de la CITI Révision 2, "Bâtiment et travaux publics".

Quantités produites

Les chiffres de la *production de lignite* couvrent le charbon brun et le lignite. Pour le charbon brun, il s'agit de la production des mines nette des déchets retirés et lavés dans les installations de préparation du charbon. Pour le lignite, qui n'est pas lavé, le chiffre retenu est celui de la production brute.

La série concernant la *production de houille* indique la production nette de houille, c'est-à-dire la somme des chiffres de production des différentes entreprises minières, moins le charbon livré aux lavoirs pour raffinage, plus la production des lavoirs.

La *production d'acier brut* couvre les matériaux ferreux autres que ceux obtenus par réduction directe, qui sont malléables et qui contiennent un poids de carbone ne dépassant pas 2 pour cent.

La série concernant le *ciment* couvre la production de ciments Portland, ciments de laitier, ciments aux pouzzolanes, ciments alumineux, ciments spéciaux et autres types de ciment (par exemple, ciment de magnésie et ciment à forte expansion).

La série concernant la *production de voitures particulières* couvre les voitures de tourisme et les camions, y compris les châssis complets séparés, les voitures à usage spécial et les minibus.

Construction

Logements

Sont considérés comme des logements les pièces ou ensembles de pièces qui, selon les autorités de tutelle, ont été conçus pour l'habitation et qui peuvent constituer des unités indépendantes à cet effet. Les chambres individuelles des pensionnats, résidences et foyers d'étudiants qui ne sont pas gérés par des administrations locales ne sont pas comptées parmi les logements.

Les logements achevés sont les logements qui ont été réceptionnés en bonne et due forme. Les séries de la RFTS sur les logements excluent les maisons individuelles, les logements construits par des membres de coopératives eux-mêmes et les logements construits par des organismes n'appartenant pas au secteur du bâtiment.

Commerce intérieur

Jusqu'à la fin de 1990, les indices mensuels de ventes de détail en valeur se rapportent aux ventes de biens et de services, aux prix de détail courants, assurées par le réseau public de commerce de détail et les entreprises de restauration des secteurs étatique et coopératif (c'est-à-dire les entreprises des ministères du commerce, les coopératives de consommateurs, les restaurants et les fournisseurs de combustibles). Il s'agit de produits vendus aux consommateurs pour leur propre usage ou aux consommateurs collectifs et aux organisations du secteur socialisé pour une consommation intermédiaire. Les recettes au titre des services rendus sont incluses. Les chiffres mensuels représentent environ 85 pour cent du commerce total.

Les chiffres trimestriels et annuels jusqu'à la fin de 1990 couvrent aussi les activités commerciales des entreprises non commerciales des secteurs étatique et coopératif.

Depuis le début de 1991, la couverture de l'enquête sur les ventes de détail avait changé, se limitant aux entreprises d'au moins 100 salariés en 1991, aux entreprises d'au moins 25 salariés en 1992. Depuis 1991, les données mensuelles représentent une estimation des ventes totales pour prendre en compte les unités déclarantes qui n'étaient pas soumises à l'enquête statistique.

Les données sont présentées en deux séries distinctes. La première, qui couvre la période 1980-90, a pour base 100 la même période de 1980. La deuxième, qui débute en 1991, a pour base 100 la même période de 1990. Bien que les deux séries représentent les ventes totales de détail, comme il y a eu un changement dans la structure de l'échantillon à partir de janvier 1991, il n'est pas souhaitable de raccorder les séries avant et après cette période.

Main-d'oeuvre

Emploi

Les données sur l'emploi en RFTS couvrent l'emploi des secteurs étatique et coopératif, à l'exception des coopératives agricoles et des entrepreneurs du secteur privé. A partir du début de 1991, la série couvre les entreprises et organisations d'au moins 100 salariés et, à partir de 1992, les entreprises et organisations d'au moins 25 salariés. Les données se réfèrent au nombre moyen de salariés, occupés à temps plein et à temps partiel, à l'exclusion des apprentis et des femmes en congé de maternité.

L'emploi dans l'industrie couvre les salariés des entreprises industrielles nationales, des entreprises privées, des coentreprises, des organisations sociales et professionnelles (y compris les maisons d'édition). Il exclut les entreprises gérées par les autorités municipales, les coopératives de production et les entreprises de distribution des eaux des secteurs étatique et coopératif. Les apprentis ne sont pas pris en compte.

En 1992, la classification nationale tchécoslovaque était remplacée par la CITI-88.

Chômage

L'enregistrement des chômeurs a commencé en décembre 1989. Il était nécessaire de s'inscrire pour pouvoir bénéficier d'un recyclage et d'une aide financière. Les chômeurs étaient d'autant plus incités à s'inscrire que c'est le même service qui s'occupait de l'inscription au chômage et des offres d'emploi.

Le chômage total se réfèrait aux personnes qui n'avaient pas de contrat de travail et n'exerçaient aucune activité indépendante lucrative et qui avaient demandé au service local de l'emploi de leur trouver un emploi susceptible de leur convenir.

Les données se réfèrent à la fin de la période et proviennent du Ministère fédéral du travail et des affaires sociales.

Le taux de chômage représente la proportion de demandeurs d'emploi dans la population active totale.

Entreprises privées

Jusqu'à la fin de 1989, les données couvraient les personnes assurant des services avec l'autorisation des comités nationaux conformément à l'ordonnance émanant des gouvernements de la République tchèque et de la République slovaque. Depuis le début de 1990, elles couvrent les entrepreneurs inscrits conformément à la Loi No. 105/1990.

Plusieurs phénomènes obscurcissent l'interprétation des données sur le nombre d'entrepreneurs du secteur privé. De nombreuses personnes font enregistrer une entreprise puis, pour des raisons diverses, n'exercent finalement aucune activité. D'autres peuvent ne poursuivre une activité qu'à temps partiel, en particulier à titre de consultants. Autre complication, il arrive, par exemple dans le cas d'un supermarché privé ayant un personnel d'une centaine de personnes, que chaque membre du personnel s'inscrive comme entrepreneur si l'entreprise fonctionne selon la formule du partenariat.

Le ré-enregistrement a été obligatoire pour tout entreprise au cours de l'année selon la Loi sur les petites entreprises, No. 455/1991.

Salaires

Gains mensuels

Les statistiques trimestrielles et annuelles de *gains mensuels totaux* se réfèrent aux gains des secteurs étatique et coopératif, à l'exception des coopératives agricoles. Depuis le début de 1991, la couverture a changé, se limitant, en 1991, aux entreprises et organisations d'au moins 100 salariés et, à partir de 1992, aux entreprises et organisations d'au moins 25 salariés.

Les chiffres se rapportent aux salaires mensuels moyens par travailleur. Il s'agit de salaires bruts, c'est-à-dire les salaires et traitements de base, plus les primes et autres gratifications, mais hors allocations familiales et autres prestations sociales.

Prix

Prix à la production

L'indice des prix à la production industrielle se réfère aux prix à la production des produits industriels fabriqués en RFTS. Jusqu'à la fin de 1990, les données se référaient aux prix catalogue, alors que, à partir de 1991, il s'agissait des prix relevés mensuellement sur environ 6 000 articles représentatifs auprès d'un échantillon d'entreprises industrielles représentant environ 410 branches de la Classification type des activités industrielles. N'étaient pas couverts les produits ou les branches de production non standard des constructions mécaniques et de la métallurgie, les travaux de montage et de démontage, les services industriels, les réparations et la distribution d'énergie.

Les prix indiqués sont la moyenne arithmétique des prix de transaction effectifs, nets des taxes sur le chiffre d'affaires et autres taxes sur les ventes, de tous les contrats importants observés en milieu de mois.

 OECD
OCDE
SHORT-TERM ECONOMIC INDICATORS, SOURCES AND DEFINITIONS
OECD/CCET © April 1996

262

INDICATEURS ÉCONOMIQUES A COURT TERME, SOURCES ET DÉFINITIONS
OCDE/CCET © avril 1996

Les articles représentatifs pouvaient être remplacés par d'autres, de qualité similaire, mais, quand des écarts de qualité importants étaient observés, les prix étaient corrigés en conséquence.

Il s'agit d'un indice de Laspeyres, calculé à partir de simples rapports de prix pondérés par la valeur de la production de la branche concernée en 1989. La base nationale était janvier 1989=100.

Prix à la consommation

L'indice des prix à la consommation (IPC) reflète les mouvements des prix des produits alimentaires, des produits industriels, de la restauration et des autres services achetés par la population. Les relevés de prix portaient sur un échantillon de 827 biens et services en 1992.

Grands groupes	Nombre d'articles
Produits alimentaires	191
Produits industriels	387
Restauration publique	63
Services (y compris loyers, transports et communications)	186
Total	827

Les agents des services statistiques relevaient les prix dans un certain nombre de points de vente de détail et de services dans tous les districts de la République tchèque et de la République slovaque, vers le 15 du mois, sauf pour les fruits et légumes, dont les prix étaient relevés trois fois par mois (les 1er, 10ème et 20ème jours). Un panier distinct de fruits et légumes frais était constitué chaque mois, réunissant diverses variétés de saison. L'indice se référait aux prix payés dans les magasins étatiques, coopératifs et privés pour des marchandises de première main ; les prix des marchandises d'occasion n'étaient pas pris en compte.

Si le produit observé disparaissait des étalages, il était remplacé par un autre, de qualité comparable. Si la qualité du nouvel article n'était pas vraiment comparable, on procédait à un ajustement. En général, les prix des produits qui suivent les nouvelles tendances de la mode étaient introduits directement dans l'indice.

L'IPC est de type Laspeyres. Les prix relevés dans les différentes unités déclarantes servaient à calculer des moyennes arithmétiques non pondérées. Les indices élaborés pour divers groupes et agrégats étaient calculés sous forme de moyennes arithmétiques pondérées par des coefficients constants se rapportant à l'année de base. La pondération se référait, pour les produits, à la structure des ventes de détail, et pour les services, à la structure des dépenses de la population, en 1989. Des indices distincts étaient calculés pour la République tchèque et la République slovaque.

En 1991, on est passé d'un système trimestriel à un système mensuel d'observation et de calcul des indices de prix, et la nouvelle base nationale du 1er janvier 1989=100 a été introduite.

R F T S

Finances internes

La masse monétaire au sens étroit (M1) englobe la monnaie nationale en circulation en dehors du secteur bancaire et les dépôts à vue, sauf ceux des administrations centrales.

La quasi-monnaie englobe les dépôts à terme, les dépôts d'épargne et les dépôts en devises des résidents, à l'exclusion des administrations centrales.

Taux d'intérêt

Le taux d'escompte officiel correspond au taux, observé en fin de période, auquel la Banque d'État prête aux banques commerciales.

Finances extérieures

Le taux de change du dollar des États-Unis correspond au taux principal en fin de période.

Jusqu'à la fin de 1988, le système de change comprenait un taux officiel, un taux commercial et un taux non commercial. Le taux officiel et la parité or ont été supprimés le 1er janvier 1989. En janvier 1990, les taux commercial et non commercial ont été fusionnés en un taux unique, le taux principal, fondé sur un panier des cinq devises représentant la plus grande part du montant des transactions au titre de la balance des paiements. Un taux touristique a été instauré en 1990, fondé sur les taux des marchés parallèles de la couronne en Autriche et en Suisse. Le taux principal et le taux touristique ont été fondus en un seul taux de change à la fin de 1990.

Les données sur *les réserves officielles, or exclu,* sont conformes à la définition du Fonds monétaire international.

Commerce extérieur

Dans les statistiques du commerce extérieur de la RFTS, les exportations étaient enregistrées fab et les importations sur la base d'une parité à la frontière. Les importations excluant les transports et les assurances, étaient donc essentiellement aussi enregistrées fab. Pour la période 1980-88, les valeurs de transaction étaient converties en couronnes tchécoslovaques sur la base du taux de change en vigueur jusqu'à la fin de 1988. Depuis le début de 1989, on utilise les taux de change courants.

1980-90

Jusqu'à la fin de 1990, les statistiques *d'exportations, d'importations* et *de solde commercial* provenaient d'une enquête auprès des exportateurs et importateurs détenant une licence. Cela signifie que certains services étaient inclus dans ces données. Les travaux effectués à l'étranger par des entreprises de construction tchécoslovaques étaient inclus dans les exportations.

Depuis 1991

Depuis le début de 1991, les statistiques du commerce extérieur s'appuyaient sur les déclarations douanières. Les réexportations directes et les exportations et importations de services étaient exclues.

Le changement de système de notification a entraîné un changement dans les délais d'enregistrement. Les marchandises exportées étaient enregistrées à la date où elles traversaient la frontière tchécoslovaque. Les importations de marchandises étaient ensuite enregistrées à la date de sortie des entrepôts sous douane et non plus à la date du passage de frontière. Il y avait un délai de traitement de un à quinze jours avant que les déclarations soient acheminées. Les données étaient tenues à jour en permanence par l'Administration centrale des douanes.

Prix

Les prix, fab pour les exportations, caf pour les importations, étaient observés pour un échantillon d'environ 1 800 articles représentatifs, choisis pour leur importance et leur part relativement constante dans les transactions commerciales avec l'étranger. Les informations de prix étaient communiquées chaque trimestre par 28 établissements commerciaux sélectionnés.

L'indice est de type Laspeyres et les rapports de prix individuels étaient pondérés par la valeur correspondante des exportations et des importations en 1985, au niveau de détail à quatre chiffres de la Classification tchécoslovaque du commerce extérieur.

Volumes

On obtient *les indices de volume des exportations et des importations* en déflatant les valeurs courantes du commerce extérieur par les indices de prix décrits ci-dessus.

Les données présentées à partir de 1991 sont approximatives puisque les indices de prix n'ont pas encore été repondérés pour tenir compte des changements intervenus depuis janvier 1991 dans la couverture des données aux prix courants.

ESTONIE

Production industrielle

Jusqu'en 1993, la production industrielle était classée selon la Nomenclature des branches de l'économie nationale (NBNE) du CAEM. La Classification internationale type, par industrie, de toutes les branches d'activité économique (CITI, Révision 3) des Nations Unies a été introduite en 1993 et les données de 1992 ont été recalculées sur cette base.

Les valeurs de la production de 1985 à fin 1990 sont calculées à partir de données en volume évaluées aux prix de gros de 1982. Les séries ne sont pas corrigées du nombre de jours ouvrables dans le mois.

Depuis 1994, les données se réfèrent aux ventes industrielles privées. Les enquêtes annuelles couvrent tout le secteur public et les entreprises du secteur privé de plus de 20 salariés. Les enquêtes mensuelles couvrent toutes les entreprises de plus de 50 salariés ce qui représente environ 85 pour cent des ventes industrielles totales.

La production industrielle exclut les variations de stocks, de produits non finis et la production non principale. L'Office statistique d'Estonie publie les données des ventes industrielles en valeur courante uniquement.

Les ventes industrielles en valeur courante sont déflatées par le Secrétariat de l'OCDE à l'aide de l'Indice des prix à la production en base 1993 = 100.

La production industrielle totale dans la NBNE couvre, globalement, les industries extractives, les industries manufacturières et l'électricité. Ne sont pas inclus les services "non productifs", la distribution de gaz, d'énergie thermique et d'eau à usage domestique (une partie de 342, de 4102, de 4103 et de 4200 de la CITI).

L'indice de la production industrielle d'électricité couvre la totalité de la production nationale d'électricité des centrales brûlant du schiste bitumineux.

Quantités produites

Le *ciment* se réfère au ciment Portland P400.

Enquêtes de conjoncture

On trouvera une description des techniques de réalisation de ces enquêtes et la liste des questions harmonisées dans le chapitre de cette publication consacré aux *Enquêtes de conjoncture*.

Construction

Logements

Par logements, on entend des locaux à usage d'habitation distincts et indépendants, comportant une ou plusieurs pièces (principales et de service) et une entrée indépendante donnant directement accès à une partie commune (escalier, palier, passage, etc.), ou à la rue.

On considère que la construction d'un logement débute lorsque le permis de construire est délivré. Le total des *logements mis en chantier* inclut les maisons construites par leur propriétaire.

Le nombre de *logements achevés* par les entreprises du bâtiment est relevé chaque trimestre dans les bureaux de construction de chaque région (15 régions et Tallin). Les logements sont considérés comme achevés une fois qu'ils ont été enregistrés (auprès des services de la construction) conformément aux procédures obligatoires ou, dans le cas des logements construits par des particuliers, lorsqu'ils sont prêts à être habités.

Commerce intérieur

Jusqu'à la fin de 1992, tous les établissements de vente de détail et de restauration, y compris ceux du secteur privé, faisaient l'objet d'une enquête. Les données couvraient le chiffre d'affaires des commerces de détail et coopératives appartenant à l'État, y compris la restauration publique (cantines de travailleurs, etc.) ainsi que les ventes directement effectuées par les entreprises industrielles et les sociétés de transport. Étaient également couvertes les ventes de détail des organismes, entreprises et institutions (sanatoriums, crèches, hôpitaux, etc.) à leur personnel.

Les données couvraient la vente de produits par les coopératives alimentaires sociales, les coopératives de vente et les coopératives d'achat et de vente ainsi que la vente de produits fabriqués par des particuliers en dehors du lieu de travail mais vendus par le biais d'entreprises commerciales. Étaient également inclus tous les produits agricoles, sauf ceux qui étaient vendus de façon informelle sur les marchés urbains.

Depuis 1993, une enquête par sondage est mise en oeuvre. Tous les commerces de détail comptant au moins 20 salariés sont couverts. Une enquête menée à partir d'un échantillonnage stratifié est conduite auprès des entreprises privées de moins de 20 salariés. Jusqu'à la fin de 1994, la taille de l'échantillon pour les entreprises de commerce de détail était de 350 pour un total approximatif de 1 200. Depuis 1995, la taille de l'échantillon pour les entreprises de commerce de détail est de 600 sur une population d'environ 3 400.

Les *statistiques du commerce intérieur* ne couvrent que les commerces de détail (elles excluent les établissements de restauration), elles incluent l'ensemble des entreprises étatiques et municipales.

La *valeur des ventes de détail* est exprimée en roubles jusqu'en décembre 1991 et en couronnes par la suite. Pour plus de précisions, voir ci-dessous la section sur les finances internes et le chapitre *Introduction de nouvelles monnaies*.

La série sur le *volume des ventes de détail* est présentée en base 1992 = 100. L'indice des prix de détail est utilisé comme déflateur.

ESTONIE

Main-d'oeuvre

Emploi

Jusqu'à la fin de 1991, les chiffres de l'*emploi total* couvraient l'ensemble des personnes travaillant dans le secteur étatique, les fermes collectives, les coopératives privées et les exploitations agricoles privées, ainsi que les travailleurs indépendants. Seul l'emploi civil était couvert, et les étudiants étaient exclus. Jusqu'à la fin de 1989, les salariés à temps partiel étaient comptés à part entière et non en équivalent plein temps. Depuis 1990, ils sont pris en compte en fonction du nombre d'heures travaillées. L'emploi durant cette période correspond au nombre annuel moyen de salariés des entreprises et organismes de chaque secteur de l'économie. Les salariés étaient classés par secteur selon le système de classification de l'ex-Union soviétique. Pour le secteur étatique, un tableau des effectifs figurant sur les registres de chaque entreprise et organisme des républiques de l'ex-Union soviétique était communiqué chaque mois aux services statistiques. Les moyennes annuelles étaient calculées sur la base des chiffres mensuels.

Depuis 1991, les entreprises enregistrées remplissent un questionnaire trimestriel sur le nombre de salariés, leur salaire et le nombre d'emplois vacants. Il n'y a pas de limite inférieure de taille pour les entreprises, même celles qui n'ont qu'un seul travailleur doivent remplir le questionnaire. Jusqu'au troisième trimestre 1993, l'enquête couvrait toutes les entreprises enregistrées. Depuis le quatrième trimestre 1993, un échantillon d'entreprises enregistrées est utilisé. On estime que 80 pour cent des salariés sont ainsi couverts. On procède ensuite à une extrapolation pour obtenir le nombre total de salariés.

Les données sont classées selon la CITI à partir de 1991.

Les séries englobent tous les salariés civils détenteurs d'un contrat de travail, y compris ceux qui sont temporairement inactifs : personnes en congé de maternité ou en congé parental, personnes en chômage technique ou dont le contrat de travail est suspendu pour une raison quelconque. Les salariés à temps partiel sont comptés en équivalent plein temps. Le personnel des coentreprises et les travailleurs indépendants ne sont pas encore inclus.

Chômage

Le nombre des *allocataires* est recueilli par l'intermédiaire de l'Office du travail dans six grandes villes et les 15 régions d'Estonie le premier jour de chaque mois.

Pour être enregistré comme chômeur, il faut :

-- être un résident permanent de l'Estonie ;

-- avoir entre 16 ans et l'âge de la retraite ;

-- avoir effectué un travail ou une activité équivalente pendant au moins 180 jours au cours des 12 derniers mois ;

-- chercher activement un emploi.

Un chômeur inscrit dont les revenus sont inférieurs aux indemnités de chômage versées par l'État est en droit de percevoir une allocation mensuelle. Le montant de cette allocation est établi à 180 couronnes estoniennes depuis 1991. La période minimum de non activité avant de recevoir des allocations est de 10 jours, 60 jours dans certains cas exceptionnels. Généralement, la durée maximale des allocations (c'est-à-dire de la période ouvrant droit à l'inscription en tant que chômeur auprès d'une agence

OECD
OCDE
SHORT-TERM ECONOMIC INDICATORS, SOURCES AND DEFINITIONS
OECD/CCET © April 1996

268

INDICATEURS ÉCONOMIQUES A COURT TERME, SOURCES ET DÉFINITIONS
OCDE/CCET © avril 1996

nationale pour l'emploi) est de 180 jours civils et elle peut cesser ou être prolongée dans certains cas conformément à la "loi sur la protection sociale des chômeurs". Les intéressés perdent leur droit à recevoir l'allocation s'ils ne se présentent pas en personne à une agence nationale pour l'emploi au moins une fois tous les 10 jours ouvrables, ou s'ils obtiennent un revenu au moins égal aux indemnités de chômage versées par l'État.

La série du *taux de chômage* représente le nombre de chômeurs en pourcentage de la population en âge de travailler. La définition de la population en âge de travailler est en train de changer. Depuis 1994, l'âge de la retraite est repoussé de six mois tous les ans, de sorte qu'en 2003 il sera de 60 ans (56,5 ans en 1996) pour les femmes et de 65 ans (61,5 ans en 1996) pour les hommes. Les données sont fournies par l'Office du travail.

Des informations sur le nombre d'*offres d'emploi* sont recueillies à l'occasion de l'enquête "emploi" menée auprès des entreprises (voir plus haut).

Temps travaillé

La semaine de travail normale compte 40 heures.

Salaires

Gains mensuels

Les statistiques sur les salaires sont collectées à l'aide d'une enquête trimestrielle auprès des entreprises, des institutions et des organisations (à l'exclusion des exploitations agricoles et des travailleurs indépendants). Les données par branche d'activité économique sont classées selon les catégories de la CITI. L'enquête couvre toutes les entreprises, institutions et organisations étatiques, municipales et autres de plus de 19 salariés. Celles de moins de 20 salariés (à l'exclusion des entreprises et des institutions étatiques et municipales) font l'objet d'une enquête par sondage. La principale activité économique de l'entreprise, institution ou organisation et le nombre de salariés engagés dans celle-ci constituent les critères d'échantillonnage.

Le *salaire brut total moyen* inclut :

-- B_1 : gains des salariés au titre des heures effectivement travaillées, qui correspondent à la rémunération perçue par les salariés à temps complet et à temps partiel (rétribution du travail réalisé, primes et autres gratifications régulières) en fonction de la durée effective du travail ;

-- B_2 : rémunération des salariés au titre des heures non travaillées, dont les congés payés, les indemnités, les primes occasionnelles et la rémunération des arrêts de travail, etc. ;

-- R : prestations maladie versées aux salariés par la caisse de sécurité sociale ;

Il est calculé de la façon suivante :

$$B_{moyen} = \frac{B_1 + B_2 + R}{t_{trimestre} * 3}$$

ESTONIE

où :

-- $t_{trimestre}$: nombre moyen de salariés par mois au cours d'un trimestre ;

-- B_{moyen} : salaire mensuel brut moyen par trimestre.

Les gains totaux sont exprimés en roubles jusqu'à la fin de 1991, puis en couronnes par la suite. Les gains dans l'industrie et le secteur manufacturier sont exprimés en roubles jusqu'au deuxième trimestre de 1992, et en couronnes par la suite. Pour plus de précisions, voir ci-dessous la section sur les finances internes et le chapitre *Introduction de nouvelles monnaies*.

Prix

Prix à la production

"Ancien indice"

Les données de prix destinées à l'établissement de l'*indice des prix à la production dans les industries manufacturières* ayant pour base 100 la période correspondante de 1990, sont recueillies directement auprès des entreprises, chaque mois, principalement par questionnaire postal. Environ 300 produits industriels étaient couverts, et ce, dans un tiers des plus grandes entreprises. L'indice, de type Laspeyres, était pondéré par la valeur de la production des grandes entreprises des principales branches industrielles en 1989. Les prix s'entendaient hors taxes.

Les *indices des prix à la production dans les industries manufacturières* ayant comme base 100 la période précédente étaient pondérés par la valeur de la production des grandes entreprises des principales branches industrielles en 1992.

"Nouvel indice"

Depuis 1993, la méthodologie utilisée pour le calcul de l'indice des prix à la production a changé pour être en accord avec les recommandations internationales. L'indice est de type Laspeyres.

Pour calculer l'indice des prix à la production, on prend en compte les prix de biens manufacturés autant destinés au marché intérieur qu'à l'exportation. Jusqu'en mai 1995, les prix étaient relevés directement auprès de 100 entreprises tous les mois par le moyen de questionnaires postaux. Environ 350 produits industriels étaient couverts. Les prix moyens de 1992 des produits de l'échantillon étaient choisis comme prix de base et les volumes de la production industrielle par activité de 1992 avaient été choisis comme poids.

Depuis juin 1995, les prix moyens de 1994 des produits de l'échantillon sont retenus comme prix de base et les volumes de la production industrielle par activité de 1994 sont utilisés comme poids. L'enquête porte sur environ 440 produits industriels et sur 110 entreprises.

Dans l'index, on utilise les prix nets : hors taxes d'accise et TVA. Aucun traitement n'est effectué pour prendre en compte les changements de qualité ou les produits saisonniers.

Les indices des prix à la production sont exprimés dans les publications nationales en base fixe 1992 = 100 et 1994 = 100.

OECD / OCDE
SHORT-TERM ECONOMIC INDICATORS, SOURCES AND DEFINITIONS
OECD/CCET © April 1996

270

INDICATEURS ÉCONOMIQUES A COURT TERME, SOURCES ET DÉFINITIONS
OCDE/CCET © avril 1996

Les poids utilisés dans l'IPP sont les suivants :

Branche d'activité	1992	1993	1994
Industries manufacturières	84.7	82.6	81.0
Industries extractives	4.3	4.7	4.6
Énergie	11.0	12.7	14.4
TOTAL	100.0	100.0	100.0

Prix à la consommation

L'*indice des prix à la consommation (IPC)* reflète les mouvements de prix des produits alimentaires, des biens manufacturés et des services achetés par la population. Les enquêteurs effectuent trois relevés par article dans un échantillon de points de vente et d'établissements de service situés dans dix villes d'Estonie. Depuis 1994, les prix sont relevés sur environ 317 biens et 93 services durant la semaine qui comprend le 15 du mois. Trente-trois relevés de prix sont effectués pour chacun de ces biens et services.

De 1990 à juin 1992, la série correspondait à un indice du coût de la vie. A partir de juillet 1992, il s'agit d'un indice des prix à la consommation. On notera certaines différences entre les deux périodes (par exemple, les réparations et l'entretien des logements ne sont inclus dans la composante "logement" de l'indice que dans la seconde période ; les tabacs et alcools et le coût des automobiles ont aussi été introduits en juillet 1992), mais la plupart des principaux indices partiels (alimentation, habillement et chaussures, logements) sont considérés comme comparables.

Une autre différence entre les chiffres de juin et ceux de juillet 1992 tient à l'augmentation, de 10 à 18 pour cent, de la taxe sur les ventes. Comme les prix s'entendent toutes taxes comprises, cela explique une partie de la hausse des prix entre les deux périodes.

L'IPC était un indice à pondération fixe du premier trimestre de 1990 jusqu'en décembre de 1993.

De juin 1992 à décembre 1993, les pondérations de l'IPC étaient tirées de l'enquête sur les dépenses familiales pendant la période allant de mars à mai 1992. La répartition des dépenses des mois précédents n'a pas été prise en compte parce que la structure des dépenses des ménages a connu un brusque changement en mars 1992 du fait d'une hausse spectaculaire du coût des logements. La configuration des dépenses de juin n'a pas non plus été retenue, la réforme imminente de la monnaie ayant entraîné une transformation radicale des modes de consommation.

Depuis janvier 1994, l'indice est de type Laspeyres. Les coefficients de pondération se réfèrent à l'enquête sur le budget des ménages de 1993, avec des corrections prenant en compte les récentes variations des prix et des droits de douane. Les indices sont calculés par rapport aux prix moyens de 1993 et sont présentés en base 1993=100. Les chiffres des tabacs et alcools sont révisés pour tenir compte d'une probable sous-déclaration des articles concernés.

Quand des articles saisonniers sont rares ou indisponibles, on utilise le prix moyen des autres articles du groupe de produits que l'on attribue à l'article saisonnier manquant.

ESTONIE

Les produits importés ont reçu un poids plus important, mais la plupart des relevés de prix sont faits sur des articles produits à l'intérieur du pays. Les changements de qualité sont minimes sur ces articles et seulement quelques ajustements sont faits sur les IPC pour traiter le changement de qualité.

Les services sont compris dans chacun des groupes énumérés ci-dessous ; ils en sont également extraits de façon à permettre la construction d'un indice partiel distinct, l'*IPC des services*. Le coefficient de pondération attribué à l'ensemble des services en 1994 est 32.75.

Le poste *habillement et chaussures* englobe les vêtements de confection, la bonneterie, les chaussures, les tissus (hors tissus d'ameublement) et les services des tailleurs et cordonniers.

Le poste *logement* inclut le logement lui-même et les services municipaux, les combustibles, les produits d'entretien et de réparation. Il exclut la construction et l'achat de logements, lesquels sont considérés comme un investissement en capital.

Le groupe *transports et communications* peut se subdiviser en trois : les transports privés, catégorie essentiellement nouvelle, dont l'ancien indice du coût de la vie ne prenait en compte que les dépenses concernant les bicyclettes, les transports publics et les communications.

Les *loisirs* englobent des éléments aussi divers que les produits radiophoniques et photographiques, les articles de voyage et de sport, les dépenses de garde d'enfants, les jouets, les graines, plantes et fleurs, les publications, y compris les périodiques, et les services liés au cinéma, au théâtre, etc.

Les *dépenses domestiques* comprennent les meubles, les textiles d'ameublement, l'électroménager, les ustensiles de cuisine, la vaisselle, les lessives, les ampoules électriques, etc. Les *soins et effets personnels* incluent les autres services nécessaires, les produits d'hygiène et la restauration publique. Le poste *soins médicaux* inclut les médicaments, les produits de soins et les services des professions médicales.

La pondération des groupes de produits dans l'IPC total est la suivante :

Poste	Poids mars à mai 1992 (utilisés de juin 92 à déc. 93)	Poids 1993 (utilisés depuis jan. 94)
Alimentation	43.46	37.85
Habillement et chaussures	11.77	7.61
Logement : dont combustibles et électricité	11.25 5.98	19.73 9.99
Transports et communications	9.84	13.04
Loisirs, spectacles et publications	7.76	6.56
Dépenses domestiques	6.06	3.20
Tabacs et alcools	5.12	4.33
Soins et effets personnels	3.99	5.67
Soins médicaux	0.75	2.01
TOTAL	100.00	100.00

Finances internes

Les données concernant les finances internes sont calculées par la Banque d'Estonie et se réfèrent à la fin de la période.

Une nouvelle monnaie, la couronne estonienne, a été introduite le 20 juin 1992. Le facteur de conversion, quand cette monnaie a été introduite, était d'une couronne pour 10 roubles. Les données sont donc exprimées en roubles avant le deuxième trimestre 1992, et en couronnes estoniennes par la suite. Pour plus de précisions, voir le chapitre *Introduction de nouvelles monnaies*.

Les *disponibilités monétaires au sens étroit (M1)* comprennent la monnaie en circulation en dehors du secteur bancaire et les dépôts à vue.

La *quasi-monnaie* comprend les dépôts à terme et dépôts d'épargne et les dépôts en devises convertibles et non convertibles, à l'exclusion des dépôts de l'administration centrale et des administrations locales.

Les *dépôts personnels* incluent les dépôts à vue, les dépôts d'épargne et les dépôts à terme des ménages.

Finances extérieures

Les données sont calculées par la Banque d'Estonie.

Toutes les séries relatives *au taux de change* sont des moyennes des taux officiels publiés quotidiennement par la Banque d'Estonie.

La série *réserves officielles* se réfère aux avoirs totaux nets en devises de la Banque d'Estonie en fin de période c'est-à-dire aux réserves nettes (les engagements extérieurs sont soustraits des réserves de devises de la Banque d'Estonie). Les devises non convertibles ne sont pas comprises dans les réserves totales. L'or est inclus dans les chiffres jusqu'à la fin de 1993.

La *dette extérieure brute* comprend toutes les dettes endossées par le gouvernement et certains crédits du Fonds monétaire international. Les données se réfèrent à la fin de la période.

Commerce extérieur

Les données de 1987-1990 ont été calculées par le Goskomstat de l'ex-URSS. La classification des échanges était celle de l'ex-Union soviétique. Les produits étaient évalués aux prix intérieurs en roubles courants. Les prix intérieurs des produits exportés étaient les prix payés par les exportateurs aux producteurs nationaux ; les prix intérieurs des produits importés étaient les prix effectivement payés par les acheteurs finals nationaux.

Les échanges en *monnaies non convertibles* incluent les échanges avec toutes les républiques de l'ex-Union soviétique, y compris la Lettonie et la Lituanie. Les échanges en *monnaies convertibles* se réfèrent aux échanges avec tous les autres pays.

Les statistiques du commerce extérieur de 1991 et du premier semestre de 1992 étaient élaborées à partir des rapports statistiques des entreprises et des organisations sises sur le territoire de l'Estonie.

OECD
OCDE
SHORT-TERM ECONOMIC INDICATORS, SOURCES AND DEFINITIONS
OECD/CCET © April 1996

273

INDICATEURS ÉCONOMIQUES A COURT TERME, SOURCES ET DÉFINITIONS
OCDE/CCET © avril 1996

ESTONIE

Depuis juillet 1992, les statistiques du commerce extérieur sont basées sur les déclarations douanières.

Les exportations sont comptabilisées fab et les importations caf. Les statistiques du commerce extérieur excluent les services ainsi que les marchandises destinées aux ambassades. Les réexportations et les réimportations sont incluses.

Les statistiques du commerce extérieur de 1991 et du premier semestre de 1992 étaient élaborées à partir de la Nomenclature des branches de l'économie nationale (NBEN) de l'ex CAEM. Le commerce extérieur est classifié selon le système harmonisé (SH) depuis juillet 1992. Les pays de destination ou d'origine sont classés selon la norme ISO3166.

Les données sur les échanges extérieurs sont exprimées en roubles jusqu'au second trimestre de 1992 et en couronnes par la suite. Pour plus de précisions, voir ci-dessus la section sur les finances internes et le chapitre *Introduction de nouvelles monnaies*.

Publications

Certaines des séries décrites ici figurent aussi, mais avec une présentation conforme à la pratique nationale, dans les publications suivantes, en anglais, de l'Office statistique d'État de l'Estonie :

Estonian Statistics, Monthly Statistical Bulletin (Statistiques de l'Estonie, Bulletin statistique mensuel)

Statistical Yearbook (Annuaire statistique)

Estonia in Figures (L'Estonie en chiffres)

National Accounts in Estonia (Comptes nationaux de l'Estonie)

Régional Statistics (Statistiques des régions)

Government Finance Statistics (Statistiques des finances publiques)

Foreign Trade (Commerce extérieur).

HONGRIE

Production industrielle

L'*indice de la production industrielle* (IPI) se réfère aux activités de production définies dans les divisions 10 à 41 (groupes C, D et E) de la Classification internationale type, par industrie, de toutes les branches d'activité économique (CITI) des Nations Unies, Révision 3. Les activités de production comprennent les industries extractives, les industries manufacturières, l'électricité, le gaz et l'eau. Cette définition correspond à la grande branche "industrie" de la classification hongroise des activités, intitulée Classification type, par industrie, de toutes les branches d'activité économique (TEAOR).

Jusqu'à la fin de 1988, les données mensuelles couvrent toutes les entreprises dotées de la personnalité juridique, c'est-à-dire à l'exclusion des entreprises non constituées en sociétés. Pour 1989 et 1990, la couverture englobait toutes les entreprises d'au moins 50 salariés, toujours à l'exclusion des entreprises non constituées en sociétés. A partir de 1991, cependant, on a observé les entreprises de moins de 50 salariés au moyen d'une enquête par sondage. En 1992, les statistiques industrielles ont été étendues aux entreprises non constituées en sociétés et aux entreprises individuelles. En 1993, les entreprises de 21 à 50 salariés ont fait l'objet d'une enquête par sondage et l'on a estimé la production des entreprises de moins de 20 salariés. Depuis 1994, l'enquête couvre les entreprises de 11 à 50 salariés et l'on estime, à partir des déclarations fiscales, la production industrielle des entreprises de 10 salariés ou moins pour établir l'IPI total. Les indices de branche, de sous-branche et de division sont toutefois calculés sur la base d'évaluations de la production de toutes les entreprises de plus de 20 salariés (1994) ou de plus de 10 employés (1995). Aussi la couverture de l'IPI total est-elle plus large que celle de ses composantes.

La production prise en compte est la production brute des activités industrielles, couvrant les ventes de biens et services finals et intermédiaires, à l'exclusion des transactions entre établissements de la même entreprise, et de la production subsidiaire de l'entreprise. Les données sont corrigées de la variation des quantités de produits en cours de fabrication et des stocks de produits finis. Les impôts sur la consommation et les taxes sur la valeur ajoutée sont exclus.

Les données exprimées en valeur sont déflatées aux prix constants de janvier 1985 à l'aide de l'indice des prix à la production (IPP).

L'indice de la production industrielle est un indice-chaîne de type Paasche ; les séries sont pondérées par la production brute, les coefficients de pondération étant modifiés chaque année.

Les indices corrigés des variations saisonnières sont calculés par l'Office central des statistiques de Hongrie, qui utilise à cet effet la méthode X11 Arima/88, en prenant les moyennes mobiles calculées pour chaque indicateur.

L'*indice de la production industrielle pour les industries extractives* se réfère aux divisions 10 à 14 (groupe C) de la CITI Révision 3, y compris l'extraction de matériaux de construction (pierre à bâtir, argile et sable).

HONGRIE

L'*indice de la production industrielle pour les industries manufacturières* se réfère aux dimensions 15 à 37 (groupe D) de la CITI Révision 3. Avant 1985, les chiffres excluaient l'édition.

L'*indice de la production industrielle pour l'électricité et le gaz* se réfère aux divisions 40 et 41 (groupe E) de la CITI Révision 3. Avant 1985, la distribution et les installations de distribution d'eau étaient exclues.

Quantités produites

Les séries relatives aux quantités produites sont établies au moyen d'un recensement qui collecte les données des entreprises de plus de 50 salariés sur leur production.

La *production de charbon* couvre tous les types de charbon de qualités diverses, avec un pouvoir calorifique net variant entre 6.2 et 26.4 MJ par kilogramme. La houille anthraciteuse (y compris l'anthracite) et le charbon brun (y compris le lignite) sont inclus.

La *production d'acier brut* couvre les produits contenant du fer, élaborés à partir de fer brut, de ferraille (avec additifs et fondants) et, dans le cas des aciers alliés, les produits contenant des additifs d'alliage et dont la teneur en carbone ne dépasse pas 1,7 pour cent.

La *production de ciment* couvre les ciments de tous types comportant du clinker comme matériau de base, quels que soient les additifs et la quantité de clinker mis en oeuvre, et indépendamment de la solidité du ciment.

La *production de pétrole brut* couvre l'huile de schiste, mais pas les condensats de gaz naturel.

La *production de gaz naturel* couvre principalement le méthane, mais aussi une petite proportion d'autres gaz. Les données couvrent les gaz non associés (provenant de gisements produisant des hydrocarbures liquides et gazeux), le méthane récupéré sur les têtes de puits ou dans les mines de charbon et les gaz d'égout. Dans la mesure où ils sont isolés, l'éthane, le propane, le butane et autres condensats sont exclus. Il n'est pas tenu compte des pertes dues à des raisons techniques.

La *production de voitures particulières* exclut les véhicules militaires. Cette série a été suspendue afin de protéger l'anonymat des constructeurs.

Enquêtes de conjoncture

On trouvera une explication des techniques de réalisation de ces enquêtes et la liste des questions harmonisées dans le chapitre de cette publication consacré aux *Enquêtes de conjoncture*.

Ventes

Ventes en volume

Les indices de *ventes en volume* se réfèrent aux livraisons industrielles totales et à leurs deux composantes, les ventes intérieures et les livraisons destinées à l'exportation. On obtient le volume des ventes en déflatant les valeurs courantes par un indice de prix. L'indice de prix utilisé à cet effet est tiré de l'indice des prix des ventes industrielles (voir, plus loin, l'indice des prix à la production).

Les valeurs courantes proviennent de la même enquête que les données servant à établir l'indice de la production industrielle (voir ci-dessus). Les séries corrigées des variations saisonnières sont établies par l'Office central des statistiques de Hongrie.

Les *ventes totales en volume* se réfèrent à la somme des recettes au titre des ventes de produits transformés et semi-transformés et des services commandés (tels que montage, réparations et maintenance, travail rémunéré) dans l'industrie (industries extractives et manufacturières et électricité et gaz). Les recettes des activités non industrielles, telles que la construction, la revente de produits achetés et les services de transports intra-entreprise, ne sont pas incluses.

Les *ventes en volume de biens d'exportation* se réfèrent à la valeur des biens et services facturés à des acheteurs étrangers et, jusqu'en 1991, aux entreprises de commerce extérieur. Depuis 1992, seuls les biens et services effectivement facturés aux acheteurs étrangers sont pris en compte.

Les *ventes du commerce intérieur* se réfèrent au volume de tous les biens et services consommés dans le pays.

Construction

Logements

Les données concernant le nombre de logements sont établies à partir des registres des administrations locales.

Les *logements mis en chantier* se réfèrent au nombre de logements pourvus d'un permis de construire et dont la construction a effectivement commencé.

Les *logements achevés* se réfèrent à l'ensemble des logements dont la mise en service a été autorisée. Sont compris tous les logements construits par les administrations locales, l'administration centrale, les entités économiques dotées de la personnalité juridique et les particuliers. Jusqu'en 1995, le nombre de logements achevés au premier trimestre de chaque année est inclus dans les chiffres du deuxième trimestre.

Commerce intérieur

Des enquêtes mensuelles sur les *ventes de détail* et la restauration sont effectuées auprès des grands magasins, boutiques, stations-service, vendeurs de matériaux de construction, restaurants, cafés, cantines et autres établissements de restauration qui vendent des marchandises neuves ou d'occasion aux particuliers, aux entreprises et autres organismes. Le chiffre d'affaires est enregistré sur la base des prix payés par les acheteurs, c'est-à-dire des prix à la consommation, TVA comprise. La population de référence comprend tous les points de vente de détail et les établissements de restauration, quelle que soit leur taille. Les points de vente d'entités économiques dont le commerce de détail ou la restauration ne constitue pas la principale activité, ainsi que les entreprises individuelles, sont couverts.

Les ventes des entreprises productrices aux consommateurs qui sont effectuées soit directement, soit par l'intermédiaire d'agents, sont exclues.

La population de référence des enquêtes conduites de 1991 à 1993 se composait des unités de vente de détail (magasins, restaurants et établissements de restauration). Les unités qui formaient

HONGRIE

l'échantillon étaient choisies en fonction de leur taille, définie par leur chiffre d'affaires passé. Les ventes par correspondance étaient exclues.

Depuis 1994, c'est une enquête de conception nouvelle qui est mise en oeuvre. Au premier niveau d'échantillonnage, on utilise une liste d'entreprises complétée au deuxième niveau par une stratification géographique. Toutes les entreprises ayant une activité dans le commerce de détail et/ou la restauration entrent dans l'un des deux cadres d'échantillonnage. Le chiffre d'affaires des sociétés de vente par correspondance est pris en compte. Les unités de la liste d'entreprises sont sélectionnées au moyen d'un échantillonnage stratifié. L'échantillon par secteurs géographiques est constitué grâce à un échantillonnage aléatoire simple de chacun des 200 secteurs géographiques délimités en Hongrie. Il est mis à jour en permanence. Les unités d'échantillonnage sont les entreprises dans le cas de la liste d'entreprises et les points de vente dans celui de la stratification géographique.

Le chiffre d'affaires estimé est classé par branche d'activité selon la Classification type, par industrie, de toutes les branches d'activité économique (TEAOR) de la Hongrie. Les résultats obtenus à partir de 1994 ne sont donc pas comparables avec les données des périodes antérieures au niveau des branches d'activité détaillées.

On obtient le *volume des ventes de détail* en déflatant les valeurs courantes à l'aide de l'indice des prix de détail, en base janvier 1991 = 100. Les données en volume pour 1993 et 1994 sont comparables.

Investissements étrangers

Les données relatives aux investissements étrangers correspondent au total cumulé des investissements effectués depuis le début de l'année. La série *coentreprises nouvelles* ne comprend ni les entreprises hongroises existantes qui sont devenues des coentreprises du fait de l'association de capitaux étrangers, ni les capitaux étrangers investis dans des opérations d'emprunts. Elle ne couvre de ce fait que 20 à 30 pour cent du total des investissements directs étrangers.

Main-d'oeuvre

Emploi

Jusqu'à la fin de 1991, les données sur l'*emploi total* englobaient les salariés de toutes les entreprises dotées de la personnalité juridique et de toutes les institutions budgétisées. En 1992 et 1993, les entreprises de moins de 20 salariés étaient exclues. Toutes les institutions budgétisées continuaient à être couvertes, indépendamment de leurs effectifs. A partir de 1994, les chiffres sur l'emploi se rapportent aux entreprises de plus de 10 salariés. Toutes les entreprises de plus de 50 salariés sont interrogées et un échantillon est tiré parmi les unités qui occupent de 11 à 50 salariés. Bien que la couverture de l'enquête ait été différente en 1993, puisqu'elle ne comprenait que les unités employant plus de 20 salariés, les tendances générales en 1993 et 1994 sont considérées comparables.

Les salariés en congé de longue durée (congé de maternité ou congé parental, service militaire actif, congé de maladie de plus de trois mois, etc.) sont exclus. Les personnes qui ne font pas partie des effectifs réguliers mais ont travaillé de façon continue (étudiants venant travailler pendant les vacances, travailleurs "prêtés" par d'autres employeurs, etc.) sont inclus.

OECD
OCDE
SHORT-TERM ECONOMIC INDICATORS, SOURCES AND DEFINITIONS
OECD/CCET © April 1996

278

INDICATEURS ÉCONOMIQUES A COURT TERME, SOURCES ET DÉFINITIONS
OCDE/CCET © avril 1996

Les données trimestrielles sur l'*emploi dans les branches matérielles* précédemment publiées se réfèrent aux salariés de l'agriculture, des industries extractives et manufacturières, de la branche électricité, du gaz et eau, de la construction, du commerce, des transports, des communications et du traitement de données. Jusqu'à la fin de 1988, elles couvrent toutes les unités économiques dotées de la personnalité juridique et, à partir de 1989, seulement celles d'entre elles qui comptent au moins 50 salariés.

On note des différences de couverture entre les séries trimestrielles et annuelles de l'*emploi dans l'industrie* et de l'*emploi dans les industries manufacturières*. Les données trimestrielles couvrent, jusqu'à la fin de 1988, toutes les entreprises ayant la personnalité juridique et, de 1989 à 1992, les entreprises de plus de 50 salariés. Quant aux données annuelles, jusqu'à la fin de 1991 elles couvrent les entreprises de toute taille et, en 1992, les entreprises de plus de 20 salariés et toutes les institutions budgétisées.

La population d'âge actif en Hongrie se réfère aux femmes âgées de 15 à 54 ans et aux hommes âgés de 15 à 59 ans.

Chômage

Les statistiques sur le nombre de chômeurs inscrits et d'allocataires s'appuient sur les chiffres en fin de mois des registres administratifs des agences locales pour l'emploi, qui sont ensuite agrégés par région. Les *chômeurs inscrits* englobent par définition :

-- les personnes disponibles pour travailler et qui cherchent un emploi ;

-- les personnes qui ne perçoivent pas de pension ;

-- les personnes qui ne sont pas inscrites comme étudiants ;

-- les personnes inscrites à une agence locale pour l'emploi pendant le mois en cours.

On obtient le chômage déclaré en y ajoutant :

-- les personnes qui ont droit à des allocations de chômage ;

-- les personnes inscrites au chômage, mais qui n'ont plus droit aux allocations ;

-- les personnes qui participent à un programme actif du marché de l'emploi.

La couverture du chômage déclaré a été modifiée en mai 1995. Depuis cette date, les demandeurs d'emploi qui se trouvent temporairement dans l'incapacité de travailler, en raison par exemple de la garde de leurs enfants ou d'obligations militaires, sont exclus du décompte des chômeurs inscrits. En mai 1995, on dénombrait 27 288 personnes dans ce cas.

Les *allocataires* sont les personnes qui ont cotisé à l'assurance-chômage pendant au moins 360 jours au cours des quatre années précédant leur période de chômage, qui n'ont pas droit à une pension et qui répondent aux offres d'emploi adaptées à leur profil que leur propose l'agence pour l'emploi. La durée maximum de l'indemnisation est proportionnelle à la période de cotisation à la caisse d'assurance-chômage au cours de ces quatre années. Les personnes qui ont cotisé sans interruption durant les quatre années précédentes perçoivent des allocations pendant un an au maximum. Celles qui n'ont cotisé que 12 à 16 mois en perçoivent que pendant trois mois au maximum.

Les diplômés de l'enseignement secondaire ou post-secondaire peuvent bénéficier d'allocations de chômage s'ils sont diplômés depuis moins de 18 mois, sont inscrits en tant que chômeurs auprès des

HONGRIE

services de l'emploi depuis au moins trois mois et n'ont pas droit à des allocations à un autre titre. Ils touchent alors 75 pour cent du salaire minimum pendant un maximum de six mois.

Un allocataire perd ses droits s'il refuse un emploi ou une formation appropriés proposés par l'agence pour l'emploi, s'il exerce une activité lucrative ou s'il touche une pension.

Le paiement des allocations est suspendu si la personne :

-- ne coopère pas avec l'agence pour l'emploi afin de trouver du travail ;

-- reçoit des allocations de maternité ou une allocation de garde d'enfant ;

-- est emprisonnée ;

-- effectue son service militaire ou civil ;

-- fait un travail d'utilité collective proposé par l'agence pour l'emploi.

Le *taux de chômage* se réfère au nombre de chômeurs inscrits auprès des services nationaux de l'emploi le dernier jour du mois donné, divisé par la population active totale au 1er janvier de l'année précédente.

Temps travaillé

Le nombre moyen mensuel d'*heures effectuées dans les industries manufacturières* se rapporte aux travailleurs manuels, non compris les travailleurs à domicile et les retraités, des entreprises manufacturières (divisions 15 à 37, groupe D, de la CITI Révision 3). Jusqu'à décembre 1988, toutes les entreprises étaient couvertes ; à partir de janvier 1989, la couverture a été réduite aux entreprises de plus de 50 salariés. En 1993, elle a été étendue à toutes les entreprises de plus de 20 salariés, et en 1994 à celles de plus de 10 salariés. Ces données ne sont pas corrigées des variations du nombre de jours ouvrables dans le mois.

Dans les publications statistiques nationales, certaines séries mensuelles, trimestrielles et annuelles sont corrigées des variations du *nombre de jours ouvrables*. Ces données peuvent être utilisées pour évaluer des taux mensuels de croissance de la production et des ventes industrielles.

Salaires

Gains mensuels

Les *gains mensuels*, *total* et les gains dans les *branches matérielles* se réfèrent aux salaires mensuels bruts moyens des employés et ouvriers occupés à plein temps, avant déduction de l'impôt sur le revenu des personnes physiques et des cotisations de retraite et de sécurité sociale. Les sommes versées au titre des programmes de participation aux bénéfices sont incluses. Depuis 1992, les primes et autres gains sont compris dans les chiffres, qui ne couvraient auparavant que les salaires de base.

Les séries relatives aux gains mensuels proviennent des mêmes enquêtes que celles qui concernent l'emploi (pour le champ couvert, voir plus haut, la section Emploi).

Les *gains mensuels dans les industries manufacturières* se rapportent aux salaires bruts moyens versés aux travailleurs manuels.

OECD
OCDE
SHORT-TERM ECONOMIC INDICATORS, SOURCES AND DEFINITIONS
OECD/CCET © April 1996

280

INDICATEURS ÉCONOMIQUES À COURT TERME, SOURCES ET DÉFINITIONS
OCDE/CCET © avril 1996

Prix

Prix à la production

L'*indice des prix à la production (IPP) de l'industrie* reflète les variations des prix des ventes des biens industriels. Les relevés sont effectués par courrier, par le biais d'une enquête mensuelle obligatoire concernant les produits vendus sur les marchés intérieur et extérieur par les industries minières, extractives et manufacturières, ainsi que par les branches de la distribution de gaz, de vapeur et d'eau. Le questionnaire est adressé à quelques 800 des principaux producteurs des produits sélectionnés. Environ 5 500 observations sont recueillies pour 800 articles. Les variétés sélectionnées sont généralement produites en grandes quantités. Les prix indiqués sont les prix mensuels moyens de chaque variété vendue.

Le critère utilisé pour la sélection des produits est le niveau des ventes totales. Jusqu'en 1994, l'IPP reflétait non seulement les variations du niveau des prix mais aussi l'évolution de la configuration des ventes intérieures et des ventes à l'exportation. Depuis 1994, l'IPP est calculé sous forme de moyenne pondérée des indices des prix intérieurs et des prix à l'exportation, il n'est donc pas affecté par les changements de structure des ventes intérieures et des ventes à l'exportation au niveau du produit.

Les prix se rapportent aux ventes à d'autres producteurs, aux grossistes et détaillants, et sont définis par le prix de vente des biens et services vendus au cours du mois. Les prix n'incluent pas la taxe à la valeur ajoutée, introduite en janvier 1988, ni la taxe sur le chiffre d'affaires qui existait précédemment. Une majoration des prix en fonction du chiffre d'affaires est cependant appliquée. Dans le cas d'une vente à l'étranger, c'est le prix fab des marchandises à la frontière hongroise qui est retenu.

L'IPP est un indice-chaîne de Laspeyres. Les indices de produit sont des moyennes des rapports de prix individuels correspondants. Ils sont agrégés au niveau des indicatifs à 4 chiffres de la classification hongroise des activités (TEAOR), avec une pondération par la valeur des ventes. Les indices par sous-branche sont pondérés par les ventes annuelles de l'avant-dernière année précédant la période de référence. Les pondérations par produits sont établies à partir des statistiques annuelles de la production industrielle et sont révisées tous les quatre ans. A partir de 1993, les indices de certains groupes de produits sont pondérés par les ventes annuelles réalisées deux ans avant l'année de référence, avec une révision en fonction de la production industrielle annuelle.

On procède en fin d'année à un examen systématique des produits représentatifs. Pour les produits saisonniers, le dernier prix observé est reconduit hors saison. En cas de changement de qualité, la nouvelle série de rapports de prix est raccordée à l'ancienne sans ajustement.

Prix à la consommation

L'*indice des prix à la consommation (IPC)* hongrois est établi mensuellement et se rapporte à tous les groupes socio-économiques de l'ensemble du pays. Les dépenses de consommation englobent la plupart des biens et services acquis par les ménages. En particulier, le loyer fictif des logements occupés par leur propriétaire, les réparations et les redevances télévision sont inclus. L'auto-consommation, les biens et les services reçus à titre gratuit, les cartes grises des voitures particulières, le coût du crédit à la consommation, les primes d'assurance vie, les impôts directs, les services de santé gratuits et les transactions sur les biens d'occasion (à l'exception des voitures) sont exclus.

Les coefficients de pondération des articles sélectionnés sont tirés de l'enquête sur les dépenses des ménages avec certains ajustements pour raison de conformité avec les comptes nationaux, et sont

HONGRIE

révisés chaque année. L'enquête porte sur un échantillon de 12 000 ménages. Chaque ménage tient un décompte journalier et détaillé de ses dépenses.

Les coefficients de pondération de l'enquête sur les dépenses des ménages sont corrigés à l'aide des statistiques de la consommation pour tenir compte de la sous-déclaration de certains articles comme par exemple l'alcool et le tabac, ainsi que de la sous-représentation des ménages à faible revenu en réajustant le coefficient de pondération du sous-échantillon des ménages à faible revenu grâce à une décomposition des chiffres correspondant à l'ensemble de la population.

En 1996, la pondération utilisée pour le calcul de l'IPC est tirée de l'enquête sur les dépenses des ménages de 1994. En 1995, les poids étaient tirés de l'enquête de 1993, et en 1994 de celle de 1992 ; jusqu'à la fin de 1993, ils étaient dérivés de l'enquête de 1990.

La pondération et la composition de l'indice sont les suivantes :

Grands groupes	Poids de 1990 (utilisés jusqu'à la fin de 1993)	Poids de 1992 (utilisés en 1994)	Poids de 1993 (utilisés en 1995)	Poids de 1994 (utilisés depuis 1996)
Produits alimentaires	28	26.6	27.4	28.4
Boissons et tabac	12	10.3	9.6	9.6
Combustibles et électricité	5	8.5	6.9	6.5
Habillement	8	7.8	7.8	7.5
Biens de consommation durables	10	7.7	8.1	7.4
Autres produits industriels	17	17.5	17.5	17.2
Services	20	21.6	22.7	23.4
TOTAL	100	100.0	100.0	100.0

Les prix sont relevés pour environ 1 800 articles représentatifs. Les relevés de prix sont effectués par environ 145 agents sur des points de vente sélectionnés dans 86 villes. Les prix des fruits et légumes sont aussi relevés sur différents marchés. Plus de 100 000 observations (entre 30 et 150 par produit) sont recueillies chaque mois dans 8 000 points de vente. Pour les produits alimentaires saisonniers les pondérations mensuelles varient à l'intérieur d'un panier fixe de produits.

L'IPC est un indice de Laspeyres modifié. Le prix mensuel d'un article donné correspond à la moyenne arithmétique de tous les prix relevés pour l'article en question pendant le mois considéré. L'indice est obtenu à partir des rapports de prix moyens calculés pour chacun des articles spécifiés, toute observation manquante étant omise.

Finances internes

Les *disponibilités monétaires au sens large (M2)* englobent la masse monétaire au sens étroit (M1) et la quasi-monnaie. Pour les périodes récentes, il n'est pas possible de mesurer séparément M1 et la quasi-monnaie parce que la Banque nationale de Hongrie ne fait pas la distinction entre les dépôts à vue et les dépôts à terme ou d'épargne.

La *masse monétaire au sens étroit (M1)* englobe la monnaie en circulation en dehors du secteur bancaire et les dépôts à vue excepté ceux de l'administration centrale. Cette série a été interrompue.

La *quasi-monnaie* englobe les dépôts à terme, les dépôts d'épargne et les dépôts en devises, excepté les dépôts en devises des non résidents. Cette série a été interrompue.

Les *dépôts personnels* englobent les dépôts des ménages à l'exception des bons d'épargne et dépôts en devises détenus par des non résidents. Les données incluent les comptes enregistrés par la Banque nationale de Hongrie, les banques commerciales et les établissements financiers spécialisés.

Taux d'intérêt

Le *taux d'escompte* se réfère au taux de base que la Banque nationale applique aux établissements financiers pour le refinancement des crédits à échéance de plus d'un an. Ce taux, conformément à la politique monétaire de 1993, doit être aligné chaque trimestre sur les rendements à moyen terme du marché des capitaux.

Le *taux de l'argent au jour le jour* se réfère au taux du marché monétaire interbancaire pour les crédits à deux jours au maximum. Il s'agit d'une moyenne mensuelle des taux quotidiens.

Le *taux d'intérêt à court terme* se réfère au rendement des bons du Trésor à 90 jours. Il s'agit d'une moyenne des rendements observés lors des adjudications bimensuelles de bons du Trésor à 90 jours.

Finances extérieures

Taux de change : le forint suit un régime de parité ajustable, rattachée à un panier de devises composé du dollar des États-Unis (à 50 pour cent) et de l'Écu (à 50 pour cent).

Les *réserves officielles, or exclu,* se rapportent aux avoirs en devises convertibles en fin de période.

Commerce extérieur

1980-1990

Les *exportations*, les *importations* et le *solde commercial* sont exprimés aux prix courants pour la période 1980-1990. Les chiffres de cette période, qui reposaient en principe sur les statistiques douanières, provenaient en pratique des données d'une enquête auprès des exportateurs et importateurs agréés. Les données couvraient les échanges directs, c'est-à-dire les biens importés en vue de leur consommation ou de leur transformation et les biens exportés par la Hongrie.

La définition du commerce extérieur couvrait les éléments suivants :

-- le paiement des biens d'origine étrangère, ainsi que les biens reçus en paiement (troc) ;

-- le paiement des équipements, y compris les coûts d'étude et de montage ;

OECD
OCDE
SHORT-TERM ECONOMIC INDICATORS, SOURCES AND DEFINITIONS
OECD/CCET © April 1996

283

INDICATEURS ÉCONOMIQUES À COURT TERME, SOURCES ET DÉFINITIONS
OCDE/CCET © avril 1996

HONGRIE

  -- la valeur des films de cinéma, y compris la licence d'exploitation ;

  -- la valeur des achats effectués en devises par des organismes étrangers en Hongrie et par des organismes hongrois à l'étranger, pour leur usage propre ;

  -- la valeur des carburants vendus à des bateaux, avions, etc., étrangers sur le territoire hongrois, ou achetés à l'étranger par des compagnies hongroises ;

  -- l'aide publique en nature découlant d'un traité inter-gouvernemental ;

  -- la valeur des investissements achevés et la valeur nette des travaux de construction et de montage (à l'exclusion de la valeur des matières premières) ;

  -- la valeur de l'or non monétaire, de l'argent et du platine.

Les échanges directs excluaient :

  -- les paiements au titre de la propriété intellectuelle (licences de fabrication, redevances, etc.) ;

  -- les bagages personnels ;

  -- l'aide en nature d'organisations internationales telles que la Croix-Rouge ;

  -- la valeur de l'or monétaire.

Les importations étaient enregistrées caf et les exportations fab, à la frontière hongroise, en forints.

Depuis 1991

Les données sur *les exportations, les importations et le solde commercial*, qui reposent sur les déclarations douanières, conformément au Système harmonisé, sont fournies depuis le 1er janvier 1991 par les services douaniers. Les données sont conforme à la Nomenclature Combinée depuis 1994. Les exportations et importations se rapportent aux échanges de marchandises quelle qu'en soit l'origine ou la destination, selon la définition présentée ci-après.

Depuis 1991, la couverture des données du commerce extérieur est étendue aux éléments suivants :

  -- les ventes et achats de biens libellés en forints ;

  -- toutes les formes d'aide en nature reçue ou octroyée ;

  -- les matériaux et produits exportés ou importés en vue d'une transformation, à leur valeur hors douane ;

  -- les biens loués ;

  -- les échanges au titre d'opérations de finition ou de réparation : depuis 1995, la valeur des moyens de transport (comme les avions et les bateaux), temporairement importés pour réparation, qui est évaluée à plus de cinq millions de dollars, est exclue des statistiques du commerce extérieur. Pour des raisons de comparabilité, un indice-chaîne a été calculé sur la base des données de 1994 recalculées au moyen de la méthodologie adoptée en 1995.

Sont désormais exclus les éléments suivants :

  -- les achats et ventes des organismes étrangers extraterritoriaux ;

 SHORT-TERM ECONOMIC INDICATORS, SOURCES AND DEFINITIONS   284   INDICATEURS ÉCONOMIQUES A COURT TERME, SOURCES ET DÉFINITIONS

OECD/CCET © April 1996   OCDE/CCET © avril 1996

-- les carburants destinés à l'usage de bateaux, avions, etc., étrangers sur le territoire hongrois ou achetés à l'étranger par des sociétés hongroises ;

-- le commerce effectué à bord de bateaux ou d'avions.

Depuis 1991, les éléments suivants sont classés dans le commerce extérieur de services et non de marchandises :

-- les opérations de construction et de montage (à l'exclusion de la valeur des matières premières) ;

-- la valeur des films de cinéma (exportés ou importés), y compris la licence d'exploitation ;

-- la valeur des logiciels (hormis leur support physique, qui est inclus dans le commerce de marchandises).

Pour obtenir une certaine comparabilité dans le temps, l'Office central des statistiques de Hongrie a ajusté les données du commerce extérieur de 1990, qui s'appuyaient sur des informations tirées d'une enquête auprès des exportateurs et importateurs agréés, en fonction des nouvelles définitions. On notera toutefois qu'on ne disposait pas des sources statistiques actuelles et que la comparabilité exacte ne peut donc être garantie.

Depuis 1995, si des réparations sont effectuées sur des moyens de transport (comme les avions et les bateaux), temporairement importés ayant une valeur supérieure à cinq millions de dollars, cette valeur est alors incluse dans les chiffres des échanges de service.

Les importations sont évaluées caf et les exportations fab aux prix courants à la frontière hongroise. Les échanges en devises sont convertis en forints en utilisant les taux de change officiels.

Prix

Les *indices des prix à l'exportation et à l'importation* pour le commerce extérieur sont élaborés à partir des valeurs unitaires obtenues grâce aux déclarations douanières. Les indices des prix à l'exportation et à l'importation ne reflètent pas uniquement les variations des prix effectivement payés, mais aussi l'évolution de la structure des produits et des groupes de produits qui entrent dans les échanges internationaux.

Les valeurs unitaires se réfèrent aux prix à l'exportation et à l'importation sur la même base à la frontière, c'est-à-dire aux valeurs caf pour les importations et fab pour les exportations, à la frontière hongroise. Les transactions en devises sont recalculées en forints à l'aide des taux de change officiels.

Les indices trimestriels des prix du commerce extérieur sont de type Paasche, alors que les indices annuels sont des indices de Fischer.

Volumes

On a établi, à partir de l'indice de valeurs unitaires décrit ci-dessus, des indices trimestriels du volume des importations et des exportations. Pour obtenir une comparabilité dans le temps, l'Office central des statistiques de Hongrie a raccordé les données de 1990, converties sur la base des nouveaux contenus et définitions, à l'indice de volume fondé sur les définitions et observations précédentes, en utilisant

HONGRIE

comme lien le rapport du premier trimestre 1990 (données observées), au premier trimestre 1990 (données converties).

Formation brute de capital fixe

La principale composante de la *formation brute de capital fixe* (FBCF) est constituée par l'achat d'actifs corporels neufs. Depuis 1991, les rénovations de grande envergure des biens d'équipement existants sont également prises en compte. Les données relatives à l'investissement sont obtenues au moyen d'enquêtes trimestrielles et annuelles auprès des entreprises et des institutions dont les investissements annuels dépassent dix millions de forints. Des estimations de l'investissement total sont alors effectuées à l'aide d'autres sources statistiques incluant les déclarations de TVA, ainsi que des estimations d'experts.

Publications

Certaines des séries décrites ci-dessus figurent aussi, mais avec une présentation conforme à la pratique nationale, dans les publications suivantes de l'Office central des statistiques de Hongrie :

Statisztikai Havi Közlemények (Bulletin statistique mensuel)

Main Economic Indicators (Principaux Indicateurs Economiques)

Fogyasztoi árindex füzetek (Bulletin de l'indice des prix à la consommation)

Munkaeröpiaci Helyzetkép (Statistiques de la population active)

Statisztikai Evkönyv (Annuaire statistique)

ainsi que dans le :

Rapport mensuel de la Banque nationale de Hongrie.

LETTONIE

Production industrielle

La production industrielle se réfère à la production de produits finis et semi-finis destinés à la vente, ainsi qu'aux services fournis à d'autres entreprises et aux services gratuits rendus à l'intérieur d'une entreprise donnée. La production industrielle comprend la variation des stocks de produits finis et la production non principale.

Depuis 1985, les chiffres de la production industrielle renvoient à la classification internationale type, par industrie, de toutes les branches d'activité économique (CITI) des Nations Unies. La distribution d'eau est prise en compte dans les enquêtes mensuelles à partir de 1995.

A partir de 1991, les enquêtes mensuelles couvrent 90 pour cent de la production. Toutes les entreprises d'État et les administrations locales font l'objet d'une enquête, quel que soit le nombre de leurs salariés ; toutes les autres entreprises de plus de 50 salariés en font également l'objet. Par contre, les enquêtes annuelles couvrent 100 pour cent de la production.

Jusqu'en 1994, les valeurs étaient déflatées par les entreprises elles-mêmes et les séries étaient raccordées d'année en année par la méthode de l'indice chaîne. Depuis 1995, l'indice de la production industrielle est un indice de Laspeyres et est calculé au moyen de données exprimées aux prix constants de janvier 1992.

Quantités produites

La production de ciment se réfère au ciment Portland.

La production de *textiles* comprend tous les tissus, tissés et non tissés, en coton, soie, lin et laine.

Enquêtes de conjoncture

On trouvera une description des techniques de réalisation de ces enquêtes et la liste de questions harmonisées dans le chapitre de cette publication consacré aux *Enquêtes de conjoncture*.

Construction

Logements

Un logement est défini comme une unité d'habitation pourvue d'une entrée indépendante donnant accès à la rue, à une cour, à un escalier ou à un passage commun. Les foyers collectifs ayant une cuisine et des installations communes ne sont pas considérés comme des logements séparés.

LETTONIE

Les *logements achevés* incluent la construction effectuée par des entreprises d'État et les administrations locales, des coopératives, des sociétés par actions salariales, des organisations de consommateurs et les particuliers eux-mêmes. Les entreprises du secteur privé ne sont pas incluses.

Un logement est considéré comme achevé lorsque le certificat d'achèvement des travaux, obligatoire, a été déposé.

Commerce intérieur

Jusqu'à la fin de 1992, un recensement était effectué sur tous les points de vente de détail, établissements de restauration, marchés et kiosques. Au 1er janvier 1992, les points de vente de détail étaient au nombre d'environ 7 200 et les établissements de restauration au nombre de 3 500. Comme de nouveaux points de vente se créaient, un nouveau type d'enquête a été lancé à la fin de 1992. Des données sont recueillies chaque mois auprès de tous les magasins étatiques et municipaux, quelles que soient leur taille ou leur spécialité. Les sociétés d'intérêt économique, entreprises à capital mixte, entreprises en régie et entreprises privées prévoyant un chiffre d'affaires annuel de plus de 10 000 lats font l'objet d'une enquête trimestrielle ; celles qui prévoient un chiffre d'affaires annuel inférieur à 10 000 lats font l'objet d'une enquête annuelle. Le chiffre des ventes de détail sur les marchés est établi à partir des résultats d'enquêtes effectuées sur les quatre principaux marchés de Lettonie.

Depuis janvier 1995, la couverture de l'enquête a changé. Tous les magasins étatiques et municipaux ainsi que les entreprises du secteur privé dont le chiffre d'affaires annuel dépasse 100 000 lats sont couverts ; pour toutes les autres entreprises, un échantillon de 10 pour cent est enquêté et le chiffre d'affaires total est estimé. Le chiffre d'affaires du commerce de détail s'entend à l'exclusion de la restauration publique.

Les données mensuelles sont corrigées après réception des données trimestrielles et les données trimestrielles après réception des données annuelles.

Les ventes de détail en valeur sont exprimées en roubles lettons jusqu'au deuxième trimestre de 1993 et en lats par la suite. Pour plus de précisions, voir la section finances internes ci-dessous et le chapitre *Introduction de nouvelles monnaies*.

Les ventes de détail en volume sont exprimées aux prix constants de janvier 1991 ; elles sont obtenues en déflatant les données en valeur à l'aide de l'indice des prix à la consommation "ensemble des biens". La série est présentée, dans les *Indicateurs économiques à court terme : Économies en transition*, en base 1993=100.

Main d'oeuvre

Emploi

L'emploi total comprend le personnel du secteur étatique, des sociétés d'intérêt économique, y compris d'intérêt agricole, des entreprises privées (fermes paysannes, lopins individuels et fermes satellites privées, ainsi que les travailleurs indépendants). Les entreprises et organisations de toute taille sont incluses.

Avant 1992, l'emploi correspondait au nombre annuel moyen de salariés des entreprises et organisations de chaque secteur de l'économie. Les salariés étaient classés par secteur en fonction du système de classification de l'ex-Union soviétique. Dans le secteur étatique, les tableaux d'effectifs ouvriers et employés de chaque entreprise ou organisation des républiques de l'ex-Union soviétique étaient communiqués à l'agence statistique. Les données annuelles étaient les moyennes des données mensuelles.

Depuis 1992, la classification des branches d'activité concorde avec la CITI. Des questionnaires statistiques sont adressés tous les mois et tous les trimestres aux unités publiques et d'économie mixte, tous les ans aux entreprises privées. Pour 1992, toutefois, les chiffres du secteur privé sont des estimations.

Les militaires de carrière et les appelés du contingent ainsi que les personnes en congé de maternité ou en congé parental sont compris dans les chiffres de l'emploi. Les travailleurs à temps partiel sont inclus au même titre que les travailleurs à temps complet. Les étudiants d'âge actif effectuant un travail rémunéré sont aussi inclus.

Chômage

Conformément à la loi sur l'emploi, adoptée en décembre 1991, et à la législation ultérieure, un chômeur est une personne qui :

-- ne travaille pas ;

-- est de nationalité lettone ou, si elle est étrangère, a obtenu un permis de séjour permanent ;

-- est âgée de 15 à 54 ans pour les femmes ou de 15 à 59 ans pour les hommes ;

-- n'est pas installée à son compte ;

-- gagne moins que le salaire minimum ;

-- recherche activement un emploi ;

-- est inscrite auprès de l'agence publique pour l'emploi du lieu de sa résidence permanente et s'y présente au moins une fois par mois.

Pour s'inscrire au chômage, les intéressés doivent se présenter avec leur certificat d'état de services et leur passeport. La décision de les considérer comme chômeurs incombe au chef de l'agence locale pour l'emploi et doit intervenir dans les deux semaines qui suivent la date d'inscription.

Tout chômeur inscrit a droit à des *allocations de chômage*, et à une bourse pendant la durée d'une formation professionnelle. Les allocataires reçoivent leurs premières indemnités quatorze jours après l'inscription. Ces prestations ne peuvent être perçues plus de six mois au cours d'une période de 12 mois. La durée des droits peut être portée à douze mois à la demande des autorités locales. Les prestations de chômage correspondent à 90 pour cent du salaire minimum pour les personnes ayant cotisé six mois au cours des 12 derniers mois. Le niveau des prestations tombe à 70 pour cent du salaire minimum si l'intéressé n'a pas cotisé et si, pendant cette période, il s'est trouvé dans l'un des cas suivants :

-- il a obtenu le diplôme d'un établissement d'enseignement ;

-- il est sorti de prison ;

-- il s'agit d'une femme qui avait des enfants âgés entre 3 ans et 3 ans et demi ;

-- il a cessé d'être entièrement pris en charge par l'État, ou a pris sa retraite du service actif des armées ;

-- il était précédemment considéré invalide et a recouvré son aptitude physique.

LETTONIE

Les allocataires doivent pointer une fois par mois pour continuer à percevoir leurs prestations.

Les allocations ne sont pas accordées aux personnes qui ont volontairement rompu leur contrat de travail ou qui ont été renvoyées pour infraction aux règles prévues par celui-ci ou pour des raisons disciplinaires.

Un chômeur perd ses droits à allocation si :

-- il refuse deux offres d'emploi correspondant à son profil, ou une formation professionnelle ou des cours de requalification s'il ne lui est pas possible de trouver pareil emploi ;

-- sans raison valable, il n'assiste pas aux cours de formation professionnelle ou de requalification, ou n'honore pas son contrat de travail, ou effectue un travail social temporaire rémunéré ;

-- il cesse de résider de façon permanente en Lettonie ;

-- il ne peut plus être classé comme chômeur (comme défini ci-dessus).

Le *taux de chômage* est le rapport entre le nombre des chômeurs inscrits et la population active (population occupée plus personnes sans emploi inscrites).

Les agences publiques pour l'emploi enregistrent également le nombre d'*offres d'emploi*. Tous les employeurs, quelle que soit la forme de propriété de l'unité de production doivent fournir des informations sur les emplois vacants. Toutes les données mensuelles relatives au chômage et aux offres d'emploi se réfèrent à la fin de la période, les données trimestrielles et annuelles sont des moyennes mensuelles.

Salaires

Gains mensuels

Les *gains mensuels* sont calculés en divisant une estimation de la masse salariale, y compris les primes régulières ou exceptionnelles, les gratifications et autres versements provenant du fonds d'encouragement de la production par le nombre moyen d'ouvriers et d'employés de la période considérée (mois, trimestre, année). Les versements de la caisse de sécurité sociale ne sont pas inclus. La collecte des données mensuelles ne concerne que les entreprises d'État.

Les données se réfèrent aux salaires bruts, c'est-à-dire avant retenue de l'impôt sur le revenu et des cotisations de sécurité sociale. Les paiements en nature (soins de santé, repas ou transports gratuits) sont exclus. Les primes trimestrielles sont incluses dans les chiffres trimestriels et annuels. Les primes annuelles sont comprises à la fois dans les chiffres annuels et dans ceux du quatrième trimestre ou du premier trimestre de l'année suivante, selon la période où elles ont été calculées.

Les données sur les salaires sont exprimées en roubles lettons jusqu'au deuxième trimestre de 1993 et en lats par la suite. Pour plus de précisions, voir la section finances internes ci-dessous et le chapitre *Introduction de nouvelles monnaies*.

Les *gains mensuels dans l'industrie* se réfèrent aux unités publiques et d'économie mixte.

OECD
OCDE
SHORT-TERM ECONOMIC INDICATORS, SOURCES AND DEFINITIONS
OECD/CCET © April 1996

290

INDICATEURS ÉCONOMIQUES A COURT TERME, SOURCES ET DÉFINITIONS
OCDE/CCET © avril 1996

Prix

Prix à la production

En 1993 et 1994, l'enquête permettant de calculer l'*indice des prix à la production (IPP) des industries manufacturières* couvrait 469 produits et groupes de produits dont les prix étaient observés dans 90 entreprises manufacturières représentant 57 classes de la CITI, y compris quelques entreprises du secteur privé. Avant 1993, l'enquête couvrait 274 produits.

Depuis janvier 1995, l'*indice des prix à la production* est calculé selon un nouveau système de pondération. Il couvre 709 produits dont les prix sont observés dans 166 entreprises manufacturières représentant 69 classes de la CITI. Il est basé sur les prix du mois de décembre de l'année précédente.

Les prix à la production ne sont enregistrés que pour les produits fabriqués en Lettonie. Mais des matières premières, produits semi-finis, composants et ressources énergétiques d'importation peuvent être utilisés pour leur fabrication. Les produits industriels destinés à l'exportation sont inclus. Les prix s'entendent hors taxes.

Le choix des produits est fait par le Bureau central de statistique de Lettonie, en coordination avec les entreprises individuelles elles-mêmes. Les entreprises visées ont pour instruction de corriger les prix pour tenir compte des changements de qualité.

Pour les produits saisonniers, les prix du dernier mois de production sont reconduits hors saison.

Avant 1995, les différents produits étaient pondérés par le volume des ventes de l'année précédente. A partir de 1995, ils sont pondérés par le volume des ventes de 1993.

L'IPP est un indice-chaîne de type Laspeyres.

Prix à la consommation

L'*indice* mensuel *des prix à la consommation* (IPC) a été introduit en janvier 1991.

Jusqu'à juin 1992, il s'agissait d'un indice de Paasche calculé à partir des prix de 950 produits (300 produits alimentaires et 650 produits non alimentaires) et de 150 services, relevés dans 150 points de vente de détail de 15 régions réparties sur le territoire.

En juin 1992, un nouvel indice, de type Laspeyres, a été introduit. En 1993, des relevés de prix ont été effectués sur 388 biens et services (379 en 1992) dans 775 points de vente répartis dans 15 des 26 régions lettones. Les points de vente se répartissent en 257 magasins d'État, 243 magasins municipaux, 212 coopératives (dont 155 coopératives de consommation), 49 magasins privés, 4 établissements syndicaux et 10 marchés.

Fin 1995, la situation a changé à la suite de privatisations et un plus grand nombre de points de vente privés ont été inclus dans l'enquête. La part des points de vente étatiques et municipaux est tombée à 32 pour cent et celle des points de vente privés est passée à 48 pour cent. Les données sur les prix ont été recueillies auprès de 1120 points de vente au total.

De quatre à huit observations de prix sont enregistrées chaque mois pour les produits agricoles, et de une à quatre pour les autres produits.

LETTONIE

Certains biens et services ont été reclassés en décembre 1993 conformément aux classifications internationales usuelles des dépenses.

Les chiffres des mois de janvier à juin 1992 ont été recalculés en cohérence avec le nouvel indice de Laspeyres. Pour 1991, seuls les indices concernant *l'alimentation* et les *alcools et tabacs* sont considérés comme comparables avec les chiffres ultérieurs.

Pour les produits saisonniers qui ne sont pas "de saison" pendant un mois donné, on retient le prix moyen de saison, même si l'on ne dispose que de quelques relevés pour le mois en question. Cela s'applique notamment aux produits alimentaires importés en période hivernale.

Quelques ajustements ont été apportés aux IPC pour tenir compte de l'évolution de la qualité.

Les indices sont calculés à partir des rapports de prix moyens. Tous les prix s'entendent toutes taxes comprises.

Ils sont pondérés par les dépenses des ménages ; depuis 1994, l'IPC est pondéré à l'aide de la structure des dépenses du milieu de l'année 1992 au milieu de l'année 1993. Auparavant, l'IPC était pondéré en fonction des résultats de l'enquête sur les dépenses des ménages de 1991. Les chiffres ont été corrigés pour tenir compte de la sous-déclaration des dépenses de tabac et d'alcool par les ménages.

Les pondérations tirées des enquêtes auprès des ménages sont les suivantes :

Article	Poids 1991 (utilisés en 1992-1993)	Poids Mi-1992 à mi-1993 (utilisé à partir de 1994)
Alimentation	48.72	49.67
Vêtements et chaussures	11.12	8.68
Entretien courant de la maison	4.23	2.67
Tabacs et alcools	9.54	7.37
Transports et communications	6.39	7.18
Loisirs, activités culturelles, éducation	5.09	4.32
Biens et services divers	8.72	4.93
Soins de santé	0.92	1.09
Logement	5.27	14.09
TOTAL	100.00	100.00

Le poids total des services est de 23,65 dans l'enquête de 1992-1993.

Tous les IPC sont exprimés sous la forme d'indices en base fixe : décembre 1993=100, et sous forme de taux de variation mensuels dans les publications nationales.

L'indice des prix pour le *logement* couvre les loyers et les matériaux de construction.

Finances internes

Le rouble letton était devenu monnaie officielle le 7 mai 1992, à parité avec le rouble russe, qui continuait d'avoir cours. Le 20 juillet 1992, le rouble letton est devenu la seule monnaie légale. A partir du 5 mars 1993, le lat a été progressivement mis en circulation, 1 lat valant 200 roubles lettons. Le rouble letton a été démonétisé à compter du 18 octobre 1993 et totalement retiré de la circulation le 1er juillet 1994.

Les données de finances internes sont exprimées en roubles lettons jusqu'au deuxième trimestre de 1993 et en lats par la suite. Pour plus de précisions, voir aussi le chapitre *Introduction de nouvelles monnaies*.

Les *disponibilités monétaires* au sens large *(M2)* comprennent la monnaie en circulation en dehors du secteur bancaire, les dépôts personnels et les dépôts en devises. Les chiffres se rapportent à la fin de la période.

Taux d'intérêt

Le *taux d'escompte* est le taux du crédit de la Banque centrale aux banques commerciales.

Finances extérieures

Les séries de *taux de change* retracent l'évolution du cours de la monnaie lettone, le lat, par rapport au dollar des États-Unis, au deutsche mark et à l'Écu.

Le lat est une monnaie à parité librement ajustable, rattachée au droit de tirage spécial (DTS, unité monétaire du Fonds monétaire international) et à un panier de monnaies comprenant le dollar des États-Unis, le deutsche mark, le yen, le franc français et la livre sterling.

Les *réserves officielles, or exclu*, comprennent les avoirs en devises détenus en Lettonie comme à l'étranger et sont comptabilisées en fin de période.

Commerce extérieur

Jusqu'à la fin de 1990, les statistiques du commerce extérieur étaient établies par le Goskomstat et les organismes soviétiques de commerce extérieur, aux prix intérieurs courants en roubles. La classification du commerce était celle utilisée par les républiques de l'ex-Union soviétique. Les données de la période 1988-1990 sont des estimations fondées sur les tableaux d'entrées-sorties de 1987 concernant 120 secteurs.

Jusqu'en 1990, les exportations de biens étaient évaluées aux prix payés aux producteurs nationaux par les organismes d'exportation ; les importations de biens étaient évaluées aux prix effectivement payés par les acheteurs finals locaux, à savoir les prix à l'importation pour les organismes de commerce extérieur, corrigés à l'aide de coefficients de conversion spécifiques fixés pour chaque groupe de produits par les autorités compétentes.

A partir de 1991, les entreprises d'import-export ont fait l'objet d'une enquête trimestrielle, qui a couvert cette année-là environ 80 pour cent du commerce extérieur. Les échanges de gaz et d'énergie

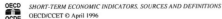

LETTONIE

électrique, font l'objet d'une notification, mais les services de recherche et développement sont exclus. En 1992, des documents de déclaration douanière ont été mis en place conformément au Système harmonisé. Depuis 1993, toutes les données sont recueillies par le biais de ces déclarations, complétées par des enquêtes spécifiques sur les échanges d'énergie électrique et de gaz naturel, les ventes de poisson effectuées à l'étranger par des bateaux de pêche lettons. Avant 1995, les statistiques trimestrielles incluent les ventes et les achats de biens aux militaires russes en poste sur le territoire letton, ainsi qu'un ajustement pour tenir compte des importations de combustibles minéraux.

Dans les séries *exportations*, *importations* et *solde commercial*, les données mensuelles ne couvrent pas le même champ que les données trimestrielles. Les données mensuelles ne comprennent ni les livraisons aux troupes russes qui stationnaient auparavant en Lettonie, ni les transactions de la flotte de pêche lettone à l'étranger, ni aucun ajustement pour tenir compte des importations de combustibles minéraux.

Les services importés ou exportés et l'aide étrangère ne sont pas inclus.

Les exportations comme les importations sont enregistrées fab.

Les données sont exprimées en roubles lettons jusqu'au second trimestre de 1993, et en lats par la suite. Pour plus de précisions voir ci-dessus la section sur les finances internes, ainsi que le chapitre *Introduction de nouvelles monnaies*.

En ce qui concerne les *exportations et importations à destination et en provenance des NEI*, la Lituanie et l'Estonie étaient considérées comme faisant partie de la zone rouble jusqu'en 1992 ; ensuite elles sont comptées parmi les pays n'appartenant pas à cette zone. Les échanges avec le reste du monde à l'exception de l'ex-Union soviétique sont couverts par les séries du *commerce avec les pays autres que les NEI*.

Publications

Certaines des séries décrites ci-dessus figurent aussi, mais avec une présentation conforme à la pratique nationale, dans les publications suivantes du Bureau central de statistique de Lettonie :

Bulletin of Latvian Economic Statistics (Bulletin de statistiques économiques de Lettonie).
Statistical Yearbook of Latvia (Annuaire statistique de la Lettonie).

LITUANIE

Production industrielle

L'*indice de la production industrielle (IPI) dans les industries manufacturières* se réfère aux ventes de produits industriels, non corrigées de la variation des stocks de produits finis; la production non principale est exclue. Les volumes des ventes sont déclarés chaque mois par les entreprises couvertes par l'enquête. Si une entreprise produit des biens à partir de matières premières fournies par le consommateur, la valeur de ces matières premières n'est pas soustraite de la valeur finale. Les volumes des ventes du mois courant sont ensuite pondérés à l'aide de l'indice des prix à la production correspondant (voir plus bas), et le résultat est exprimé en taux de variation par rapport au mois précédent. L'indice en base fixe est calculé directement à partir des taux mensuels de variation. Les séries annuelles et trimestrielles sont calculées à partir des séries mensuelles.

L'enquête, menée auprès d'environ 600 entreprises, permet d'enregistrer les ventes de 1 100 produits industriels. Jusqu'à la fin de 1994, elle couvrait toutes les entreprises publiques, privées et d'économie mixte de plus de 100 salariés. Depuis janvier 1995, elle est effectuée auprès des entreprises de plus de 20 salariés. On estime que la production industrielle est ainsi couverte à 90 pour cent.

Depuis janvier 1994, la production industrielle est classée selon la Classification internationale type, par industrie, de toutes les branches d'activité économique (CITI, Révision 3) et comprend la production des activités extractives et de fabrication, la production et la distribution d'électricité, ainsi que la distribution de gaz et d'eau.

Quantités produites

La *production de ciment* englobe tous les types de ciment.

Enquêtes de conjoncture

On trouvera une explication des techniques de réalisation de ces enquêtes et la liste des questions harmonisées dans le chapitre de cette publication consacré aux *Enquêtes de conjoncture*.

Construction

Logements

La définition d'un logement est en accord avec celle du Conseil d'assistance économique mutuelle (CAEM), qui remonte à 1980 ; elle couvre tous les appartements et maisons individuelles. Les habitations collectives comme les sanatoriums, les foyers d'étudiants et de travailleurs, etc., sont exclues.

LITUANIE

Une fois la construction achevée, un document officiel est délivré par la commission locale de la construction, qui se compose d'entrepreneurs en bâtiment, d'architectes et de représentants des entreprises de service public. Ce document énonce les caractéristiques du logement et confirme qu'il est dûment achevé. Un logement est considéré comme achevé dès l'enregistrement de ce document. Pour les logements construits directement par des particuliers, l'achèvement est notifié au Département des statistiques par les services d'architecture des administrations locales. Tous les entrepreneurs, qu'ils appartiennent au secteur privé ou au secteur public, doivent certifier de l'achèvement d'un logement.

Le total des *logements achevés* comprend les logements construits par les entreprises de bâtiment de tous les secteurs, c'est-à-dire y compris le secteur privé, ainsi que les logements construits par des particuliers.

Les *logements achevés par les entreprises* ne comprennent pas les logements construits par des particuliers, qui sont généralement des maisons individuelles.

Commerce intérieur

Les données sur le commerce de détail sont recueillies à l'aide de questionnaires statistiques mensuels envoyés aux entreprises ; les réponses sont ensuite regroupées par catégorie de points de vente (publics, semi-publics, etc.). Toutes les entreprises d'État et les coopératives sont couvertes, quelle que soit leur taille. Les ventes des fermes collectives sont toutefois exclues des chiffres avant 1992. Les sociétés de personnes à vocation agricole qui ont commencé à remplacer les fermes collectives en 1992 sont prises en compte.

A partir de 1992, les enquêtes ont englobé une partie du secteur privé ; les entreprises d'État privatisées ont été prises en compte, mais les entreprises privées nouvellement créées sont restées exclues. Celles-ci ont été couvertes à partir de 1993 lorsqu'elles comptaient plus de 20 salariés. On estime que, en 1993, environ 55 à 70 pour cent du commerce de détail était couvert par les enquêtes. A côté de cela, 30 pour cent des biens vendus au détail qui étaient écoulés sur les marchés en plein air et dans les points de vente privés employant moins de 20 salariés, étaient exclus du champ de l'enquête. Depuis avril 1994, les entreprises privées d'au moins 5 salariés sont interrogées. Les ventes de détail effectuées sur les marchés ont commencé à être prises en compte, de même que des estimations de l'économie "souterraine" sur la base des revenus déclarés des personnes physiques diminués des dépôts et de l'épargne personnels, des dépenses de location, de combustible et d'énergie, des prélèvements fiscaux, ainsi que des estimations officielles du commerce de détail. Depuis janvier 1995, les ventes de commerce de détail de toutes les entreprises privées ainsi que les ventes sur les marchés sont incluses.

Les chiffres trimestriels des *ventes de détail en valeur* sont corrigés pour tenir compte des déclarations tardives, etc., et ne correspondent donc pas à la somme des chiffres mensuels. Il n'y a en revanche pas de différence de couverture entre les enquêtes mensuelles et trimestrielles.

La valeur du commerce de détail s'entend toutes taxes comprises.

Les *ventes de détail en valeur* sont exprimées en roubles, ou en talonas jusqu'à la fin de 1992, et en litas par la suite. Pour plus de précisions, voir la section finances internes ci-dessous et le chapitre *Introduction de nouvelles monnaies*.

Le *volume des ventes de détail* est obtenu en déflatant la valeur du commerce de détail aux prix courants à l'aide d'un indice des prix à la consommation recalculé suivant les groupes inclus dans les statistiques du commerce intérieur en base mai 1992=100. Contrairement à la série de ventes de détail en

OECD
OCDE
SHORT-TERM ECONOMIC INDICATORS, SOURCES AND DEFINITIONS
OECD/CCET © April 1996

296

INDICATEURS ÉCONOMIQUES A COURT TERME, SOURCES ET DÉFINITIONS
OCDE/CCET © avril 1996

valeur qui inclut, depuis janvier 1995, les ventes sur les marchés et les ventes des petites entreprises, la série en volume n'inclut pas ces ventes. La couverture de la série en volume est la même avant et après janvier 1995 pour des raisons de comparabilité historique.

Main-d'oeuvre

Emploi

L'emploi total comprend toutes les personnes travaillant dans le secteur étatique, les coopératives et les entreprises privées, ainsi que les travailleurs indépendants. Toutes les entreprises sont couvertes par l'enquête, quels que soient leurs effectifs. Dans le secteur étatique comme dans le secteur privé, le nombre des ouvriers et employés est communiqué chaque trimestre à l'Office statistique. Le nombre de salariés des petites entreprises (de moins de quatre salariés) est connu grâce aux déclarations fiscales ; celui des exploitants agricoles privés est fourni par le registre des exploitations agricoles. En 1995, le taux de non réponse des entreprises interrogées était estimé à 15 pour cent.

Avant 1992, les entreprises et organismes étaient classés par secteur selon le système de classification de l'ex-CAEM. En 1992, la Nomenclature générale des activités économiques des Communautés européennes (NACE) a été introduite.

Le personnel en congé de maternité ou en congé parental et le personnel militaire sont pris en compte. Les travailleurs à temps partiel sont compris dans les chiffres de l'emploi après conversion en équivalent plein temps. Les personnes qui sont en dehors de l'âge actif (16-55 ans pour les femmes, 16-60 ans pour les hommes) mais qui conservent un emploi rémunéré sont incluses.

Les chiffres de l'*emploi total* englobent tous les secteurs de l'économie, y compris l'agriculture et le secteur non marchand (services de santé, administration publique, activités culturelles, etc.).

L'*emploi dans l'industrie* englobe les activités de fabrication, les activités extractives, la production et la distribution d'eau, de gaz et d'électricité, la transformation de produits agricoles, la construction, les transports et les communications.

Chômage

Les statistiques du chômage sont établies depuis mars 1991, date d'entrée en vigueur de la Loi sur le chômage. Les Bourses du travail inscrivent les chômeurs, distribuent les allocations de chômage et pourvoient les emplois vacants. Elles inscrivent également les demandeurs d'emploi qui ont délibérément quitté leur travail, mais ils ne sont pas considérés comme des "chômeurs inscrits pour raisons économiques". En 1994 et 1995, deux enquêtes pilotes ont été effectuées chaque année sur la population active. D'après leurs résultats, les personnes sans emploi sont à peu près deux fois plus nombreuses que celles qui se sont inscrites dans les Bourses du travail.

Le *chômage total* se réfère aux chômeurs inscrits, ainsi qu'aux personnes qui ont volontairement quitté leur emploi, qui n'ont pas de travail rémunéré ou ne sont pas établis à leur compte au moment considéré, et qui sont disponibles pour travailler.

LITUANIE

Le *chômage déclaré* recense les personnes ayant perdu leur travail malgré elles et les nouveaux diplômés inscrits à la Bourse du travail. Le pointage, plusieurs fois par mois, dans les Bourses du travail est obligatoire pour conserver le statut de chômeur.

Les chômeurs inscrits qui ont travaillé au moins 24 mois au cours des trois dernières années, les nouveaux diplômés et les personnes revenant du service militaire peuvent recevoir des allocations. La période minimale de non activité avant de recevoir des allocations est de 8 jours pour ceux qui travaillaient précédemment. Cette période minimale est de 6 mois pour les personnes inscrites qui ont quitté leur travail volontairement.

Les *allocataires* perçoivent des prestations pendant six mois au maximum. Celles-ci ne peuvent pas dépasser le double du minimum vital. En 1994, l'allocation minimale était d'à peu près 20 litas, l'allocation maximale de 100 litas et l'allocation moyenne de 50 litas. Le 1er janvier 1995, le plancher de l'allocation a été fixé à 75 litas. Au 1ᵉʳ janvier 1996, l'allocation minimale était de 90 litas, et l'allocation maximale de 180 litas. Le montant actuel de l'allocation est défini en pourcentage du salaire antérieur de l'intéressé. Pendant les deux premiers mois, un chômeur précédemment salarié perçoit 70 pour cent de son ancien salaire, dans la limite de deux fois le minimum vital. Au cours des deux mois suivants, il ne touche plus que 60 pour cent du salaire précédent ; pendant les deux derniers mois, les indemnités de chômage sont égales à 50 pour cent du salaire antérieur. Les personnes qui n'ont jamais travaillé perçoivent l'allocation minimale.

Un allocataire perd ses droits à percevoir des indemnités s'il ne pointe pas tous les mois, refuse trois offres d'emploi ou un stage de formation proposé par les Bourses du travail afin de lui permettre d'acquérir les nouvelles qualifications qui lui sont nécessaires pour trouver un emploi rémunéré.

Le *taux de chômage total* représente le nombre total de chômeurs, en proportion de la population active (personnes occupées et personnes sans emploi) moyenne de l'année précédente.

Le *taux de chômage déclaré* correspond au nombre de chômeurs inscrits, en proportion de la population active (personnes occupées et personnes sans emploi) moyenne de l'année précédente.

Le nombre d'*offres d'emploi* se rapporte aux emplois vacants enregistrés par les Bourses du travail dans le secteur public et le secteur privé.

Temps travaillé

Dans les publications statistiques nationales, certaines séries mensuelles, trimestrielles ou annuelles sont publiées en données corrigées par le *nombre de jours ouvrables* de la période considérée. Ces données peuvent servir à évaluer les taux de croissance des ventes et de la production industrielles.

Salaires

Gains mensuels

Les données relatives aux gains mensuels sont collectées dans le cadre de l'enquête sur l'emploi (voir ci-dessus). Les données mensuelles, trimestrielles et annuelles couvrent les entreprises du secteur privé. Des estimations concernant les entreprises individuelles sont également incluses dans les données trimestrielles et annuelles.

OECD
OCDE *SHORT-TERM ECONOMIC INDICATORS, SOURCES AND DEFINITIONS*
OECD/CCET © April 1996

298

INDICATEURS ÉCONOMIQUES A COURT TERME, SOURCES ET DÉFINITIONS
OCDE/CCET © avril 1996

Les gains mensuels représentent les salaires bruts perçus par les salariés avant paiement de l'impôt sur le revenu. Les rémunérations des heures supplémentaires, des congés payés et de toutes les primes, y compris les primes d'intéressement aux bénéfices, sont prises en compte. Les chiffres mensuels sont corrigés de façon à étaler les primes trimestrielles ou annuelles sur tous les mois du trimestre ou de l'année. Il existe peu de paiements en nature, mais ils sont estimés aux prix courants et inclus dans les gains mensuels.

Les prestations sociales ne sont pas prises en compte dans les gains, ni les indemnités versées par les entreprises en cas de catastrophe, telle qu'un incendie ou un décès dans la famille.

Les *salaires* sont exprimés en roubles ou en talonas, jusqu'à la fin de 1992 et en litas par la suite. Pour plus de précisions, voir la section finances internes ci-dessous et le chapitre *Introduction de nouvelles monnaies*.

Prix

Prix à la production

L'*indice des prix à la production* (IPP) est construit à l'aide des réponses de 270 entreprises à une enquête couvrant 890 produits industriels et groupes de produits. Les prix s'entendent hors taxe à la valeur ajoutée à partir de janvier 1995, auparavant la TVA était comprise. En 1993, 82 pour cent de la production industrielle était assurée par les entreprises couvertes par l'enquête. En 1994-95, les prix des produits industriels sont pondérés par la valeur des ventes correspondantes enregistrées en 1993. Jusqu'en 1996, les produits ayant subi des changements de qualité étaient considérés comme de nouveaux produits. Depuis 1996, les prix sont pondérés par la valeur des ventes en 1994 ; et sont corrigés pour tenir compte de l'évolution de la qualité. Pour les produits ayant un cycle de production saisonnier, le dernier relevé est reconduit pendant la période hors saison.

L'indice des prix à la production est de type Laspeyres.

La classification de la CITI a été utilisée jusqu'à la fin de 1995. Depuis 1996, le système de classification de la NACE a été adopté.

Prix à la consommation

Un nouvel *indice des prix à la consommation* (IPC) est en place depuis mai 1992. C'est un indice de Laspeyres modifié, et les sous-groupes sont pondérés à l'aide des résultats de l'enquête sur le budget des ménages. L'indice précédent, utilisé avant mai 1992, était un indice de Paasche, pondéré par le chiffre d'affaires des magasins de détail du secteur étatique et coopératif.

Le nouvel IPC est calculé à partir des prix relevés sur 369 biens et services dans sept grandes villes et neuf régions de Lituanie. L'échantillon de points de vente est sélectionné par les enquêteurs en coopération avec le Département des statistiques. Il se compose d'environ 1 060 points de vente des secteurs étatique, coopératif et privé : magasins de détail, cantines, restaurants et cafés, ainsi que kiosques et marchés en plein air. Les prix des biens alimentaires et non alimentaires sont aussi relevés sur les marchés. Les points de vente sont choisis de manière à constituer un échantillon représentatif sur le plan géographique et comprenant des grandes et moyennes surfaces, ainsi que de petits commerces spécialisés. Il n'existe pas de registres du commerce de détail permettant de procéder mathématiquement à l'échantillonnage.

LITUANIE

Tous les articles font l'objet d'un relevé de prix par mois. Les prix des biens alimentaires sont relevés entre le 21 et le 23 du mois, ceux des biens non alimentaires entre le 17 et le 20, ceux des services le 15 ou le 16.

Les prix enregistrés sont les prix effectivement payés par les consommateurs, c'est-à-dire y compris les taxes sur le chiffre d'affaires et les taxes d'accise. Certains prix sont encore fixés par le gouvernement, à savoir ceux de l'électricité et du gaz, des services postaux et de télécommunications, des produits pharmaceutiques et des transports (à l'exclusion des transports publics urbains de voyageurs). Les loyers des logements et les tarifs des transports publics urbains de voyageurs sont réglementés par les administrations locales.

Si un article saisonnier est indisponible dans un point de vente de détail, on reconduit le prix relevé le mois précédent ou on lui affecte le prix moyen du sous-groupe de produits correspondant de façon que le prix manquant soit neutre pour ce sous-groupe. Les prix ne sont pas ajustés pour tenir compte des changements de qualité.

L'enquête sur les dépenses des ménages utilisée pour pondérer l'IPC de 1994 a été réalisée d'août 1992 à juillet 1993. Quant à l'IPC pour 1992 et 1993, il a été pondéré à l'aide de l'enquête sur les dépenses des ménages de 1991.

Les coefficients de pondération correspondants sont présentés ci-après :

Groupes	Poids 1991 (utilisés en 1992-1993)	Poids 1992-1993 (utilisés depuis 1994)
Alimentation, tabacs et alcools	53.81	65.82
Habillement et chaussures	15.38	9.61
Entretien courant de la maison	6.48	3.15
Transports et communications	5.70	5.91
Logement et combustibles	4.93	8.07
Loisirs, culture, éducation et divers	13.22	6.57
Dépenses médicales et soins de santé	0.48	0.87
TOTAL	100.00	100.00

La structure des dépenses est corrigée pour tenir compte de la sous-déclaration de la consommation d'alcools et de tabacs, à l'aide du chiffre d'affaires du commerce de détail pour ces produits.

A partir de janvier 1994, la composante *alimentation* de l'IPC s'entend à l'exclusion de la restauration.

La composante *entretien courant de la maison* comprend les meubles, les revêtements de sol et leur réparation, les articles de literie, les ustensiles de cuisine, les détergents, ainsi que d'autres services.

La composante *logement* comprend le loyer, les réparations et l'entretien de l'habitation, ainsi que l'électricité et les combustibles.

La composante *services* comprend des éléments de la plupart des principaux sous-groupes de l'enquête sur les dépenses des ménages : cordonnerie, entretien courant de la maison, services de soins de santé, etc.

Finances internes

Toutes les données monétaires et financières sont établies par la Banque nationale de Lituanie.

Le talonas lituanien a été adopté à titre de monnaie provisoire le 1er octobre 1992 pour remplacer le rouble de l'ex-Union soviétique. Le litas a remplacé le talonas le 25 juin 1993 avec une parité flottante. A l'époque, il équivalait à 100 talonas. Les données de la série du taux de change concernent, pour l'année 1992, le cours du talonas et, à partir de 1993, celui du litas. Voir également le chapitre *Introduction de nouvelles monnaies*.

Les séries monétaires sont exprimées en roubles, ou en talonas, jusqu'à la fin de 1992 et en litas par la suite.

Les *disponibilités monétaires au sens étroit* (M1) désignent la monnaie en circulation, augmentée des dépôts à vue des particuliers, des entreprises d'État et des coopératives ainsi que d'institutions financières non bancaires telles que les compagnies d'assurance.

La *quasi-monnaie* recouvre les dépôts à terme et les dépôts en devises des particuliers et des entreprises. Les dépôts en devises sont convertis en litas à l'aide du taux de change officiel.

Les *dépôts personnels* désignent les dépôts à vue, à terme et en devises, des particuliers et des entreprises du secteur privé qui ne tiennent pas de comptabilité d'entreprise. Les dépôts en devises sont convertis en litas à l'aide du taux de change officiel. Les dépôts personnels sont placés dans les 25 banques commerciales et l'unique caisse d'épargne de Lituanie.

Taux d'intérêt

Le *taux d'escompte officiel* est le taux moyen du crédit de la Banque centrale aux banques commerciales, il se rapporte à la fin de la période.

Finances extérieures

Le *taux de change du dollar des États-Unis en litas* se réfère au taux de change officiel consenti par la Banque centrale. Il se situe à peu près à mi-chemin entre le cours acheteur et le cours vendeur du dollar des États-Unis dans les banques commerciales.

LITUANIE

Commerce extérieur

Les statistiques du commerce extérieur sont tirées des déclarations douanières depuis 1993, à l'exception des données relatives aux importations d'énergie électrique, qui sont encore communiquées par les entreprises importatrices. En 1992, elles ont toutes été établies à partir des factures des entreprises de commerce extérieur, parmi lesquelles figuraient la totalité des entreprises d'État et une fraction, estimée de 20 à 30 pour cent des entreprises du secteur privé. Les entreprises d'import-export du secteur privé étaient identifiées grâce au registre du commerce.

Environ 480 produits et groupes de produits sont couverts par les statistiques du commerce extérieur. Le Système harmonisé a été mis en oeuvre en 1993 ; auparavant, les échanges étaient classés selon le système de l'ex-CAEM. Les exportations de marchandises étaient évaluées aux prix payés aux producteurs nationaux par les organismes d'exportation, et les importations de marchandises aux prix effectivement payés par les acheteurs finals locaux.

Les quelques biens exclus des statistiques du commerce extérieur sont les suivants :

-- les biens expédiés par le gouvernement lituanien aux forces armées et aux représentations diplomatiques à l'étranger ; les importations de marchandises des ambassades étrangères en Lituanie ;

-- l'or monétaire, les valeurs mobilières et les billets de banque ;

-- les marchandises importées ou exportées à titre temporaire ou pour une durée limitée, par exemple à des fins de présentation, de démonstration ou d'utilisation dans le cadre de foires-expositions ; le matériel de promotion du tourisme ; les machines, le matériel et l'outillage envoyés pour inspection et démonstration, etc.

-- le poisson pêché en dehors des eaux territoriales ;

-- la réparation de biens d'équipements ;

-- les approvisionnements destinés aux navires ou aux avions lituaniens assurant des liaisons internationales.

Les importations destinées à la réexportation sont incluses.

Les importations sont évaluées caf, les exportations fab.

Les *totaux* indiqués pour les *exportations*, les *importations* et le *solde commercial* sont exprimés en roubles, ou en talonas, jusqu'à la fin de 1992, et en litas par la suite. Pour plus de précisions, voir la section finances internes ci-dessus et le chapitre *Introduction de nouvelles monnaies*. Les séries relatives au commerce extérieur total existent aussi en dollars des États-Unis.

La série statistique sur le *commerce avec les pays autres que les NEI* autrefois publiée était exprimée en dollars des États-Unis et comprenait la totalité des transactions libellées en monnaies convertibles. La couronne estonienne et le lat letton sont traités comme des monnaies convertibles depuis le quatrième trimestre de 1992.

La série statistique sur le *commerce avec les NEI* qui était auparavant publiée représentait la totalité des échanges effectués dans des monnaies comme le rouble russe et le karbovanets ukrainien.

Publications

Certaines des séries décrites ci-dessus figurent aussi, mais avec une présentation conforme à la pratique nationale, dans les publications suivantes du Département des statistiques de Lituanie :

Gyventoju Idarbinimas Ir Bedarbyste (Emploi et chômage)

Lietuvos Uzsienio Prekyba (Le commerce extérieur de la Lituanie)

Lietuvos Ekonomine ir Socialine Raida (Développement économique et social en Lituanie)

Lietuvos Statistikos metrastis (Annuaire statistique de la Lituanie)

Main Economic Indicators of Lithuania (Principaux indicateurs économiques de Lituanie).

POLOGNE

Production industrielle

Les indices de la production industrielle (IPI) sont des indices de volume couvrant l'ensemble des activités, industrielles ou non, des entreprises industrielles du pays.

Avant 1994, les informations étaient fournies par les entreprises classées dans l'industrie selon la Classification de l'économie nationale (KGN). En janvier 1994, la classification de la Nomenclature générale des activités économiques dans les Communautés européennes (NACE) a été introduite. Les données de 1993 ont été calculées à partir des deux classifications, la NACE et la KGN. En accord avec la NACE, les entreprises sont classées selon leur activité première.

Jusqu'à la fin de 1990, les séries mensuelles et trimestrielles se référaient aux entreprises industrielles de l'ancien secteur socialiste de l'économie, c'est-à-dire les entreprises d'État, les coopératives, les organisations sociales et les entreprises à capital mixte. En 1988, par exemple, ces entreprises représentaient 98 pour cent de la production. Bien que le secteur privé, en expansion, n'ait pas été totalement couvert avant 1991, la production non décomptée était assez minime. Pour cette raison, la discontinuité entre l'ancien et le nouveau champs couverts n'est pas jugée très importante. Les données annuelles se référaient à la fois au secteur public et au secteur privé.

Depuis janvier 1991, les séries mensuelles et trimestrielles couvrent les entreprises industrielles des secteurs public et privé comptant au moins six salariés. Une déclaration mensuelle est obligatoire pour toutes les grandes entreprises (plus de 50 salariés) et un échantillon au dixième est tiré pour les entreprises de taille moyenne (de 6 à 50 salariés). L'ensemble des moyennes entreprises est couvert une fois par an, tandis qu'une enquête, ayant lieu en même temps, permet de couvrir 5 pour cent des petites entreprises. Les résultats de ces enquêtes servent à établir les statistiques de la production annuelle. Les entreprises des branches de la construction, du commerce et des services qui fabriquent des produits industriels ne sont cependant prises en compte que si elles ont au moins 6 salariés.

Les entreprises déclarent mensuellement le produit de leurs ventes aux prix courants, cumulé depuis le début de l'année. Les valeurs courantes sont converties en données à prix constants par l'Office central de statistique à l'aide de l'indice des prix de la production industrielle décrit ci-après dans la rubrique Prix à la production. Cet indice est utilisé comme déflateur de la production industrielle de chaque branche, avant agrégation à un niveau supérieur de la classification. Les flux mensuels sont obtenus par différence entre deux valeurs cumulées successives.

Les données sur les ventes couvrent tous les produits finis et semi-finis, les pièces de rechange et les biens et services, industriels ou non. Contrairement aux données annuelles, les données mensuelles ne sont pas corrigées de la variation des stocks. Les indices sont de type Laspeyres.

Pour la période 1985-1990, on a utilisé les prix constants de 1984 pour calculer les indicateurs de volume ; de 1991 à 1993, on a utilisé les prix constants de 1990. A partir de 1994, on utilise les prix de 1992.

OECD
OCDE
SHORT-TERM ECONOMIC INDICATORS, SOURCES AND DEFINITIONS
OECD/CCET © April 1996

304

INDICATEURS ÉCONOMIQUES A COURT TERME, SOURCES ET DÉFINITIONS
OCDE/CCET © avril 1996

Pour la période 1986-1990, le volume de chaque mois ou trimestre était exprimé par rapport à la moyenne mensuelle ou trimestrielle du volume des ventes de 1985. Pour 1991, les indices mensuels et trimestriels ont été raccordés à la période correspondante de 1990.

Les indices de volume ne sont pas corrigés des variations de la durée effective du travail.

La *production industrielle totale* couvre les ventes des produits des industries extractives et des industries manufacturières, ainsi que les ventes d'électricité et de gaz. La construction n'est pas comprise. A partir de 1994, la production totale fait référence aux sections C, D et E de la NACE.

L'*IPI des industries extractives* pour la période 1980-1993 englobait toutes les branches de l'industrie définies par la KGN comme ayant un lien avec l'extraction des ressources naturelles :

-- Extraction du charbon : extraction de la houille et de l'anthracite et production de briquettes de houille (branche 011), extraction du lignite et production de briquettes de lignite (branche 014) ;

-- Combustibles : extraction du pétrole et du gaz naturel (branche 023), extraction et préparation de la tourbe, extraction et traitement des schistes bitumineux et de l'huile minérale (branche 028) ;

-- Métallurgie du fer : extraction et préparation du minerai de fer (branche 041) ;

-- Minerais non ferreux : extraction et préparation des minerais non ferreux (branche 051), extraction et préparation du minerai de cuivre (branche 052) ;

-- Industrie chimique : extraction du sel et d'autres minéraux pour l'industrie chimique sauf les matières premières contenant du soufre (branche 121), extraction des matières premières contenant du soufre (branche 138) ;

-- Industrie minière : extraction d'agrégats, de matières premières minérales et exploitation des carrières (branche 141).

Depuis 1994, ces activités sont classées par référence à la section C de la NACE.

La *composante électricité et gaz* de l'IPI couvre la production d'énergie électrique (branche 03), et la production de gaz (branche 022), ces deux branches faisant partie des industries manufacturières dans la KGN. La KGN ne comporte pas de branche spécifique pour la production, l'épuration et la distribution de l'eau.

A partir de 1994, l'indice recouvre toutes les activités classées dans la section E de la NACE.

Les autres branches de l'industrie, selon la classification KGN, à savoir essentiellement les industries manufacturières, sont couvertes par l'*IPI des industries manufacturières*. Depuis 1994, ces activités sont classées par référence à la section D de la NACE.

L'*IPI de la construction* se réfère à la production des entreprises de bâtiment et travaux publics, à savoir les travaux de construction, les travaux de réparation et d'entretien, le forage et les travaux d'excavation pour l'exploitation de mines en profondeur.

Avant 1994, la construction était définie comme suit :

-- construction générale (KGN, section 31, branches 311 à 314)

POLOGNE

-- construction pour l'industrie et les services (section 32, branches 321 à 328)

-- construction spécialisée (section 34, branches 341 à 348)

-- autres (branches 381 à 388).

Les classifications de la NACE ont été introduites en 1994. L'IPI de la construction concorde avec la section F de la NACE.

Jusqu'à la fin de 1990, les séries mensuelles, trimestrielles et annuelles se référaient aux entreprises de bâtiment et travaux publics (BTP) de l'ancien secteur socialiste de l'économie, c'est-à-dire les entreprises d'État, les coopératives, les entreprises municipales, les organisations sociales et les entreprises à capital mixte. A partir de janvier 1991, les séries mensuelles et trimestrielles couvrent toutes les entreprises de BTP des secteurs public et privé (entreprises d'État, coopératives, entreprises municipales, personnes morales et personnes physiques) employant au moins six salariés.

Les entreprises, classées dans le secteur de la construction, déclarent chaque mois les revenus, aux prix courants, de leurs activités de construction. La conversion en prix constants est effectuée par l'Office statistique à l'aide de l'indice des prix de la construction.

Depuis 1990, cet indice est calculé à partir d'enquêtes sur les prix menées auprès d'un échantillon représentatif du BTP et composé d'environ 500 entreprises. Avant 1990, l'indice des prix était établi à partir d'enquêtes sur les variations du coût des matériaux et de la main-d'oeuvre, menées auprès d'une centaine d'entreprises représentatives du bâtiment.

Quantités produites

Les statistiques des quantités produites sont des données mensuelles collectées séparément. C'est sur elles que l'on se fonde pour calculer les chiffres trimestriels et annuels. Elles sont obtenues auprès des unités employant au moins 50 personnes.

Les données sur *la production de lignite* se réfèrent aux quantités totales extraites des mines à ciel ouvert et souterraines. Elles excluent la production de briquettes de lignite.

La série sur *la production de houille* couvre la production totale de toutes les qualités d'anthracite et de charbon bitumineux extraites du sous-sol, à l'exclusion des déchets retirés sur place, des briquettes de charbon et du poussier.

Les données sur *la production de gaz naturel* se réfèrent au gaz naturel issu des champs pétrolifères et des gisements de gaz ainsi qu'au gaz obtenu par déméthanisation dans les gisements à forte teneur en méthane.

La série sur *la production d'acier brut* couvre l'acier brut obtenu en four Martin, en four électrique et en convertisseur ainsi que l'acier brut de deuxième fusion.

La série sur *la production de ciment* couvre tous les ciments hydrauliques utilisés pour la construction : ciments Portland, ciments métallurgiques, ciments alumineux et ciments naturels.

La *production de pétrole brut* comprend la totalité de l'extraction de pétrole brut, y compris la part consommée dans le processus de production.

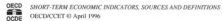

La *production de voitures particulières* comprend la production destinée à l'usage général. Les véhicules spéciaux -- ambulances, voitures de police, véhicules militaires spéciaux -- sont exclus.

La *production de matières plastiques* comprend toutes les matières plastiques à l'état brut, que ce soit sous forme de liquide ou de granulats. Elle ne comprend pas la transformation des produits en plastique.

Enquêtes de conjoncture

On trouvera une description des techniques de réalisation de ces enquêtes et la liste des questions harmonisées dans le chapitre de cette publication consacré aux *Enquêtes de conjoncture*.

Construction

Logements

On entend par logement un lieu d'habitation structurellement distinct, composé d'une ou de plusieurs pièces principales complétées par des pièces de service (telles qu'entrée, salle de bains, cabinet de toilette). Il doit comporter une entrée indépendante donnant accès à un escalier, à un couloir commun, ou directement à une cour ou à la rue.

Les combles et les sous-sols destinés à être habités et affectés à cet usage sont considérés comme des logements dans la mesure où ils répondent à la définition ci-dessus. Les séries sur les logements couvrent aussi les logements existants reconstruits et les logements créés par transformation de bâtiments, qui, au départ, n'étaient pas destinés à être habités.

Les zones d'habitation de bâtiments aménagés pour un hébergement collectif (foyers de travailleurs, dortoirs d'étudiants, résidences pour personnes âgées, etc.) ne sont pas considérées comme des logements.

L'appellation "logement et communs" fait référence à des bâtiments réunissant sous un même toit une zone à usage d'habitation et une zone utilitaire (étable, grange). Dans les statistiques, ce type de bâtiment n'est mentionné que dans le cas de maisons individuelles.

Les informations concernant les logements coopératifs, municipaux et d'entreprise sont fournies par les investisseurs qui en déclarent la mise en chantier et l'achèvement. En ce qui concerne les maisons individuelles, des rapports mensuels sur les logements achevés sont établis par les administrations locales, sur la base des déclarations des investisseurs.

Les données sur les *logements mis en chantier dans le secteur public* se réfèrent uniquement aux logements coopératifs, municipaux et institutionnels. La pose des fondations est considérée comme le point de départ de la construction d'un logement ou d'un logement avec communs.

Les statistiques sur les *logements en cours de construction dans le secteur public* se réfèrent uniquement aux logements coopératifs, municipaux et institutionnels compris dans des immeubles collectifs.

POLOGNE

Le *total des logements en cours de construction*, en revanche, couvre toute l'économie, c'est-à-dire les logements coopératifs, municipaux et d'entreprise comme les maisons individuelles, et les appartements comme les logements avec communs.

Le *total des logements achevés* couvre aussi toute l'économie, c'est-à-dire les logements coopératifs, municipaux et d'entreprise ainsi que les maisons individuelles. En 1993 sont apparues les premières entreprises privées de construction. Depuis janvier 1984, les données mensuelles, trimestrielles et annuelles sur les appartements achevés englobent aussi les appartements situés dans des bâtiments à usage autre que d'habitation, de même que les appartements créés par transformation de combles et les reconstructions de logements existants. Avant 1984, ces informations ne figuraient que dans les données annuelles.

Les *logements achevés du secteur public* se réfèrent aux logements coopératifs, municipaux et institutionnels. Les données mensuelles et trimestrielles de la période 1981-1983 n'englobaient pas les appartements situés dans des bâtiments à usage autre que d'habitation.

Un logement est considéré comme achevé lorsque :

-- l'investisseur (coopérative, municipalité ou entreprise) reconnaît par écrit que le bâtiment est prêt à l'usage ; ou

-- l'occupant (ou le propriétaire, dans le cas des maisons individuelles) s'installe dans tout ou partie des lieux quel qu'en soit l'état d'achèvement.

Commerce intérieur

On regroupe dans les ventes de détail et ventes à la commission les ventes effectuées par les boutiques de détaillants, les grands magasins, les établissements de restauration et les autres points de vente de détail. La *valeur des ventes de détail* est établie à partir du chiffre d'affaires déclaré chaque mois, aux prix courants, par ces établissements.

Les statistiques mensuelles et trimestrielles de la valeur des ventes de détail présentent une rupture de série entre la fin de 1990 et le début de 1991, et ce pour deux raisons.

Premièrement, l'enquête de la première période ne couvre que les unités de l'ex-secteur socialiste (points de vente de détail appartenant à l'État, des coopératives, des municipalités ou des organisations collectives ou sociales), alors que depuis le début de 1991 l'obligation de déclaration mensuelle est étendue à tous les établissements de vente employant au moins 20 employés, quel qu'en soit le propriétaire, à quoi s'ajoute un sondage aléatoire au dixième parmi les établissements de six à 20 salariés, à partir duquel sont estimées les ventes de l'ensemble de ce groupe.

La série annuelle couvre l'ensemble de l'économie (donc y compris le secteur privé) aussi bien avant qu'après 1991. A partir de 1991, les ventes des établissements de moins de six salariés sont estimées une fois par an sur la base du chiffre d'affaires moyen par salarié, tiré d'une enquête représentative, et du nombre de salariés.

Deuxièmement, depuis janvier 1991, la définition des ventes est restreinte car les ventes déclarées par les détaillants du secteur public n'englobent plus les ventes à des entités du secteur privé telles que commerçants, sociétés commerciales et artisans ; elle n'inclut pas, non plus, les ventes de détail des unités classées dans le secteur agricole.

Par conséquent, les données mensuelles et trimestrielles sur les ventes de détail de la période 1980-1990 se réfèrent aux établissements de l'ancien secteur socialiste, alors que les données annuelles de la même période couvrent l'ensemble de l'économie (y compris le secteur privé). A partir de 1991, les données se réfèrent aux ventes de détail correspondant à la nouvelle définition et à la nouvelle couverture.

Le *volume des ventes de détail* fait référence à la valeur desdites ventes aux prix de 1992. Le calcul est effectué par le Secrétariat de l'OCDE à l'aide de l'indice des prix à la consommation des biens. Il est présenté en base 1993=100 dans *Indicateurs économiques à court terme : Économies en transition*.

Main d'oeuvre

Emploi

Les données se réfèrent au nombre moyen de personnes salariées, c'est-à-dire occupant un emploi à temps plein ou à temps partiel durant une période de référence donnée, d'après une preuve d'emploi ou un contrat de travail. Ne sont prises en compte que les personnes ayant un contrat de travail et non les travailleurs à domicile, les agents payés à la commission, les membres des coopératives de production agricole, les propriétaires ou copropriétaires d'établissements ou unités employant des salariés, les travailleurs indépendants et les propriétaires d'exploitations agricoles individuelles. Les données concernant les personnes appartenant à ces catégories ne sont disponibles qu'annuellement dans les publications nationales.

Les effectifs de travailleurs à temps partiel non saisonniers sont exprimés en équivalent plein temps, sur la base du rapport entre la durée du travail à temps partiel et la durée du travail à temps plein, entreprise par entreprise. La durée du travail à temps plein est définie par l'horaire nominal de travail exigé par l'entreprise de la part d'un travailleur à temps plein. La durée du travail à temps partiel se réfère à tout horaire de travail inférieur au plein temps nominal défini par l'entreprise.

Les données sur le nombre moyen de personnes salariées sont tirées des rapports mensuels, trimestriels et annuels émanant des entités économiques.

Jusqu'à la fin de 1990, l'information sur l'emploi salarié moyen ne couvrait que les établissements de l'ancien secteur socialiste, c'est-à-dire les établissements appartenant à l'État, aux coopératives, aux organisations sociales et politiques et aux syndicats. Depuis janvier 1991, toutefois, les données mensuelles et trimestrielles couvrent tous les établissements employant au moins six personnes, quel qu'en soit le propriétaire ; les données annuelles comprennent tous les établissements, quel que soit le nombre de personnes qu'ils emploient.

Pour permettre une comparaison entre l'ancienne et la nouvelle série, les données de 1990 sont disponibles avec l'une et l'autre couverture.

En 1994, les emplois ont été classés par branches d'activité par référence à la NACE. Les données de 1993 ont été calculées à la fois à partir de la NACE et de l'ancienne KGN.

La série trimestrielle concernant *l'emploi total* couvre tous les établissements de l'économie nationale employant au moins six personnes, quel qu'en soit le propriétaire, à l'exception des entités de la Défense nationale et des Affaires intérieures financées par le budget central. Sont exclues les personnes employées à l'étranger, les personnes employées dans les unités budgétaires de la sphère de la production

POLOGNE

matérielle et les personnes exerçant des activités statutaires dans des organisations politiques ou sociales ou des syndicats. La série annuelle couvre toutes les unités de production.

Les séries -- *emploi dans les branches de la production matérielle, dans l'industrie et dans le secteur manufacturier* -- font référence à l'emploi dans le secteur marchand, c'est-à-dire à l'exclusion des personnes occupées dans l'éducation, les activités culturelles, l'administration publique, etc.

L'emploi couvre l'emploi moyen dans tous les établissements d'au moins six salariés, dans six grandes branches de l'économie :

- -- industrie ;
- -- construction ;
- -- transports ;
- -- communications ;
- -- commerce ;
- -- à partir de 1991, services collectifs des municipalités.

La série *emploi dans les branches matérielles* n'est plus publiée depuis 1993.

L'emploi dans l'industrie couvre les salariés des industries extractives des industries manufacturières et de l'électricité, du gaz et de l'eau, pour toutes les unités de production comptant au moins six salariés.

L'emploi dans les industries manufacturières couvre toutes les entreprises manufacturières d'au moins six salariés. La série annuelle peut contenir des données corrigées, ne correspondant donc pas aux moyennes calculées à partir des données mensuelles et trimestrielles qui elles, ne sont pas révisées.

Chômage

Le *chômage* est enregistré depuis janvier 1990. D'après la loi sur l'emploi du 16 octobre 1991 (et ses modifications ultérieures), en vigueur depuis décembre 1991, une personne est considérée comme étant au chômage si elle est apte au travail et prête à prendre un emploi à temps complet sur la base d'un contrat de travail, est actuellement sans travail et ne suit pas une scolarité (sauf dans les conditions spécifiées par la loi).

La "nouvelle Loi pour l'emploi et pour la lutte contre le chômage" du 14 décembre 1994, est en vigueur depuis le 1er janvier 1995. Le terme "chômeur" tel qu'il figure dans cette Loi, désigne une personne sans emploi qui ne suit pas de cours pendant la journée dans un établissement d'enseignement, apte au travail, prête à accepter un emploi à plein temps, et inscrite à une agence locale pour l'emploi. Une personne peut être inscrite si :

- -- elle a plus de 18 ans, sauf dans le cas des diplômés des établissements d'enseignement secondaire ;
- -- elle a moins de 60 ans s'il s'agit d'une femme, moins de 65 ans s'il s'agit d'un homme ;
- -- elle n'a pas droit au versement d'une pension de vieillesse ou d'une pension d'invalidité ou a cessé de travailler et ne reçoit pas d'allocations maladie, d'allocations maternité, d'allocations pour la garde des enfants ou d'allocations d'autre nature ;

-- elle ne possède pas une exploitation agricole (selon la définition figurant dans la loi susmentionnée) ;

-- elle n'a pas droit aux prestations de sécurité sociale, elle ne travaille pas dans une exploitation familiale de plus de 2 ha ;

-- elle ne s'engage pas dans une activité économique non agricole ni ne bénéficie d'assurances sociales ni du système de retraite ;

-- elle est handicapée et son état de santé lui permet de travailler au moins à mi-temps ;

-- elle n'est pas temporairement détenue ou incarcérée.

Les données se rapportent à la fin de chaque période et couvrent les personnes inscrites comme demandeurs d'emploi auprès des agences locales pour l'emploi de la région où elles résident.

Les *allocataires* sont des personnes :

-- qui sont inscrites comme chômeurs dans les conditions précitées ;

-- auxquelles ne sont proposés ni un emploi correspondant à leur profil, ni une formation en cours d'emploi ou qualifiante en vue d'un nouveau type d'emploi, ni des travaux d'utilité publique,

-- qui ont travaillé au moins 180 jours au cours des 12 mois précédant leur inscription.

La période minimale de non activité avant de recevoir des allocations est de trois mois pour les nouveaux diplômés.

Un allocataire perd ses droits s'il :

-- ne se présente pas à son agence locale pour l'emploi sans justification ;

-- refuse, sans motif, une offre d'emploi correspondant à son profil ou de suivre une formation ou d'effectuer des travaux d'utilité collective ;

-- a été licencié pour des motifs disciplinaires par son employeur ;

-- a perçu, à son départ de la mine un certain montant fixé par la convention collective applicable aux salariés du secteur minier.

Depuis décembre 1992, la durée de l'indemnisation du chômage est limitée à 12 mois. Cette durée est prolongée dans les cas prévus dans la Loi.

Le montant de l'allocation de chômage est égal à 36 pour cent du salaire mensuel moyen du trimestre précédent (sauf dans les cas prévus dans la Loi).

Le *taux de chômage* est mesuré par le nombre de chômeurs inscrits en fin de période, en pourcentage de la population active civile :

-- à la fin de 1989 pour l'année 1990 ;

-- à la fin de la même période, et présumée constante toute l'année, pour 1991 et les années suivantes.

POLOGNE

Le nombre d'*offres d'emploi* correspond aux offres des agences de l'emploi, y compris les créations d'emploi dans le secteur public comme dans le secteur privé.

Salaires

Gains mensuels

Les gains mensuels se réfèrent aux traitements et salaires mensuels moyens nets dans différents secteurs de l'économie polonaise, en correspondance avec les données sur l'emploi (pour le détail de la couverture des secteurs et branches, se reporter à la rubrique Emploi). Toutes les séries sur les salaires sont calculées trimestriellement pour l'ensemble des secteurs de l'économie et mensuellement pour le secteur des entreprises.

Les traitements et salaires se définissent comme la rémunération des personnes employées pour le travail fourni conformément à leur contrat de travail.

Le calcul des traitements et salaires mensuels moyens par personne employée prend en compte :

-- les traitements et salaires du personnel (à l'exclusion de la rémunération des travailleurs à domicile et des apprentis) ;

-- les bénéfices distribués et les sommes versées au titre de l'excédent d'exploitation des coopératives ;

-- les bourses distribuées par les fonds de primes des établissements ;

-- les honoraires payés à certains groupes de personnes, telles que journalistes et producteurs de films et de programmes de radio, au titre de l'exécution de leur contrat.

De 1992 à 1994, les gains mensuels étaient nets d'impôt sur le revenu des personnes physiques.

Depuis 1995, les séries se rapportent aux gains mensuels bruts.

Les données sur les salaires sont exprimées en anciens zlotys jusqu'à la fin de 1994 et en nouveaux zlotys par la suite. Pour plus de précisions, voir ci-dessous la section sur les finances internes.

Prix

Prix à la production

Des enquêtes représentatives sur les *prix à la production dans l'industrie* sont menées mensuellement dans les entreprises depuis 1982. Elles se réfèrent aux prix départ-usine, identiques pour tous les acheteurs jusqu'à la fin de 1984 et aux prix de vente effectivement négociés par la suite. Jusqu'en 1994, les prix de vente comprennent les taxes sur les produits. En 1994-95, les prix étaient observés hors TVA. Depuis 1996 les prix sont relevés hors TVA et taxes d'accise. Les producteurs de biens et de services représentatifs couverts par l'enquête sont choisis sur la base d'informations statistiques concernant le montant de leurs ventes et leur gamme de produits. L'enquête couvre environ 3 500 entreprises des secteurs public et privé de l'économie.

Les entreprises choisissent les biens et services dont elles notifient les prix en fonction des indications fournies par l'Office central de statistique. Les biens et services représentatifs doivent être choisis parmi ceux qui dominent dans la valeur des ventes de l'entreprise déclarante, c'est-à-dire qui représentent environ 75 pour cent de son chiffre d'affaires mensuel. Le nombre moyen d'articles représentatifs couverts chaque mois par l'ensemble des entreprises déclarantes est d'environ 19 000. Celles-ci communiquent chaque mois le prix et le montant des ventes de chaque article retenu.

Ces informations sont utilisées pour calculer, tout d'abord, un rapport de prix mensuel par article, avec le mois précédent pour période de référence, puis un indice de prix mensuel, de type Paasche, pour chaque entreprise. Les indices de prix d'entreprise sont donnés par la moyenne des indices élémentaires par article représentatif, pondérée par la valeur des ventes du mois considéré. La pondération évolue donc de mois en mois. Les indices synthétiques mensuels globaux sont les moyennes des indices synthétiques d'entreprise, pondérées par la valeur des ventes durant le mois considéré. La pondération utilisée pour calculer les indices des prix à la production est tirée de la valeur des ventes en 1992, actualisée à l'aide de la variation des prix et de la modification de la structure des ventes observées pendant le mois courant. En 1996, la pondération utilisée est tirée de la structure des ventes de 1994.

Lorsqu'un produit connaît une modification sensible de sa qualité, il est traité comme un produit nouveau, dont le prix n'est pas enregistré le premier mois. L'évolution de ce prix est donc calculée à partir du deuxième mois de son existence. Toutefois, lorsqu'elles notifient le prix d'un nouveau produit pour le mois d'observation, les entreprises indiquent une estimation du prix de ce produit pour le mois précédent et l'indice des prix est donc calculé dès son premier mois d'apparition dans l'enquête. Aucun traitement particulier n'est effectué concernant les produits saisonniers.

Prix à la consommation

L'*indice des prix à la consommation (IPC)* reflète les taux mensuels de variation des prix des biens de consommation et des services fournis aux consommateurs, pondérés depuis 1991 par les résultats de l'enquête sur les budgets des ménages qui couvre toute la population depuis 1993. Avant 1991, l'IPC se référait aux ventes de détail de biens et de services destinés à la consommation finale.

Les données sur les mouvements des prix et leur niveau sont collectées dans 28 000 points de vente de détail ainsi que des centres de restauration et de services situés dans 307 zones d'enquête, à savoir les villes et les districts urbains. Les relevés sont effectués par des enquêteurs des offices statistiques des différentes régions. Le choix des points de vente sondés est effectué par les enquêteurs eux-mêmes, sous la supervision des responsables régionaux. Les catalogues et la réglementation nationale des changements de prix permettent de disposer de sources d'information supplémentaires en ce qui concerne :

-- le gaz et l'électricité ;

-- le chauffage central et l'eau chaude ;

-- les loyers des logements appartenant aux communes ou à l'État ;

-- certaines catégories de médicaments ;

-- les tarifs des transports publics (ferroviaires et routiers) ;

-- les services des postes et des télécommunications ;

-- les redevances de radio et de télévision ;

-- les alcools (contenant au moins 30° d'alcool pur).

POLOGNE

L'enquête sur les prix couvre de 1 400 à 1 800 biens et services représentatifs, dont la liste est révisée chaque année. Les prix de l'alimentation, restauration comprise, des boissons alcoolisées et du tabac sont relevés trois fois par mois, ceux des autres biens et services une fois par mois.

Depuis 1991, les pondérations sont établies à partir des enquêtes sur les budgets des ménages, avec certains ajustements visant à rectifier, par exemple, la sous-déclaration des dépenses consacrées aux boissons alcoolisées, au tabac et à la restauration et correspondent à la structure annuelle des dépenses de l'année précédente. Les coefficients de pondération sont révisés chaque année au mois de janvier. Plus de 200 sous-groupes sont pris en compte dans le système de pondération.

Les pondérations utilisées pour le calcul de l'IPC, sont les suivantes :

Principaux groupes	1990	1991	1992	1993	1994
Ensemble des biens	88.4	85.6	79.9	72.5	73.4
Alimentation	37.0	48.0	41.8	38.9	39.2
Alcools	10.6	6.4	5.9	4.6	4.2
Autres biens	40.8	31.2	32.2	29.0	30.0
Services	11.6	14.4	20.1	27.5	26.6
TOTAL	100.0	100.0	100.0	100.0	100.0

Des ajustements distincts sont effectués pour les articles saisonniers, tels que les fruits et légumes. Le coefficient de pondération global du groupe auquel appartiennent ces produits reste constant toute l'année, mais les coefficients affectés aux différents articles du panier sont modifiés tous les mois en fonction de l'évolution saisonnière de la répartition des dépenses des consommateurs.

L'IPC est un indicateur du taux de variation des prix, et non de leur niveau absolu. Il est calculé de la façon suivante : on obtient le prix moyen d'un article représentatif k dans une région r en faisant la moyenne arithmétique des observations. L'IPC mensuel correspondant, calculé pour le mois t, est égal au rapport de ce prix moyen au prix moyen de l'année précédente. Le prix annuel moyen est calculé comme la moyenne arithmétique des douze prix mensuels.

L'indice national de chaque article s'obtient comme moyenne géométrique des indices élémentaires pour toutes les régions. Au niveau d'agrégation supérieur, c'est-à-dire au niveau du groupe d'articles, l'IPC partiel est la moyenne arithmétique des indices de sous-groupe pondérée par les dépenses, selon la formule de Laspeyres.

L'IPC est exprimé dans les sources nationales sous la forme d'un taux de variation par rapport à la période précédente, ou à la période correspondante de l'année précédente, ou au mois de décembre précédent. Le calcul de l'indice à base fixe est effectué par le Secrétariat de l'OCDE.

L'IPC des services recouvre les loyers (sauf ceux des logements du secteur privé), l'électricité et le gaz, la rémunération des services de santé, les dépenses culturelles, les redevances mensuelles au titre des services de télévision, postes et télécommunications, les dépenses personnelles de transport, les frais de réparation de vêtements et de chaussures, le coût des services de coiffure, de blanchisserie, etc.

La composante *restauration* de l'IPC comprend les cantines destinées aux travailleurs, les cafétérias et les restaurants.

Finances internes

Les informations sur la masse monétaire sont établies par la Banque nationale de Pologne.

Les *disponibilités monétaires au sens étroit (M1)* englobent la monnaie nationale en circulation (à l'exclusion des encaisses bancaires) et les dépôts à vue en zlotys du secteur non financier (incluant les compagnies d'assurance), comprenant les entreprises d'État et le secteur privé (ménages et entreprises privées).

Depuis 1992, les données sont présentées sur la base d'un nouveau plan comptable et ne sont donc pas comparables avec les données des années précédentes. Pour le mois de décembre, le quatrième trimestre et l'année 1991, le chiffre comparable avec les résultats de l'ancienne méthode est 127 006 milliards d'anciens zlotys.

La *quasi-monnaie* se compose des dépôts à terme et d'épargne en zlotys, des dépôts en devises du secteur non financier (à savoir des entreprises d'État et du secteur privé dont ménages et compagnies d'assurance), ainsi que des bons de caisse.

Depuis 1992, les données sont présentées sur la base du nouveau plan comptable et ne sont donc pas comparables avec les données des années précédentes. Pour le mois de décembre, le quatrième trimestre et l'année 1991, le chiffre comparable avec les résultats de l'ancienne méthode est 160 175 milliards d'anciens zlotys.

Les *dépôts personnels* comprennent les dépôts en zlotys et en devises des ménages (dépôts à vue, d'épargne et à terme, plus les bons de caisse, à l'exclusion des intérêts acquis). Avant décembre 1991, ils englobaient également les dépôts en zlotys et en devises des entreprises privées. Les dépôts en devises sont convertis en zlotys à l'aide du taux de change officiel de la Banque nationale de Pologne en fin de mois.

Depuis 1992, les données sont présentées sur la base du nouveau plan comptable et ne sont donc pas comparables avec les données des années précédentes. Pour le mois de décembre, le quatrième trimestre et l'année 1991, le chiffre comparable avec les résultats de l'ancienne méthode est 129 829 milliards d'anciens zlotys.

Les séries statistiques portant sur les finances internes sont exprimées en anciens zlotys jusqu'à la fin de 1994 et en nouveaux zlotys par la suite. Une nouvelle dénomination du zloty a été introduite le 1er janvier 1995, le nouveau zloty équivalant à 10 000 anciens zlotys.

Taux d'intérêt

Le *taux d'escompte officiel* désigne le taux du refinancement, en fin de période. Il s'agit du taux annuel appliqué aux banques commerciales par la Banque nationale de Pologne.

POLOGNE

Finances extérieures

Outre *le taux de change du dollar des États-Unis en zlotys*, la Banque nationale de Pologne publie les cours de l'Écu, des droits de tirages spéciaux (DTS -- monnaie du FMI) et des monnaies de 28 pays à économie de marché. Jusqu'à la fin de 1990, les taux de change étaient publiés une fois par semaine par la Banque nationale de Pologne. Depuis le début de 1991, ils sont publiés quotidiennement. Le zloty est une monnaie à parité mobile rattachée à un panier de cinq monnaies : le dollar des États-Unis, le deutsche mark, la livre sterling, le franc français et le franc suisse.

Les séries des taux de change sont exprimées en anciens zlotys jusqu'à la fin de 1994 et en nouveaux zlotys par la suite. Pour plus de précisions, voir ci-dessus la section sur les finances internes.

Les réserves officielles, or exclu, couvrent les réserves de change des autorités monétaires.

La *dette extérieure brute totale* englobe la dette extérieure en devises convertibles et en roubles transférables.

La *dette extérieure brute en monnaies convertibles* couvre la dette extérieure libellée en dollars des États-Unis et dans d'autres devises convertibles converties en dollars des États-Unis.

La *dette extérieure brute en monnaies non convertibles* représente l'ensemble de la dette extérieure brute libellée en roubles transférables.

Commerce extérieur

Les séries sur les *exportations, les importations et le solde commercial* indiquent la valeur courante des biens et services achetés et vendus à l'étranger.

1980-1991

Les exportations et les importations étaient ventilées dans les sources nationales selon le pays partenaire. Pour les importations, le pays partenaire est le pays d'achat, i.e. le pays du fournisseur. Pour les exportations, c'est le pays de vente, i.e. le pays de l'acquéreur. Par fournisseur ou acquéreur on entend l'entité avec laquelle la transaction est effectuée conformément à un accord international signé antérieurement. En l'absence de pareil accord, le pays d'achat ou de vente est celui où l'autre partie contractante a son siège légal.

Les marchandises étaient classées selon la Nomenclature des produits du commerce extérieur (NHTZ) et représentaient à peu près 12 000 articles. Environ 1 700 articles exportés et 2 100 articles importés faisaient l'objet d'observations dans le cadre des enquêtes sur les prix.

Les échanges couvraient notamment les documentations scientifiques et techniques, les services techniques (savoir-faire), et les licences. Les données du commerce extérieur excluaient les aides, dons et donations de l'État, des associations et du secteur privé, les colis et bagages privés et les marchandises apportées par des voyageurs.

Pendant la période 1980-1989, seules des entreprises spécialement désignées du secteur public (étatique et coopératif) pouvaient commercer avec l'étranger. Pour cette période, les statistiques du commerce extérieur s'appuyaient sur les formulaires statistiques (dits factures FE et FI) qui étaient remplis pour chaque livraison effectuée par ces entreprises et traités par l'Office statistique. Pour les importations, ces formulaires étaient les documents de douane prouvant que les marchandises avaient franchi la frontière polonaise ; pour les exportations, il s'agissait de certificats de prise en charge remis par les transporteurs internationaux.

En 1990-1991, quand d'autres entreprises ont commencé à commercer avec l'étranger, le système des déclarations en douane a été retenu comme principale source des statistiques du commerce extérieur. Les déclarations en douane couvrent les transactions effectuées par des sociétés agréées (à l'exception des sociétés issues de la restructuration d'entreprises d'État), de petits fabricants étrangers, des fondations et des personnes physiques. Ces déclarations douanières étaient complétées par les formulaires de facturation. Les données de 1990 sont toutefois des estimations. En 1991, la moitié de la valeur des échanges a été réalisée par des entreprises privées. A cette époque, il y avait 60 000 unités exportatrices, contre 100 unités en 1989.

Les valeurs des exportations et des importations étaient comptabilisées fab. La date de comptabilisation était généralement la date de remise des documents appropriés, et non pas la date de franchissement de la frontière. En décembre 1991, notamment, de nombreuses déclarations en douane ont été remises avant l'introduction du Document administratif unique. On considère donc que les statistiques du commerce extérieur pour décembre 1991 sont surestimées.

Les séries correspondant aux *échanges en devises convertibles et non convertibles* sont classées par types de devises utilisées dans les transactions, et non par zones géographiques.

Depuis 1992

En janvier 1992, le Document administratif unique a été institué pour les déclarations douanières. Les exportations sont comptabilisées fab et les importations caf.

A partir de 1992 également, les groupes d'échanges par pays et régions sont définis par rapport aux pays d'origine ou de destination des produits échangés, et non plus en fonction de la location de l'acheteur ou du fournisseur.

Le système utilisé pour la classification des biens échangés est la Nomenclature combinée (NC), qui comprend à peu près 9 500 articles. Plus de 2 000 articles exportés et de 3 000 articles importés font l'objet d'observations dans le cadre des enquêtes sur les prix.

Conformément à la méthodologie des Nations Unies, les ventes de produits du commerce extérieur en Pologne sont basées sur la formule des "échanges spéciaux" qui couvre les importations et les exportations de tous les produits – quelle que soit la forme de paiement – définitivement dédouanées, ou dédouanées à titre conditionnel (en cas d'opérations de finition), sur le Document administratif unique, y compris :

-- les réexportations indirectes et les importations pour réexportation indirecte ;

-- les donations d'organisations sociales ;

-- les aides bénévoles ;

-- les importations et exportations de marchandises correspondant à des apports de matériel d'entités étrangères ;

-- les achats dans les ports étrangers de fournitures pour bateaux tel que le combustible de soute ;

-- le commerce des produits de la pêche en mer ;

-- les marchandises importées ou exportées dans le cadre d'un contrat ou d'une opération de location pour une période d'exploitation supérieure à un an ;

-- les échanges au titre d'opérations de finition calculés selon la méthode brute.

Conformément à la formule des "échanges spéciaux", le chiffre d'affaires courant du commerce extérieur exclut :

-- le chiffre d'affaires des transactions des zones franches et des entrepôts sous douane avec l'étranger ;

-- les réexportations directes et importations pour réexportation directe ;

-- les services (sauf les opérations de finition), calculés selon la méthode brute ;

-- les réparations ;

-- la construction ;

-- les brevets, licences et savoir-faire.

A partir de 1992, toutes les transactions commerciales avec l'étranger ont été libellées en devises convertibles, à l'exception des importations de gaz de la Fédération de Russie. Ce contrat est en effet payable en partie en roubles jusqu'en 2005.

Les statistiques du commerce extérieur sont exprimées en anciens zlotys jusqu'à la fin de 1994 et en nouveaux zlotys par la suite. Pour plus de précisions, voir ci-dessus la section sur les finances internes.

Prix

Jusqu'à la fin de 1991, les prix sont enregistrés par rapport aux prix moyens de la période précédente. Ils font référence aux prix de transaction pour 1991, et reposent sur les "valeurs unitaires" pour les années antérieures.

A partir de 1992, les prix représentent les valeurs unitaires, que l'on obtient en divisant la valeur totale par le coefficient de pondération de chaque produit correspondant au niveau inférieur de la classification des biens dans la NC. Ces valeurs unitaires sont <u>cumulées</u> depuis le début de l'année courante. Elles sont pondérées par les quantités cumulées (elles-mêmes pondérées) et rapportées aux prix mensuels moyens correspondants de l'année précédente. Les indices de prix ainsi obtenus pour les différentes rubriques élémentaires de la NC sont agrégés par branches au sens de la Liste uniforme des marchandises (SWW), pour former des séries mensuelles cumulatives. Aux niveaux supérieurs d'agrégation, les indices synthétiques sont pondérés par la valeur, cumulée depuis le début de l'année, des biens échangés.

Les prix, exprimés en zlotys, s'entendent fab pour les prix à l'exportation et caf pour les prix à l'importation.

L'indice est de type Paasche, pondéré par les données de l'année courante.

Volumes

Pour calculer *les indices de volume des exportations et des importations*, à prix constants, on utilise les informations fournies par l'enquête sur les prix et, pour les années antérieures, les valeurs unitaires. Les données mensuelles et trimestrielles à prix constants sont obtenues par différence entre les valeurs cumulées. Pour la période 1980-1990, les prix constants sont ceux de 1984 et, depuis 1991, ceux de 1990.

En 1991, les réexportations et réimportations n'étaient pas comprises dans les échanges en volume, sauf en cas d'opération de finition. Les services étaient exclus du commerce extérieur, hormis les services d'impression. En 1992, les échanges à titre gratuit (dons, etc.) ont été exclus du volume total des échanges.

D'autres différences de couverture des échanges entre 1991 et 1992 sont signalées plus haut (voir les sections "1980-1991" et "Depuis 1992").

Formation brute de capital fixe

La *formation brute de capital fixe* fait référence aux dépenses consacrées à l'achat et à la modernisation de bâtiments, machines et équipements et de tous les moyens de transport. Les bâtiments et machines agricoles sont compris, mais l'achat de bétail est exclu. Les dépenses de réparation et d'entretien ne sont pas comptabilisées.

Depuis 1991, tous les établissements de plus de 50 salariés sont couverts dans le secteur manufacturier, et tous ceux de plus de 20 salariés dans l'ensemble des autres branches.

Publications

Certaines des séries décrites ci-dessus figurent aussi, mais avec une présentation conforme à la pratique nationale, dans les publications suivantes de l'Office central de la statistique polonais :

Biuletyn Statystyczny (Bulletin statistique)

Concise Statistical Yearbook of Poland (Annuaire statistique concis de la Pologne)

Information on the Social and Economic Situation in Poland (Informations sur la situation sociale et économique de la Pologne)

Kwartalnik Statystyki Miedzynarodowej (Statistiques internationales trimestrielles)

Monitoring Rynku Pracy (Situation du marché du travail)

ainsi que dans la publication :

Monthly Report of the National Bank of Poland (Bulletin mensuel de la Banque nationale de Pologne).

RÉPUBLIQUE DE SLOVÉNIE

Production industrielle

L'*Indice de la production industrielle totale* se décompose par branches selon la Classification nationale des activités industrielles (la Classification unifiée des activités industrielles de l'ex-Yougoslavie) et couvre les industries extractives, les industries manufacturières (sauf l'édition) et la distribution d'électricité. La distribution de gaz, de vapeur et d'eau est exclue.

Les produits industriels sont classés selon la Nomenclature nationale des produits industriels, qui comprend environ 3 400 produits finis et semi-finis. La production non principale est incluse.

Jusqu'à 1990 toutes les entreprises industrielles étaient couvertes par l'enquête. Depuis 1992, on interroge chaque mois les entreprises publiques, ainsi que toutes les entreprises privées employant au moins cinq salariés d'après le Registre des entreprises de Slovénie. En 1994, ces entreprises privées étaient environ 1 800 en Slovénie.

Les entreprises notifient le volume de leur production, exprimé en quantités (tonnes, pièces, etc.). Les quantités sont pondérées par la valeur des ventes facturées en 1993, corrigée à l'aide de leur part dans la valeur ajoutée de la branche correspondante en 1993. On combine les indices de branche pour obtenir l'indice de la production industrielle totale en utilisant comme pondération la répartition de la valeur ajoutée des activités industrielles de l'année précédente. Les coefficients de pondération des produits et des branches changent tous les ans en fonction de l'évolution de la part de la valeur ajoutée dans les différentes branches au cours des deux années précédentes. Les indices de branche comme l'indice d'ensemble sont des indices de Laspeyres.

Quantités produites

La *production de charbon* recouvre le lignite.

Le *gaz naturel* comprend le gaz associé et le gaz non associé.

Le *pétrole brut* représente l'huile minérale constituée d'un mélange d'hydrocarbures d'origine naturelle.

L'*acier brut* fait référence à l'acier utilisé pour les moulages et les lingots.

Le *ciment* couvre uniquement le ciment Portland.

L'*électricité* comprend la production des centrales hydrauliques, traditionnelles, thermiques et nucléaires.

La série *textiles* englobe la production d'étoffes de coton, de laine et de soie artificielle.

OECD
OCDE
SHORT-TERM ECONOMIC INDICATORS, SOURCES AND DEFINITIONS
OECD/CCET © April 1996

320

INDICATEURS ÉCONOMIQUES A COURT TERME, SOURCES ET DÉFINITIONS
OCDE/CCET © avril 1996

Dans la *production de réfrigérateurs* sont inclus les réfrigérateurs et congélateurs à usage domestique exclusivement.

Construction

L'indice du *nombre d'heures de travail effectuées dans la construction* mesure l'activité des entreprises de construction d'au moins 10 salariés. Les entreprises couvertes par l'enquête sont celles qui sont inscrites dans le Registre des entreprises de Slovénie comme exerçant une activité de construction. L'enquête mensuelle couvre 160 entreprises et l'on estime que la production totale de la construction est ainsi couverte à 90 pour cent.

Logements

Par logement on entend un ensemble à usage d'habitation possédant une unité structurelle, comptant une ou plusieurs pièces principales, complétées ou non par des espaces utilitaires appropriés (cuisine, vestibule, salle de bains, toilettes) et ayant au moins une entrée indépendante. Les dortoirs d'étudiants et de travailleurs, les résidences pour personnes âgées, etc., ne sont pas pris en compte dans le nombre de logements.

Le nombre de *logements achevés* fait référence aux logements certifiés habitables par les autorités locales dans lesquels la totalité des travaux de construction, d'aménagement et de finition prévus ont été effectués dans tous les intérieurs.

Le nombre de *logements achevés par les entreprises* s'entend à l'exclusion de tous les logements construits pour le compte de particuliers. Les données sont également tirées de l'enquête utilisée pour connaître le nombre d'heures de travail effectuées dans la construction (voir ci-dessus).

Commerce intérieur

Le commerce de détail fait référence à la vente de biens dans les points de vente publics et privés, y compris les pharmacies, les boutiques de commissionnaires-détaillants, les kiosques, les stations d'essence, ainsi qu'aux ventes de détail effectuées directement par des entrepôts. Les ventes des producteurs privés aux consommateurs effectuées sur les marchés d'alimentation ne sont pas couvertes.

Le commerce de détail est mesuré à l'aide d'une enquête par sondage trimestrielle auprès des principaux points de vente de détail comptant pour 50 pour cent du volume des ventes. Le taux de réponse à l'enquête atteint 100 pour cent. Les entreprises sont classées par catégories et branches d'après la Classification nationale des activités. Les changements qui interviennent en cours d'année dans les entreprises et autres organisations ne sont pas pris en compte avant le début de l'année suivante.

L'indice de *volume des ventes de détail* se réfère à la valeur des ventes de détail déflatée à l'aide de l'indice des prix de détail. Celui-ci est construit à partir des prix des biens, à l'exclusion des services, et est pondéré par la répartition du chiffre d'affaires (voir, plus loin, la rubrique Prix de détail).

RÉPUBLIQUE DE SLOVÉNIE

Main-d'oeuvre

Emploi

Par salariés des entreprises et autres organisations on entend les personnes qui ont signé un contrat de travail de durée déterminée ou indéterminée, qu'ils travaillent à temps complet ou à temps partiel dans l'entreprise, établissement privé ou autre organisation qui les emploie, et ce, y compris les stagiaires. Les titulaires d'un contrat de travail temporaire ou occasionnel, ainsi que les citoyens slovènes travaillant à l'étranger, ne sont pas compris dans ces chiffres.La population d'âge actif se réfère aux femmes âgées de 15 à 58 ans et aux hommes âgés de 15 à 63 ans.

Jusqu'à la fin de 1991, les enquêtes statistiques sur les salariés des entreprises et autres organisations couvraient la totalité des entreprises et organisations non privées ainsi que leurs unités constitutives. A partir de 1992, leur couverture a été étendue aux entreprises privées d'au moins trois salariés, et aux services des forces armées. Depuis 1993, les services des administrations chargés des affaires internes sont également interrogés. Les travailleurs indépendants et leurs salariés sont exclus du champ de l'enquête mensuelle sur l'emploi. Les statistiques sur les travailleurs indépendants et leurs salariés sont des estimations qui s'appuient sur des données tirées du Registre de l'assurance maladie et du recensement de 1991. On estime que les travailleurs à temps partiel qui sont comptabilisés de la même façon que les travailleurs à temps complet, représentent moins de 2 pour cent de la population active occupée.

Les registres administratifs de l'assurance vieillesse et invalidité, ainsi que de l'assurance maladie, sont utilisés pour vérifier par recoupement les chiffres sur l'emploi.

Une classification des branches d'activité conforme à la Nomenclature générale des activités économiques (NACE) a été mise en service en janvier 1995.

Chômage

Les données relatives aux *chômeurs inscrits* et aux *offres d'emploi* sont fournies à l'OSC par l'Agence nationale pour l'emploi (ANPE).

Un demandeur d'emploi est considéré chômeur inscrit s'il :

-- n'est ni pourvu d'un emploi régulier ni travailleur indépendant, n'est ni propriétaire ni copropriétaire d'une entreprise exploitante et n'a ni la propriété ni la jouissance de biens qui pourraient lui assurer un revenu ;

-- est capable et désireux de travailler, et est prêt à accepter un emploi correspondant à son niveau professionnel ou à ses compétences ;

-- s'est inscrit à l'ANPE comme demandeur d'emploi.

En vertu de la loi sur l'emploi et l'assurance contre le chômage, les chômeurs inscrits qui ont perdu leur emploi contre leur gré et sans qu'il y ait eu faute de leur part ont droit à des allocations de chômage s'ils s'inscrivent à l'ANPE dans les 30 jours qui suivent la perte de leur emploi.

Peuvent faire valoir leur droit aux allocations les personnes sans emploi qui ont travaillé au moins neuf mois sans interruption, ou 12 mois avec des interruptions, au cours des 18 derniers mois. Le montant de l'allocation est défini en pourcentage des gains moyens du chômeur calculés sur ses trois derniers mois de travail. Pendant les trois premiers mois de leurs droits, les allocataires reçoivent 70 pour cent desdits gains moyens. Ensuite, le pourcentage diminue, sans que le montant de l'allocation puisse devenir inférieur à 80 pour cent du salaire minimum.

La durée de l'indemnisation du chômage est, par exemple, de trois mois pour les personnes qui n'ont travaillé que 12 mois sur les 18 derniers mois, de neuf mois pour celles qui ont travaillé de 5 à 10 ans et de 18 mois pour celles qui ont occupé un emploi pendant 15 à 20 ans. Un chômeur en fin de droits peut faire une demande d'allocations supplémentaires dans un délai de 30 jours si, au cours des trois mois précédant le dépôt de la demande, son revenu total, ajouté aux gains totaux des membres de sa famille n'a pas dépassé par personne 80 pour cent du minimum garanti. Un allocataire perd ses droits s'il refuse trois emplois proposés par l'ANPE.

Le *taux de chômage* représente le nombre de chômeurs exprimé en pourcentage de la population active totale (personnes pourvues d'un emploi et chômeurs) de la période correspondante.

Salaires

Gains mensuels

Les informations sur les salaires sont recueillies avec la même enquête que celle de l'emploi (voir ci-dessus). Les salaires des collaborateurs extérieurs et des consultants ne sont pas couverts. Outre les revenus du travail effectivement fourni dans le cadre de l'horaire normal, on prend en compte les catégories de revenus suivantes : la rémunération des heures supplémentaires, le paiement des congés annuels, des congés de maladie ne dépassant pas 30 jours, des ralentissements d'activité dont les salariés ne sont pas responsables, des jours fériés, de l'accomplissement des devoirs nationaux, des congés rémunérés, des rappels de salaire, des primes de productivité et autres primes et gratifications.

Avant 1992, on disposait seulement de données sur les gains officiels nets (gains bruts, diminués des cotisations de sécurité sociale et de l'impôt sur le revenu). A partir de 1992, les données concernent les salaires bruts. Il y a donc rupture de série entre les chiffres de la période antérieure à 1992 et ceux de la période postérieure à 1991.

Les données trimestrielles et annuelles ne sont pas toujours égales à la moyenne mensuelle, à cause de couvertures différentes dans les données de base.

Prix

Prix à la production

Les prix à la production sont recueillis tous les mois au moyen de questionnaires envoyés par courrier. Les prix observés sont ceux d'un échantillon de quelque 450 produits vendus en Slovénie par environ 300 des plus grandes entreprises de production. La liste des produits est en harmonie avec la nomenclature utilisée pour les statistiques industrielles (voir, plus haut, la rubrique Production industrielle). Pour construire *l'indice des prix à la production* qui est un indice de Laspeyres, on pondère les prix hors taxe des produits au moyen de coefficients dérivés de la part de chaque produit dans la production. On obtient ensuite l'indice d'ensemble des prix à la production en pondérant chacun des 30 groupes de produits industriels en fonction de sa part dans la valeur des ventes de l'année précédente.

RÉPUBLIQUE DE SLOVÉNIE

Pour les produits ayant un cycle de production saisonnier, le dernier relevé est reconduit pendant la période hors saison.

Prix à la consommation

Les prix à la consommation sont relevés pour 354 biens et 91 services dans 150 points de vente de détail, marchés permanents et établissements de service situés dans quatre grandes villes et zones rurales. Un relevé de prix est effectué une fois par mois, entre le 3 et le 25, dans chaque unité de l'échantillon et pour tous les biens et services. L'observation des prix est bimensuelle dans le cas des produits agricoles. Les prix utilisés pour calculer l'indice sont les prix payés par les consommateurs, c'est-à-dire toutes taxes comprises. Les prix des soldes et des ventes au rabais ne sont pas pris en compte.

L'observation des loyers est effectuée une fois par mois sur un échantillon de 64 logements loués. Ces logements sont répartis en huit groupes selon l'ancienneté de la construction. Les loyers sont calculés par mètre carré. Les logements occupés par leur propriétaire ne sont pas représentés dans l'indice.

Quand un changement intervient dans la qualité d'un article, celui-ci est remplacé par un article similaire censé ne pas introduire un changement de prix, ou bien on applique une méthode de raccordement. Quand un produit disparaît, (1) il est remplacé au début de l'année par le nouveau produit, ou bien (2) son poids est ajouté à celui d'un autre article, ou bien encore (3) son poids est réparti entre les différents postes du sous-groupe. On introduit de nouveaux articles lorsque leurs ventes deviennent significatives.

Les prix des articles saisonniers, comme les fruits et légumes frais, ne sont relevés qu'en saison. Hors saison, leurs poids sont enlevés du panier fixe de fruits et légumes saisonniers.

L'IPC est un indice de Laspeyres. Pour chaque article, on calcule la moyenne arithmétique simple des prix relevés dans chaque agglomération urbaine ; on affecte ensuite aux prix moyens ainsi obtenus des coefficients de pondération représentant la part des ventes des différentes agglomérations dans le total des ventes de détail de cet article, ce qui donne le prix national moyen. Au niveau du groupe de produits, *l'indice des prix à la consommation* est le rapport du prix moyen de la période courante au prix moyen de la période de base. En combinant ces indices élémentaires à l'aide de la pondération des dépenses fournies par l'enquête sur les budgets familiaux, on arrive à l'IPC national d'ensemble.

La pondération actuellement utilisée pour calculer l'IPC est tirée des résultats de l'enquête de 1993 sur les budgets familiaux. Cette enquête a été menée auprès de 3 270 ménages choisis par échantillonnage aléatoire simple. Les coefficients de pondération sont actualisés au début de chaque année au moyen de la variation de prix présentée par les groupes de produits correspondants au cours de l'année précédente.

Les coefficients de pondération tirés des résultats des enquêtes sur les budgets familiaux sont les suivants :

Groupes principaux	Enquête de 1990		Enquête de 1993	
	Nombre d'articles	Poids	Nombre d'articles	Poids
Alimentation	121	34.0	132	31.8
Vêtements et chaussures	82	15.0	82	9.8
Transports et communications	38	12.3	38	18.5
Éducation et loisirs	48	8.2	47	8.3
Boissons et tabacs	17	6.6	17	5.3
Soins personnels et médicaux	30	6.5	30	8.4
Équipement ménager	61	6.2	66	5.7
Combustibles et électricité	17	6.1	14	7.5
Loyer	19	5.1	19	4.7
TOTAL	433	100.0	445	100.0

Prix de détail

Les prix moyens utilisés pour calculer l'*indice des prix de détail* sont les mêmes que ceux qui servent à établir l'*IPC* (voir, ci-dessus, la rubrique Prix à la consommation). Le panier de l'indice des prix de détail comprend toutefois quelques biens supplémentaires, par exemple les matériaux de construction. *L'indice des prix de détail* inclut aussi quelques services : services liés à l'artisanat, services municipaux et de logement, services culturels, services de santé et soins personnels, services de transport et de communication, services financiers et autres services. La principale différence entre les deux indices réside dans leur pondération. Les coefficients utilisés pour pondérer l'*IPD* sont extraits de la structure du chiffre d'affaires du commerce de détail de biens et de services.

L'indice des prix de détail est utilisé pour calculer le taux d'inflation officiel. C'est aussi l'indice utilisé par le secteur bancaire pour l'ajustement mensuel des taux d'intérêt. L'indexation des allocations et l'ajustement des salaires, en particulier du salaire minimum, se réfèrent en revanche à l'indice des prix à la consommation.

Finances internes

Les *disponibilités monétaires au sens étroit (M1)* comprennent la monnaie en circulation, les dépôts à vue (comptes courants bancaires) du secteur non bancaire, y compris les institutions publiques, et les dépôts des entreprises et institutions financières non monétaires à la Banque de Slovénie. La seconde catégorie de dépôts se compose essentiellement des réserves constituées à la Banque de Slovénie par les caisses et coopératives d'épargne ; elles ne sont pas considérées dans les statistiques comme des réserves bancaires, car les établissements en question ne figurent ni parmi d'autres ni en tant que groupe distinct dans la définition des banques de dépôt.

RÉPUBLIQUE DE SLOVÉNIE

La *quasi-monnaie* englobe tous les dépôts à terme et dépôts d'épargne du secteur non bancaire, y compris les dépôts en devises qui sont principalement des dépôts des ménages. Les dépôts en devises sont convertis en tolars au moyen des taux de change officiels en fin de mois.

Les *dépôts personnels* se composent de l'ensemble des dépôts des ménages : dépôts à vue, d'épargne et à terme, y compris les dépôts en devises. Les dépôts en devises sont convertis en tolars au moyen des taux de change officiels en fin de mois.

Taux d'intérêt

Le *taux d'escompte officiel* n'est appliqué directement à aucune des opérations de la Banque centrale. Il peut être considéré comme un indicateur implicite des orientations que celle-ci souhaite imprimer à son action.

Le *taux de l'argent au jour le jour* se réfère à la moyenne, calculée sur la période considérée, des taux d'intérêt pratiqués sur le marché monétaire interbancaire pour les crédits au jour le jour.

Finances extérieures

La Slovénie a adopté le tolar comme unité monétaire le 8 octobre 1991. A cette époque, le rapport de conversion du tolar en dinar yougoslave était de 1 pour 1. Les *taux de change* du dollar des États-Unis, du deutsche mark et de l'Écu s'entendent en fin de période. Ce sont les taux de change officiels de la Banque de Slovénie.

Les *réserves officielles, or exclu*, recouvrent les avoirs en devises convertibles détenus par la Banque de Slovénie sous forme de monnaie fiduciaire et de dépôts dans les banques étrangères et sous forme de titres. En sont exclus les Droits de Tirage Spéciaux et la position de réserve au FMI, de même que les réserves liquides de change détenues par les banques commerciales.

La *dette extérieure brute* englobe tous les engagements à long et à moyen terme du secteur public comme du secteur privé en monnaie convertible, y compris la dette envers le FMI. L'attribution d'une partie de la dette extérieure de l'ancienne Yougoslavie fait toujours l'objet de négociations entre les États successeurs.

Commerce extérieur

Les déclarations douanières constituent la source de toutes les statistiques du commerce extérieur. Le Système harmonisé et la Classification type pour le commerce international, Révision 3, ont été mis en oeuvre en 1988. La Nomenclature combinée a été mise en place en 1996.

Les exportations couvrent tous les biens exportés par la Slovénie, en provenance des unités de production intérieures ou des zones de libre circulation du pays. Les importations représentent tous les biens mis sur le marché en vue de leur consommation dès leur arrivée en Slovénie ou à leur sortie des entrepôts. Les échanges à titre gratuit sont pris en compte. Les exportations et importations temporaires sont exclues, (sauf s'il s'agit de biens exportés ou importés en vue de leur transformation ou de leur location) ; sont également exclus l'approvisionnement des missions diplomatiques slovènes à l'étranger,

OECD
OCDE
SHORT-TERM ECONOMIC INDICATORS, SOURCES AND DEFINITIONS
OECD/CCET © April 1996
326
INDICATEURS ÉCONOMIQUES A COURT TERME, SOURCES ET DÉFINITIONS
OCDE/CCET © avril 1996

l'approvisionnement en carburants des transporteurs slovènes à l'étranger et des transporteurs étrangers sur le territoire national, les échantillons commerciaux et les bagages des voyageurs. Les échanges de services ne sont pas couverts.

Les données sur la valeur des biens échangés se fondent sur les documents d'origine (contrats, factures) des entreprises exportatrices ou importatrices. Elles se réfèrent aux valeurs facturées qui ont été stipulées au moment du contrat. Ces valeurs ont été recalculées sur une base uniforme à la frontière slovène, les exportations étant évaluées fab et les importations, caf. Les valeurs exprimées en monnaies étrangères sont converties en tolars et en dollars des États-Unis d'après les taux de change en vigueur le jour du dédouanement. Avant 1987, toutefois, la conversion se faisait au moyen des taux de change annuels en dinars yougoslaves.

Un certain nombre de changements méthodologiques ont été introduits dans les statistiques du commerce extérieur entre 1991 et 1992. Avant 1992, elles étaient en effet établies séparément pour chacune des républiques de l'ex-Yougoslavie. Les courants d'échanges étaient imputés à la république dans laquelle étaient produits les biens exportés, ou consommés les biens importés. Il n'était toutefois pas tenu compte des échanges entre les républiques de l'ex-Yougoslavie.

A partir de 1992, les séries englobent également les biens exportés ou importés en vue de leur transformation, ainsi que les échanges avec les pays qui faisaient auparavant partie du territoire de la Yougoslavie. En outre, les échanges étaient comptabilisés à leur valeur du mois courant, que les biens aient été dédouanés pendant cette période ou pendant un mois antérieur. A partir de 1992, les échanges sont imputés au mois du dédouanement. Recalculés suivant la méthode utilisée pour 1991, les totaux annuels de 1992 deviennent : exportations, 4 181 millions de dollars des États-Unis ; importations, 4 133 millions de dollars des États-Unis.

Publications

Certaines des séries décrites ci-dessus figurent aussi, mais avec une présentation conforme à la pratique nationale, dans les publications suivantes de l'Office statistique de Slovénie :

Statistical Yearbook (Annuaire statistique)

Mesicni Statisticni Pregled (Bulletin statistique mensuel)

divers numéros de *Statisticne Informacije* (Informations statistiques)

ainsi que dans le

Monthly Bulletin of the Bank of Slovenia (Bulletin mensuel de la Banque de Slovénie).

ROUMANIE

Production industrielle

L'indice de la production industrielle (IPI) se réfère aux activités de production physique, décrites dans les catégories 10 à 41 (groupes C, D et E) de la Classification internationale type, par industrie, de toutes les branches d'activité économique des Nations Unies (CITI), Révision 3 (industries extractives, industries manufacturières, électricité, gaz et distribution d'eau). La classification détaillée par activité s'appuie sur la Nomenclature industrielle générale des activités économiques dans les Communautés européennes (NACE), introduite en février 1991.

Une nouvelle méthode de calcul a été adoptée en février 1991. Des données en volume sont collectées pour un panier de 1 030 produits et groupes de produits. Les entreprises privées, bien que relativement marginales (7 pour cent de la production en 1993) sont comprises. Toutefois, pour quelques produits, on utilise les données en valeur déflatées par les indices de prix. Le nouvel indice est de type Laspeyres. A partir de 1993, les données sont pondérées par la valeur ajoutée brute de 1991 et, au niveau de chaque produit, par le prix moyen au cours de la période 1981-1993. Avant 1993, par contre, les données en volume des séries individuelles par produit étaient pondérées par les prix moyens des produits en 1989. Ce sont en effet les seuls prix dont on dispose et cette période s'est révélée assez stable du point de vue des fluctuations de prix. Les indices pour les années précédentes ont été recalculés dans l'année de base courante selon la méthode de l'indice chaîne.

L'indice de la production industrielle inclut l'auto-consommation au sein de l'entreprise considérée et exclut les variations de stocks de produits finis et la production en cours.

Les indices de la période 1990-1993 étaient publiés auparavant en données corrigées de l'incidence du nombre de jours ouvrables dans le mois, compte tenu du travail posté. La correction par le nombre de jours ouvrables est un ajustement effectué, non seulement à l'intérieur d'une même année, mais aussi d'une année à l'autre, le nombre de jours ouvrables variant légèrement selon les années. Tous les indices de production industrielle sont désormais publiés non ajustés du nombre de jours ouvrables de la période considérée.

L'indice de la production industrielle totale correspond aux catégories 10 à 41 (groupes C, D et E) de la CITI, Révision 3. Cette série se compose d'indices de la production physique, qui ne sont pas comparables aux indices de la production de biens précédemment publiés pour la période 1981-1990, lesquels représentaient des données en valeur exprimées à prix départ-usine "comparables", conformément à l'ancienne méthode. Les chiffres annuels pour 1981-1990 ont cependant été recalculés par l'Office statistique roumain à l'aide de la nouvelle méthode.

L'indice de la production industrielle pour les industries manufacturières correspond aux catégories 15 à 37 (groupe D) de la CITI, Révision 3.

L'*indice de la production industrielle dans les industries extractives* correspond aux catégories 10 à 14 (groupe C) de la CITI, Révision 3. Une série annuelle et une série semestrielle fondées sur l'ancienne méthode de calcul sont également disponibles pour la période antérieure à 1990.

L'*indice de la production industrielle pour l'électricité* correspond aux catégories 40 à 41 (groupe E) de la CITI, Révision 3. Une série annuelle et une série semestrielle fondées sur l'ancienne méthode de calcul sont également disponibles pour la période antérieure à 1990.

L'*indice de la production industrielle spécifique* à la *construction* correspond à la catégorie 45 (groupe F) de la CITI, Révision 3. La série s'appuie sur l'ancienne méthode de calcul (utilisant des données en valeur). Elle se rapporte à la valeur déflatée des nouveaux travaux de construction, du gros entretien et des réparations courantes, ainsi que de la maintenance des structures existantes assurés par les agents économiques, les unités administratives et les particuliers. Les données trimestrielles pour 1993 et 1994 correspondent à l'indice des travaux de construction, incluant les services, elles sont calculées sur la base d'un échantillon de 1 633 unités dont l'activité principale est la construction. L'échantillon couvre également les unités qui mènent des travaux de construction sous contrôle de l'État, ainsi que les unités exécutant des travaux de construction pour compte propre.

Quantités produites

Les données sur les quantités produites sont obtenues au moyen d'enquêtes auprès de toutes les entreprises productrices de plus de 50 salariés. Un échantillon représentatif des entités de moins de 50 salariés est également couvert. Les données sont révisées tous les ans pour tenir compte des quantités produites par les entreprises dont la principale activité ne relève pas des catégories 10 à 41 (groupes C, D et E) de la CITI, Révision 3.

La *production de charbon* se rapporte au charbon net (préparé), c'est-à-dire à l'anthracite trié, à la houille et au lignite nets, et au charbon brun trié.

La *production de gaz naturel* se rapporte au gaz naturel extrait (à une température de 15°C et une pression de 770 mm de mercure), y compris le méthane, le gaz de puits de pétrole et le gaz non associé.

La *production de pétrole brut* concerne la production totale à l'exception du gaz de pétrole liquéfié.

La *production d'acier brut* se rapporte à la production totale d'acier en lingots, coulé en continu ou en pièces. Le fer doux (puddlé) est exclu.

La *production de ciment* couvre tous les types de ciment, y compris le ciment contenant 80 pour cent de clinker comme matériaux de base.

Enquêtes de conjoncture

On trouvera une explication des techniques de réalisation de ces enquêtes et la liste des questions harmonisées dans le chapitre de cette publication consacré aux *Enquêtes de conjoncture*.

ROUMANIE

Construction

Logements

Toutes les séries sur le nombre de logements concernent exclusivement les logements construits par des entreprises du secteur public. Un logement est une unité composée d'une ou plusieurs pièces principales situées au même étage ou à différents étages d'un même bâtiment, généralement équipée d'une cuisine, d'une salle de bains, etc., qui est fonctionnellement indépendante, ayant une entrée indépendante donnant accès à un escalier, à un hall, à une cour ou à la rue, et construite, transformée ou aménagée pour l'usage d'un seul ménage.

Les *logements mis en chantier* font référence aux constructions résidentielles pour lesquelles un permis de construire a été délivré et dont les fondations sont déjà commencées.

Le nombre de *logements en cours de construction* est celui qui a été décompté en fin de période.

Les *logements achevés* font référence aux constructions résidentielles complètement terminées dont le gros oeuvre, y compris les fondations, n'existait pas auparavant.

Ces trois séries, *logements mis en chantier*, *logements achevés* et *logements en cours de construction*, ne concordent pas si l'on considère les périodes correspondantes, et ce pour plusieurs raisons. Dans les logements en cours de construction sont inclus ceux qui font l'objet d'un transfert, d'un achat ou d'une vente entre le secteur public et le secteur privé ; les logements transférés du secteur public au secteur privé disparaissent donc des statistiques officielles. En outre, les omissions que comportent les séries sont souvent rectifiées dans la période suivante, de sorte que le calcul du nombre de logements en cours de construction se fonde sur un chiffre révisé en ce qui concerne les logements mis en chantier et les logements achevés.

Commerce intérieur

Le commerce de détail correspond à l'activité de revente de marchandises neuves ou d'occasion, principalement à la population, par des magasins, des kiosques, des ventes par correspondance, de représentants de commerce, des coopératives de consommation, des ventes aux enchères et des ventes de détail dans les magasins des entreprises productrices. Les données sont collectées à l'aide d'enquêtes statistiques auprès des entités dont le commerce de détail constitue la principale activité et des entreprises productrices qui vendent leurs produits dans leurs propres magasins.

La *valeur des ventes de détail* était enregistrée aux prix généraux fixés par l'État jusqu'au mois d'avril 1990. Depuis 1990, la restauration publique n'est plus prise en compte dans le calcul de la valeur des ventes au détail.

Actuellement, la valeur des ventes de détail est enregistrée aux prix courants de détail, TVA comprise. Dans les ventes de détail figurent les produits, alimentaires et non alimentaires, vendus dans 3 000 points de vente de détail des secteurs public, coopératif et d'économie mixte et, depuis 1990, du secteur privé. Depuis 1993, les associations familiales et les travailleurs indépendants dont l'activité principale fait partie du commerce de détail (par exemple les producteurs d'articles ménagers, meubles, produits artisanaux, bijoux, tissus, vêtements, articles de bonneterie, chaussures, articles en cuir) sont couverts. Des estimations sont établies en ce qui concerne l'activité de l'économie "souterraine". Les produits agricoles vendus par des particuliers sur les marchés en plein air ne sont pas pris en compte ; ne sont pas comprises non plus les ventes d'énergie électrique ou thermique et de gaz naturel.

Les séries de données mensuelles sont complétées par les résultats d'une enquête statistique trimestrielle effectuée auprès des points de vente de détail du secteur privé. L'échantillon se compose de 722 points de vente, qui ont été choisis en fonction de leur revenu parmi une population de 60 000 agents économiques de telle façon que leur répartition par classes de revenu soit représentative de celle de la population de référence.

La série de *ventes de détail en volume* correspond à la série de ventes de détail en valeur déflatée par l'indice des prix en base "Mois correspondant de 1989 = 100", ou celui en base "Mois précédent = 100".

Investissements étrangers

Les séries relatives aux *investisseurs étrangers et aux capitaux étrangers* sont établies par l'Agence pour le développement de la Roumanie. Elles ont pour but de recenser l'ensemble des investisseurs étrangers dans toutes les branches de l'économie, quelle que soit la taille de leur investissement.

Main d'oeuvre

Emploi

Les séries sur l'emploi se rapportent aux personnes occupées dans les unités du secteur étatique, du secteur semi-public, que les capitaux de la composante privée soient roumains ou étrangers, et du secteur coopératif, à l'exclusion de l'emploi dans le secteur privé jusqu'en 1994. Sont considérées comme pourvues d'un emploi les personnes âgées de 14 ans et plus qui ont exercé une activité économique pendant au moins une heure au cours de la période de référence. Les personnes temporairement absentes de leur travail, pour cause d'accident ou de maladie, de congé payé ou de grève, sont comptées dans la population active occupée.

Le nombre moyen de salariés n'est pas le même dans les séries annuelles et dans les séries mensuelles parce que les premières incluent les personnes qui font un travail à la commission, saisonnier ou occasionnel et celles qui travaillent à l'étranger, la statistique concernant ces personnes n'étant pas établie mensuellement. En 1990, par exemple, ces catégories représentaient environ 110 000 personnes pourvues d'un emploi.

Les données sur l'*emploi total* se réfèrent au nombre moyen de salariés et couvrent l'ensemble de l'économie.

La série sur l'*emploi dans l'industrie* se réfère au nombre moyen de salariés et couvre les activités des divisions 10 à 41, (groupes C, D et E) de la CITI, Révision 3, ainsi que la sylviculture, qui fait partie de la division 2.

Les chiffres sur l'*emploi dans les industries manufacturières* se rapportent au nombre moyen de salariés et couvrent les divisions 15 à 37 (groupe D) de la CITI, Révision 3.

ROUMANIE

Chômage

Tous les chiffres concernant le chômage proviennent du Ministère du travail et de la protection sociale.

Le nombre de *chômeurs inscrits* est celui des personnes inscrites dans les agences pour l'emploi, qu'elles reçoivent des allocations de chômage, qu'elles bénéficient d'une aide sociale ou qu'elles n'aient droit à aucune de ces prestations selon la Loi 1/1991.

La série sur les *allocataires* se rapporte au nombre de personnes ayant droit à des prestations de chômage en vertu de la Loi 1/1991 relative à la protection sociale des chômeurs et à leur réinsertion professionnelle.

Les allocations sont accordées aux personnes de plus de 18 ans, inscrites au chômage, qui ont perdu leur emploi ou n'ont encore jamais travaillé (parce qu'elles ont récemment terminé leurs études ou leur service militaire obligatoire), dont les revenus d'autre source ne dépassent pas 50 pour cent du salaire minimum brut, dont la famille ne possède pas plus de 20 000 m² de terres agricoles (40 000 m² dans les zones de montagne) et qui sont physiquement aptes au travail. Les personnes qui ont volontairement quitté leur emploi, ou qui ont été renvoyées pour des raisons disciplinaires, ne perçoivent pas d'allocation. La durée de l'indemnisation du chômage est limitée à 270 jours.

Tout allocataire qui refuse un emploi correspondant à ses qualifications et à son expérience professionnelle ou une formation à une distance ne dépassant pas 50 km de son domicile que lui propose le Bureau de chômage perd ses droits. Les allocataires sont tenus de pointer une fois par mois.

Le montant de l'allocation versée aux personnes qui ont travaillé pendant cinq ans est par exemple égal à 50 pour cent de leur salaire moyen des trois derniers mois, mais ne peut être inférieur à 75 pour cent du salaire minimum, net d'impôts. Les diplômés de l'enseignement secondaire reçoivent 60 pour cent du salaire minimum mensuel, ceux de l'université 70 pour cent.

Les *non allocataires* sont les personnes sans emploi qui n'ont pas droit aux allocations de chômage et celles qui n'en reçoivent plus à cause de l'expiration de leurs droits. Depuis avril 1992, les nouvelles dispositions de la loi 1/1991 permettent aux chômeurs en fin de droits qui n'ont pas encore trouvé d'emploi de bénéficier durant 18 mois d'une aide sociale, indexée et imposable, fixée à 60 pour cent du salaire minimum national. Les titulaires d'une aide sociale doivent pointer une fois par mois dans les agences pour l'emploi.

Le *taux de chômage* exprime le nombre total de chômeurs inscrits en pourcentage de la population active civile (personnes pourvues d'un emploi et chômeurs inscrits) au 31 décembre de l'année précédente.

Salaires

Gains mensuels

Les données se rapportent aux gains mensuels nets, c'est-à-dire aux gains mensuels bruts diminués des impôts. A partir de 1993, les primes provenant des fonds salariaux, des fonds de participation aux bénéfices et autres fonds sont comprises. Jusqu'à la fin de 1993, les données sur les gains mensuels se rapportent aux secteurs public et coopératif seulement, et depuis 1994 le secteur privé est inclus.

La série des *gains mensuels totaux* se rapporte aux gains mensuels nets moyens nominaux, tels qu'ils sont définis ci-dessus.

Les *gains mensuels dans l'industrie* se rapportent aux gains mensuels nets moyens nominaux (voir ci-dessus) des salariés des divisions 10 à 41 (groupes C, D et E) de la CITI, Révision 3. Les activités de production d'électricité, d'énergie thermique, de gaz et d'eau n'étaient pas couvertes avant 1994.

La série des *gains mensuels dans les industries manufacturières* se rapporte aux gains mensuels nets moyens nominaux (voir ci-dessus) des salariés des divisions 15 à 37 (groupe D) de la CITI Révision 3.

Prix

Prix à la production

L'*indice de la production industrielle* ne couvre pas les armes, l'uranium, les métaux rares, les produits ayant un cycle de production long, les prototypes, les réparations de travaux industriels et les produits consommés au sein même de l'entreprise productrice. Le prix à la production se compose des coûts de production, des bénéfices, de certains honoraires et droits d'accise (impôts sur la consommation appliqués à certains biens importés ou produits sur le territoire national). Le prix des produits exportés correspond au prix négocié et acquitté, converti au taux de change en vigueur au moment de la transaction. Le prix à la production ne comprend pas la TVA.

L'IPP mensuel établi depuis 1993, n'est pas comparable avec l'indice qui était publié antérieurement. Les chiffres annuels de la période 1990-1992 sont des indices de Paasche. A partir de 1993, tous les chiffres sont des indices de Laspeyres ayant pour base les prix moyens de 1992. Les prix des produits sont pondérés par la valeur des livraisons en 1992.

En 1993, environ 840 unités industrielles et 1 753 produits comprenant 9 000 articles fabriqués en Roumanie étaient représentés. En 1994, l'échantillon est constitué de 1 030 unités industrielles représentatives, de 2 450 produits et groupes de produits et d'environ 12 000 articles. En 1995, environ 740 unités et 1 700 groupes de produits constitués de 9 000 produits sont enquêtés. Sont inclus les produits destinés au marché intérieur comme les produits destinés à l'exportation.

L'*indice des prix de gros*, publié antérieurement, se composait des coûts de production, des bénéfices et des taxes sur la circulation des marchandises. L'indice synthétique était un indice de Laspeyres, obtenu par agrégations successives : en suivant la Classification des activités de l'économie nationale (CAEN), on passait des indices d'article aux indices de produit, de classe de produits, de division, et enfin à l'indice d'ensemble pour l'industrie.

Prix à la consommation

La source de toutes les séries d'*indices des prix à la consommation (IPC)* est l'Indice roumain officiel des prix à la consommation. Les chiffres annuels indiqués pour la période 1980-1990 s'appuient sur la méthode dite des "prix comparables", ayant 1980 pour année de base. Ce sont des indices de prix qui n'intègrent pas la forme d'inflation la plus courante, i.e. traitement des changements de qualité en cours de période, et ils ne sont donc pas comparables avec les chiffres mensuels publiés depuis octobre 1990.

ROUMANIE

Le nouvel IPC, mis en place en octobre 1990, est un indice de Laspeyres calculé chaque mois. Dans le cadre de la nouvelle méthode, le traitement des changements de qualité est conforme à l'usage courant de l'OCDE : le prix d'un produit est corrigé de la variation due à l'amélioration de ses caractéristiques fonctionnelles intégrée dans un nouveau modèle, de sorte que l'effet-qualité n'est pas présenté comme une hausse de prix.

Les prix relevés sont les "prix de transaction", qui comprennent les marges commerciales et la TVA au taux de 18 pour cent (depuis le 1er juillet 1993).

Les prix de 1 800 biens et services sont observés dans un échantillon de plus de 4 300 points de vente et de service comprenant des marchés, des commerces de détail, des coopératives et des établissements de service. Les prix sont relevés dans 40 chefs-lieux de districts et dans la municipalité de Bucarest. Les prix sont relevés deux fois par mois, pour tous les biens et services. Un problème préalable, commun aux économies de pénurie est que les différents articles de la liste des biens et services représentatifs ne sont pas tous disponibles en toutes périodes. Pour en tenir compte, les prix de nombreux biens étaient auparavant relevés chaque semaine, ce qui augmentait les chances de disposer au moins d'une observation par mois. En outre, la liste des articles était plus longue que d'ordinaire. Elle comportait plusieurs variétés pour un même article de façon qu'il reste possible, si certaines d'entre elles étaient manquantes au cours d'un mois donné, de calculer un rapport de prix en se fondant sur les variétés disponibles.

Les tarifs des transports et des télécommunications, les loyers des logements publics, les tarifs de l'électricité, du gaz, de l'eau et des services postaux, qui sont fixés par des organismes publics, sont directement fournis par ces organismes. Le poste *"logement"* est représenté par les loyers, tant publics que privés. Il n'est pas tenu compte des logements occupés par leur propriétaire. Les articles saisonniers comme les fruits et légumes frais et les articles en laine sont regroupés dans un panier mensuel dont la pondération globale reste constante.

Le mois d'octobre 1990 a été retenu comme période de base parce qu'aucune mesure de libéralisation des prix n'était encore entrée en vigueur à cette date. Les dernières subventions appliquées à des biens de consommation ou à des services essentiels ont été supprimées dans le courant de 1993.

Les principales composantes de la consommation des ménages sont toutes représentées dans l'IPC. Les éléments qui en sont exclus sont les biens et services produits par les ménages eux-mêmes, les taxes, droits et amendes, les jeux de hasard, les intérêts des crédits, les assurances et la rémunération des dépôts d'épargne, les dépenses des ménages d'ouvriers agricoles et les dépenses d'acquisition de matériaux de construction usagés pour construire des logements neufs.

La pondération de l'IPC est tirée des résultats d'une enquête nationale sur les dépenses familiales menée auprès de 9 000 ménages dont le chef de famille est salarié, exploitant agricole ou retraité. Pour la période 1990-1993 l'IPC est pondéré par la structure des dépenses révélée par l'enquête de 1990 et, depuis 1994, par celle de l'enquête de 1993.

Les coefficients de pondération utilisés dans le calcul de l'IPC sont les suivants :

Groupes de dépenses	Poids 1990 (utilisés entre 1990-1993)	Poids 1993 (utilisés depuis 1994)
Alimentation	40.5	47.1
Autres biens	43.7	40.9
Services	15.8	12.0
TOTAL	100.0	100.0

Finances internes

Toutes les données sont calculées par la Banque nationale de Roumanie et se rapportent à la fin de la période considérée. A partir de janvier 1993, tous les agrégats monétaires comprennent les dépôts effectués dans les banques étrangères établies en Roumanie.

La *masse monétaire au sens étroit (M1)* englobe les pièces et billets à l'exclusion des encaisses des banques, et les dépôts à terme.

La *quasi-monnaie* se rapporte aux dépôts à terme et aux dépôts à vue des ménages, aux dépôts à terme des agents économiques, ainsi qu'aux dépôts en devises des ménages résidents.

Les *dépôts personnels* englobent les dépôts à vue et les dépôts à terme des ménages.

Taux d'intérêt

Par *taux d'escompte officiel* on entend le taux appliqué par la Banque nationale de Roumanie au refinancement des lignes de crédit accordées par les banques commerciales. Les taux sont pondérés par le volume des crédits accordés au cours du mois correspondant.

Finances extérieures

Jusqu'en janvier 1990, le *taux de change du dollar des États-Unis en leu* était le taux commercial, appliqué à toutes les opérations commerciales ou en capital libellées en devises convertibles. En février 1990, le taux commercial et le taux non commercial ont été remplacés par un taux unique, le taux officiel. Depuis novembre 1991, les données se réfèrent au cours flottant du marché interbancaire.

Les *réserves officielles, or exclu*, couvrent les réserves de change de la Banque nationale de Roumanie et de l'ensemble des banques commerciales.

ROUMANIE

Commerce extérieur

Dans les séries *exportations, importations et solde commercial*, les données de la période 1980-1989 ont été révisées d'après les taux de change commerciaux en vigueur. Depuis 1990, les données relatives au commerce extérieur sont calculées à l'aide du taux de change officiel de la Banque nationale de Roumanie.

Les exportations sont évaluées fab ; les importations s'entendent fab jusqu'à la fin de 1990, et caf à partir de 1991.

Le mode de collecte des données sur le commerce extérieur a été modifié en janvier 1991. A partir de ce mois, on s'est en effet servi, à des fins statistiques, d'informations tirées des déclarations douanières selon le Système harmonisé (au niveau de classification à six chiffres). C'est en 1994 qu'a été adoptée la classification de la Nomenclature combinée (NC) au niveau de classification à huit chiffres. Les clefs de conversion de la CTCI, Révision 3, sont utilisées pour établir une correspondance entre les deux systèmes de classification.

Les produits transportés par câble ou par canalisations (énergie électrique ou gaz naturel, par exemple) sont directement enregistrés par les entreprises importatrices/exportatrices.

Le commerce extérieur fait référence aux échanges de marchandises ; il comprend les importations destinées à être réexportées, ainsi que les marchandises qui sortent des zones franches et des entrepôts en douane pour entrer en Roumanie. Les services productifs comme les brevets, licences d'utilisation, de savoir-faire technique, travaux de conception et de recherche, travaux de montage et de construction, les produits alimentaires et le carburant destinés à l'approvisionnement des navires, l'impression de livres, de brochures, de matériel publicitaire, etc., ne sont pas pris en compte.

Dans les sources nationales, les exportations sont classées en fonction de leur pays de destination, par quoi l'on entend, le pays dans lequel s'effectue la consommation finale. Les importations sont classées en fonction du pays d'origine, défini comme celui dans lequel la marchandise a été produite, ou a subi sa dernière transformation.

Formation brute de capital fixe

Des questionnaires statistiques sont remplis chaque trimestre par un échantillon d'entreprises des secteurs public, coopératif et d'économie mixte, d'entités socio-culturelles, d'administrations publiques, d'organisations politiques et de mouvements associatifs.

La *formation brute de capital fixe totale* comprend les investissements en biens d'équipement et moyens de transport, les dépenses de construction, d'installation et d'assemblage, ainsi que tous les autres investissements en actifs immobilisés neufs, y compris l'achat de bétail, de même que l'extension et la modernisation des actifs existants. La valeur des actifs immobilisés importés est prise en compte ; la valeur des terrains est exclue de la formation brute de capital fixe. La valeur des services fournis en vue d'un transfert de propriété des actifs immobilisés et des terrains existants est cependant incluse.

Les investissements en *biens* d'*équipement* recouvrent les achats de machines et outillage de toutes sortes, ordinateurs, machines et matériel électriques, matériel de radio, télévision et communications, matériel médical et optique, montres et horloges, et tous moyens de transport.

Publications

      Certaines des séries décrites ci-dessus figurent aussi, mais avec une présentation conforme à la pratique nationale, dans les publications de la Commission nationale pour les statistiques :

      Buletin Statistic Trimestrial (Bulletin statistique trimestriel)

      Situation sociale et économique de la Roumanie

      Monthly Statistical Bulletin (Bulletin statistique mensuel)

      Statistical Bulletin -- Prices (Bulletin statistique -- Prix)

      Statistical Bulletin -- Industry (Bulletin statistique -- Industrie)

      Statistical Bulletin -- Foreign Trade (Bulletin statistique -- Co mmerce extérieur)

ainsi que dans de nombreux numéros thématiques de :

      Informatii Statistice Operative (Informations statistiques rapides).

RÉPUBLIQUE SLOVAQUE

Introduction

La République slovaque est devenue un État indépendant le 1er janvier 1993. Avant cette date, elle faisait partie de la République fédérative tchèque et slovaque (RFTS).

En règle générale, les données relatives à la RFTS étaient obtenues par agrégation des données concernant chacune des deux républiques. Les données historiques sont donc disponibles pour de nombreuses séries slovaques.

Les données en valeurs sont exprimées en couronnes de la RFTS jusqu'à la fin de 1992 et en couronnes slovaques à partir de janvier 1993, époque à laquelle des monnaies distinctes ont été introduites dans les deux républiques. Les deux monnaies étaient à parité jusqu'à la dévaluation de 10 pour cent de la couronne slovaque le 9 juillet 1993.

Production industrielle

Les indices de la production industrielle couvrent les entreprises des industries extractives et manufacturières, y compris l'électricité, le gaz et l'eau, et ce quelle que soit la forme de propriété des entreprises.

Pour 1990, la structure des branches industrielles est conforme à la Classification uniforme tchécoslovaque des branches de l'économie nationale. A partir de 1992, la structure se réfère à la Nomenclature générale des activités économiques (NACE), Révision 1 qui correspond à la CITI, Révision 3 au niveau de chaque division ; les données de 1991 ont été recalculées sur cette base.

Jusqu'à la fin de 1990, un recensement de toutes les entreprises industrielles était effectué. Depuis 1991, la couverture des entreprises a changé. En 1991, étaient concernées les entreprises d'au moins 100 salariés. En 1992 et 1993, les entreprises d'au moins 25 salariés ont fait l'objet d'enquêtes trimestrielles. Depuis 1993, le chiffre mensuel de la production industrielle totale incorpore une estimation de la production industrielle des entreprises de moins de 25 salariés et de la production des entrepreneurs indépendants. Les entreprises de moins de 25 salariés font l'objet d'une enquête trimestrielle dont les résultats permettent d'affiner les estimations mensuelles de la production industrielle totale. Depuis 1991, toutes les données ont été recalculées pour inclure les estimations de ces unités.

En revanche, les indices de la production par branche ne couvrent que les entreprises de plus de 25 salariés.

Depuis 1991, la production est mesurée par la production finale de l'entreprise. Elle inclut la variation des stocks ainsi que la variation des quantités des produits en cours de fabrication mais exclut la production non principale.

Dans le passé, les données mesuraient la variation du volume de la production par rapport à la période correspondante de l'année précédente. Si la structure industrielle changeait, on recalculait la valeur de la production de la période correspondante de l'année précédente sur une base comparable et on raccordait le taux de variation obtenu à l'indice avec la base d'origine. Par conséquent, si l'on pouvait valablement comparer une même période sur différentes années, on ne pouvait en faire autant, à strictement parler, à l'intérieur d'une même année.

Les valeurs de la production aux prix de 1989 étaient enregistrées de façon cumulative depuis le début de l'année jusqu'au mois en cours. Les chiffres mensuels étaient ensuite calculés par soustraction des données cumulées successives. Depuis 1993, on dispose directement de données mensuelles sur la valeur de la production. L'indice des prix à la production est utilisé pour obtenir des données en volume. Les indices sont de type Laspeyres.

A partir de 1992, les indices ont pour base de prix le 1er janvier 1989=100. Ils sont publiés dans les *Indicateurs économiques à court terme : Économies en transition* avec pour année de base 1990=100.

L'*indice de la production industrielle totale* couvre les industries extractives, les industries manufacturières (sauf l'édition avant 1992) et l'électricité, le gaz et l'eau.

L'*indice de la production industrielle pour les industries extractives* se réfère aux subdivisions de la NACE, Révision 1 concernant les industries minières et extractives.

L'*indice de la production industrielle pour les industries manufacturières* pour 1991 se réfère aux subdivisions de la NACE, Révision 1 concernant les activités manufacturières, excepté l'édition. A partir de 1992, l'édition est incluse.

L'*indice de la production industrielle pour l'électricité et le gaz* se réfère aux subdivisions de la NACE, Révision 1 concernant l'électricité, le gaz et l'eau et inclut la production et la distribution d'eau depuis 1991.

L'*indice de la production industrielle pour la construction* se réfère aux subdivisions de la NACE, Révision 1 concernant la construction, et couvre les entreprises de construction enregistrées dans la République slovaque.

Quantités produites

La *production de lignite* couvre le charbon brun et le lignite. Pour le charbon brun, il s'agit de la production des mines nette des déchets retirés et lavés dans les installations de préparation du charbon. Pour le lignite, qui n'est pas lavé, le chiffre retenu est celui de la production brute. Cette série a été suspendue.

La *production d'acier brut* couvre les matériaux ferreux autres que ceux obtenus par réduction directe, qui sont malléables et qui contiennent un poids de carbone ne dépassant pas 2 pour cent.

La série concernant le *ciment* couvre la production de ciment Portland, ciments de laitier, ciments aux pouzzolanes, ciments alumineux, ciments spéciaux et autres types de ciment (tels que ciment de magnésie et ciment à forte expansion).

La série concernant le *gaz naturel* se réfère à la production des mines.

RÉPUBLIQUE SLOVAQUE

La *production de voitures particulières* couvre principalement la production de camionnettes à plateau.

Enquêtes de conjoncture

On trouvera une explication des techniques de réalisation de ces enquêtes et la liste des questions harmonisées dans le chapitre de cette publication consacré aux *Enquêtes de conjoncture*.

Construction

Logements

Un logement est constitué d'une ou plusieurs pièces qui, selon les autorités de tutelle, sont destinées à l'habitation et qui peuvent constituer des unités indépendantes. Les chambres individuelles des pensionnats et résidences et les logements gérés par des administrations locales ne sont pas pris en compte.

Les *logements mis en chantier* sont établis sur la base des permis de construire délivrés par les Bureaux de district du Ministère de l'environnement.

Les *logements achevés* sont ceux pour lesquels un document certifiant qu'ils sont en état d'être habités a été délivré. Le certificat en question n'est obligatoire que pour les organismes et les entreprises de construction, mais les données incorporent aussi des estimations tirées d'enquêtes sur les investissements qui permettent de couvrir tous les logements construits dans le cadre de la formation de capital, y compris les maisons individuelles.

Étant donné la diversité des sources, il n'est pas possible d'utiliser les données disponibles pour connaître directement le nombre de *logements en cours de construction*. Des estimations étaient tout de même faites dans le passé sur la base des enquêtes sur les investissements, et les séries obtenues couvraient tous les logements mis en chantier durant la période considérée et ceux qui restaient inachevés à la fin de la période.

Depuis 1993, seul le nombre des logements achevés est comptabilisé par l'Office statistique. Les données sont collectées semestriellement.

Commerce intérieur

Jusqu'à la fin de 1990, la série *ventes de détail en valeur* se rapportait aux ventes de biens et services, aux prix de détail courants, assurées par le réseau public de détaillants et les entreprises de restauration des secteurs étatique et coopératif (c'est-à-dire les entreprises du Ministère du commerce, les coopératives de consommation, les restaurants et les fournisseurs de combustibles). Elle couvrait aussi les activités commerciales des entreprises non commerciales des secteurs étatique et coopératif.

Il s'agit de produits vendus directement aux consommateurs pour leur propre usage ou pour un usage collectif, ainsi qu'aux organismes du secteur public pour une consommation intermédiaire. Les recettes au titre des services sont incluses. Les chiffres mensuels représentent environ 85 pour cent du commerce total.

OECD
OCDE SHORT-TERM ECONOMIC INDICATORS, SOURCES AND DEFINITIONS
OECD/CCET © April 1996

340

INDICATEURS ÉCONOMIQUES A COURT TERME, SOURCES ET DÉFINITIONS
OCDE/CCET © avril 1996

Depuis 1991, les ventes de détail incluent les ventes et les recettes des secteurs de l'hôtellerie et de la restauration, ainsi que des services, y compris la réparation de véhicules automobiles. Les données représentent la valeur des biens et services vendus directement aux consommateurs pour leur propre usage. Une TVA a été instaurée le 1er janvier 1993 et les données correspondent à la valeur des ventes totales, taxes comprises.

Jusqu'à 1990, un recensement de tous les établissements commerciaux était effectué. Depuis le début de 1991, la couverture de l'enquête a changé. En 1991, elle se limitait aux entreprises d'au moins 100 salariés. De 1992 à 1995, les entreprises d'au moins 25 salariés ont fait l'objet d'enquêtes mensuelles et trimestrielles. Les petites entreprises de moins de 25 salariés étaient soumises à une enquête trimestrielle ; les données ainsi obtenues étaient utilisées pour affiner les estimations mensuelles. Depuis 1996, les entreprises d'au moins 20 salariés font l'objet d'une enquête mensuelle. Des corrections ont été apportées aux données depuis 1991 afin d'inclure une estimation des ventes totales des entités qui n'étaient pas soumises à l'enquête statistique.

Une série *ventes de détail en volume* a été calculée par le Secrétariat de l'OCDE à partir de la série en valeur déflatée par l'indice des prix à la consommation. Cette série est exprimée en base 1993 = 100.

Main-d'oeuvre

Emploi

Les données sur l'*emploi total* et sur l'*emploi dans l'industrie* proviennent des enquêtes trimestrielles auprès des entreprises qui permettent de déterminer la production industrielle. La couverture des entreprises est donc la même. Les données sur l'emploi total ont également été corrigées à partir de 1991 pour inclure des estimations relatives aux petites entreprises et aux entrepreneurs indépendants (par exemple sur la base des données concernant le nombre de licences d'exploitation délivrées aux petits commerçants).

Les données couvrent donc l'emploi dans les secteurs étatique, coopératif (pour les données rétrospectives) et privé, ainsi qu'une estimation du nombre d'entrepreneurs indépendants et de leurs salariés. Elles indiquent le nombre moyen de salariés civils, qu'ils travaillent à temps plein ou à temps partiel. Les apprentis et les salariés en congé de maternité ou en congé parental sont exclus.

Une enquête sur la population active auprès de 10 000 ménages a été instaurée en décembre 1992. Ces données sont actuellement collectées trimestriellement. Elles sont utilisées à des fins comparatives et pour élargir le champ des indicateurs de l'emploi de manière à couvrir l'emploi par niveau d'instruction, le sous-emploi, etc. Pour plus de précisions sur cette enquête, voir plus haut dans ce volume le chapitre *Indicateurs du marché du travail*.

La population d'âge actif se réfère aux femmes âgées de 15 à 54 ans et aux hommes âgés de 15 à 59 ans.

Chômage

L'enregistrement des chômeurs a commencé en février 1990 dans le cadre du Bureau de la main-d'oeuvre du Ministère du travail, des affaires sociales et de la famille, alors nouvellement créé. Le *chômage total* se réfère aux personnes qui n'ont pas de contrat de travail, n'exercent aucune activité indépendante lucrative et qui ont demandé au service local de l'emploi de leur trouver un emploi susceptible de leur convenir.

Il est nécessaire de s'inscrire au chômage pour pouvoir bénéficier d'un cours de recyclage et d'une aide financière ; les intéressés sont d'autant plus incités à s'inscrire que c'est le même service qui s'occupe de l'inscription au chômage et des offres d'emploi. Toutefois, les personnes qui travaillent à temps partiel ou souhaitent changer d'emploi ne peuvent pas s'inscrire au chômage.

Les données concernant les *allocataires* se réfèrent aux personnes qui perçoivent des allocations versées par le Bureau de la main-d'oeuvre. Pour être allocataire, il faut avoir travaillé au moins 12 mois au cours des trois dernières années. Les personnes qui ne se réinscrivent pas régulièrement perdent leurs droits aux allocations. Les intéressés peuvent être indemnisés pendant un maximum de six mois. Les trois premiers mois, ils touchent 60 pour cent du salaire moyen de leur emploi précédent, avec un plafond de 3 000 couronnes slovaques. Les trois mois suivants, le pourcentage passe à 50 pour cent du salaire moyen de leur emploi précédent. Les allocataires peuvent gagner jusqu'à 800 couronnes sans que cela modifie le niveau de leur prestation.

Au bout de six mois, le chômeur peut se voir proposer un travail d'utilité publique. Il continue alors à percevoir 50 pour cent de son salaire moyen précédent, plus un supplément de 800 couronnes slovaques. S'il n'y a pas de travail d'intérêt public à lui proposer, il peut, le cas échéant, avoir droit à des allocations sociales, versées par une autre administration.

Le *taux de chômage* représente le rapport entre le nombre de chômeurs inscrits et l'ensemble de la population active civile, (à savoir, chômeurs plus personnes pourvues d'un emploi, c'est-à-dire ayant travaillé plus d'une heure par semaine durant la période de référence, y compris les personnes en congé de maternité ou congé parental mais excluant les forces armées).

Les *offres d'emploi* incluent tous les emplois vacants à pourvoir immédiatement, déclarés aux services de l'emploi le jour de référence.

L'enquête sur la population active précédemment mentionnée, et décrite plus haut dans le chapitre *Indicateurs du marché du travail* de ce volume, fournit plus d'informations sur les chômeurs (par exemple leur répartition par sexe et par âge, la durée du chômage, etc.).

Entreprises privées

Jusqu'à la fin de 1989, les données couvrent les personnes assurant des services avec l'autorisation des comités nationaux, conformément à l'ordonnance émanant des gouvernements de la République tchèque comme de la République slovaque. Depuis le début de 1990, les données se réfèrent au nombre d'entrepreneurs inscrits conformément à la Loi N°105/1990.

Les données concernant les *entrepreneurs* du secteur privé inscrits en 1990 et 1991 émanent du Ministère de l'intérieur slovaque. Depuis 1992, elles proviennent du Registre des unités statistiques de l'Office statistique de la République slovaque. Les entrepreneurs enregistrés couvrent aussi les ouvriers qualifiés et les agriculteurs indépendants. Une estimation est également faite pour les entrepreneurs individuels qui ne sont pas couverts par le registre.

Plusieurs phénomènes obscurcissent l'interprétation des données sur le nombre d'entrepreneurs du secteur privé. De nombreuses personnes déclarent une entreprise privée, puis, pour des raisons diverses, n'exercent en fait aucune activité. D'autres peuvent ne poursuivre une activité qu'à temps partiel.

Pour vérifier le degré d'(in)activité des entrepreneurs privés inscrits, ceux-ci ont dû se réinscrire jusqu'à la fin de 1992, conformément à la Loi sur les petites entreprises N°455/1991. A la fin de 1992, une nouvelle législation est entrée en vigueur, exigeant le versement de cotisations sociales et d'une assurance pour les locaux loués par les entrepreneurs privés. Ces procédures ont entraîné une diminution du nombre d'entrepreneurs inscrits ; seuls les entrepreneurs actifs étant en mesure de faire face à ces charges se sont réinscrits.

Salaires

Gains mensuels

Les données sur les *gains mensuels totaux* sont tirées des enquêtes auprès des entreprises dont déjà les statistiques de la production industrielle et de l'emploi sont également extraites, et leur couverture est donc la même. Par ailleurs, l'Office statistique de la République slovaque corrige ces données depuis 1991 pour y inclure une estimation des gains mensuels dans les petites entreprises du secteur privé (celles comptant de 1 à 24 salariés). Aucun ajustement n'est fait pour tenir compte des salaires des petits commerçants engagés dans une activité indépendante et non inscrits au registre des entreprises. Grâce à l'enquête sur la population active, on dispose aussi, depuis 1993, d'estimations des gains des entrepreneurs indépendants, mais pour l'instant ces données ne sont pas publiées ni directement intégrées aux statistiques de gains.

Les données se rapportent uniquement aux salariés des entreprises (et non à leurs dirigeants). Les gains visés correspondent au salaire mensuel moyen brut par salarié et englobent le salaire ou traitement de base, les primes et gratifications, mais excluent les allocations familiales et autres prestations sociales.

Les gains dans l'*industrie totale* et les gains dans les *industries manufacturières* sont exclusivement établis à partir de données sur les entreprises d'au moins 25 salariés.

Prix

Prix à la production

L'*indice des prix à la production* (IPP) se réfère aux prix des produits industriels fabriqués dans la République slovaque. Jusqu'à la fin de 1990, les données concernaient les prix catalogue et faisaient l'objet d'une collecte trimestrielle. A partir de 1991, il s'agit des prix relevés mensuellement sur environ 1 890 articles représentatifs auprès de 382 producteurs représentant 270 branches d'activité. Ne sont pas couverts les productions non standard des constructions mécaniques et de la métallurgie, les travaux de montage et de démontage, les services industriels, les réparations et la distribution d'électricité.

Les prix indiqués sont la moyenne arithmétique des prix de transaction effectifs de tous les contrats importants observés en milieu de mois. Jusqu'en 1993, les prix excluent l'impôt sur le chiffre d'affaires.

Les articles choisis peuvent être remplacés par d'autres, de qualité similaire, mais quand des écarts de qualité importants sont observés, les prix sont corrigés en conséquence. Aucun traitement particulier n'est effectué concernant les produits saisonniers. Les prix excluent la TVA, instaurée le 1er janvier 1993, mais incluent les taxes à la consommation imposées sur certains produits.

OECD
OCDE
SHORT-TERM ECONOMIC INDICATORS, SOURCES AND DEFINITIONS
OECD/CCET © April 1996
343
INDICATEURS ÉCONOMIQUES A COURT TERME, SOURCES ET DÉFINITIONS
OCDE/CCET © avril 1996

RÉPUBLIQUE SLOVAQUE

L'indice est de type Laspeyres, calculé à partir de simples rapports de prix individuels pondérés par la valeur de la production de la branche concernée en 1989. Dans les statistiques nationales, l'indice a pour base 100 le 1er janvier 1989 et des données mensuelles sont disponibles sur cette base à partir de 1991.

Prix à la consommation

L'*indice des prix à la consommation* (IPC) reflète les mouvements des prix des produits alimentaires, des produits industriels, de la restauration et d'autres services achetés par la population. Les prix de 836 biens et services sont observés, comme le montre le tableau ci-dessous.

Grands groupes	Nombre d'articles	Poids
Produits alimentaires	160	29.9
Produits industriels	423	44.6
Restauration publique	59	11.5
Services (y compris loyers, transports et communications)	194	14.0
TOTAL	836	100.0

Les agents des services statistiques relèvent les prix dans un certain nombre de commerces de détail et d'établissements de services de 38 districts de la République slovaque, pendant les vingt premiers jours du mois. Les fruits et légumes font l'objet de trois relevés mensuels (les 1er, 10 et 20 du mois). Un panier distinct de fruits et légumes frais est constitué chaque mois, réunissant diverses variétés couramment en vente pendant le mois en question. On relève entre trois et cinq prix pour les produits alimentaires, non alimentaires et certains services. Pour d'autres services, tels que les transports et communications, on fait un seul relevé. L'indice se réfère aux prix payés dans les magasins et points de vente des secteurs étatique, coopératif et privé ; les prix des marchandises d'occasion ne sont pas pris en compte.

Si le produit observé disparaît des étalages, il est remplacé par un autre, de qualité comparable à la précédente. Si la qualité du nouvel article n'est pas vraiment comparable à la précédente, on procède à un ajustement. En général, les prix des produits qui suivent les nouvelles tendances de la mode sont introduits directement dans l'indice.

L'IPC est de type Laspeyres. Les prix relevés dans les différentes unités déclarantes servent à calculer des moyennes arithmétiques non pondérées. Les indices élaborés pour divers groupes et agrégats sont calculés sous forme de moyennes arithmétiques pondérées par des coefficients constants se rapportant à l'année de base.

La pondération se réfère, pour les produits, à la structure des ventes de détail de 1989, et, pour les services, à la structure des dépenses en service de la population en 1989.

Le système de suivi et de calcul des indices des prix a été modifié en 1991, où l'on est passé d'une périodicité trimestrielle à une périodicité mensuelle, et une nouvelle base 100 en janvier 1989 a été introduite dans les statistiques nationales. Dans les *Indicateurs économiques à court terme : Économies en transition*, les séries publiées ont pour base l'année 1990=100.

OECD
OCDE
SHORT-TERM ECONOMIC INDICATORS, SOURCES AND DEFINITIONS
OECD/CCET © April 1996

344

INDICATEURS ÉCONOMIQUES A COURT TERME, SOURCES ET DÉFINITIONS
OCDE/CCET © avril 1996

Finances internes

La *masse monétaire au sens étroit* (M1) englobe la monnaie nationale en circulation en dehors du secteur bancaire et les dépôts à vue, sauf ceux des administrations centrales.

La *quasi-monnaie* englobe les dépôts à terme, les dépôts d'épargne et les dépôts en devises des résidents, à l'exclusion des administrations centrales.

Les *dépôts personnels* englobent tous les dépôts d'épargne des ménages résidents dans toutes les institutions financières, notamment les banques et compagnies d'assurances, du territoire slovaque.

Taux d'intérêt

Le *taux d'escompte officiel* désigne le taux, observé en fin de période, auquel la Banque nationale prête aux banques commerciales. Le montant des prêts bénéficiant de ce taux est plafonné, les crédits excédant le plafond étant consentis par la Banque nationale au taux du marché.

Finances extérieures

Le *taux de change du dollar des États-Unis* correspond au taux moyen de la période. Jusqu'à la fin de 1992, il se réfère à la parité de la couronne de la RFTS. A partir de 1993, il se réfère au taux de change de la couronne slovaque.

Commerce extérieur

Jusqu'à 1990, les données du commerce extérieur sont tirées d'une enquête auprès des exportateurs et importateurs ayant une licence. Depuis le début de 1991, les statistiques du commerce extérieur s'appuient sur les déclarations en douane, et le Système harmonisé est utilisé. Le Document administratif unique est entré en vigueur en République slovaque le 1er janvier 1992. Les déclarations sont traitées par l'Administration centrale des douanes, également mise en place de façon autonome par la République slovaque au début de l'année 1993.

Depuis le 1er janvier 1991, les marchandises exportées sont enregistrées à la date où elles traversent la frontière. Les importations de marchandises sont enregistrées à la date de sortie des entrepôts sous douane et non à la date du passage de frontière. Le traitement des déclarations connaît certains retards qui entraînent de fréquentes révisions des données.

Les données incluent les réexportations et les réimportations, mais excluent les exportations et importations de services. Depuis 1993, le commerce avec la République tchèque est inclus.

Depuis 1991, les importations et les exportations sont évaluées fab.

La ventilation du commerce extérieur en *monnaies convertibles* et *monnaies non convertibles* dépend du statut du pays de provenance ou de destination, défini ou non comme une économie "de marché". La somme des deux peut ne pas coïncider avec le chiffre du commerce total du fait des difficultés d'identification du pays de provenance ou de destination ou de la monnaie de référence sur certaines déclarations.

RÉPUBLIQUE SLOVAQUE

Formation brute de capital (investissement en équipements)

Les données concernant la *formation brute de capital (investissement en équipements)* font l'objet d'une collecte trimestrielle. Jusqu'en 1991, les données concernent uniquement les investissements immobilisés principalement machines et équipements. Depuis 1992, d'autres investissements (la recherche, les logiciels, etc.) ont été mesurés. Une nouvelle enquête a été mise en place en 1994. Toutes les catégories d'unités figurant au registre du commerce sont prises en compte, y compris celle des entrepreneurs indépendants.

Les travaux de *construction* englobent les travaux réalisés par les organismes budgétaires et les administrations, les travaux de construction des entreprises privées et les constructions réalisées pour compte propre. Toutes les constructions sont prises en compte, qu'il s'agisse de l'activité primaire ou d'une activité secondaire de l'entité considérée.

La définition slovaque de la série des *autres éléments de la formation brute de capital* inclut la valeur des achats et ventes de terres faisant suite à un changement de propriétaire, qui constitue la plus importante composante de cette catégorie.

Publications

Certaines des séries décrites ci-dessus figurent aussi, mais avec une présentation conforme à la pratique nationale, dans les publications suivantes de l'Office statistique de la République slovaque :

Slovak Economic Monitor (Le Moniteur économique slovaque)
Slovak Statistical Review (Revue statistique slovaque)

DIX NOUVEAUX ÉTATS INDÉPENDANTS

Le chapitre qui suit est consacré aux notes méthodologiques et définitions des données relatives à 10 nouveaux États indépendants (NEI) : Arménie, Azerbaïdjan, Bélarus, Kazakstan, République Kirghize, République de Moldova, Fédération de Russie, Tadjikistan, Turkménistan et Ouzbékistan.

Ces informations sont fournies à l'OCDE par le Comité interétatique de statistique de la Communauté des nouveaux États indépendants.

Production industrielle

La production industrielle totale et la production des différentes branches représentent la production brute notifiée régulièrement par les établissements industriels à partir de leurs enregistrements statistiques. La production brute d'un établissement industriel couvre la valeur des produits fabriqués par l'établissement durant la période comptable, y compris la valeur des produits semi-finis vendus, ou destinés à être vendus à d'autres entités. Sont également inclus la valeur des services industriels rendus à d'autres entités sur une base contractuelle ainsi que les services rendus à des unités du secteur non matériel et à des établissements au sein d'une entreprise. Sont exclus la valeur de la production de l'établissement consommée dans le processus de production, les produits non finis et la variation des stocks. La variation de la production en cours est prise en compte dans les branches d'industrie caractérisées par un cycle de production long.

Les séries mensuelles et trimestrielles couvrent les établissements industriels du secteur public, ceux qui sont détenus collectivement et les sociétés par actions. Les entreprises caractérisées par d'autres formes de propriété sont généralement incluses dans les séries annuelles.

Les séries annuelles couvrent également la production auxiliaire qui inclut par exemple la production industrielle des fermes collectives, des fermes d'État et des entreprises de construction. La part de la production auxiliaire dans la production totale est estimée à 6-7 pour cent.

Les chiffres annuels ne correspondent pas toujours aux moyennes des chiffres mensuels et trimestriels notamment à cause de différence dans la couverture des entreprises.

L'*Indice de la Production Industrielle totale (IPI)* est fondé sur la valeur totale de la production exprimée à prix "comparables". La production industrielle à prix "comparables" est calculée par les entreprises en multipliant le volume de production en unités physiques par des prix à la production "comparables" hors taxe sur le chiffre d'affaires, TVA et droits d'accise.

Les prix du 1er janvier 1982 ont été utilisés pour déflater la production de la période 1980-1990. A partir de 1991, ce sont les prix de janvier de chaque année qui sont utilisés, et les indices sont chaînés.

Différences par rapport à cette définition :

-- *Fédération de Russie (à partir de 1993), Azerbaïdjan et Kazakstan (à partir de 1994)* : l'indice de la production industrielle (IPI) est une moyenne pondérée des variations du volume de la production. Des indices sont calculés pour un panier constant d'articles représentatifs puis combinés pour donner les indices de branche et l'indice d'ensemble. En Azerbaïdjan, au Kazakstan et en Fédération de Russie, le nombre de produits utilisés pour le calcul de l'indice est, respectivement, de 300, 400 et 430.

-- *République Kirghize et Turkménistan* : Depuis 1992, les séries en valeur sont déflatées par les prix du mois courant.

La classification de la production industrielle est basée sur la Nomenclature des branches de l'économie nationale (NBEN), élaborée par l'ex-Conseil d'assistance économique mutuelle (CAEM).

L'*IPI total* couvre en gros les branches industries minières, extractives et manufacturières et électricité, gaz et eau (branches 2, 3 et 4) de la Classification internationale type par industrie (CITI, Rév. 2). Il inclut en outre l'exploitation forestière et la pêche, les services de nettoyage, la réparation et l'entretien de véhicules à moteur ainsi que la réparation d'articles personnels et domestiques. L'imprimerie et l'édition sont exclues.

L'*IPI des industries extractives* couvre les établissements assurant l'extraction de produits minéraux, de minerais métalliques, ferreux et non ferreux, et de matières premières, autres que les minerais, utilisées dans l'industrie métallurgique, l'extraction de pétrole brut, l'extraction de minerais non métalliques, de gaz, charbon, tourbe, schiste, sel et de matériaux de construction, autres que des minerais, de remplissage légers et de chaux.

Le forage, la prospection minière et le raffinage de pétrole brut et de gaz naturel sur place sont exclus.

L'*IPI des industries manufacturières* couvre les établissements assurant la transformation de produits miniers, de produits ayant déjà subi une transformation et de produits agricoles. Cette classification propres aux NEI diffère de la division 3 de la CITI, Rév. 2, en ce qu'elle inclut la production d'électricité (à l'exclusion de l'hydro-électricité) et la réparation de véhicules à moteur, de meubles et d'appareils ménagers et qu'elle exclut l'imprimerie et l'édition.

Dans l'*IPI de la construction*, la définition de la production se limite à la valeur des investissements en constructions nouvelles, travaux d'agrandissement et travaux de reconstruction. Sont inclus les travaux d'installation, les fouilles, les travaux d'architecture, de conception et de dessin et autres grandes composantes de l'activité de construction, ainsi que la réparation importante de bâtiments et d'ouvrages. La valeur des constructions non terminées est incluse. La valeur des machines et outillages et des plantations est exclue.

Les données sur la construction sont recueillies auprès des entreprises d'État et des coopératives, des entreprises privées, des coentreprises ainsi que des projets de logements agricoles et de logements individuels, quel que soit leur mode de financement.

Pour la période 1980-1984, les données sont exprimées aux prix constants de 1973, pour la période de 1985-1988 aux prix constants de 1983, et depuis 1989 aux prix de l'année précédente.

OECD
OCDE
SHORT-TERM ECONOMIC INDICATORS, SOURCES AND DEFINITIONS
OECD/CCET © April 1996

348

INDICATEURS ÉCONOMIQUES A COURT TERME, SOURCES ET DÉFINITIONS
OCDE/CCET © avril 1996

Quantités produites

La *production de charbon* couvre la houille et le lignite, en données brutes des pertes dues à la production de briquettes, au tri, au nettoyage, etc.

La *houille* comprend le charbon à coke, l'anthracite et le charbon utilisé dans les centrales thermiques. La tourbe, le coke et le semi-coke obtenus à partir du charbon sont exclus.

Le *lignite* exclut le coke et le semi-coke obtenus à partir de lignite ou de tourbe.

La *production de gaz naturel* couvre le gaz naturel obtenu à partir de puits de gaz et le gaz de pétrole obtenu à la tête des puits.

Selon la méthode adoptée dans les NEI, la production de gaz est mesurée à 20°C et à une pression de 760 mm de mercure.

La *production de pétrole brut* couvre le pétrole brut obtenu par toute méthode, à l'exclusion de la production de condensat de gaz.

La *production d'acier brut* couvre tous les types d'acier (fours Martin, acier électrique, convertisseurs, acier Bessemer, etc.), les lingots d'acier destinés à être laminés, forgés et martelés par l'entreprise et livrés ailleurs, les lingots d'acier obtenus par fonte continue, les lingots pour refonte (à l'exclusion de l'acier pour traitement en procédé duplex dans l'entreprise même). L'acier liquide utilisé pour le moulage est inclus.

Différences par rapport à cette définition :

-- *Tadjikistan* et *République Kirghize* : depuis 1992, l'acier est produit en totalité par des établissements industriels auxiliaires, qui ne fournissent un rapport statistique qu'une fois par an.

Tous les types de *production de ciment* sont couverts, à l'exclusion des matériaux visqueux locaux obtenus à partir de scories et de schiste. La production auxiliaire des branches industrielles non spécialisées dans les matériaux de construction est prise en compte.

La *production d'électricité* mesure tous les types de production d'électricité : hydroélectrique, hydraulique, classique, thermique, nucléaire, géothermique, solaire, marémotrice. La production brute des centrales comprend les réseaux d'électricité indépendants et les systèmes de chauffage électrique.

La *production de machines à usiner les métaux* recouvre tous les types de tours, raboteuses, perceuses, fraiseuses, affûteuses, machines de brochage et autres, y compris les machines à ultrasons et à électroérosion (à l'exclusion des machines à main et des machines portables).

La *production de camions* couvre tous les types de camions et de semi-remorques (à l'exclusion des engins à moteur à usage spécifique) ainsi que les camions fabriqués à partir de châssis de voitures particulières.

La *production d'engrais minéraux* comprend tous les types d'engrais minéraux à base de nitrates, de phosphates, de potassium, de bore ou associant du bore et du magnésium.

La *production de réfrigérateurs* ne couvre que les réfrigérateurs et congélateurs d'aliments à usage domestique et ceux qui sont destinés aux automobiles.

La *production de voitures particulières* comprend toutes les catégories de voitures, à l'exclusion des camions fabriqués à partir de châssis de voitures particulières.

Il existe certaines différences dans la couverture des entreprises entre les séries trimestrielles et les séries annuelles de quantités produites.

Enquêtes de conjoncture

Des résultats d'enquêtes de conjoncture sont disponibles pour la Fédération de Russie depuis le premier trimestre de 1992 et pour le Bélarus depuis le second trimestre de 1994. On trouvera une description des techniques de réalisation de ces enquêtes et la liste des questions harmonisées dans le chapitre de cette publication consacré aux *Enquêtes de conjoncture*.

Construction

Logements

Sont inclus tous les *logements achevés*, indépendamment du type d'entreprise chargée de leur construction. Les logements achevés comprennent la construction des entreprises d'État, des coopératives de construction de logements, des organisations sociales et des syndicats, des kolkhozes et autres entreprises de construction de logements agricoles ainsi que celle des entreprises privées et des logements construits par des particuliers, indépendamment de la source de financement. Il peut y avoir certaines différences dans la couverture des entreprises entre les données trimestrielles et les données annuelles.

Par logements on entend des locaux destinés à l'habitation permanente, physiquement séparés d'autres locaux et ayant une entrée indépendante donnant directement accès à un escalier, à une partie commune, à un hall ou à la rue. Un logement peut comprendre, sous un même toit, une ou plusieurs pièces, un couloir, une cuisine, une buanderie, une entrée et un débarras.

Deux séries sont présentées pour les logements : la première indique le nombre de *logements achevés*, la seconde la *surface totale des logements achevés*, à l'inclusion des appartements, des hôtels et logements similaires et des dortoirs. La surface habitable totale englobe les pièces principales et toutes les pièces de service comme la cuisine, le couloir, le débarras et la buanderie. Dans le cas des foyers, les pièces de service peuvent aussi inclure les locaux médicaux et culturels. Les vérandas, loggias, terrasses et balcons peuvent être partiellement inclus, au moyen d'un coefficient déterminé par les indicateurs techniques et économiques du projet de logement. Sont exclus de la surface habitable les halls d'entrée, les escaliers et les couloirs communs.

Commerce intérieur

La *valeur des ventes de détail* est définie comme la valeur totale des biens de consommation vendus par des commerces de détail et des établissements de restauration publique ou livrés directement par des entreprises industrielles, des entreprises de transport et d'autres entreprises. Tous les points de vente, quel que soit leur régime de propriété, sont inclus. Le chiffre d'affaires du commerce de détail comprend les ventes de produits alimentaires et d'autres biens aux sanatoriums, hôpitaux, établissements pour les enfants et autres institutions.

Les données sur les ventes de détail sont collectées directement auprès de toutes les entreprises qui écoulent des biens de consommation par l'intermédiaire de points de vente officiellement agréés, indépendamment du régime de gestion ou de propriété. Les marchés urbains sont exclus.

Avant 1990, le chiffre d'affaires du commerce de détail englobait les recettes de certains services rendus aux ménages, notamment la confection individuelle de vêtements, la réparation de vêtements et de chaussures ou la réparation de biens de consommation durables. La part de ces services dans le total avoisinait 2 pour cent, mais depuis 1991 le chiffre d'affaires du commerce de détail ne comprend plus de services.

Le total annuel des ventes peut dépasser la somme des recettes des mois ou des trimestres correspondants en raison d'une couverture plus large des entreprises de commerce.

La valeur des ventes de détail a été exprimée dans les nouvelles monnaies nationales à mesure que celles-ci ont été instituées. Pour plus de précisions, voir le chapitre *Introduction de nouvelles monnaies*.

Depuis 1995, une nouvelle série portant sur la *valeur totale des ventes de détail* est disponible pour tous les pays à l'exception de la République de Moldova et du Tadjikistan. Cette série indique le chiffre d'affaires total du commerce de détail réalisées par l'ensemble des points de vente et elle inclut des estimations des ventes effectuées sur les marchés parallèles par les particuliers et les entreprises non immatriculées.

On obtient l'indice du *volume des ventes de détail* en corrigeant le chiffre d'affaires du commerce de détail de la variation des prix. Le déflateur utilisé à cet effet est l'indice des prix à la consommation de l'ensemble des biens en Arménie, au Bélarus et dans la Fédération de Russie et l'indice des prix de détail dans les autres pays (voir plus loin la section Prix).

Main d'oeuvre

Emploi

L'*emploi total* indique l'effectif moyen des personnes employées dans les entreprises et organisations d'État ou contrôlées par l'État, les coopératives et institutions sociales et les coentreprises, ainsi que des travailleurs indépendants, comme les agriculteurs privés, les personnes assurant une production agricole pour auto-consommation et les personnes exerçant une activité individuelle. Le personnel militaire est exclu. Les institutions sociales comprennent, par exemple, les clubs sportifs, les syndicats, les associations d'écrivains et de journalistes, la Croix rouge et le Croissant rouge, le Fonds pour la paix, le Fonds pour l'enfance. A partir de 1991, les personnes travaillant dans des entreprises privées sont également couvertes.

Les données sont tirées des déclarations trimestrielles et annuelles concernant les effectifs des entreprises, organisations et institutions. Toutes les entreprises, indépendamment de leur régime de propriété, sont tenues de notifier leurs effectifs. Ces informations sont généralement comparées avec les données similaires recueillies par l'administration fiscale et les banques d'État. Le nombre des personnes assurant une production agricole pour auto-consommation fait l'objet d'une estimation.

Toutes les branches de l'économie nationale sont incluses, que l'activité en cause soit matérielle ou immatérielle.

Les travailleurs à temps partiel, y compris ceux qui sont placés en tant que tels par les agences pour l'emploi, sont comptabilisés comme équivalent plein temps. Les pluriactifs sont comptabilisés d'après leur lieu de travail principal. Les effectifs civils des complexes industriels militaires, les personnes en congé de maladie, les apprentis, les travailleurs à domicile et les travailleurs occasionnels sont pris en compte.

L'*emploi dans les branches matérielles* couvre les branches suivantes de l'économie nationale :

-- industrie ;

-- agriculture ;

-- sylviculture ;

-- transports et communications, dans la mesure où ces services sont utilisés par les activités productives dans le secteur de la production matérielle ;

-- commerce, restauration publique, approvisionnements matériels, passation de marchés ;

-- services informatiques et services d'information ;

-- autres branches de la production matérielle : édition, production et distribution de films, transformation des déchets, pêche, chasse, etc.

Cette série a été interrompue depuis le deuxième trimestre de 1993.

L'*emploi dans l'industrie* couvre tous les salariés travaillant dans les établissements industriels d'entreprises industrielles ainsi que dans les établissements industriels d'entreprises classées dans d'autres branches. Les salariés d'établissements non industriels d'entreprises industrielles sont inclus dans la branche d'activité à laquelle appartient l'établissement considéré. La couverture des branches est la même que dans le cas de l'IPI total (voir plus haut la section Production industrielle).

L'*emploi dans les industries manufacturières* représente le nombre moyen d'ouvriers et d'employés participant directement au processus de production des entreprises manufacturières, d'après leur registre des salaires. La couverture des branches est la même que dans le cas de l'IPI des industries manufacturières (voir plus haut la section Production industrielle).

Chômage

Le nombre *total des chômeurs inscrits* représente le nombre de personnes enregistrées comme chômeurs par les agences publiques pour l'emploi en fin de mois, conformément à la législation sur l'emploi en vigueur dans chaque nouvel État indépendant.

Les personnes valides en âge de travailler (de 16 à 60 ans pour les hommes et de 16 à 55 ans pour les femmes) sont considérées comme chômeurs, quelles que soient les raisons pour lesquelles elles n'exercent pas d'emploi rémunéré, à condition d'avoir été dûment enregistrées comme demandeurs d'emploi par une agence publique pour l'emploi, d'être aptes et prêtes à exercer toute activité rémunérée et de n'avoir pas reçu de propositions d'emploi correspondant à leur profil.

L'enregistrement des chômeurs par les agences publiques pour l'emploi a commencé aux dates suivantes :

-- 1er juillet 1991 au Bélarus, au Kazakstan, en République Kirghize, en République de Moldova, dans la Fédération de Russie ;

-- 1er octobre 1991 en Azerbaïdjan ;

-- 1er mars 1992 en Arménie ;

-- 16 avril 1992 au Tadjikistan ;

-- 1er juillet 1992 en Ouzbékistan.

Selon la réglementation en vigueur dans les différents pays, les agences pour l'emploi statuent au sujet de l'inscription d'un demandeur d'emploi au plus tard 10 jours après sa demande. Les personnes précédemment employées doivent présenter leur passeport, leur livret de travail et les bulletins de salaire de leur dernier employeur. Les primodemandeurs d'emploi sont tenus de présenter leur passeport et leurs diplômes. Un chômeur reste inscrit jusqu'à ce qu'il trouve du travail.

Les personnes qui ont perdu leur emploi ne sont pas tenues de s'inscrire au chômage. Celles qui désirent changer d'emploi, de même que les travailleurs à temps partiel à la recherche d'un emploi à plein temps, ne sont pas considérés comme chômeurs, mais peuvent s'inscrire comme demandeurs d'emploi dans les agences pour l'emploi. Dans tous les pays, les chômeurs sont tenus de pointer périodiquement dans les agences publiques pour l'emploi. L'obligation de pointage est :

-- hebdomadaire au Kazakstan et au Tadjikistan ;

-- bimensuelle en Arménie, en République Kirghize, en République de Moldova, dans la Fédération de Russie et en Ouzbékistan ;

-- mensuelle au Bélarus.

Les allocataires reçoivent leur allocation, à la suite de leur inscription au chômage, à partir :

-- du premier jour au Bélarus et dans la Fédération de Russie ;

-- du deuxième jour au Tadjikistan ;

-- du huitième jour au Kazakstan ;

-- du onzième jour en Arménie, Azerbaïdjan, République Kirghize, République de Moldova et Ouzbékistan.

Le montant de l'allocation et la durée des droits varient beaucoup d'un pays à l'autre et selon la catégorie à laquelle appartient le bénéficiaire. En général, l'allocation versée à un primodemandeur d'emploi est d'au moins 70 pour cent du salaire minimum légal et lui est payée pendant une période allant de 12 semaines, en Arménie, à 12 mois, dans la Fédération de Russie. Quant aux personnes qui occupaient précédemment un emploi, elles reçoivent généralement 50 pour cent, au moins, du salaire payé par leur ancien employeur pendant une période qui va de 24 semaines, en Arménie, à 12 mois, dans la Fédération de Russie.

Les *non allocataires* sont les personnes inscrites au chômage qui n'ont pas droit à l'allocation et celles dont les droits ont été annulés ou suspendus pour refus de deux offres d'emploi correspondant à leur profil (une seule en République de Moldova), non pointage dans les agences pour l'emploi, perception illégale d'allocations ou travail non déclaré.

Le *taux de chômage* représente le rapport entre le nombre de chômeurs inscrits et la population active civile (personnes pourvues d'un emploi et chômeurs). Les estimations mensuelles de l'emploi utilisées pour calculer la population active sont tirées des statistiques trimestrielles de l'emploi.

Salaires

Gains mensuels

Les chiffres relatifs aux *gains mensuels* ne proviennent pas des mêmes sources que ceux qui concernent l'emploi (voir le paragraphe précédent) : les gains des agriculteurs privés, des personnes réalisant une production agricole d'auto-consommation et des autres travailleurs indépendants sont exclus.

Les données expriment le salaire brut moyen par salarié, calculé en divisant la masse salariale totale par le nombre total de salariés. Pour le calcul du salaire moyen, les salariés à temps partiel sont enregistrés en équivalent plein temps, tandis que les personnes en congé maternité ou en congé parental sont exclues. La masse salariale englobe des paiements tels que les prestations de santé, les indemnités de subsistance et les frais de déplacement, les paiements en nature, les primes d'intéressement aux bénéfices, la rémunération des heures supplémentaires et des congés payés. Les versements au titre de la sécurité sociale n'en font toutefois pas partie.

Les séries sur les *gains mensuels dans les branches de la production matérielle* ont été suspendues depuis le deuxième trimestre de 1993.

Les gains mensuels ont été exprimés dans les nouvelles monnaies nationales à mesure que celles-ci ont été instituées. Pour plus de précisions, voir le chapitre *Introduction de nouvelles monnaies*.

Prix

"Ancien" indice des prix à la consommation

Des indices mensuels des *prix à la consommation* (IPC) ont été mis en place en janvier 1991.

Pour tous les pays (à l'exception de la Fédération de Russie depuis 1991 et de la République de Moldova : voir ci-dessous) les prix de 1 030 biens représentatifs choisis dans l'ensemble des groupes de produits inclus dans les ventes de détail ont été observés jusqu'en décembre 1993. En ce qui concerne l'IPC *des services*, l'évolution des prix de 72 articles représentatifs de la structure des ventes de services marchands aux ménages était suivie dans plus de 250 villes.

Dans la Fédération de Russie, l'IPC était calculé à partir des relevés de prix d'un ensemble de 409 groupes élargis de biens et services. Dans la République de Moldova, les prix de 1 585 biens et services étaient inclus dans l'IPC.

Les prix comprenaient les taxes et étaient relevés tous les mois dans environ 5 000 points de vente répartis dans l'ensemble des NEI et dont l'éventail s'étendait des grands magasins qui vendaient une large gamme de produits jusqu'aux petits points de vente spécialisés (librairies ou magasins d'articles pour enfants, etc.). Les indices reflétaient l'évolution des prix dans les points de vente des secteurs public, coopératif et privé, ainsi que celle des prix des biens produits par les coopératives et par les travailleurs indépendants.

Aucune estimation n'était effectuée pour tenir compte du secteur informel. Les marchés non couverts urbains étaient exclus du calcul des sous-groupes de l'IPC, mais étaient inclus dans l'IPC total.

Les coefficients de pondération attachés aux produits alimentaires saisonniers dans les indices agrégés variaient toutefois selon qu'ils étaient cultivés sous serre et vendus en tant que primeurs, ou qu'ils étaient "de saison". Pour ce qui est des services, quelques entreprises accordaient des remises pour certains d'entre eux au cours de la période de baisse saisonnière de la demande. Ces remises étaient prises en compte dans les relevés de prix.

Dans tous les pays, sauf la Fédération de Russie, l'Ouzbékistan et la République Kirghize, l'IPC des biens de consommation est un indice de Paasche jusqu'en décembre 1992 et un indice de Laspeyres depuis janvier 1993. En Ouzbékistan et dans la République Kirghize, l'IPC est un indice de Paasche, quelle que soit la période.

Pour tous les pays, à l'exception de la Fédération de Russie et de la République de Moldova, les coefficients de pondération utilisés pour agréger les données relatives aux régions et aux groupes sont basés sur la structure des ventes de détail de l'année en cours. L'IPC des services est un indice de Laspeyres et les coefficients de pondération sont basés sur les ventes de services aux ménages pendant la période de référence.

Dans la Fédération de Russie, l'IPC est de type Laspeyres depuis janvier 1991 (voir aussi ci-dessous la section "Nouvel indice des prix à la consommation"). Les coefficients de pondération utilisés sont basés sur la structure des dépenses de consommation effectives de la population russe au cours de l'année précédente. Les indices élémentaires sont agrégés en trois grands sous-groupes : produits alimentaires, produits non alimentaires et services. L'IPC total est une moyenne pondérée des indices élémentaires.

Dans la République de Moldova, l'IPC est de type Laspeyres depuis janvier 1993, et les coefficients de pondération sont basés sur la structure des dépenses de consommation des ménages au cours de l'année précédente (voir aussi ci-dessous la section "Nouvel indice des prix à la consommation").

Un indice annuel montrant le taux de variation au cours de l'année précédente est également publié. En raison de la libéralisation des prix et de leur hausse spectaculaire, ainsi que des changements qui se sont produits dans la structure de la production et des ventes, les indices mensuels et annuels des prix à la consommation ne sont pas compatibles, sauf ceux de la Fédération de Russie.

Dans la Fédération de Russie, les 409 groupes élargis de biens et services étaient choisis de façon à ce que les changements structurels liés aux très importantes hausses de prix soient pris en compte dans les indices mensuels, de sorte que les chiffres annuels calculés par comparaison directe des prix de décembre avec ceux du même mois de l'année précédente peuvent être compatibles avec les chiffres mensuels.

"Nouvel" indice des prix à la consommation

De nouveaux IPC mensuels ont été introduits en 1991 dans la Fédération de Russie, 1993 dans la République de Moldova et en 1994 dans tous les autres NEI.

Les indices sont de type Laspeyres.

Ils sont calculés à partir de relevés des prix de détail et des droits de douane de biens et de services représentatifs.

Les paniers de référence utilisés ont été composés à l'image de la structure des dépenses des consommateurs. Ils sont composés de 300 à 400 articles comprenant tous les produits alimentaires, les produits non alimentaires, et les services achetés par les ménages.

Différence par rapport à cette définition :

-- *Ouzbékistan* : les bijoux et l'épicerie fine sont exclus.

La population de référence retenue pour le calcul des dépenses des consommateurs est l'ensemble de la population résidente.

Pour chaque région on calcule un prix global par article qui est la moyenne arithmétique de toutes les observations. Au niveau national, chaque région est assortie d'un coefficient de pondération qui correspond à sa part dans la population.

Les pondérations utilisées pour construire les indices synthétiques sont tirées des enquêtes sur les dépenses de consommation des ménages de l'année précédente.

Différence par rapport à cette définition :

-- *Azerbaïdjan :* dépenses de consommation des ménages en 1993.

Les prix des services sont relevés dans des points et organisations de vente et de service, quel que soit leur propriétaire : secteur public, secteur privé, marchés informels.

Les prix sont observés tous les 7 ou 10 jours dans le cas des produits alimentaires, une fois par mois dans celui des autres biens et des services.

Différences par rapport à cette définition :

-- *Arménie* : les prix des produits non alimentaires et des services sont suivis tous les 10 jours ;

-- *Bélarus, République Kirghize* : l'observation des prix des produits alimentaires est mensuelle ;

-- *République de Moldova* : les prix des produits non alimentaires et des services sont relevés deux fois par mois.

Finances internes

Les *dépôts personnels* couvrent les dépôts à terme et les dépôts d'épargne détenus en fin de période dans les caisses d'épargne. Les annuités d'intérêt sont incluses dans les chiffres de décembre, du quatrième trimestre et de l'année entière.

Depuis le 1er septembre 1991, dans tous les pays, les dépôts personnels englobent une compensation de 40 pour cent destinée à dédommager les déposants d'une forte hausse des prix. Dans la limite de 200 roubles, cette compensation a été versée sur le compte de dépôt principal. Lorsque la compensation dépassait 200 roubles, elle a été déposée sur un compte spécial. Les dépôts placés sur les comptes spéciaux ont été inclus dans les dépôts personnels.

Différence par rapport à cette définition :

-- *Kazakstan* : les données sur les dépôts personnels n'incluent pas les paiements compensatoires.

La population est autorisée à retirer ces dépôts compensatoires depuis mars 1994 en Arménie, avril 1994 en République de Moldova et en Ouzbékistan, 1992 dans la Fédération de Russie et au Turkménistan, 1993 au Bélarus.

Les dépôts personnels ont été exprimés dans les nouvelles monnaies nationales à mesure que celles-ci ont été instituées. Pour plus de précisions, voir le chapitre *Introduction de nouvelles monnaies*.

Finances extérieures

Des séries concernant les *taux de change* du dollar des États-Unis, du nouveau rouble ou de ces deux monnaies en unités monétaires des NEI sont publiées. Ces cours sont fixés par la banque nationale de chacun des pays en cause, et les chiffres indiqués correspondent à la fin de la période, ou à la moyenne de la période s'agissant du taux de change du rouble. On trouvera des informations supplémentaires sur la mise en service des nouvelles monnaies dans le chapitre *Introduction de nouvelles monnaies*.

Commerce extérieur

Les données sur les *exportations* et les *importations* sont tirées des rapports statistiques soumis par les organismes de commerce extérieur, ainsi que des déclarations douanières. Les exportations et importations sont enregistrées à la date où elles franchissent la frontière. Les exportations sont exprimées en données fab, les importations en données caf. Les biens faisant l'objet d'un troc sont évalués aux prix du marché mondial pour des produits similaires.

Les données du commerce extérieur excluent les services, sauf dans la Fédération de Russie où les services de construction, les services financiers, l'édition, l'enseignement, la formation et les services de santé sont inclus jusqu'en 1994. En Ouzbékistan, les statistiques du commerce extérieur englobaient jusqu'en 1992 les services matériels. Les recettes touristiques sont exclues dans tous les NEI. Les exportations d'or, d'argent, d'autres métaux précieux et de diamants sont en principe incluses, mais dans la pratique elles ne sont que partiellement couvertes.

Les réexportations et réimportations ne sont enregistrées qu'au moment où les biens entrent dans le pays.

Les statistiques du commerce extérieur ont commencé en 1991, sauf dans la Fédération de Russie où elles ont commencé en 1988.

Jusqu'en 1994, on disposait uniquement de données sur le commerce avec les pays autres que les NEI. Depuis 1994, les statistiques du commerce extérieur sont ventilées en commerce avec les NEI et commerce avec les pays autres que NEI.

Les statistiques du commerce extérieur avec les NEI ne couvrent que les échanges avec les pays de l'ex-Union soviétique, à l'exception de ceux avec l'Estonie, la Lettonie et la Lituanie, lesquels sont inclus dans les statistiques du commerce avec les pays autres que NEI.

Dans le cas du commerce extérieur avec les pays autres que les NEI, les chiffres annuels comprennent certaines statistiques douanières non prises en compte dans les données trimestrielles pour 1993 et 1994 au Kazakstan, et pour 1993 au Bélarus. Les chiffres annuels ne correspondent donc pas à la somme des statistiques trimestrielles et mensuelles dans ces pays.

Les exportations et importations de la Fédération de Russie entre 1988 et 1990, évaluées au taux de change officiel, sont exprimées en dollars des États-Unis sur la base des taux annuels moyens suivants :

-- 1988 à 0.61 rouble/dollar ;

-- 1989 à 0.63 rouble/dollar ;

-- 1990 à 0.58 rouble/dollar.

En 1991 leur mode d'évaluation en dollars a été révisé et s'est fondé sur la moyenne du taux de change officiel et du taux de change commercial, à savoir 1,26 rouble/dollar.

Pour les autres NEI, les transactions commerciales avec l'étranger sont estimées en dollars des États-Unis depuis 1992. Pour tous les NEI, les taux de change sont calculés sur la base des taux de change officiels fixés par les banques nationales.

Formation brute de capital

La *formation brute de capital totale* représente les dépenses consacrées à l'achat de biens d'équipement neufs, ainsi qu'à l'extension, la reconstruction et la rénovation d'actifs immobilisés en service. La valeur des investissements en équipements représente le coût de la construction et des installations, l'achat du matériel et de l'outillage et les dépenses d'infrastructure.

L'investissement en équipements est évalué à son coût initial, à savoir son prix d'acquisition, brut de tout amortissement. Les bâtiments et ouvrages non terminés qui ont été payés par les entrepreneurs sont inclus dans l'investissement en équipements ; la réparation de biens d'équipement est exclue.

Les équipements sont inclus quel que soit leur mode de financement : dépenses d'investissement des entreprises et institutions étatiques, des entreprises en régie, des coopératives de consommation et organisations publiques de consommateurs, des coopératives, des fermes collectives, des coopératives de construction de logements et constructions individuelles auto-financées.

Les dépenses d'équipement sont enregistrées aux prix courants et recalculées aux prix constants de 1984, soit sur la base des données fournies par les entreprises soit à l'aide d'indices de prix. Les séries de la période 1984-1990 s'appuient sur les données fournies par les entreprises.

OECD
OCDE

SHORT-TERM ECONOMIC INDICATORS, SOURCES AND DEFINITIONS
OECD/CCET © April 1996

358

INDICATEURS ÉCONOMIQUES A COURT TERME, SOURCES ET DÉFINITIONS
OCDE/CCET © avril 1996

La *formation brute de capital au titre de la construction et des installations* comprend les travaux liés à la construction, à l'agrandissement et à la reconstruction de bâtiments et d'ouvrages permanents ou temporaires, ainsi que les activités d'installation de modules de construction et d'équipements.

Depuis 1991, les indices du volume des dépenses d'investissement sont calculés dans la plupart des pays de la CEI comme le rapport des valeurs aux prix constants obtenues en déflatant la valeur des dépenses d'investissement aux prix courants par l'indice des prix des dépenses d'investissement. Cet indice des prix est élaboré à partir des données sur la variation des prix des principaux éléments des dépenses d'investissement (travaux de construction et d'aménagement, machines et outillage, grosses réparations, autres dépenses d'investissement).

Les statistiques sur la formation brute de capital ont été exprimées dans les monnaies nationales à mesure que celles-ci ont été instituées. Pour plus de précisions, voir le chapitre *Introduction de nouvelles monnaies*.

Publications

Certaines des séries décrites ci-dessus, mais avec une présentation conforme à la pratique nationale, dans diverses publications du Comité interétatique de statistique de la CEI ou dans des publications des Offices statistiques nationaux de chacun des pays.

OECD
OCDE
SHORT-TERM ECONOMIC INDICATORS, SOURCES AND DEFINITIONS
OECD/CCET © April 1996
359
INDICATEURS ÉCONOMIQUES A COURT TERME, SOURCES ET DÉFINITIONS
OCDE/CCET © avril 1996

UKRAINE

Production industrielle

La production industrielle totale et la production des différentes branches de l'industrie représentent la production brute notifiée régulièrement par les établissements industriels à partir de leurs enregistrements statistiques. La production brute d'un établissement industriel couvre la valeur des produits fabriqués par l'établissement durant la période comptable, y compris la valeur des produits semi-finis vendus, ou destinés à être vendus, à d'autres entités. Sont également inclus la valeur des services industriels rendus à d'autres entités sur une base contractuelle ainsi que la valeur des services rendus à des unités du secteur non matériel et à des établissements au sein d'une entreprise. Sont exclus la valeur de la production de l'établissement consommée dans le processus de production, les produits non finis et la variation des stocks. La variation des travaux en cours est prise en compte dans les branches d'industrie caractérisées par un cycle de production long.

Les indices annuels de la production industrielle sont calculés à partir des statistiques de production industrielle totale établies par les entreprises fonctionnant de façon indépendante, au sens comptable, par les unités de production manufacturière, les entreprises à participation étrangère, les petites entreprises et coopératives, les établissements industriels auxiliaires (financièrement non autonomes) d'organisations non industrielles, par les fermes collectives et fermes d'État, ainsi que par les organisations multisectorielles de toutes formes et de tous types de propriété (propriété étatique, privée, collective et mixte).

Les séries mensuelles et trimestrielles sont tirées des formulaires statistiques sur la production industrielle totale qui sont remplis par les entreprises fonctionnant de façon indépendante et par les unités relevant de toutes les formes de propriété ; la production des établissements auxiliaires des unités de production manufacturière est comprise dans les chiffres qu'elles fournissent.

La classification de la production industrielle se fonde sur la Nomenclature par branches de l'économie nationale de l'ex-Union soviétique (NBEN), élaborée par l'ex-Conseil d'assistance économique mutuelle (CAEM).

Les indices de la production industrielle sont de type Paasche.

L'*indice de la production industrielle (IPI) totale* couvre en gros les industries extractives, manufacturières et l'électricité, le gaz et l'eau de la Classification internationale type par industrie (CITI, divisions 2, 3 et 4). Il inclut en outre l'exploitation forestière et la pêche, les services de nettoyage, la réparation et l'entretien de véhicules à moteur ainsi que la réparation d'articles personnels et domestiques. L'édition est exclue.

L'IPI total est fondé sur la valeur totale de la production exprimée aux prix constants de janvier 1989. La production industrielle à prix constants est évaluée directement par les entreprises. Celles-ci déflatent la valeur de la production en utilisant les prix de gros qui excluent les taxes sur les ventes, la TVA et les taxes d'accise.

Les observations portent sur environ 90 000 entreprises et le panier de l'indice total se compose de 500 articles.

Pour tous les indices de branche, ce sont les prix de janvier de l'année précédente qui ont été utilisés pour déflater la production industrielle.

L'*IPI des industries extractives* couvre les établissements assurant l'extraction de produits minéraux, de minerais métalliques, ferreux et non ferreux, et de matières premières autres que les minerais utilisées dans l'industrie métallurgique, l'extraction de pétrole brut, l'extraction de minerais non métalliques, de gaz, charbon, tourbe, schistes, sel et de matériaux de construction autres que des minerais, de matériaux de remplissage légers et de chaux. Le forage, la prospection minière et le raffinage de pétrole brut et de gaz naturel sur place sont exclus.

L'*IPI des industries manufacturières* couvre les établissements assurant la transformation de produits miniers, de produits ayant déjà subi une transformation et de produits agricoles. Il exclut la production d'électricité, la réparation de véhicules à moteur, de meubles et d'appareils ménagers et l'édition.

L'*IPI de l'électricité* mesure tous les types de production d'électricité : hydro-électrique, hydraulique, classique, thermique, nucléaire, géothermique, solaire, marémotrice. La production brute des centrales électriques comprend les réseaux d'électricité indépendants et les systèmes de chauffage électrique.

L'*IPI de la construction* recouvre le ciment, le ciment à base d'amiante, les matériaux de couverture en rouleaux et matériaux d'étanchéité, le béton armé précontraint et les structures et produits en béton, les matériaux de construction de murs, les terres cuites, les matériaux et produits de construction à base de polymères, l'extraction et la taille de dalles de parement en pierre naturelle, les agrégats poreux, le gypse calcaire, les liants et produits de source locale et les matériaux d'isolation thermique. Il recouvre aussi d'autres matériaux de construction comme les bétons et mortiers prêts à l'emploi et le béton asphaltique.

Les données sur la construction sont recueillies auprès des entreprises d'État et des coopératives, des entreprises privées, des entreprises mixtes, des projets de logements agricoles et entrepôts, et de logements individuels, indépendamment de leur mode de financement.

Quantités produites

La *production de charbon* couvre la houille et le lignite, en données brutes des pertes dues à la production de briquettes, au tri, au nettoyage, etc.

La *houille* comprend le charbon à coke, l'anthracite et le charbon utilisé dans les centrales thermiques. La tourbe, le coke et le semi-coke obtenus à partir du charbon sont exclus.

Le *lignite* exclut le coke et le semi-coke obtenus à partir de lignite ou de tourbe.

La *production de gaz naturel* couvre le gaz naturel obtenu à partir de puits de gaz et le gaz de pétrole obtenu à la tête des puits. Selon la méthode adoptée en Ukraine, la production de gaz est mesurée à 20°C et à une pression de 760 mm de mercure. Les données ont été recalculées compte tenu de la norme internationale (0°C et 760 mm de mercure) à l'aide d'un coefficient de 1 073.

UKRAINE

La *production de pétrole brut* couvre le pétrole brut obtenu par toute méthode, incluant la production de condensat de gaz.

La *production d'acier brut* couvre tous les types d'acier (fours Martin, acier électrique, convertisseurs, acier Bessemer, etc.), les lingots d'acier destinés à être laminés, forgés et martelés par l'entreprise ou livrés ailleurs, les lingots d'acier obtenus par fonte continue, les lingots pour refonte (à l'exclusion de l'acier pour traitement en procédé duplex dans l'entreprise même). L'acier liquide utilisé pour le moulage est inclus.

Tous les types de *production de ciment* sont couverts, à l'exclusion des matériaux visqueux locaux obtenus à partir de scories et de schiste. La production auxiliaire de ciment des branches d'industrie non spécialisées dans les matériaux de construction est incluse.

La *production de voitures particulières* comprend toutes les catégories de voitures, à l'exclusion des camions fabriqués à partir de châssis de voitures particulières. Les voitures particulières produites par des entreprises militaires sont exclues.

Construction

Logements

Plusieurs séries sont présentées pour les *logements achevés* : une série indiquant la superficie des logements achevés dans le secteur public et deux séries indiquant, l'une le nombre, l'autre la superficie des logements achevés par les entreprises de tout type.

Dans le nombre total des *logements achevés* sont compris les logements construits par les entreprises d'État, les coopératives de construction de logements, les organisations sociales et les syndicats, les kolkhozes et autres entreprises de construction de logements agricoles, les entreprises privées, ainsi que les logements construits par des particuliers, indépendamment de la source de financement. Par logements on entend des locaux destinés à l'habitation permanente, physiquement séparés d'autres locaux et ayant une entrée indépendante donnant directement accès à un escalier, à une partie commune, à un hall ou à la rue. Un logement peut comprendre, sous un même toit, une ou plusieurs pièces, un couloir, une cuisine, une buanderie, une entrée et un débarras.

La *superficie totale des logements achevés* s'entend y compris les appartements, les hôtels et établissements similaires, et les dortoirs. La surface habitable totale englobe les pièces principales et toutes les pièces de service comme la cuisine, le couloir, le débarras et la buanderie ; dans le cas des foyers, les pièces de service peuvent aussi inclure les locaux médicaux et culturels. Les vérandas, loggias, terrasses et balcons peuvent être partiellement inclus, au moyen d'un coefficient déterminé par les indicateurs techniques et économiques du projet de logement. Sont exclus de la surface habitable les halls d'entrée, les escaliers et les couloirs communs.

Commerce intérieur

La valeur des *ventes de détail* est définie comme la valeur totale (à l'inclusion des taxes sur les ventes) des biens de consommation vendus par des commerces de détail et des établissements de restauration, ou vendus directement par des entreprises industrielles, des entreprises de transport et autres entreprises. Les points de vente aussi bien publics que privés sont inclus. Le chiffre d'affaires du commerce de détail comprend les ventes de produits alimentaires et d'autres biens aux sanatoriums, hôpitaux, établissements pour enfants et autres institutions. Sont également inclus le revenu de la vente de biens par des coopératives de restauration, ainsi que les produits résultant d'un travail individuel et vendus par l'intermédiaire du réseau général de distribution.

Les données sur les ventes de détail sont collectées directement auprès de toutes les entreprises qui écoulent des biens de consommation par l'intermédiaire de points de vente spécialement établis et officiellement agréés, indépendamment du régime de gestion ou de propriété. Les rapports statistiques fournis par tous les points de ventes de détail, kiosques et marchés sont pris en compte chaque trimestre.

Jusqu'à 1990 inclus, le chiffre d'affaires du commerce de détail englobait les recettes de certains services rendus aux ménages, notamment la confection individuelle de vêtements, la réparation de vêtements et de chaussures ou la réparation de biens de consommation durables. La part de ces services dans le total avoisinait 2 pour cent. Depuis 1991, le chiffre d'affaires du commerce de détail ne comprend plus de services.

Les données annuelles et les données trimestrielles de la série sur le chiffre d'affaires du commerce de détail sont parfois supérieures à la somme des recettes des trimestres ou des mois correspondants en raison d'une couverture plus large des entreprises de commerce.

Le montant des ventes de détail est affecté au mois et au trimestre durant lesquels a lieu la livraison des marchandises, et non le paiement.

La valeur des ventes au détail est exprimée en roubles jusqu'en novembre 1992 et en karbovanets par la suite. Pour plus de précisions, voir la section finances internes ci-dessous et le chapitre *Introduction de nouvelles monnaies.*

L'indice des ventes de détail en volume est calculé en corrigeant le chiffre d'affaires du commerce de détail de la variation des prix. Le déflateur utilisé est l'indice des prix de détail (voir, plus loin, la section Prix). Jusqu'en 1990 inclus, toutes les variations de prix étaient réglementées par le gouvernement. Depuis 1991, les indices de prix sont établis au moyen d'un échantillon de points de vente de détail.

Main-d'oeuvre

Emploi

A partir de 1991, les chiffres annuels de toutes les séries sur l'*emploi*, sauf celle de l'industrie, couvrent le secteur public, les petites entreprises, les coopératives, les entreprises mixtes, les kolkhozes, les personnes engagées dans une activité agricole pour compte propre et le secteur semi-public, semi-coopératif. Les données trimestrielles ne couvrent que le secteur public et les kolkhozes.

En ce qui concerne l'*emploi dans l'industrie*, les données ne couvrent que le secteur public, qui représente environ 95 pour cent de la population occupée par cette branche.

Toutes les branches de l'économie nationale sont incluses, que l'activité soit matérielle ou non matérielle.

Les données sont tirées des déclarations trimestrielles et annuelles concernant les effectifs des entreprises, organisations et institutions. Toutes les entreprises, indépendamment de leur régime de propriété, sont tenues de notifier leurs effectifs. Ces informations sont généralement recoupées avec des

UKRAINE

données similaires recueillies par l'administration fiscale et les banques d'État. Le nombre des personnes assurant une production agricole pour auto-consommation est estimé.

Les travailleurs à temps partiel sont comptabilisés en équivalent plein temps. Les pluriactifs sont comptabilisés d'après leur lieu de travail principal. Les effectifs civils des complexes industriels militaires, les personnes en congé de maladie, les apprentis, les travailleurs à domicile et les travailleurs occasionnels sont pris en compte, tandis que les personnes en congé de maternité ou en congé parental sont exclues.

L'*emploi dans les branches matérielles* couvre les branches suivantes de l'économie nationale :

-- industrie ;

-- agriculture incluant la production agricole pour compte propre ;

-- sylviculture ;

-- transports et communications, dans la mesure où ces services sont utilisés par les activités productives dans le secteur de la production matérielle ;

-- commerce, restauration publique, négoce interindustriel et négoce de produits agricoles ;

-- services informatiques et services d'information ;

-- autres branches de la production matérielle : édition, production et distribution de films, transformation des déchets, pêche, chasse, etc.

L'*emploi dans l'industrie* couvre tous les salariés travaillant dans les établissements industriels d'entreprises industrielles ainsi que dans les établissements industriels d'entreprises classées dans d'autres branches. Les salariés d'établissements non industriels d'entreprises industrielles sont inclus dans la branche d'activité à laquelle appartient l'établissement considéré. La couverture des branches est la même que dans le cas de l'IPI total (voir, plus haut, la section Production industrielle).

L'*emploi dans les industries manufacturières* représente le nombre moyen d'ouvriers et d'employés participant directement au processus de production dans les établissements manufacturiers. La couverture des branches est la même que dans le cas de l'IPI des industries manufacturières (voir, plus haut, la section Production industrielle).

Chômage

Le total des *chômeurs inscrits* représente le nombre de personnes enregistrées comme chômeurs par les agences publiques pour l'emploi en fin de mois, conformément à la législation en vigueur en Ukraine.

La législation relative au chômage est entrée en vigueur le 1er juin 1991. Selon cette législation, l'agence nationale pour l'emploi statue au sujet de l'inscription d'un demandeur au plus tard 11 jours après sa demande. Les personnes précédemment employées doivent présenter leur passeport, leur livret de travail et les bulletins de salaire de leur dernier employeur. Les primodemandeurs d'emploi sont tenus de présenter leur passeport et leurs diplômes. Un chômeur reste inscrit jusqu'à ce qu'il trouve du travail.

Les personnes valides en âge de travailler (de 16 à 54 ans pour les femmes et de 16 à 59 ans pour les hommes) sont considérées comme chômeurs, quelles que soient les raisons pour lesquelles elles n'exercent pas d'emploi rémunéré, n'ont pas de revenu provenant d'une activité; à condition d'avoir été dûment enregistrées comme demandeurs d'emploi par une agence publique, d'être aptes et prêtes à exercer toute activité rémunérée et de n'avoir pas reçu de propositions d'emploi correspondant à leur profil.

Les personnes qui ont perdu leur emploi ne sont pas tenues de s'inscrire au chômage. Celles qui désirent changer d'emploi, de même que les travailleurs à temps partiel à la recherche d'un emploi à plein temps, ne sont pas considérés comme chômeurs, mais peuvent s'inscrire comme demandeurs d'emploi dans les agences pour l'emploi.

Les chômeurs inscrits sont tenus de pointer périodiquement à l'agence publique pour l'emploi.

Les *allocataires* se réfèrent aux chômeurs inscrits qui n'ont pas d'autres sources de revenu. Selon la législation en vigueur en Ukraine, les personnes sans emploi qui n'ont <u>pas</u> droit à l'allocation de chômage sont :

-- les personnes de moins de 16 ans, sauf celles qui ont déjà travaillé et ont été licenciées à cause de changements dans l'organisation de la production et du travail, de la réorganisation ou de la fermeture de l'entreprise, institution ou organisation, ou de la réduction du nombre de salariés ;

-- les primodemandeurs d'emploi qui n'ont pas de qualification professionnelle, y compris les jeunes sortis du système scolaire, s'ils ont refusé un programme de formation ou un travail rémunéré, même temporaire ;

-- les personnes qui ont refusé deux offres d'emploi correspondant à leur qualification depuis leur inscription comme demandeurs d'emploi à l'agence pour l'emploi. Ces personnes peuvent se réinscrire, mais perdent pour trois mois le droit d'être considérées comme sans emploi ;

-- les personnes percevant une pension en vertu du droit ukrainien.

Les *allocataires* reçoivent leur allocation à partir du onzième jour suivant leur inscription. La période maximale de droit à ces allocations est d'un an.

Pour les personnes ayant déjà exercé un emploi, les allocations sont supérieures au salaire minimum, et atteignent au moins 50 pour cent de la moyenne des salaires et traitements versés par leur dernier employeur durant les 12 derniers mois de travail mais ne dépassant pas le salaire annuel moyen. Pour les personnes nouvellement diplômées et s'étant inscrites au chômage moins d'un mois après l'obtention du diplôme, ou pour celles ayant terminé leurs obligations nationales et s'étant inscrites au chômage moins de trois mois après leur libération, le montant des allocations est au moins égal au salaire minimum. Pour les personnes ayant perdu leur emploi à cause d'un accident de travail ou pour cause de maladie, et qui ont besoin d'une formation professionnelle, les allocations représentent 75 pour cent du salaire moyen perçu pendant au moins 6 mois dans leur dernier emploi. Pour les autres personnes, y compris les primodemandeurs d'emploi ou ceux en arrêt depuis plus d'un an, le montant des allocations est au moins égal à 75 pour cent du salaire minimum.

Salaires

Gains mensuels

Le champ couvert par les données est le même que dans le cas des données trimestrielles sur l'emploi.

UKRAINE

Les données expriment le salaire brut moyen par salarié, calculé en divisant la masse salariale totale par le nombre global de salariés. La masse salariale englobe des paiements tels que les prestations de santé, les indemnités de subsistance et les frais de déplacement, les paiements en nature, les primes d'intéressement à la productivité, l'indexation des salaires compensant la hausse des prix, la rémunération des heures supplémentaires et des congés payés. Les versements au titre de la sécurité sociale n'en font toutefois pas partie.

Les gains mensuels sont exprimés en roubles jusqu'en novembre 1992 et en karbovanets par la suite. Pour plus de précisions, voir la section finances internes ci-dessous et le chapitre *Introduction de nouvelles monnaies*.

Prix

Prix de gros

L'*indice des prix de gros* (IPG) est calculé à partir des prix de produits destinés au marché intérieur, recueillis dans le cadre d'une enquête sur 6 200 articles représentatifs effectuée auprès de 1 500 entreprises industrielles. Chaque mois les entreprises interrogées fournissent les prix courants et les prix du mois précédent.

L'IPG est un indice de type Laspeyres modifié. La pondération utilisée entre 1991 et 1993, pour son calcul est tirée de la structure de la valeur de la production de 1991 par types de production, branches et sous-branches. Pour 1994, la pondération utilisée est tirée de la structure de la valeur totale des ventes de 1993.

Les prix s'entendent hors taxes.

Du fait de la forte inflation et de changements très importants intervenus dans la structure des ventes et de la production, certaines catégories de produits ont dû être remplacées par d'autres. C'est pourquoi les indices annuels ne peuvent pas être recalculés par chaînage des indices mensuels. Le Ministère des statistiques d'Ukraine compose actuellement un nouveau panier de biens représentatifs.

Prix à la consommation

1990-1993

Un *indice des prix de détail* (IPD) mensuel a été introduit en janvier 1991. L'observation des prix porte sur 1 200 biens et services représentatifs choisis dans tous les groupes de produits inclus dans les données du commerce de détail. Les prix (taxes comprises) étaient relevés chaque mois dans quelque 10 000 points de vente répartis dans toute l'Ukraine, qui vont des plus gros établissements, distributeurs d'un large éventail de produits, aux petits points de vente spécialisés (librairies, articles pour enfants, etc.)

Les indices reflètent la variation des prix dans les points de vente des secteurs étatique, coopératif et privé, ainsi que celle des prix des biens produits par les coopératives et par les personnes au titre du travail individuel.

De nouveaux articles ou services peuvent être introduits dans l'indice. Le prix d'un nouveau produit ou d'un service au cours du mois précédent est alors estimé d'après le prix d'un produit similaire ayant des caractéristiques analogues. Aucun ajustement n'est opéré si un produit présente un changement de qualité ou devient rare.

Les prix des produits non alimentaires sont relevés toute l'année, que ces articles soient saisonniers ou non. Les produits alimentaires saisonniers, en revanche, sont assortis dans les indices synthétiques de coefficients de pondération différents selon qu'ils sont produits en serre et écoulés comme primeurs, ou vendus en saison. S'agissant des services, quelques entreprises font des prix réduits sur certains services en période de demande creuse. Ces prix réduits sont pris en compte dans les relevés.

En ce qui concerne l'*IPD des services*, des rapports de prix étaient observés pour 72 articles représentatifs de la structure des ventes de services rendus aux ménages à titre onéreux.

L'IPD était un indice de Paasche dans lequel la pondération des regroupements régionaux et par classe de produits était fondée sur la structure des échanges du commerce de détail de l'année courante. Les indices annuels publiés font apparaître le taux de variation par rapport à l'année précédente. Ces chiffres ne peuvent pas être dérivés des chiffres mensuels puisque les indices mensuels de type Paasche ne sont pas transitifs sur un an. Une chaîne de 12 indices mensuels de ce type, aboutissant au mois courant, ne donne généralement pas l'indice de Paasche du mois courant rapporté au mois correspondant de l'année précédente.

En 1994

Des *indices des prix à la consommation (IPC)* sont désormais disponibles, depuis janvier 1994. Ils diffèrent de l'indice des prix de détail, calculé antérieurement.

L'IPC exprime le taux mensuel de variation des prix des biens et des services, pondérés par la structure des dépenses de consommation de la population en 1993. Cet indice est de type Laspeyres modifié. Le tableau suivant indique les pondérations utilisées pour calculer les indices :

Grands groupes	Poids
Biens	93
Alimentation	47
Non alimentation	46
Services	7
TOTAL	100

Les prix de 300 articles sont relevés entre le 10 et le 25 de chaque mois dans 29 villes d'Ukraine et 54 000 points de vente de détail couvrant toutes les formes de propriété. L'échantillon de points de vente a été choisi par les experts des services statistiques régionaux.

UKRAINE

A partir de 1995

A partir de janvier 1995, l'IPC est calculé en utilisant les prix observés de 345 biens et 80 services. Les prix sont observés entre le 5 et le 25 de chaque mois dans toutes les villes et chefs-lieux d'Urkaine.

L'IPC est calculé selon la formule de Laspeyres modifié, utilisant comme pondération la structure de la consommation de la population de l'année précédente. Le tableau suivant montre les poids des principaux groupes correspondant à la structure de la consommation de 1994 :

Grands groupes	Poids
Biens	88
Alimentation	65
Non alimentation	23
Services	12
TOTAL	100

Finances internes

Les *dépôts personnels* recouvrent les dépôts à terme et les dépôts à vue, en karbovanets uniquement, détenus en fin de période dans les caisses d'épargne. Les annuités d'intérêts sont incluses dans les chiffres de décembre, ceux du quatrième trimestre et celui de l'année entière. Depuis 1994, la série inclut les dépôts des banques commerciales y compris la banque commerciale d'État de l'Ukraine.

Les dépôts personnels représentent plus de 99 pour cent des dépôts observés en Ukraine.

Depuis le 1er juillet 1993, les dépôts personnels englobent une compensation de 40 pour cent pour les hausses massives de prix. Cette compensation est créditée sur le compte de dépôt principal.

Les dépôts personnels sont exprimés en roubles jusqu'en novembre 1992 et en karbovanets par la suite. Pour plus de précisions, voir le chapitre *Introduction de nouvelles monnaies*.

Finances extérieures

Le *taux de change* officiel du dollar des États-Unis en karbovanets est établi par la Banque nationale d'Ukraine. Les chiffres indiqués se rapportent à la fin de période.

Commerce extérieur

1990-91

La comptabilisation des *exportations* et *importations* a commencé en 1991. Les statistiques ukrainiennes du commerce extérieur, pour cette période, ne comprennent pas les chiffres des échanges avec les pays de l'ex-Union soviétique.

Les données sur les exportations et les importations étaient tirées des rapports statistiques soumis par les organismes de commerce extérieur, ainsi que des déclarations douanières. Les exportations et importations étaient enregistrées à la date où elles franchissaient la frontière. Les exportations étaient exprimées en données fab, les importations en données caf. Les biens faisant l'objet d'un troc étaient évalués aux prix du marché mondial pour des produits similaires.

Les données du commerce extérieur excluent les services matériels et non matériels ainsi que les revenus du tourisme. Les exportations d'or, d'argent, d'autres métaux précieux et de diamants sont en principe incluses, mais dans la pratique elles ne sont que partiellement couvertes.

Les réexportations et réimportations ne sont enregistrées seulement si les biens entrent dans le pays.

1992-1993

Les statistiques du commerce extérieur se fondaient sur la comptabilité des sociétés, harmonisée avec les documents de déclarations douanières. Les données n'incluaient pas le commerce avec les pays de l'ex-Union soviétique. Les marchandises échangées étaient classées selon le Système harmonisé.

Depuis le 12 janvier 1993, par décret ministériel, les données sur le commerce extérieur excluent 200 produits de première nécessité qui sont jugées non exportables (tels que le sucre, l'huile, le pétrole, etc.). Les transactions étaient affectées au mois au cours duquel les biens passaient la frontière. Les réimportations et les réexportations étaient exclues.

Les statistiques étaient converties directement en dollar des États-Unis par le Ministère des statistiques d'Ukraine.

Depuis 1994

Depuis 1994, les données du commerce extérieur sont disponibles ventilées en commerce avec les pays de l'ex-Union soviétique et avec les pays autres que ceux de l'ex-Union soviétique. Les données sont tirées des rapports mensuels des entreprises quelle que soit leur forme de propriété, harmonisés avec les documents des déclarations douanières.

L'exportation des biens suivants est limitée depuis le 1er Novembre 1994 :

-- céréales ;

-- fonte brute ;

-- charbon ;

-- résidus de métaux précieux et semi-précieux ;

-- résidus de métaux ferreux et non ferreux ;

-- minerais de fer et concentré de métaux précieux ;

-- pierres et métaux précieux et semi-précieux et produits dérivés.

En 1995, seules les exportations des métaux précieux et semi-précieux et de leurs résidus sont limitées.

UKRAINE

Le commerce pour 1994, qui inclut celui avec l'ex-Union soviétique, est estimé par types de biens selon la Nomenclature des biens, fondée sur le Système Harmonisé, introduite le 1er janvier 1994. Elle couvre 5 000 biens.

Les exportations sont exprimées fab, les importations caf.

Les biens exportés et importés sont évalués au prix effectivement payé. Les biens échangés par troc sont évalués au prix des biens similaires sur le marché mondial. Depuis le 1er janvier 1995, la valeur des matières premières fournies par le client en vue d'une transformation est incluse dans les données du commerce extérieur.

Les données sont converties en dollars américains par le Ministère des statistiques d'Ukraine au moyen des taux de change moyens mensuels calculés par la Banque nationale d'Ukraine.

Les échanges de services sont mesurés à partir des notifications des entreprises, organisations et institutions. La collecte de ces informations est trimestrielle.

Les données sont converties en dollars américains par le Minsitère des statistiques d'Ukraine au moyen des taux de change moyens trimestriels calculés par la Banque nationale d'Ukraine.

Formation brute de capital

La *formation brute de capital totale* représente les dépenses consacrées à l'achat de biens d'équipement neufs, ainsi qu'à l'extension, la reconstruction et la rénovation d'actifs immobilisés en service. La valeur des investissements en équipements représente le coût de la construction et des installations, l'achat du matériel et de l'outillage et les dépenses d'infrastructure.

L'investissement en équipements est évalué à son coût initial, à savoir son prix d'acquisition, brut de tout amortissement. Les bâtiments et ouvrages non terminés qui ont été payés par les entrepreneurs sont inclus dans l'investissement en équipements ; la réparation de biens d'équipement est exclue.

Les équipements sont inclus quel que soit leur mode de financement : dépenses d'investissement des entreprises et institutions étatiques, des entreprises en régie, des coopératives de consommation et organisations publiques de consommateurs, des coopératives, des fermes collectives, des coopératives de construction de logements et constructions individuelles autofinancées.

Les dépenses d'équipement sont enregistrées aux prix courants et recalculées aux prix de 1984, soit sur la base des données fournies par les entreprises soit à l'aide d'indices de prix. Les séries de la période 1984-1990 s'appuient sur les données fournies par les entreprises.

La *formation brute de capital au titre de la construction et des installations* comprend les travaux liés à la construction, à l'agrandissement et à la reconstruction de bâtiments et d'ouvrages permanents ou temporaires, ainsi que les activités d'installation de modules de construction et d'équipements.

Les statistiques sur la formation brute de capital sont exprimées dans la monnaie nationale, en karbovanets.

Publications

Certaines des séries décrites ci-dessus figurent aussi, mais avec une présentation conforme à la pratique nationale, dans *Statistical Yearbook* (Annuaire Statistique) et d'autres publications du Ministère des statistiques d'Ukraine.

MAIN SALES OUTLETS OF OECD PUBLICATIONS
PRINCIPAUX POINTS DE VENTE DES PUBLICATIONS DE L'OCDE

ARGENTINA – ARGENTINE
Carlos Hirsch S.R.L.
Galería Güemes, Florida 165, 4° Piso
1333 Buenos Aires   Tel. (1) 331.1787 y 331.2391
Telefax: (1) 331.1787

AUSTRALIA – AUSTRALIE
D.A. Information Services
648 Whitehorse Road, P.O.B 163
Mitcham, Victoria 3132   Tel. (03) 9210.7777
Telefax: (03) 9210.7788

AUSTRIA – AUTRICHE
Gerold & Co.
Graben 31
Wien I   Tel. (0222) 533.50.14
Telefax: (0222) 512.47.31.29

BELGIUM – BELGIQUE
Jean De Lannoy
Avenue du Roi 202 Koningslaan
B-1060 Bruxelles   Tel. (02) 538.51.69/538.08.41
Telefax: (02) 538.08.41

CANADA
Renouf Publishing Company Ltd.
1294 Algoma Road
Ottawa, ON K1B 3W8   Tel. (613) 741.4333
Telefax: (613) 741.5439
Stores:
61 Sparks Street
Ottawa, ON K1P 5R1   Tel. (613) 238.8985
12 Adelaide Street West
Toronto, ON M5H 1L6   Tel. (416) 363.3171
Telefax: (416)363.59.63

Les Éditions La Liberté Inc.
3020 Chemin Sainte-Foy
Sainte-Foy, PQ G1X 3V6   Tel. (418) 658.3763
Telefax: (418) 658.3763

Federal Publications Inc.
165 University Avenue, Suite 701
Toronto, ON M5H 3B8   Tel. (416) 860.1611
Telefax: (416) 860.1608

Les Publications Fédérales
1185 Université
Montréal, QC H3B 3A7   Tel. (514) 954.1633
Telefax: (514) 954.1635

CHINA – CHINE
China National Publications Import
Export Corporation (CNPIEC)
16 Gongti E. Road, Chaoyang District
P.O. Box 88 or 50
Beijing 100704 PR   Tel. (01) 506.6688
Telefax: (01) 506.3101

CHINESE TAIPEI – TAIPEI CHINOIS
Good Faith Worldwide Int'l. Co. Ltd.
9th Floor, No. 118, Sec. 2
Chung Hsiao E. Road
Taipei   Tel. (02) 391.7396/391.7397
Telefax: (02) 394.9176

**CZECH REPUBLIC –
RÉPUBLIQUE TCHÈQUE**
Artia Pegas Press Ltd.
Narodni Trida 25
POB 825
111 21 Praha 1   Tel. (2) 242 246 04
Telefax: (2) 242 278 72

DENMARK – DANEMARK
Munksgaard Book and Subscription Service
35, Nørre Søgade, P.O. Box 2148
DK-1016 København K   Tel. (33) 12.85.70
Telefax: (33) 12.93.87

EGYPT – ÉGYPTE
Middle East Observer
41 Sherif Street
Cairo   Tel. 392.6919
Telefax: 360-6804

FINLAND – FINLANDE
Akateeminen Kirjakauppa
Keskuskatu 1, P.O. Box 128
00100 Helsinki
Subscription Services/Agence d'abonnements :
P.O. Box 23
00371 Helsinki   Tel. (358 0) 121 4416
Telefax: (358 0) 121.4450

FRANCE
OECD/OCDE
Mail Orders/Commandes par correspondance :
2, rue André-Pascal
75775 Paris Cedex 16   Tel. (33-1) 45.24.82.00
Telefax: (33-1) 49.10.42.76
Telex: 640048 OCDE
Internet: Compte.PUBSINQ @ oecd.org
Orders via Minitel, France only/
Commandes par Minitel, France exclusivement :
36 15 OCDE
OECD Bookshop/Librairie de l'OCDE :
33, rue Octave-Feuillet
75016 Paris   Tel. (33-1) 45.24.81.81
(33-1) 45.24.81.67

Dawson
B.P. 40
91121 Palaiseau Cedex   Tel. 69.10.47.00
Telefax: 64.54.83.26

Documentation Française
29, quai Voltaire
75007 Paris   Tel. 40.15.70.00

Economica
49, rue Héricart
75015 Paris   Tel. 45.78.12.92
Telefax: 40.58.15.70

Gibert Jeune (Droit-Économie)
6, place Saint-Michel
75006 Paris   Tel. 43.25.91.19

Librairie du Commerce International
10, avenue d'Iéna
75016 Paris   Tel. 40.73.34.60

Librairie Dunod
Université Paris-Dauphine
Place du Maréchal-de-Lattre-de-Tassigny
75016 Paris   Tel. 44.05.40.13

Librairie Lavoisier
11, rue Lavoisier
75008 Paris   Tel. 42.65.39.95

Librairie des Sciences Politiques
30, rue Saint-Guillaume
75007 Paris   Tel. 45.48.36.02

P.U.F.
49, boulevard Saint-Michel
75005 Paris   Tel. 43.25.83.40

Librairie de l'Université
12a, rue Nazareth
13100 Aix-en-Provence   Tel. (16) 42.26.18.08

Documentation Française
165, rue Garibaldi
69003 Lyon   Tel. (16) 78.63.32.23

Librairie Decitre
29, place Bellecour
69002 Lyon   Tel. (16) 72.40.54.54

Librairie Sauramps
Le Triangle
34967 Montpellier Cedex 2   Tel. (16) 67.58.85.15
Telefax: (16) 67.58.27.36

A la Sorbonne Actual
23, rue de l'Hôtel-des-Postes
06000 Nice   Tel. (16) 93.13.77.75
Telefax: (16) 93.80.75.69

GERMANY – ALLEMAGNE
OECD Publications and Information Centre
August-Bebel-Allee 6
D-53175 Bonn   Tel. (0228) 959.120
Telefax: (0228) 959.12.17

GREECE – GRÈCE
Librairie Kauffmann
Mavrokordatou 9
106 78 Athens   Tel. (01) 32.55.321
Telefax: (01) 32.30.320

HONG-KONG
Swindon Book Co. Ltd.
Astoria Bldg. 3F
34 Ashley Road, Tsimshatsui
Kowloon, Hong Kong   Tel. 2376.2062
Telefax: 2376.0685

HUNGARY – HONGRIE
Euro Info Service
Margitsziget, Európa Ház
1138 Budapest   Tel. (1) 111.62.16
Telefax: (1) 111.60.61

ICELAND – ISLANDE
Mál Mog Menning
Laugavegi 18, Pósthólf 392
121 Reykjavik   Tel. (1) 552.4240
Telefax: (1) 562.3523

INDIA – INDE
Oxford Book and Stationery Co.
Scindia House
New Delhi 110001   Tel. (11) 331.5896/5308
Telefax: (11) 332.5993
17 Park Street
Calcutta 700016   Tel. 240832

INDONESIA – INDONÉSIE
Pdii-Lipi
P.O. Box 4298
Jakarta 12042   Tel. (21) 573.34.67
Telefax: (21) 573.34.67

IRELAND – IRLANDE
Government Supplies Agency
Publications Section
4/5 Harcourt Road
Dublin 2   Tel. 661.31.11
Telefax: 475.27.60

ISRAEL – ISRAËL
Praedicta
5 Shatner Street
P.O. Box 34030
Jerusalem 91430   Tel. (2) 52.84.90/1/2
Telefax: (2) 52.84.93

R.O.Y. International
P.O. Box 13056
Tel Aviv 61130   Tel. (3) 546 1423
Telefax: (3) 546 1442

Palestinian Authority/Middle East:
INDEX Information Services
P.O.B. 19502
Jerusalem   Tel. (2) 27.12.19
Telefax: (2) 27.16.34

ITALY – ITALIE
Libreria Commissionaria Sansoni
Via Duca di Calabria 1/1
50125 Firenze   Tel. (055) 64.54.15
Telefax: (055) 64.12.57
Via Bartolini 29
20155 Milano   Tel. (02) 36.50.83

Editrice e Libreria Herder
Piazza Montecitorio 120
00186 Roma
Tel. 679.46.28
Telefax: 678.47.51

Libreria Hoepli
Via Hoepli 5
20121 Milano
Tel. (02) 86.54.46
Telefax: (02) 805.28.86

Libreria Scientifica
Dott. Lucio de Biasio 'Aeiou'
Via Coronelli, 6
20146 Milano
Tel. (02) 48.95.45.52
Telefax: (02) 48.95.45.48

JAPAN – JAPON
OECD Publications and Information Centre
Landic Akasaka Building
2-3-4 Akasaka, Minato-ku
Tokyo 107
Tel. (81.3) 3586.2016
Telefax: (81.3) 3584.7929

KOREA – CORÉE
Kyobo Book Centre Co. Ltd.
P.O. Box 1658, Kwang Hwa Moon
Seoul
Tel. 730.78.91
Telefax: 735.00.30

MALAYSIA – MALAISIE
University of Malaya Bookshop
University of Malaya
P.O. Box 1127, Jalan Pantai Baru
59700 Kuala Lumpur
Malaysia
Tel. 756.5000/756.5425
Telefax: 756.3246

MEXICO – MEXIQUE
OECD Publications and Information Centre
Edificio INFOTEC
Av. San Fernando no. 37
Col. Toriello Guerra
Tlalpan C.P. 14050
Mexico D.F.
Tel. (525) 606 00 11 Extension 100
Fax: (525) 606 13 07

Revistas y Periodicos Internacionales S.A. de C.V.
Florencia 57 - 1004
Mexico, D.F. 06600
Tel. 207.81.00
Telefax: 208.39.79

NETHERLANDS – PAYS-BAS
SDU Uitgeverij Plantijnstraat
Externe Fondsen
Postbus 20014
2500 EA's-Gravenhage
Tel. (070) 37.89.880
Voor bestellingen:
Telefax: (070) 34.75.778

**NEW ZEALAND –
NOUVELLE-ZÉLANDE**
GPLegislation Services
P.O. Box 12418
Thorndon, Wellington
Tel. (04) 496.5655
Telefax: (04) 496.5698

NORWAY – NORVÈGE
NIC INFO A/S
Bertrand Narvesens vei 2
P.O. Box 6512 Etterstad
0606 Oslo 6
Tel. (022) 57.33.00
Telefax: (022) 68.19.01

PAKISTAN
Mirza Book Agency
65 Shahrah Quaid-E-Azam
Lahore 54000
Tel. (42) 353.601
Telefax: (42) 231.730

PHILIPPINE – PHILIPPINES
International Booksource Center Inc.
Rm 179/920 Cityland 10 Condo Tower 2
HV dela Costa Ext cor Valero St.
Makati Metro Manila
Tel. (632) 817 9676
Telefax: (632) 817 1741

POLAND – POLOGNE
Ars Polona
00-950 Warszawa
Krakowskie Przedmieácie 7
Tel. (22) 264760
Telefax: (22) 268673

PORTUGAL
Livraria Portugal
Rua do Carmo 70-74
Apart. 2681
1200 Lisboa
Tel. (01) 347.49.82/5
Telefax: (01) 347.02.64

SINGAPORE – SINGAPOUR
Gower Asia Pacific Pte Ltd.
Golden Wheel Building
41, Kallang Pudding Road, No. 04-03
Singapore 1334
Tel. 741.5166
Telefax: 742.9356

SPAIN – ESPAGNE
Mundi-Prensa Libros S.A.
Castelló 37, Apartado 1223
Madrid 28001
Tel. (91) 431.33.99
Telefax: (91) 575.39.98

Mundi-Prensa Barcelona
Consell de Cent No. 391
08009 – Barcelona
Tel. (93) 488.34.92
Telefax: (93) 487.76.59

Llibreria de la Generalitat
Palau Moja
Rambla dels Estudis, 118
08002 – Barcelona
(Subscripcions) Tel. (93) 318.80.12
(Publicacions) Tel. (93) 302.67.23
Telefax: (93) 412.18.54

SRI LANKA
Centre for Policy Research
c/o Colombo Agencies Ltd.
No. 300-304, Galle Road
Colombo 3
Tel. (1) 574240, 573551-2
Telefax: (1) 575394, 510711

SWEDEN – SUÈDE
CE Fritzes AB
S–106 47 Stockholm
Tel. (08) 690.90.90
Telefax: (08) 20.50.21

Subscription Agency/Agence d'abonnements :
Wennergren-Williams Info AB
P.O. Box 1305
171 25 Solna
Tel. (08) 705.97.50
Telefax: (08) 27.00.71

SWITZERLAND – SUISSE
Maditec S.A. (Books and Periodicals - Livres et périodiques)
Chemin des Palettes 4
Case postale 266
1020 Renens VD 1
Tel. (021) 635.08.65
Telefax: (021) 635.07.80

Librairie Payot S.A.
4, place Pépinet
CP 3212
1002 Lausanne
Tel. (021) 320.25.11
Telefax: (021) 320.25.14

Librairie Unilivres
6, rue de Candolle
1205 Genève
Tel. (022) 320.26.23
Telefax: (022) 329.73.18

Subscription Agency/Agence d'abonnements :
Dynapresse Marketing S.A.
38, avenue Vibert
1227 Carouge
Tel. (022) 308.07.89
Telefax: (022) 308.07.99

See also – Voir aussi :
OECD Publications and Information Centre
August-Bebel-Allee 6
D-53175 Bonn (Germany)
Tel. (0228) 959.120
Telefax: (0228) 959.12.17

THAILAND – THAÏLANDE
Suksit Siam Co. Ltd.
113, 115 Fuang Nakhon Rd.
Opp. Wat Rajbopith
Bangkok 10200
Tel. (662) 225.9531/2
Telefax: (662) 222.5188

TUNISIA – TUNISIE
Grande Librairie Spécialisée
Fendri Ali
Avenue Haffouz Imm El-Intilaka
Bloc B 1 Sfax 3000
Tel. (216-4) 296 855
Telefax: (216-4) 298.270

TURKEY – TURQUIE
Kültür Yayinlari Is-Türk Ltd. Sti.
Atatürk Bulvari No. 191/Kat 13
Kavaklidere/Ankara
Tel. (312) 428.11.40 Ext. 2458
Telefax: (312) 417 24 90
Dolmabahce Cad. No. 29
Besiktas/Istanbul
Tel. (212) 260 7188

UNITED KINGDOM – ROYAUME-UNI
HMSO
Gen. enquiries
Tel. (171) 873 8242
Postal orders only:
P.O. Box 276, London SW8 5DT
Personal Callers HMSO Bookshop
49 High Holborn, London WC1V 6HB
Telefax: (171) 873 8416
Branches at: Belfast, Birmingham, Bristol,
Edinburgh, Manchester

UNITED STATES – ÉTATS-UNIS
OECD Publications and Information Center
2001 L Street N.W., Suite 650
Washington, D.C. 20036-4922 Tel. (202) 785.6323
Telefax: (202) 785.0350

Subscriptions to OECD periodicals may also be
placed through main subscription agencies.

Les abonnements aux publications périodiques de
l'OCDE peuvent être souscrits auprès des
principales agences d'abonnement.

Orders and inquiries from countries where Distribu-
tors have not yet been appointed should be sent to:
OECD Publications Service, 2, rue André-Pascal,
75775 Paris Cedex 16, France.

Les commandes provenant de pays où l'OCDE n'a
pas encore désigné de distributeur peuvent être
adressées à : OCDE, Service des Publications,
2, rue André-Pascal, 75775 Paris Cedex 16, France.

1-1996

OECD PUBLICATIONS, 2, rue André-Pascal, 75775 PARIS CEDEX 16
PRINTED IN FRANCE
(07 96 05 3) ISBN 92-64-04838-3 – No. 48726 1996